AF605798

CINEMAGRITTE

CONTEMPORARY APPROACHES TO FILM AND MEDIA SERIES

A complete listing of the books in this series can be found online at wsupress.wayne.edu.

CINEMAGRITTE

RENÉ MAGRITTE WITHIN THE FRAME OF FILM HISTORY, THEORY, AND PRACTICE

LUCY FISCHER

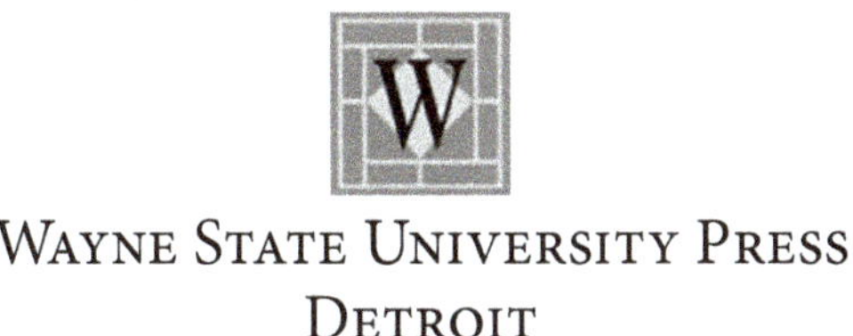

WAYNE STATE UNIVERSITY PRESS
DETROIT

ISBN 978-0-8143-4637-2 (paperback)
ISBN 978-0-8143-4636-5 (hardcover)
ISBN 978-0-8143-4638-9 (e-book)

Library of Congress Control Number: 2019941125

Published with the assistance of a fund established by Thelma Gray James of Wayne State University for the publication of folklore and English studies.

Wayne State University Press
Leonard N. Simons Building
4809 Woodward Avenue
Detroit, Michigan 48201-1309

Visit us online at wsupress.wayne.edu

For my granddaughter, Talia Sage Wicclair—
may she grow up to love and be sustained by art

Contents

Preface

Magritte and Me

My fascination with the work of René Magritte began long ago. In the 1970s, I worked in the Film Department of the Museum of Modern Art (MoMA) in New York City and spent most of my pecuniary salary at the MoMA store. Among the initial things I bought there (and the first framed print that I ever owned) was one of Magritte's *The False Mirror* (1929) (which appears on the cover of this volume)—the image of a huge eye—which hung in the museum's galleries. It was expensive and quite a splurge for me at the time. I immediately placed it on a wall above my desk in my home office. That purchase was soon followed by another, a print from the *Domain of Light* series (1949–67)—a gift for my husband. Ultimately, I bought an elegant art book about Magritte that contained myriad color reproductions—another strain on my limited finances. Finally, while working in MoMA's 16 mm Film Circulating Library, I was able to place in the collection an experimental film by Anita Thatcher titled *Homage to Magritte* (1974)—surprisingly, one of the few works of that kind (now or then) to openly engage the artist's vision.

My love of Magritte's creations continued through the years, and whenever I learned of a show that featured his art, I made a point of attending it, if possible. As for recent years, I traveled to New York in 2013 to view MoMa's exhibition *Magritte: The Mystery of the Ordinary, 1926–1938* and then later, in the summer of 2018, to San Francisco to see the SFMOMA exhibit *The Fifth Season,* focused on Magritte's late work. In between, in 2015, I journeyed to Brussels (the city in which he had long resided) to visit the Magritte Museum—one entirely devoted to the painter's oeuvre. As always, I was impressed by the beauty and wit of his work as well as the way it raised resonant (and perplexing) conceptual, artistic, and philosophical issues.

As I began my professional life as a film scholar (completing a doctorate in cinema studies at New York University), Magritte began to factor into my academic world as well. Even before working at MoMA, I had taken a stimulating course from Annette Michelson on Dada, Surrealism, and film, in which paintings by Magritte were referenced. Then, while writing a dissertation on the work of Jacques Tati,[1] I came across Magritte's painting *Hegel's Holiday* (1958), a title that bore an intriguing connection to that of Tati's *Mr. Hulot's Holiday* (1953). Furthermore, Magritte's quotidian bourgeois "man in the bowler hat" seemed ripe for comparison with the figure of Hulot, an "ordinary" guy equally known for his signature (though different) headgear. I was pleased to learn only recently that Magritte had, in fact, admired the work of Tati.[2]

When I received my PhD and began teaching, without consciously willing it, I often found myself bringing into class pictures of Magritte's work in order to highlight some aspect of a film's theme, point of view, or style. For instance, in teaching *Being John Malkovich* (Spike Jonze, 1999)—a fantastical movie about a portal that leads into the head of a famous actor—I would show slides of *Not to Be Reproduced* (1937) and *The Glass House* (1939)—paintings that got closer to the sense of subjectivity in the film than most of the critical articles written about it. (This film and these paintings are discussed briefly in chapter 20.)

Periodically, it would occur to me that there might be a rich research topic in the subject of Magritte and film, but being involved in other publishing ventures, I routinely tabled the idea. Now, however, having found myself free to contemplate a new project, the idea proposed itself again—this time, with a vengeance.

When recently I began to seriously investigate the matter in the scholarly literature, I was not entirely surprised to find a dearth of material on the subject beyond the mention of certain established facts: Magritte made Surrealist "home movies"; he painted images of Louis Feuillade's hero, Fantômas, including *The Flame Rekindled* (1943) (see figure 1.1) and *The Barbarian* (1928); and he titled one work *Blue Cinema* (1925) and another *Homage to Mack Sennett* (1934). I also found passing references to Magritte in film critics' consideration of various movies—rarely any in-depth analyses.

Given, however, that I like investigating uncharted territory, now seemed the time to face my Magritte fixation. Furthermore, my work had recently focused on cinema and the arts, having edited a volume on art direction and production design and written two separate monographs on Art Deco and Art Nouveau in relation to film history.[3] Finally, I had previously examined the links between movies and the work of another painter in my essay "The Savage Eye: Edward Hopper and the Cinema."[4]

It is my contention that of all Modernist artists, René Magritte is, perhaps, the most interesting one to examine in relation to the cinema. Rather than being an "abstract" painter or one who simply modifies modes of representation, Magritte makes "realistic" art (like the unadulterated photographic image) while, at the same time, creating myriad visual conundrums that raise intriguing conceptual and philosophical issues pertinent to cinema. This makes his work resonant for a comparative analysis with film.

Such is the task I gave myself in writing *Cinemagritte*.

Acknowledgments

In many ways completing this book has been one of the most pleasurable and difficult writing experiences of my career—pleasurable because I love the work of Magritte and the task of imagining his connections to film and media studies, difficult because of the complex and expensive process of clearing rights for the copious images required to illustrate the text. In that regard, I would like to thank the many people who helped in that endeavor, although unfortunately I have not been able to use all the images to which they gave me access. In particular, I appreciate those institutions that allowed use of their images gratis—a great help to an underfunded humanities scholar—the Menil Collection, Houston (and Kara Thoreson), the San Francisco Museum of Modern Art (and David Rozelle), the National Gallery (and Peter Huetis), the Museum of Fine Arts Houston (and Shelby Rodriguez), the Albright-Knox Gallery (and Kelly Carpenter), the Philadelphia Museum of Art (and Miriam), and the Museum of Contemporary Art Chicago (and Bonnie Rosenberg).

I would also like to thank the following other individuals and organizations who helped me secure rights to Magritte's works: Robbi Siegel of Art Resource (who had great patience in my selection of myriad images), Todd Leibowitz of the Artist Rights Society, Laura Povenelli of the New Orleans Museum of Art, and Colleen Hollister of the Baltimore Museum of Art.

As for my publisher, I am grateful to Barry Grant (editor of the Contemporary Approaches to Film and Media series) with whom I first discussed this project and Annie Martin (who was then acquisitions editor and is now editor-in-chief). I was buoyed by their enthusiastic response to it. I have had a long relationship with them as a member of Wayne State University Press's advisory board for the series and am pleased now to be one of its authors as well. I am also appreciative of the work of Marie Sweetman, who took over for Annie as acquisitions editor and has been wonderful to work with during the long and laborious preparation of the manuscript for publication. Ceylan

Akturk was helpful in vetting permissions, as was Jude Grant in dealing with the copyediting process.

There are also many individuals and institutions I need to credit at the University of Pittsburgh for supporting this project: two deans and one former dean of the Dietrich School of Arts and Sciences (Kathleen Blee, Kay Brummond, and James Knapp), the University Center for International Studies, the European Studies Program, and the Jean Monnet European Union Center of Excellence. I have also profited from help by two graduate assistants in the Department of English: John Kennedy and especially Rachel Mabe.

As ever, I have benefited from the support (mental, physical, and intellectual) of my husband, Mark Wicclair, who saw me through some very trying times during the preparation of this manuscript, and of my broader immediate family—my sister, Madeleine; my son, David; my daughter-in-law, Leigh; and my lovely, delightful granddaughter, Talia, to whom this book is dedicated.

I

BACKSTORY

I

INTRODUCTION

"A Trampoline for the Imagination"

> The true value of art is a function of its power as a liberating revelation.
>
> René Magritte[1]

IN THIS BOOK, I investigate the connections between the great Belgian Surrealist/Modernist painter René Magritte (1898–1967) and the cinema. I seek to do so in a variety of ways—by discussing the scant observations that critics have made on the topic, exploring art documentaries about Magritte, investigating explicit cinematic homages to the painter, analyzing Magritte's amateur movies, examining the broader scholarship on painting and film, and, most notably, surfacing what I deem to be "resonances" between his oeuvre and diverse films.

I choose the word *resonance* carefully because in conceiving it I am not generally claiming the direct influence of Magritte's work on the movies or vice versa (though instances of this do occur). Rather, film history is inflected by many of the thematic discourses, conceptual issues, and iconographic tropes that Magritte routinely engaged—not surprising, since he and cinema came of age in and the same era (the early twentieth century). As Xavier Canonne writes, "The Surrealists were born with the movies."[2] Such parallels between Magritte's work and the cinema exist because the artist's creative interests involved subjects having direct relevance to film theory and practice—framing, scale, montage, illusionism, the gaze, theatricality, point of view, the face, and the status of objects. In cataloging these issues, I am reminded of what Magritte once said about the cinema in a letter to a friend—that he used it as a "trampoline for the imagination," helping him to conceive his art.[3] I will honor but reverse Magritte's process, using his work as a creative jumping-off point for considering film.

In my choice of the term *resonance*, I am encouraged by its use by art historian A. M. Hammacher who applied it to Magritte's work. He states: "Magritte attempted, as it were, to achieve a controlled resonance in his work. After he had finished a painting, it set up a resonance within him.... Magritte probably attached more than usual importance to having people feel the right kind of resonance. That he could do anything about this himself was an illusion; the others were the critics, the art historians, the museums, the art dealers, the collectors, who play their own game with a variety of intentions."[4] My intentions are to take seriously the resonances of Magritte's work and foreground their implications for film history, theory, and practice.

Why Magritte?

But one may ask: Why choose Magritte out of all possible artists? I would assert that as one of the central painters of the Modernist era, he deserves more attention than the paltry consideration he has received in the annals of film studies. I would not make such a claim about many others. While the styles of Pablo Picasso or Piet Mondrian, for instance, may have relevance to experimental cinema, their methodologies do not readily apply to the dramatic fiction film. Magritte's work, on the other hand, has ties to both cinematic modes—avant-garde and mainstream. Furthermore, while one can imagine a biopic about an artist like Edward Munch or imagery marked by his visual sensibility, one cannot conceive of a unique conceptual stance that cinema might inherit from him—while, with Magritte, one can.

This is so because Magritte considered himself a philosopher more than an aesthete. As Ellen Handler Spitz states, his paintings "are questions as well as paintings, or paintings as questions.... [T]hey illustrate links between the abstract and the personal, the paradoxical and the perverse."[5] Some of the topics she asserts he confronts are: "how things living differ (and yet do not differ) from things dead; how important objects can appear small and insignificant (while others, when charged with strong feeling loom large); how looking differs from experiencing; how art differs from life; how the same object that frightens and angers us at one moment can seem funny or absurd the next; how the concrete can become suddenly abstract and the abstract all too horribly concrete."[6] Magritte's own words support this view. As he states, "My paintings are visible thoughts."[7] In fact, he conceived of his art as solving a series of "problems." As he notes (in rather awkward language): "Any object, taken as a question of a problem . . . and the right answer discovered by searching for the object that is secretly connected to the first . . . give, when brought together, a new knowledge."[8] One such search involved doors. As Magritte observes: "The problem of the door called for an opening that someone could go through. In *La Réponse imprévue* [*The Unexpected Answer*, 1933] I showed a closed door in a flat in which an odd-shaped hole unveils the night."[9]

In comparison to Magritte, some of his compatriots in Surrealism have been studied in more depth by film scholars—namely, Luis Buñuel and Salvador Dalí—because, unlike Magritte, they made experimental or narrative movies that were publicly screened and have become classics (e.g., *Un chien andalou* [1929], *L'âge d'or* [1930], *The Discreet Charm of the Bourgeoisie* [1972]), or they collaborated with mainstream directors (e.g., Dalí with Alfred Hitchcock on *Spellbound* [1945]). In a certain sense, however, in comparison to Dalí, much of whose art contains an element of abstraction or distortion (and is therefore unlike the unvarnished photographic image), Magritte's is at least superficially realistic—though the situations he creates are patently unreal. When asked why he employed this style, he responded, "Because my painting has to resemble the world in order to evoke its mystery."[10] In this regard, Magritte falls into what Bruce Elder calls the "veristic" wing of Surrealism versus the "automatist" wing (which "believed that the way to freedom in painting was to break from depiction"). The veristic artists "were interested primarily in the mind's activity of forming the world that we inhabit."[11]

Clearly, Magritte's work conforms to certain tenets of Surrealism: an interest in a world beyond the quotidian—one informed by mystery, poetry, and enchantment. As André Breton once famously asserted in his 1924 *Manifesto of Surrealism*, "Existence is elsewhere."[12] As this chapter's epigraph demonstrates, Magritte put it somewhat differently, speaking instead of liberating revelation.

While many of the Surrealists drew on dreams and the unconscious for their imagery, Magritte generally did not, gleaning his ideas instead from intense concentration. Neither did he depend on chance (also valorized by the Surrealists); rather, his paintings arose from conscious choices. Like most Surrealists, Magritte was also interested in bizarre and often humorous juxtapositions—be it an open umbrella atop of which sits a glass of water (as in *Hegel's Holiday* [1958]) or a birdcage that contains an egg rather than an avian creature (as in

Elective Affinities [1933]). It is no accident that in both of these cases Magritte utilizes an iconography of objects—also an interest of the Surrealists—though freed of their utility and always in strange contexts. Here we may think of Man Ray's *Cadeau* (1921) a sculpture comprising a clothes iron with nails jutting out of its surface. Furthermore, Magritte shares the Surrealists' interest in playing with language in ways that defy coherence and rationality (as in the *Interpretation of Dreams* series [e.g., 1927, 1930, 1935], in which pictures and word labels are often mismatched). Here a precedent may have been the Surrealist game of exquisite corpse (begun around 1925) whereby one player would write a phrase on paper, hide most of it with a fold, and pass it on to another player to continue. The result was a collectively authored nonsense composition. While Magritte generally worked alone, he did often farm out the creation of titles for his works to other members of the Belgian Surrealist circle so that the titles would not reveal authorial intent. Finally, the Surrealists (a group composed almost entirely of apparently heterosexual men) were fixated on the female erotic image. Magritte is no exception, although (perhaps in a bourgeois move), the woman he most often painted was his wife, Georgette. As previously noted, while many of the Surrealists worked in abstraction (e.g., the Chilean painter Roberto Matta), Magritte preferred a style superficially faithful to the everyday world.

Here, of course, we recall that until recently, with the advent of computer-generated imagery (CGI), film theory has stressed the verisimilitude of the cinematic image, with André Bazin deeming the latter a "decal" or "transfer" of reality onto celluloid.[13] Likewise, Siegfried Kracauer sees film as offering a "redemption of physical reality."[14] So Magritte's pictorial realism has potential ties to the ontology of the medium. Moreover, as already noted, his art is marked by a focus on objects (balls, tubas, frames, combs, etc.)—often removed from their usual framework. As Magritte has remarked, "Setting objects from reality out of context [gives] the real world from which these objects were borrowed a disturbing poetic sense by a natural exchange."[15]

Here again, film theorists have often noted the medium's ability to concentrate on things instead of people. As Bazin writes in "Theater and Cinema," "On the screen man is no longer the focus of the drama. . . . The decor that surrounds him is part of the solidity of the world. For this reason, the actor as such can be absent from it, because man in the world enjoys no a priori privilege over . . . things."[16] Again, Kracauer agrees. He sees one of cinema's special capacities as that of capturing the inanimate (a clock on a mantel or a vase on a table)—parts of material reality that would otherwise go unnoticed in daily life. Significantly, Magritte's art has been linked to the realm of the "every day." Finally, the originality of Magritte's method lies not so much in his painting skill as in the inquiries and conundrums his canvases raise about topics like vision, identity, illusionism, framing, or language versus picture—all matters that are highly relevant to filmmaking practice and theory.

But conceiving the connections between Magritte and cinema is a process that is far less literal than detecting the parallels between Dalí's *Spellbound* sequence and his painting style. Magritte's artistic signature attaches to no such movie, other than his amateur ones (see chapter 2 for further discussion). Moreover, aside from the few cases of acknowledged cinematic tributes to Magritte or documentaries about him, there are no films (to my knowledge) in which images from his canvases are literally transferred to the screen—although there are some in which his paintings themselves appear as part of the decor (one is *The Thomas Crown Affair* [1999], discussed in chapter 3). Rather, the task of unearthing cinema's ties to Magritte requires intuitive and imaginative leaps, though ones based on a knowledge of film history and discourse. Of course, such factors are always at play in successful art criticism, but they are rarely acknowledged as such.

The Critical Field: Magritte and Film

In the English language, there is little published *in any detail* about Magritte's broad relation to the cinema—barring a few articles or book chapters, to be discussed later. Instead, for the most part, we find numerous *brief comments* on the subject that tend to touch on assorted issues and move on. In part, this is the case because Magritte himself failed to write about film. As Xavier Canonne notes, "Magritte did not theorize about [the cinema], but savoured it."[17] Though except in a few cases, the prior work on Magritte and film is lacking in depth, I will summarize it thoroughly in order to survey scholarship in this area (and give credit where it is due).

Almost all biographers and authors of monographs about Magritte mention his attendance at movies during his youth in Belgium[18] and his particular love of the *Fantômas* serials directed by Louis Feuillade between 1913 and 1914.[19] Here the title of Magritte's painting *Blue Cinema* (1925)—which memorialized a childhood theater in Charleroi where he moved in 1913[20]—will be cited, as well as the subjects of *Homage to Mack Sennett* (1934) (which celebrates a famous early comedy director) and that of *The Barbarian* (1927)[21] and *The Flame Rekindled* (1943) (figure 1.1) (which picture a masked Fantômas).[22] But Canonne thinks that it would be "an exaggeration to claim any decisive influence of the cinema on his work." Rather, "it would be more accurate to see it as a general context from which Magritte extracted some memory flashes."[23]

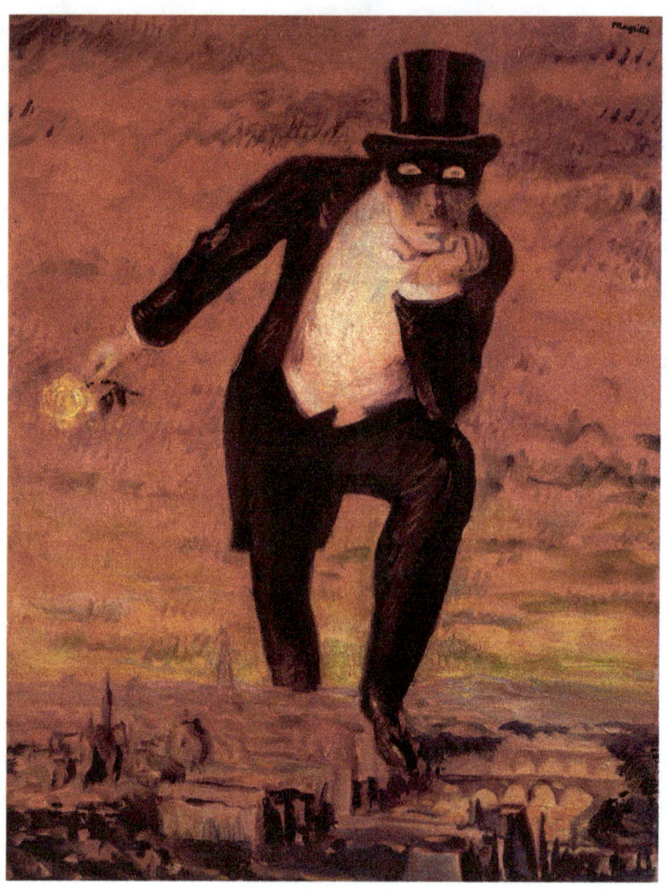

FIGURE 1.1. *The Flame Rekindled* (*Le retour de flamme*/*The Return of the Flame*) (1943)

Not surprisingly, many critics have observed aspects of Magritte's art that echo certain movies—for instance, how a split-head image in one of his illustrations for *Les chants du Maldoror* by the Comte de Lautréamont (1945) suggests a shot from Germaine Dulac's *The Seashell and the Clergyman* (1928). Often mentioned is how the scene portrayed in Magritte's *The Murderer Threatened* (1927)—with its cadaver lying on a table and armed men standing guard—seems to evoke Feuillade's crime stories.[24] In particular, Anne Umland mentions the episode, *The Murderous Corpse* (1913), for its parallels with the Magritte canvas.[25] It is possible that she does so because on one occasion in the film there is an unconscious woman reclining on a sofa and, on another, a man lying in a hospital bed. Alternatively, she may have referenced it because it involves the uncanny notion of a villain wearing a "glove of skin" made from a corpse's hand in order to leave the deceased's fingerprints at the crime scene to throw the police off track. On a similar note, Canonne sees parallels between the black body-suited figures in Magritte's *The Female Thief* and *The Man from the Sea* (both 1927) and that of actress Musidora in Feuillade's *The Vampires* (1915–16).[26] Interestingly, the latter Magritte painting has the same title as a 1920 film by Marcel L'Herbier.[27] Evidently, as late as 1952, Magritte mentioned how watching Tay Garnett's film *The Racket* (1951) reminded him of Feuillade's serials.[28]

Finally, some critics have discussed a brief period in the 1950s and 1960s when Magritte made 8 mm home movies with his wife, Georgette; fellow artists; and friends—antic comedies that often transferred the images of his paintings onto the screen. As Peter Wollen notes, "Old music hall routines like the exchange of bowler hats re-surface [from his paintings] in Magritte's films. . . . Bowler hats, umbrellas, tubas and pipes are all repeated elements in his film farces—he mimics his paintings by putting a bowler hat on a shrouded head, he puts a series of hats on a bust, he uses the shadow silhouette of a bowler hat."[29] These works (rediscovered in the 1970s) were made only for private screenings. As Canonne remarks, they were "recreational rather than creative" in the higher sense of that term, and Magritte himself claimed that he did not make "cinema," but rather "movies," crafted casually in "the good old way."[30] Thus, he remained "faithful to the cinema of his youth, [and] subsequently rooted his experience as a 'filmmaker' in the burlesque mode."[31] According to his friend and fellow Surrealist, Louis Scutenaire (who appeared in some of these films): "When Magritte painted he was calm, often bored . . . and welcomed people bursting in on him. Quite the contrary, when he put on the guise of a filmmaker, he became agitated and acerbic yet all the same infinitely amused. He was, perhaps, never so happy as when he held the camera in his hand."[32]

Aside from these biographical observations, there are numerous occasions in which a critic writing about a film finds some intimation of the work of Magritte. Such remarks are generally made in passing without any thorough analysis. Not surprisingly, articles about Surrealist cinema often refer to Magritte. Thus, Marco Borroni relates the artist's painting *The Human Condition* (1933) (see figure 8.1) to *Un chien andalou* and *L'âge d'or*.[33] Similarly, Uwe M. Scheede mentions Magritte's *One Night Museum* (1927)—with its severed hand—in relation to the 1929 Buñuel film, and Canonne connects the imagery to the painting *The Difficult Crossing* (1926).[34] We do know from Georgette Magritte that he did in fact see *Un chien andalou*, which is not surprising since Dalí and Magritte were friends and in Paris at the same time.[35] In fact, in

August 1929 Magritte visited Dalí in Cadaqués, Spain, along with other artists, including Buñuel.[36] In the same spirit, Silvano Levy in his book *Surrealism: Surrealist Visuality*, speaks of Magritte's broad interest in film: "He shared the Surrealists' approach, seeing cinema at once as a novel and popular medium not yet encumbered with academic and aesthetic paraphernalia, as uniquely competent to undermine common sense and retinal notions of reality, and, by the same token, possessing the power to endow with conviction and substance the wildest flights of the imagination."[37] Levy traces some of Magritte's imagery directly to the movies (of course, noting *Fantômas*). But he also comments on how Magritte's "strategies for displacement and enigma-making, such as framing, editing and special effects of mise-en-scène, relate to film form."[38] Predictably, he also mentions parallels between Magritte's work and the Dalí/Buñuel film collaborations. Two contributors to Levy's book find connections between cinema and Magritte. Rob Stone notes parallels to the painter's work in considering Julio Medem's *Tierra* (1996) and *Los amantes del Círculo Polar* (1998),[39] while Barbara Creed locates them in relation to David Cronenberg's *Scanners* (1981) where people with telepathic powers remind her of Magritte's painting *The Pleasure Principle* (1937).[40]

Raymond Durgnat, in writing about Georges Franju (a director sometimes associated with Surrealism, discussed in chapter 13), remarks on how a scene of junk on the street in *Blood of the Beasts* (1949) is "akin to certain paintings of Magritte."[41] And Susan Felleman, in discussing Man Ray's film *Les mystères du château du Dé* (1929) mentions that characters with veiled faces are reminiscent of those in Magritte's painting *The Lovers* (1928) (see figure 2.2).[42]

Some commentators range further afield in their remarks. In P. Adams Sitney's book on the American avant-garde, for instance, he mentions Magritte's name (though no particular paintings) in examining the work of filmmakers Gregory Markopoulos, Pat O'Neill, and Sidney Peterson.[43] Likewise, in discussing the oeuvre of experimental filmmaker, Chantal Akerman, Jonathan Rosenbaum sees elements of her style as evocative of Magritte's. As he notes:

> René Magritte's painting *Man With Newspaper* (1927–8) [see figure 20.4] tells me something about the customary disquiet of Akerman's world. In it, four panels, two on top and two on the bottom, show the same corner of a sitting room, with one difference: in the first panel a man is seated at the table by the window reading a newspaper, and in the other three panels, neither the man nor the newspaper is in evidence. . . . Similarly, many of Akerman's settings suggest absence even more than presence.[44]

Furthermore, Rosenbaum sees her focus on bourgeois quotidian existence redolent of Magritte's perspective. Similarly, Catherine Flower, in writing about Akerman's *All Night Long* (1982), talks of how the director, like Magritte, works in "clichés and stereotypes," making the familiar seem strange.[45] Significantly, Akerman was also born in Belgium.

André Delvaux is another Belgian filmmaker that some have associated with Magritte. Lenuta Giukin, for instance, deems the latter part of Delvaux's "spiritual roots." She also observes that "in parallel with the bourgeois world of Magritte, most Delvaunian characters resemble the everyday man who goes unnoticed in the street."[46] Also considering Delvaux, Georgiana M. M. Colvile finds that "foreign audiences . . . were quick to detect the impact of Magritte . . . on his early work."[47] Evidently, Delvaux "had known Magritte and was consciously influenced by the uncanny spatial juxtapositions in the latter's paintings, which he realized could be transposed temporally into film."[48] In particular, Colville mentions a "Magrittian glow of a red lantern" in Delvaux's film *Belle* (1973) and a scene in *Un soir, un train* (1968) characterized by light similar to that in Magritte's *Domain of Light* series (1949–67) (see figure 20.7). Nonetheless, she sees Delvaux's films as marked more by the style of Magic Realism than Surrealism.[49]

In examining the work of another Belgian artist, Samy Szlingerbaum, Philip Mosley discusses the film *Bruxelles-transit* (1980) which concerns the displacement and immigration of a family of Jewish Holocaust survivors. As he observes:

> Szlingerbaum's documentary style usurps the traditional monumentality of the [train] station, rendering it instead an ordinary, uninspiring place. With subtle irony he thus dedramatizes the extraordinary arrival of his family in Brussels. At the same time his gentle, cadenced montage of the station interior and of trains at night has a hypnotic, oneiric quality often found in the canvases of fellow Belgian artists Paul Delvaux and Rene Magritte. . . . Like these painters, Szlingerbaum defamiliarizes the station and its surrounding area in order to reinvest them with the emotional value of a dreamscape, a locus of enigmatic hopes and fears, of strange journeys, long waitings, and brief encounters in silent, empty, timeless space.[50]

Several critics have compared the work of Alfred Hitchcock to that of Magritte (this even though the painter once called the director "an imbecile of great talent").[51] Ágnes Pethő, writing on *Spellbound*, talks of a moment when the eyes of two lovers meet and are superimposed over images of doors.

She finds this like the "surprising substitutions or framings" that occur in the work of Magritte, lending the film sequence "an almost surrealist stylization."[52] John Walker, on the other hand, sees in *Spellbound* a borrowing of Magrittian tropes in Dalí's famous dream sequence. The latter's use of eye imagery in the beginning of the episode is suggestive of Magritte's *The False Mirror* (1929)—which appears on the cover of this volume[53]—and his depiction of a man with a shrouded face harks back to Magritte's *The Central Story* (1928) and *The Lovers* (see figure 2.2).[54] Finally, Jeffrey Longacre observes that in the 1950s, Hitchcock "achieves a uniquely modernist gothic style, combining the 'negative aesthetics' of the Gothic tradition with modernist experimentations similar to Magritte's explorations of the tenuous relationship between language and images." He continues: "One might steal Magritte's title for his painting of a pipe, which is also not a pipe, to sum up Hitchcock's dialectical structure—dialogue-heavy scenes alternating with scenes of pure cinema—as his own cinematic depiction of the treason of images. His reminder that images, as avatars of the Real always exceeding the grasp of language, betray the words that would pin them down, hold them still, and make them mean."[55] More is said about Hitchcock and Magritte in chapter 17.

In analyzing Catherine Breillat's *À ma soeur* (2001), Trevor H. Maddock and Ivan Krisjansen perceive how the film "takes up an established theme, the ambiguity of the face and the body, particularly as it is depicted in Magritte's painting *Rape* (1935) (see figure 16.3), and renders it cinematically."[56] As for the movie's main character, Anaïs, they observe: "She represents an image of self-abolition and self-effacement, precisely the image of Magritte's *Rape,* which, ironically, is no rape at all."[57]

Commenting on the wry humor of Magritte's oeuvre, Wollen concentrates on connections between the artist's use of the bowler hat and silent film comedy:

> Chaplin's antics had both an ethical and a nihilist dimension. He appealed to intellectuals as well as to vulgarians. Magritte, like almost everybody else, was an admirer of Chaplin, as well as Laurel and Hardy, whose films he collected on Super-8 and whose bowler-hatted comedy routines he enthusiastically imitated in his own home movies. . . . In one sequence, his wife Georgette (wearing a von Stroheim-style spiky military helmet) salutes a painting of a bowler-hatted man standing with his back to us.[58]

Moreover, in studying Samuel Beckett's movie *Film* (1965), Enoch Brater notes how "Beckett's opening shot resembles . . . René Magritte's *False Mirror.*"[59]

Likewise, in introducing the topic of film semiotics in *The Film Experience: An Introduction*, Timothy Corrigan and Patricia White make reference to Magritte's pioneering use of word and image.[60] Finally, in discussing François Truffaut's *Fahrenheit 451* (1966), Garrett Stewart speaks of a photo of a character named Montag that shows the subject from behind (a familiar Magrittian stance), as well as a "Magritte-like reverse mirror of the man confronted, as if from behind, by his own facelessness."[61]

Certain other scholars remark on the appearance of Magritte's paintings as part of a movie's decor or broader discourse. Maryann De Julio, for instance, mentions Agnès Varda's employment of several Magritte works in *The Beaches of Agnès* (2008)—specifically, *The Lovers* and a riff on his "famous collage of surrealists' headshots, their eyes closed, with a nude woman in the centre of the page (replaced with snapshots of *La nouvelle vague* filmmakers, all men, their eyes open)."[62]

Other writers mention the presence of the artist's painting *Not to Be Reproduced* (1937) (see figure 12.5) in Bernardo Bertolucci's *The Spider's Stratagem* (1970) (discussed in chapter 18)[63] or note the reference to Magritte's *The Treachery of Images* (1929) (see figure 7.1) in Michael Snow's *So Is This* (1982) (discussed in chapter 7).[64] Furthermore, one website compares a poster for William Friedkin's *The Exorcist* (1973) to Magritte's *Domain of Light* series.[65] To this list, I might add a painting of an eyeball (reminiscent of Magritte's *The False Mirror*) that appears in several scenes in Richard Kelly's *Donnie Darko* (2001). It functions as part of the decor of the bedroom of the main character, a teenager (and a painter).

In contrast to passing references to Magritte's relation to cinema, there are two book chapters that examine the topic in more depth. Canonne's 2017 monograph, *René Magritte: The Revealing Image* (which has already been quoted extensively), has an entire section titled "The Imitation of Photography: Magritte and the Cinematograph." The second important work is Robert Short's chapter on Magritte and film in Silvano Levy's volume on Surrealism.[66] One should note, however, that part of his work is based on earlier research by French scholars.[67] Short discusses how Magritte's love of popular cinema conformed to the preferences of the Surrealist group that admired the humorous films of Mack Sennett, Buster Keaton, Charlie Chaplin, Harry Langdon, and the serials of Pearl White.[68] Like many critics, Short mentions Magritte's affinity to Louis Feuillade's *Fantômas* films, as seen in *The Murderer Threatened*. Here he quotes David Sylvester who delves further into the influence of the serials on Magritte's oeuvre: "There is the pervasive influence of Feuillade's way of seeing the world—an impassive gaze at acts of threats or violence or aberrations of nature or states of madness presented in a tidy, formal, often symmetrical setting, a gaze from a constant position at the level of the scene and squarely facing its centre. This is how Magritte's art also coolly confronts the world in all its terrible mystery."[69] Short also observes that in the mid-1920s Magritte wrote his own *Fantômas* film scripts. A fragment of one survives (involving the hero and his nemesis, Detective Juve) and reads:

> Fantômas is close by, sleeping deeply. In a matter of seconds, Juve has tied up the sleeper. Fantômas continues to dream, of his disguises as usual. . . . Juve, in the highest of spirits, pronounces some regrettable words. They cause the prisoner to start. He wakes up, and once awake, Fantômas is no longer Juve's captive. Juve has failed again this time. One means remains for him to achieve his end: Juve will have to get into one of Fantômas's dreams—he will try to take part as one of its characters.[70]

In this imaginative scenario, one recognizes the Surrealist interest in the oneiric state, which Magritte complicates by having a detective enter a criminal's mind. Finally, Short also observes that Magritte once dressed his wife to resemble the actress Musidora—the star of another Feuillade serial—and photographed her in that attire.

In addition, Short postulates less well-known cinematic influences on Magritte's work. While acknowledging the disagreement among critics as to the origin of the bells that obsessively populate Magritte's canvases, he finds a possible source for them in a scene from Fritz Lang's *Dr. Mabuse, the Gambler* (1922). Similarly, he locates in Lang's *The Testament of Dr. Mabuse* (1933) a possible root for the bilboquets that Magritte often includes in his paintings. As for Magritte's ocular portrait, *The False Mirror*, Short cites a shot of a giant eye in Karl Grune's *The Street* (1923).

Like many other critics, Short remarks on how the four quadrants of Magritte's *Man with a Newspaper* (1928) (see figure 20.4) resemble film frames. He also notes how the "fragmented nude portrait of Georgette, titled *Eternal Evidence* [*The Eternally Obvious*] (1930), approximates a series of individual close-ups."[71] Moreover, he observes that the eye-line vectors of subjects in paintings like *Person Meditating on Madness* (1928) align their vision with something outside the frame, as is often the case with cinematic shots.[72]

Referencing the early fantasy film director Ferdinand Zecca, Short comments on how the whimsical scenarios in Magritte's paintings bear comparison to cinematic special effects.[73] And citing Georges Méliès's *The Man with the Rubber Head* (1901)—also mentioned by Canonne—he talks of Magritte's play with scale.[74] (Méliès is discussed further in chapters 6 and 16.) Taking a broader perspective, Short notes the melodramatic quality of many Magritte paintings, like *Titanic Days* (1928), in which a man appears to attack a woman (see figure18.3), and sees that tone tied to silent film narrative.[75]

Like many other scholars, Short finds parallels between Surrealist films and Magritte's work. As for a tie to *Un chien andalou*, he notes a similar substitution of one body part for another in Magritte's *Rape*, in which a torso replicates a face.[76] Commenting on *L'âge d'or*, he finds comparisons between the work's fetishistic "confusion of a dress and its wearer"—and Magritte's *Philosophy in the Boudoir* (1947).[77]

Beyond the painter's script for a *Fantômas* film, Short describes some other unrealized cinematic projects with which Magritte was involved. There was a scenario cowritten with Paul Nougé titled "The Space of Thought," variously dated 1928 or 1932, that contained "a string of descriptions of iconography which might have been drawn directly from Magritte's paintings of the time: 'The night opens on a man viewed from behind, holding in his hand a mirror in which one sees a painted picture'; 'Empty sky, a cloud, a piece of cloth blowing'; 'Seated Woman with head veiled.'"[78] In talking about the same work, Michel Draguet and Claude Goormans note that it paid tribute to *Un chien andalou* and involved themes of "ambiguous perception, mirrors, somnambulism, dead ends and the virtuality of representation."[79]

Furthermore, Short mentions a planned project with Belgian filmmaker Henri Storck in 1936, titled "L'idée fixe" (although Canonne attributes coauthorship to Nougé).[80] It was "liberally scattered with Magrittian motifs, such as the burning tuba, the locomotive in the fireplace, trees with horsebells for fruit." Moreover, it borrowed from *L'âge d'or* a "scene of an orgy with couples rolling on the ground intercut with a shot of a cemetery and a sequence of notables and priests walking with a martial step, carrying flags amid explosions."[81]

In addition, Short provides details about Magritte's amateur movies (discussed in more detail in the next chapter).[82] He quotes a 1956 letter written by Magritte to Louis Scutenaire in which the artist requests ideas for "a few scenes that will be easy to film" involving Georgette and a colleague, Irène Hamoir: "For example, Irène sucks one of Scutenaire's thumbs and Georgette the other. Or Irène and Georgette are sleepwalking with their heads leaning on pillows they are holding."[83] Evidently, however, within short order, Magritte declared himself done with filmmaking, telling Maurice Rapin that it was "tiring and hardly remunerative." Thus, he would "bury [his work on] cinema, the interest of which seems . . . more and more problematic."[84]

Although Short does not discuss the technology that Magritte used for his home movies, other sources reveal that he employed an 8 mm camera. As Daniel Urban notes, "In October 1956, Magritte acquired a Eumig C3, an 8mm camera that was made in Austria. He also owned a Kodak Instamatic M6 which could also be used for Super 8 footage."[85] Short seems less interested in Magritte's influence *on* the cinema (than the reverse dynamic). He locates some Surrealist films that he feels bear the painter's mark: Marcel Mariën's *Imitation du cinéma* (1960)[86] and Jacques Brunius's *Violons d'Ingres* (1939). While the former work does not directly reference Magritte, it concerns the whimsical pursuits of amateur inventors and artists who share his imaginative bent: "naive" sculptors and painters, makers of carnival masks, people who craft flying machines or robotic toys, model-ship builders and those who fashion ships in bottles. The latter image, of course, is the most Magrittian—given the paradox of a sailing craft housed in air and glass. While Mariën does cite canonical figures like Georges Méliès and Henri Rousseau, he privileges the work of self-taught architect and fantasist, postman Ferdinand Cheval, who built a Surrealist-inspired "ideal palace" for himself (made of carved rock) in Hauterives, France—according to the dictates of a dream. One website describes his creation as follows: "This palace looks like a cross between a temple of Angkor and La Sagrada Familia, but up close it's much like a Monet painting with small pebbles and stones replacing the intricate brush strokes. Pillars, flying buttresses and grottoes carefully crafted of found stones form the 26 meters long and 10 meters high."[87] As for more mainstream movies, Short mentions Paul Cox's *Man of Flowers* (1983), Nicolas Roeg's *Performance* (1970), Terry Gilliam's *Time Bandits* (1981), and Jaco van Dormael's *Toto the Hero* (1991)—but he never expands on these references by linking specific scenes from the films to works by Magritte.

Finally, Short observes that although the photographic realism of Magritte's style would seem to have made his imagery translatable to the screen, Magritte and film "never made a good match."[88] He concludes that "with Magritte the cinema effect can only dissipate the painting effect."[89]

I beg to differ and hope to demonstrate this point in the pages that follow. While aside from the writings of Short and Canonne, most other critical references to Magritte and film seem instances of "drive by" commentary, the sheer *number* of such remarks is testament to the fact that parallels are resonant and noteworthy.

There is one biographical issue that Short raises in passing that needs further attention, the fact that starting around 1918 (with an ad for "pot au feu Derbaix") Magritte earned a considerable portion of his income through commercial commissions.[90] Short notes the Surrealists' interest in advertising, which they accepted as part of the modern idiom and milieu.

In the early 1920s, Magritte worked for the Peters-Lacroix wallpaper factory in Haren.[91] Nonetheless, his attitude toward the applied arts was negative. In 1922, he and Victor Servranckx (a coworker) wrote an article titled "Pure Art: Defense of the Aesthetic." In one passage, they wrote emphatically "APPLIED ART KILLS PURE ART"; furthermore, in 1949 Magritte called advertisements "modern propaganda."[92] Nonetheless, Magritte sought work as a graphic designer and produced many ads for Maison Norine—a fashion house—as well as crafting a decorative mural for the company.[93]

But his most important commission came from the Samuel Fur Company (Maison Samuel). In 1927, he and a friend, poet Paul Nougé, created a groundbreaking catalog (composed of both image and text) for the business—with Magritte providing collages comprising drawings, paintings, and cutouts of photos.[94] Here is how Alastair Sooke describes it: "Containing 16 full-page designs, accompanied by enigmatic texts by . . . Nougé, it is full of inscrutable women swathed in sumptuous furs, occupying strange, indeterminate settings."[95] Sooke contradicts the notion that Magritte discounted his advertising work by stating that "Magritte was so proud of his efforts that, when he moved to Paris in September 1927, he took the [Maison Samuel] brochure with him, hoping to impress André Breton, the leader of the Surrealists. (He reported to Nougé that Breton liked what he saw.)"[96] According to Sooke, in 1930, having returned to Brussels and "worried about money, [Magritte] set up the 'Studio Dongo' advertising agency with his brother Paul, colonising the shambolic shed at the bottom of his garden as a workshop."[97] The company continued to exist until 1946.[98]

In addition to fashion ads, Magritte also designed sheet music covers and illustrated books, most notably the previously mentioned Surrealist favorite *Les chants de Maldoror*. While many art historians see little relationship between Magritte's commercial and art work, Roger Rothman sees them as tied through opposition. For him, the painter's oeuvre sought to disrupt "patterns established by the commodity culture of urban capitalism."[99] Moreover, Rothman finds Magritte's work "steeped in an urban experience of image saturation."[100] Sooke agrees that Magritte's two types of production are linked but offers different reasons. He sees the artist as favoring "bold, frontal, symmetrical compositions . . . [that] frequently combine images with words, like adverts trumpeting slogans. Objects, such as the famous pipe in *The Treachery of Images*, seem to float in mid-air like shop signs."[101]

One wonders whether Magritte's condescension toward commercial art did not factor into his love/hate for the movies. He was passionate about the medium as a viewer but dismissive of it aesthetically. According to Short, he was an avid filmgoer into old age, "patronizing any Brussels flea pit in his locality that would also tolerate his Pomeranian, Loulou."[102] But Magritte scorned the so-called Art Film (which he found pompous) and asserted that his favorite movies were *Babette Goes to War* (Christian-Jaque, 1959) and *Madame et son auto* (Robert Vernay, 1958)—the former a Brigitte Bardot potboiler and the latter a routine comedy.[103] He evidently disliked François Truffaut's *The 400 Blows* (1959), which he found a work "without cinema" equipped only with an "edifying" message.[104] With decidedly popular taste (he loved Westerns),[105] Magritte once stated that he could not "stand cinema that tries to teach me something or present an argument: that kind of cinema bores me . . . Lack of pretention paradoxically leaves the indispensable morality intact."[106] More and more, he wrote of filmgoing, "I stay fifteen minutes when I give it a try."[107] Nonetheless, he said that he "used the cinema as a kind of 'workshop of chance.'"[108]

Intermediality in Cinema: Film and Painting

> Rectangle for rectangle, much less critical attention has hitherto been paid to the interaction between the white canvas and the silver screen than to, say, the painting and the photo.
>
> Robert Short[109]

In writing on Magritte and film, I place my work within the scholarly tradition of "intermedial" criticism that relates one art form to another. In its original sense, the term meant "to come in between two things"—which is the stance I assume as a film scholar investigating other visual arts.[110] In so doing, however, a critic must nonetheless mark her "home turf," and mine is decidedly the cinema, as is emphasized in the chapters that follow. While all the books I survey below advance the interarts approach to film studies, none emphasizes Magritte's relation to the cinema—the primary argument of my volume.

The major book in this area is Pethő's *Cinema and Intermediality: The Passion for the In-Between*. As she notes, "The idea that cinema is unavoidably interconnected with other media and arts has been a constant issue addressed by theories . . . since the first moving picture shows were presented in a theatrical environment."[111] She describes the intermedial state in various ways. First, it is dynamic, involving "a system or a network of interactions . . . of media convergence and transformation."[112] Second, it is distinguished from more limited forms of textual linkage: "Where intertextuality expresses a text-text relationship, intermedial means that the reference frame of the entire system of art forms that mediates the intermedial correlation is itself included in the process of transformation."[113] Third, the critical practice of assigning intermediality to a given work "is not something one 'deciphers,' it is something one perceives or senses."[114] Finally, Pethő sees film form as becoming progressively more intermedial. As she notes, "Paradoxically, the more motion pictures engage in inter-art or intermedia 'games,' becoming increasingly 'literary,' 'theatrical,' or 'painterly,' the more they expose regarding the nature, possibilities and limitation of their own medium."[115]

Several of Pethő's points have direct relevance to my approach in *Cinemagritte*. While at times I will be dealing with intertextual relations (e.g., parallels between the use of frames in Peter Greenaway's *The Draughtsman's Contract* [1982] and in Magritte's art), such an observation would be of only minimal interest were it not that the frame also constitutes a prominent feature of film practice and theory. Hence, Pethő's notion that an art form's "entire system" is involved in intermediality is much to the point. Moreover, her sense that engaging other arts can highlight (rather than obscure) the nature of a medium is central to my project, much as André Bazin and Susan Sontag argued that there is a productive means of associating film and theater without diluting the former.[116] Finally, Pethő's assertion that ascribing intermediality to a text is something that the scholar "perceives or senses" rather than "deciphers" squares with my view that in tracing links between cinema and Magritte's art, I seek resonances of the latter in the former.

But while there is little work on the topic of intermediality and film, there has been considerable research on *cinema and painting*—largely my purview in this book, though Magritte also worked in other forms (e.g., sculpture and collage). Here I limit my discussion to English-language texts that deal with the subject on a broad level rather than as it pertains to an individual film or filmmaker.[117]

Perhaps the earliest essay on film and painting came as a chapter in Vachel Lindsay's *The Art of the Moving Picture*, published in 1915. While he sees the "action film" as amenable to "sculpture in motion,"[118] in discussing painting he focuses on the "intimate and friendly motion picture" (in other words, the drama).[119] Calling it "painting in motion," he compares an image of Mary Pickford playing Fanchon the Cricket to a Greek painting by Nikolaos Gysis.[120] Alternatively, the look of French photoplays makes him think of the canvases of Jean Charles Cazin.[121] He concludes that "the reader will find in his rounds of the picture theatres many single scenes and parts of plays that elucidate the title of this chapter"—painting in motion.[122] He goes even one step further by likening the large advertising photographs selected from films and displayed in front of theaters to the "commercial beginning of an art gallery."[123] While implicitly early film criticism and theory often drew on the other arts to "validate" the nascent cinema, later writing (including my own in this monograph), takes film's legitimacy for granted.

Some decades after Lindsay's essay was written, André Bazin published "Painting and Cinema." Here he confines himself to discussions of documentaries about artists or artworks rather than to dramatic or experimental films that draw upon a painter's style. Like other critics and practitioners, Bazin is skeptical of cinema's ability to do painting justice. As he notes, "Even should the film-maker wish to conform to the facts of art history, the instrument he uses would still be aesthetically at odds with them. As a film-maker he fragments what is by essence a synthesis while himself working towards a new synthesis never envisioned by the painter."[124]

Bazin sees a further problem in the process of rendering an artwork on screen: "Not only is the film a betrayal of the painter, it is also a betrayal of the painting and for this reason; the viewer, believing that he is seeing the picture as painted, is actually looking at it through the instrumentality of an art form that profoundly changes its nature."[125] On the other hand, Bazin realizes that films about paintings are a means of introducing the public to art, and in this sense he acknowledges their value. Thus, he praises filmmakers like Luciano Emmer, Henri Storck, Alain Resnais, and Pierre Kast who "have found a way to bring the work of art within the range of everyday seeing so that a man needs no more than a pair of eyes for the task."[126]

More recently, Angela Dalle Vacche has written an article on Bazin's broader conceptualization of the art documentary, drawing on numerous writings and reviews beyond "Painting and Cinema."[127] From this we learn that he considers the art documentary a new independent, experimental genre that bridges the gap between mass culture and the avant-garde.[128] Nuancing his concerns about cinematic technique destroying the style of a painting, he notes that "the work of art cannot be compared to a precision instrument, and it will not cease to exist even when attacked in its elements and structures."[129] Neither is Bazin troubled by the question of losing the aura when a painting is rendered on film.[130] Ultimately, he favored art documentaries that refused to depict the frame of the canvas, thereby reducing a sense of its objecthood.[131] Doing so enabled the camera to look at the painting as though through a keyhole—permitting the viewer to see the art work "not within but through the screen."[132]

Other recent works on cinema and painting take a more expansive approach. While John Walker's *Art and Artists on Screen* does consider art documentaries, it also studies biopics and dramas about fictional artists, as well as films made by artists. In the first category, he explores cinematic biographies of Vincent van Gogh (*Lust for Life* [George Cukor, 1956]), Paul Gauguin (*The Wolf at the Door* [Henning Carlsen, 1986]), and Henri de Toulouse-Lautrec (*Moulin Rouge* [John Huston, 1952]). Here it is interesting to speculate that the reason there are no well-known biopics on Magritte is because he led a rather ordinary life (married to the same woman for decades, living primarily in the country of his birth)—just like the bourgeois bowler-hatted men he pictured in his canvases. In the second group, Walker discusses fictional films about artists like *The Fountainhead* (King Vidor, 1949) and *The Rebel* (aka *Call Me Genius*; Robert Day, 1961). Finally, in the third category, he examines films made by artists—specifically László Moholy-Nagy and Andy Warhol. Walker's aim in the volume is "to provide a critical analysis of key English language films about art and artists from the 1930s to the present day."[133]

Brigitte Puecker's *Incorporating Images: Film and the Rival Arts* takes a more theoretical stance and contemplates cinema's relation to both literature and art. Her intent is to explore "the problematic space that film occupies between the established arts," which she views as an "agonistic dynamic . . . as cinema struggles for self-legitimation through the appropriation, revision, and subversion of literary and painterly tropes."[134] In speaking of F. W. Murnau's *Sunrise* (1927), for instance, she observes the film's "conflict between pictorial and cinematic space" which is "suggested by the film's opening shots."[135] She also finds the first part of the drama (which is set in the country) tied to landscape painting, while the second (set in the city) evokes the world of cinema.[136] In speaking of Murnau's later film *Tabu* (1930)—set in the South Seas—she finds its imagery curiously linked to Greek sculpture and Nicolas Poussin's mythological paintings. Finally, in Rainer Werner Fassbinder's inclusion of a famous painting in the set for *The Bitter Tears of Petra von Kant* (1972), she sees evidence that his work is characterized by "a layering of painting, sculpture, theater, and the cinematic."[137]

In Puecker's later book, *The Material Image: Art and the Real in Film*, she focuses (among other things) on the manner in which artistic texts overlay various modes of representation.[138] Thus, in discussing, Martin Scorsese's *The Age of Innocence* (1993), for instance she notes its painterly style as well as a shot with ties to a canvas by Caspar David Friedrich.[139] In another chapter, she examines films by Wim Wenders and Peter Greenaway that "'take up well-known paintings by Vermeer."[140] In considering the oeuvre of Leni

Riefenstahl, she discusses the relation of *Olympia* (1938) to Greek sculpture and architecture.[141] And in two sections concerning director Alfred Hitchcock, she investigates how sculpture and painting inform his films' representational discourse.[142]

Dalle Vacche's *Cinema and Painting: How Art Is Used in Film* examines how pictorial sources are employed by eight filmmakers. Thus, she analyzes Vincente Minnelli's *An American in Paris* (1951), Michelangelo Antonioni's *Red Desert* (1964), Eric Rohmer's *The Marquise of O* (1976), Jean-Luc Godard's *Pierrot le fou* (1965), Andrei Tarkovsky's *Andrei Rublev* (1966), F. W. Murnau's *Nosferatu* (1922), Kenji Mizoguchi's *Five Women around Utamaro* (1946), and Alain Cavalier's *Thérèse* (1986). In her introductory chapter (which proclaims a "thematic and intertextual approach"), she notes how filmmakers often "use paintings to shape or enrich the meaning of their works." Thus, she argues that "the history of art is *in* film."[143]

In her later edited collection, *The Visual Turn: Classical Film Theory and Art History*, Dalle Vacche curates canonical essays on the topic of painting and film as well as more contemporary ones that engage those critical texts.[144] Among the former is Rudolf Arnheim's "Painting and Film," which opens by talking about the difficulty of comparing a static art like painting to a moving image medium like cinema. Nonetheless, he asserts that films have learned from painting how "eye catching lines organize and unify the many visible objects" they depict with spaces "balanced according to size, form, and light." Although Arnheim is writing in the era of black-and-white cinematography, he opines that "the introduction of color film will create a new relationship between painting and film." However, he feels that film's inherent realism is at odds with painterly form. As he notes, "Whereas in painting . . . the objects of reality may seem painted—that is, they are *supposed* to seem as though they were painted—this seems to be impossible and distracting in film." He sees more possibility in the realm of abstract animation (vs. cartoons), which could "expand the means of painting into an art of time and motion."[145]

Susan Felleman's *Art in the Cinematic Imagination* explores the way movies have employed artworks and artist figures as part of their narratives (be those individuals fictional or real). In one chapter, she investigates the meaning of painted portraits in Hollywood movies (e.g., *Rebecca* [Hitchcock, 1940]). In another, she expands her focus on portraits by analyzing films (like *Pandora and the Flying Dutchman* [Albert Lewin, 1951]) in which such paintings are contextualized within a particular narrative trope (men who fall in love with women resembling their dead paramours). In a third chapter (drawing on works like *The Barefoot Contessa* [Joseph L. Mankiewicz, 1954]), she explores the way sculpture "fleshes out . . . the problematics of corporeality, carnality, and embodiment" in film.[146]

In another book, *Real Objects in Unreal Situations: Modern Art in Fiction Films*, Felleman studies the use of actual artworks in Hollywood films—primarily paintings, drawings, and sculptures.[147] She examines their fate in movies about fictional artists (e.g., a sculpture by Salvatore Cartaino Scarpitta in *The Song of Songs* [Rouben Mamoulian,1933] or a work like *Pride & Prejudice* [Joe Wright, 2005] in which a painting by Louis Laguerre appears). She contends that rather than being mere pieces of decor or props in a film, such artworks play important narrative, thematic, symbolic, and theoretical roles.

In *Framing Pictures: Film and the Visual Arts*, Steven Jacobs confronts a wide variety of issues concerning the relation between cinema and art. His first chapter focuses upon the type of art documentaries that Bazin considered, looking for how they test the boundaries between two media. His second chapter examines artist biopics, which mostly convey the familiar "romantic idea of the artist as a misunderstood genius."[148] His third chapter investigates scenes in which film characters visit museums (as in Hitchcock's *Vertigo* [1958]), which tend to address the act of looking. His fourth chapter explores the tableau vivant in post–World War II Modernist films like Jean-Luc Godard's *Passion* (1982). His fifth chapter considers the role of the film still and how it has been appropriated by artists like Cindy Sherman. His final chapter discusses the preponderance of filmic images in contemporary art museums and exhibitions.

Moving Pictures: American Art and Early Film, 1880–1910, edited by Nancy Mowll Mathews, takes a national and historical approach to the subject, examining early works of cinema for their connections to art.[149] In her introduction, Mathews makes clear that the "consistent 'rhyming' of still and moving images throughout [the book] is not intended to imply a direct influence one way or another, but rather to offer provocative new juxtapositions that broaden our understanding of each and the many ways they might be related."[150] Here (within a very different context), she echoes my thoughts about the process of apposing Magritte's oeuvre and film. The volume is divided into several sections with contributions by various scholars. In "Early Film and American Artistic Traditions," the cinema of the period is associated with paintings by Winslow Homer, John Singer Sargent, and American muralists. In "The Body in Motion," films about weight lifting or boxing are discussed in terms of the photographic work of Eadweard Muybridge and Thomas Eakins. In "The City in Motion," paintings by Childe Hassam and others by John Sloan are juxtaposed with movies about the urban scene (like *Madison Square New York* [1903] or *Panorama of Flatiron Building* [1902]). Finally, in "Art and Film: Interactions," writers consider how early movies represented art (as in J. Stuart Blackton's *The Enchanted Drawing* [1900]), and how art works represented film (e.g., paintings, magazine illustrations, and posters). One author also examines the status of trompe l'oeil in painting and film.

Perhaps the most interesting of all the books on painting and film and the one most relevant to *Cinemagritte* is a catalog published in conjunction with an exhibit, *Hitchcock and Art: Fatal Coincidences* at the Montreal Museum of Fine Arts between 2000 and 2001. Edited by Dominique Païni and Guy Cogeval, it presents a series of essays on the relationship between Hitchcock and a variety of arts (both visual and literary) and includes illustrations of the various paintings, sketches, prints, and photographs that were displayed in the exhibition.[151] Not surprisingly, the article on Hitchcock, Dalí, and Surrealism mentions Magritte twice, although only in passing.[152] But the exhibit (and hence the catalog) includes several works by Magritte: one listed as *Untitled* (1941) but a version of *Rape*, a print titled *Duo* (1928) but clearly a version of *The Lovers* (painted in the same year) and *Deep Waters* (1941). Similar to my perspective, Païni writes that the "exhibition is intended neither as a demonstration nor a sequence of comparative proofs It is meant as a reading—an *interpretation*."[153]

While all the books previously discussed are scholarly ones, *Art History for Filmmakers: The Art of Visual Storytelling* by Gillian McIver is a guide for practitioners, illustrating how to draw upon art history in creating works of cinema. As McIver says, "This book talks about art using the language of film and demonstrates the link between the two is strong and unbreakable."[154] McIver first discusses how "the cinematic can be found in art"—specifically, in paintings "in which there is a clear sense of mise-en-scène, composition, lighting and . . . color, which puts us in the frame of mind of a motion picture."[155] She also asserts that paintings can often give movie production designers an image of the past, useful in making historical dramas.[156] In discussing the Surrealist movement (and certain films that employ its aesthetic), McIver devotes a section to Magritte and "the subversion of the real."[157] As part of that, she mentions one film that might have relevance to the painter's use of *depaysment* (disorientation): Spike Jonze's *Being John Malkovich* (1999) "with its Magritte-like floor 7½."[158] (That film will is discussed in chapter 20, though from a different vantage point.) Like others, she also cites the poster for *The Exorcist* as bearing a resemblance to Magritte's *Domain of Light* series.

While these books on painting and film make extremely valuable contributions to the field and set the stage for further work in the area, *all but two make no (or scant) reference to Magritte*. I hope to change that situation by demonstrating Magritte's extraordinary relevance to the field of film and media studies.

Before I lay out precisely what areas I *will* cover in *Cinemagritte*, I should say what I will *not*.

1. There is a vast body of scholarly work by art historians and critics concerning René Magritte's life, career, oeuvre, and relation to other artists. While I will draw on this material at several points, I will not attempt to repeat it. I write as a film critic and historian, and my approach will reflect my academic field of expertise.
2. There is also an enormous archive of published work on Surrealism as well as its relation to the cinema. While I will refer to this material, I will not attempt to summarize its immense parameters.
3. While it is known that Magritte was an avid filmgoer, unfortunately I cannot report in any depth on which movies he saw since, aside from a few written or spoken allusions, he failed to discuss this. Moreover, most critics make scant reference to the specifics of this aspect of his life.
4. While at times I will perform readings of Magritte's paintings, I will not focus (to any major degree) on interpreting them—that is, seeing his flowers as signifying female genitals, his horses as signifying Nature, or his bilboquets as signifying phalluses. My approach is consonant with how Magritte felt his work should be viewed. As he remarked, "People cannot know my painting if they associate it with any kind of symbolism, whether naïve or sophisticated," since "the symbol is always the negation of poetry."[159] By this he meant that once we affix a particular meaning to an art work, its broader mystery dissolves.
5. While it is clear and well established that Magritte and other Surrealists articulate a problematic vision of Woman (potentially marked by voyeurism, fetishism, essentialism, misogyny, and idealization), I will not rehearse these arguments, except in cases where it is required for my vantage point on an individual work. Instead, I will assume it as a "given."

6. While much of this book conforms to conventional academic scholarship—for example, this introduction whose observations are rife with bibliographic citations—some of it does not. Those sections in which I seek resonances of Magritte's work in film practice and theory depend as much on my imagination as on my research skills as a traditional scholar. Through these passages (which employ creative juxtaposition), I hope to add a novel perspective to the "already known," by conceiving the conceptual and iconographic relevance of his oeuvre to the cinema.
7. Finally, the dates and titles of Magritte's work have been checked with the *Catalogue raisonné* of his work or other reliable sources (books, catalogs, etc.).[160] Sometimes, however, the information provided by the source from which I have acquired an image of a work differs from the *Catalogue*. In that case, I use the *Catalogue*'s title and date in the text. As for illustration captions, I use the title I have referenced in the text. However, if the source used a French title or a variant English title, I indicate that in parentheses.

Full credits for the Magritte illustrations are found at the end of the book. Beyond this, the process of naming and dating Magritte's work is complicated by the fact that he frequently made numerous works with the same titles at different times in his life—with similar or sometimes different iconographies (e.g., *The Domain of Light*, *The Giantess*, *The Ladder of Fire*, or *The Interpretation of Dreams*, to name but a few). Finally, I have chosen, in general, to list the titles of Magritte's works in English, given the audience for this book, unless they are always referred to in French.

Aside from the preface and introduction, part 1 of *Cinemagritte* ("Backstory") contains three additional chapters:

In chapter 2, I examine a variety of art documentaries that have been made about Magritte—some routine (presenting his biography and paintings with standard voice-over lecture) while others more inventive (involving dramatization or an attempt to convey his style using cinematic special effects). Many of them contain excerpts of the amateur home movies that Magritte, his wife, and friends shot together in the 1950s and 1960s. As my analysis will reveal, some of these films simply resemble silent comedies, while others seek to translate imagery from the artist's canvases into motion-picture discourse.

In chapter 3, I examine several films that are clear homages to Magritte—ranging from experimental ones by Anita Thatcher, to feature films by Alain Robbe-Grillet, to music videos (for a Paul Simon song) by Joan Logue. In addition, I explore some web-based YouTube videos that either attempt to re-create Magritte canvases in live action, "enter" the world of a Magritte painting, create Magritte GIFs (graphics interchange formats), or otherwise transform single or multiple Magritte artworks.

I look at the broader Belgian cinematic avant-garde in chapter 4, focusing on works by two filmmakers: Ernst Moerman and Henri Storck.

The second part of *Cinemagritte* ("Resonances") is broken down into seventeen short chapters that highlight conceptual issues that are important in Magritte's art and strive to find resonances of them in works of cinema. In most cases, no direct influence of Magritte's paintings on the films in question is asserted, or impact of movies upon his own work proclaimed (though this is always possible and, in some cases applies). Rather, what is often highlighted is the way Magritte's concerns are hospitable and familiar to the cinema and, in fact, engage topics and techniques that have been prominent in film history, theory, and practice.

In chapter 5, I foreground paintings by Magritte that stress vision and the act of illicit looking—as through a keyhole (e.g., in *The Spy* [1928]; see figure 5.1)—and compare them to films in which a similar theme of voyeurism is present (e.g., *The Blood of a Poet* [Jean Cocteau, 1932] and *The Peeping Tom* [1897]).

I take as my chapter 6 starting point Magritte's *Attempting the Impossible* (1928) (see figure 6.1), in which an artist is shown painting a "real" woman instead of a canvas. I compare this to works like Woody Allen's *The Purple Rose of Cairo* (1985) and others, in which fictional characters emerge from the movie screen into the real world.

Magritte is perhaps best known for canvases like *The Treachery of Images* (see figure 7.1) that intermix language and picture in an ironic fashion. In chapter 7, I offer a comparison of this and other such Magritte works to films like Hollis Frampton's *Zorns Lemma* (1970) and Snow's *So Is This*, which employ a similar word/image strategy.

In chapter 8, I highlight works like Magritte's *The Human Condition* (see figure 8.1), which confuses a canvas and the view through a window, as well as paintings like the 1931 version of *La belle captive* (see figure 8.2), which places a picture directly in a field identical to the painted landscape on it. I compare such works to Greenaway's *The Draughtsman's Contract*, in which an artist uses a rectangular grid device (on the grounds of an estate) to frame the scene that he is sketching.

Magritte's canvas *The Blood-letting* (1938 or 1939) (see figure 9.1), which portrays a pictureless frame that seems to provide access to the bricks behind the gallery wall (as if through X-ray vision) is the focus of chapter 9. I compare this to various films, starting with those from the primitive cinema (like *The X-Rays* [George Albert Smith, 1897]) and proceeding to more recent ones that use cinematic techniques to achieve the illusion of transparency (like Roger Corman's *X: The Man with the X-Ray Eyes* [1963]). Beyond that, I examine Hollis Frampton's ironically titled *Special Effects* (1972), which depicts nothing but a white frame devoid of any image.

In chapter 10, I foreground a poster that Magritte designed for the Second Film and Fine Arts World Festival of Belgium in 1949 (see figure 10.1), which pictures the head of a woman whose forehead contains a blank rectangle resembling a movie screen. I read this as an emblem of consciousness that dovetails with film theories that have seen parallels between cinema and the mind. I go on to highlight Michel Gondry's *Eternal Sunshine of the Spotless Mind* (2004), which uses film technique to approximate human memory. In discussing the movie's cinematic tropes, I draw parallels to many other Magritte paintings.

In the late 1940s, Magritte created a body of work that came to be known as his "stone age" paintings because they often depicted living things (people or animals) as rocks (e.g., *The Wonders of Nature* [1953]; see figure 11.3). In chapter 11, I compare such canvases to films in which characters are petrified—ranging from French art films like *Les visiteurs du soir* (Marcel Carné, 1942) to British horror movies like *The Gorgon* (Terence Fisher, 1964). But I also look to film theory for a "parallel" to petrification and find it in the freeze frame and the photograph, which I discuss in relation to such works as Chris Marker's *La jetée* (1962) and Hollis Frampton's *(nostalgia)* (1971).

While it would seem that animation (with its graphic roots and fantastic subject matter) would be amenable to borrowings from Magritte's paintings, examples are difficult to find. In chapter 12, I do discuss a commercial work that shows some relation to Magritte's Surrealist iconography, *Porky in Wackyland* (1938), directed by Robert Clampett. However, I concentrate on the avant-garde animation of Czech filmmaker Jan Švankmajer.

One of the favored pictorial elements in Magritte's work is the human face, but he often obscures it in various ways: by having the subject's back to the viewer, by blocking it with some object, or by having the individual wear a mask (as does one of the artist's film heroes—Fantômas). In chapter 13, I first discuss the importance of the face in early film theory and then move on to the ubiquity of the masked face in cinema as exemplified in such works as Max Ophüls's *Le plaisir* (1952) and two works by Georges Franju (*Eyes without a Face* [1960] and *Judex* [1963]).

Because Magritte's canvases are not bound by rules of nature or cause and effect, some of his art invokes the genre of science fiction. In many of his works, heavy objects (like boulders) float in the sky defying the rules of gravity. In discussing them in chapter 14, I draw parallels to cinema's ability to negate gravity through the midair freeze frame as well as through camera tricks (as in Fred Astaire's dancing on and walls and ceiling in *Royal Wedding* [Stanley Donen, 1951]). I also read Magritte's painting *The Double Secret* (1927) (see figure 14.1) as portraying a kind of android whose flayed skin reveals non-human interstices. I compare this work to moments in certain science-fiction films in which the robot's facial covering is ripped off to show its mechanical innards (e.g., *Ex Machina* [Alex Garland, 2015]).

Many works by Magritte take as their subject whimsical or monstrous combinations of people and animals, as in *Collective Invention* (1934) (see figure 15.1), which depicts a fish-man. In chapter 15, I compare Magritte's art to horror films involving interspecies mixings such as *The Island of Lost Souls* (Erle Kenton, 1932) and *Splice* (Vincenzo Natali, 2009).

In depicting the human body, Magritte often decapitates his subjects (e.g., *The Double Reality* [1936]; see figure 16.2), separates them into pieces (e.g., *The Eternally Obvious*), or repeats them in series (e.g., *The Month of the Grape Harvest* [1959]; see figure 3.6). In chapter 16, I relate Magritte's paintings to the trick/magic films of early cineaste Georges Méliès, whose work Magritte knew and admired.

In chapter 17, I turn to the numerous paintings in which Magritte depicts windows. Sometimes a canvas stands before them, confusing the view inside and out. At other times, a windowpane is paradoxically imprinted with the image of the landscape outside. Occasionally, people stare voyeuristically through a window into a room. I focus on the enigmatic painting *In Praise of the Dialectic* (1937) (see figure 17.1), in which the view through a window reveals another building's facade and windows inside, where I find parallels to Hitchcock's *Rear Window* (1954).

A recurrent and obsessive iconographic element of Magritte's work is the bell (as in *The Voice of the Air* [1928]; see figure 18.1), the type one finds on a horse's harness. Though generally I refrain from interpreting Magritte's imagery, in chapter 18 I read the bell as a stand-in for the female genitalia. I then proceed to relate such paintings to Luis Buñuel's film *Belle de Jour* (1967)—with its focus on female sexuality, sadomasochism, and prostitution—since whenever the heroine veers into erotic fantasy, we hear the sound of such bells.

Many of Magritte's canvases (e.g., *La belle captive* [1967]; see figure 3.2) portray red curtains opening onto the world—be it the sky or a beach. I read this as similar to the old-fashioned movie theater curtain that parted to reveal the screen, a kind of "window onto the world." In relating this to cinema, in chapter 19 I concentrate on *The Little Theater of Jean Renoir* (Jean Renoir, 1975), which uses the conceit of curtains opening to introduce its three disparate episodes. Finally, I see Magritte's *The Memoirs of a Saint* (1960) (see figure 19.2) as evocative of Cinerama.

Rather than focusing on resonances of the work of Magritte in particular films, in chapter 20 I delve into the way in which his oeuvre, in general, can be understood in terms of such film techniques as the manipulation of shot distance and scale (e.g., *The Cascade* [1961]; see figure 20.3), framing and montage (e.g., *Man with a Newspaper* [1928]; see figure 20.4), lighting (e.g., *The Domain of Light* [1954]; see figure 20.7), props (e.g., *Personal Values* [1952]; see figure 20.13), and point of view (e.g., *Not to Be Reproduced* [1937]; see figure 12.5). I also mention two instances in which Magritte's paintings can be seen to invoke signal moments of early film history (*The Lost Jockey* [1926], see figure 20.1; and *Time Transfixed* [1938], see figure 20.2).

The major ideas put forth in the book are briefly reviewed in chapter 21's conclusion.

2

ART DOCUMENTARIES ABOUT MAGRITTE/ MAGRITTE'S "HOME MOVIES"

> All the critical literature clustering round the field of art has to be seen as essentially absurd—like blundering flies, buzzing round a corpse in an advanced state of decay.
>
> René Magritte[1]

As mentioned in the previous chapter, one of film theorist André Bazin's contributions to the topic of painting and film was an essay that centered on documentaries about artists or artworks rather than dramatic or experimental films that drew upon a painter's style.[2] He found most of the documentaries lacking, but he felt that a few (e.g., those of Alain Resnais) transcended the limitations of the form.

The art documentaries about Magritte that I investigate in this chapter were made decades after those viewed by Bazin, and several of their creators had learned from mistakes of the past. Thus, while a few are pedestrian, others combine a didactic purpose with more imaginative effects, and several incorporate footage from Magritte's amateur home movies—an incredibly valuable resource. In many cases, the voice-over commentaries of the documentaries provide a means of learning about Magritte's background, as well as his aesthetic perspective and practice. Of course, as this chapter's epigraph makes clear, it is not apparent that Magritte much appreciated critical philosophizing about his work, whether in print or cinema.

Monsieur René Magritte (Adrian Maben, 1978)

Adrian Maben crafts a rather standard art film about the painter. Throughout, we hear three types of voice-over narration. One, a stand-in for Magritte's voice, reads various quotes from his writings or statements that he made. A second narrates the documentary, helping viewers to contextualize the images that they are seeing. Finally, we hear Magritte's own voice, in the form of earlier interviews that are shown in black-and-white footage.

After an opening introduction to some of Magritte's paintings, we are presented with an exterior shot of the house in which he lived in Brussels for decades of his career. We also see some of the interior furnishings: porcelain birds, clocks, family photos.

Then the film switches to a biographical/chronological mode remarking on Magritte's childhood in Lessing, his youthful love of the cinema, the family's move to Châtalet, his mother's suicide, his meeting Georgette (his future wife), his time in art school, his military service, his commercial design jobs, his association with Belgian artists, his move to Paris and association with French Surrealists, his return to Belgium, and his later recognition in the art world.

The film takes an auteurist approach to the painter, assuming that in order to understand Magritte's oeuvre, one must comprehend his life story. At certain points, the narrator makes direct connections between his biography and his paintings—relating the look of buildings in his canvases to those on his Brussels street; linking works depicting rivers, coffins, or corpses to his mother's death; associating canvases that include balloons to a strange incident in his youth when a balloonist landed on his roof; linking his painting of roses to his work as a wallpaper designer; and tying his representation of Fantômas to his early love of the movies.

At other points, the narrator makes more interpretive connections, conjoining a statement by Magritte to one of his works. Thus, the artist's discussion of dreams is linked to his painting of a castle-topped boulder hovering over the sea. Likewise, his desire to paint objects that "look like the real thing" is juxtaposed with his canvas of baguettes floating in the sky. As his "surrogate" voice notes: I want familiar objects "to utter a kind of scream."

Throughout the documentary, certain broad notions about Magritte's personality and method are proffered: that he eschewed the trappings of a bohemian life, that he utilized a "deadpan, non-painterly style," that he wanted his works to unleash a sense of "vertigo" or "anxiety" in the viewer; and that he did not seek to "reconcile" incongruous things or diverse states of being.

On a visual level, the film makes use of familiar strategies for rendering artworks—in particular, the use of zooms in or out of a canvas—to reveal sections sequentially. On occasion, footage combines an element of a Magritte's artwork with live-action material. In the opening of the film, we see the boulder from Magritte's *Castle in the Pyrenees* (1959) (see figure 14.3) conjoined with actual footage of the ocean, and later we see the bird from *The Great Family* (1963) combined with the ocean in a similar fashion.

The most valuable aspect of *Monsieur René Magritte* is its inclusion of some brief film footage that Magritte shot in the 1950s or 1960s with his wife and friends. Rather than "serious" artwork, this material is an amateur enterprise, a form of amusing home movies. One segment displays clownish behavior typical of silent film comedy (a genre that Magritte admired). Thus, there is a short episode in which Magritte makes funny faces at the camera while wearing a false mustache and another in which he blows his nose with a ragged handkerchief. Finally, in a third sequence, he tries to make his little black dog smoke a cigarette.

René Magritte (Episode of *Artists of the 20th Century* Series, 2004/Kultur)

Very traditional (and rather uninteresting), this Kultur art documentary entails a male voice-over lecturing the viewer, accompanied by images of Magritte's art. In the beginning, the narrator recites Magritte's biography as random pictures of his paintings are displayed. Subsequently, the documentary proceeds in a chronological fashion—discussing Magritte's work from the 1920s through the 1960s. Every now and then, the narrator concentrates on one particular painting as the camera lingers on certain details—for example, *The Lost Jockey* (1926) (see figure 20.1), which is discussed in terms of its break from Magritte's early Cubist style. Here the narrator highlights such elements as the horse, the dummy, and the bilboquet—which will recur in Magritte's later work. Other paintings to which the narrator attends include *Panorama for the Populace* (1926), for its trees; *The Six Elements* (1929) (see figure 20.5), for its Baroque frames within a frame; *The False Mirror* (1929) (which appears on the cover of this volume), for its reflective eye; *Time Transfixed* (1938) (see figure 20.2), for its substitution of locomotive for stove pipe; *Perspective: David's Madame Recamier* (1951), for its focus on death; *Carte Blanche* (1965), for its simultaneous presentation of two planes; and *Good Fortune* (1937), for its "misplaced" crescent moon. The narrator also examines some of Magritte's bronze sculptures crafted in the 1960s—ones that often transposed elements from his prior paintings. For example, *Megalomania* (1967), which portrays sections of a woman's body that are nested like Russian dolls, clearly draws upon his painting *Megalomania (Delusions of Grandeur)* from 1962. Beyond this, the narrator talks of Magritte's ironic realism, his recourse to a dream-like world, his engagement of metamorphosis, his focus on common objects, his erasure of differences between interior and exterior, his obsession with the grain of wood, his use of cutouts, the influence of Italian Modernist artist Giorgio de Chirico, and his interest in the fiction of Edgar Allan Poe.

René Magritte: An Attempt at the Impossible (Bernard Crutzen and Pierre Sterckx, 1999, color and black-and-white, Kultur)

Eschewing an overabundance of biographical detail in favor of a commentary that illuminates Magritte's artistic point of view and aspects of his iconography and style, this art documentary also conjoins live-action dramatization, imagery of Magritte's paintings, clips from an extended interview with the artist, documentary footage from various eras in which he lived, and animated material.

Over a pan shot of numerous Magritte canvases on the wall, a narrator (Alexandre von Sivers) talks of the artist's predilection for mystery and producing "one seemingly impossible image after another." Turning to Magritte's *Attempting the Impossible* (1928) (see figure 6.1), in which an artist seems to be painting or creating a real woman, the narrator discusses Magritte's interest in crossing the boundaries between life and death.

When the time period invoked is the 1920s, a photo frame on a table (ostensibly part of a set) suddenly is matted with documentary movies of the era, as viewers learn about Magritte's early flirtation with Fauvism and Futurism (and view accompanying images of his canvases). At this point, the audience sees the first black-and-white clip of an interview with Magritte during which he discusses Modernist art's desire to formulate "an original way of painting"; he singles out Giorgio de Chirico as an influence on his work. A few of Magritte's paintings are considered in some depth (e.g., *The Difficult Crossing* [1926]), with its iconography of storms, an amputated hand, and a bird. Following this, we see a real bird fly in front of a red curtain, both recurrent images in Magritte's oeuvre.

The narrator also discusses how Magritte's wife, Georgette, served as his "discreet muse," evidenced by the fact that he rarely used professional models. This statement, however, is counterpoised with the artist's somber painting

The Eternally Obvious (1930), in which a woman's body is "dismembered" and sectioned into separate frames. At one point, some of the static images in the frames are replaced with live-action footage of a female body moving.

Through voice-over narration illustrated with images, we learn of Magritte's collaboration with the Belgian Surrealist magazine *Oesophage* as well as with the group's gallery Le Centaur, and cafe, Le Feuille de Papier Doré. We also are told the names of the members of the Belgian Surrealist circle: Marcel Mariën, E. L. T. Mesens, Louis Scutenaire, Paul Nougé, and André Souris. Some were poets or musicians; Magritte was the only painter of the lot. Periodically, we see a female singer accompanied by a pianist performing a piece that was composed by a member of the group. The piano is encircled with a huge woman's ring, mimicking Magritte's canvas *The Happy Hand* (1953).

The narrator speaks of how Magritte supervised comic and satirical photo and movie sessions with his colleagues, and we see footage of some motion pictures—including one of a man crossing himself and another of women raising their skirts to reveal their legs. We also learn about Magritte's time as part of the French Surrealist circle and how a painting of his, *The Hidden Woman* (1929) was used for the cover of an issue of *La revolution surrealist.* Surrounding a picture of a naked woman and the words "I do not see the . . . hidden in the forest" are photographs of Louis Aragon, André Breton, Luis Buñuel, Paul Éluard, Paul Nougé, and Magritte himself. When the narrator confronts the topic of word and image, we see relevant Magritte paintings (like *The Interpretation of Dreams* [1935]) and view a clip of Magritte talking about his practice.

One of the more novel aspects of the film's commentary is its focus on the ties between Magritte's work and magic (examined in chapter 16). The narrator discusses how, like prestidigitation, some of the artist's canvases entail images of levitation, smoke and mirrors, and sleights of hand (e.g., *The Magician* [1951]; see figure 16.1). We also learn that Magritte was fascinated by magic as a child. Moreover, the commentary points out that he borrowed from the trick films of Georges Méliès, utilizing superimposition and other optical techniques. Specifically, it compares the latter's *The Man with the Rubber Head* (1901) and Magritte's use of an oversized apple in *The Listening Room* (1952).

As with other art documentaries, the film connects the suicide of Magritte's mother to his painting *The Musings of a Solitary Walker* (1926), as well as to those in which faces are shrouded in white cloth (as was his mother's when dragged from the river). Similarly, the film makes the common association of silent screen hero Fantômas and such canvases as *The Murderer Threatened* (1927).

Accompanying an inventive sequence employing animation, the narrator discusses Magritte's obsession with transformation, which he asserts anticipates "the morphing of today's computer animation" (some of which is discussed in the next chapter). On a visual level, we see an apple turn into a bowler hat and then into a bell—drawing upon objects Magritte repeatedly utilized in his paintings. Framed pictures on a wall suddenly fill with World War II newsreel footage of bombers flying, and we see several Magritte canvases with airplane-like contraptions. We are also told about Magritte's unsuccessful postwar shift to a Renoiresque style and his eventual return to his familiar mode.

Interestingly, the narration claims that Magritte's style (with its sharp, clear lines and realistically rendered objects) was amenable to reproduction. This statement is accompanied by a sheet of Belgian postage stamps containing images of one of the artist's works, *Castle in the Pyrenees* (see figure 14.3). Evincing a similar theme, between 1951 and 1953 Magritte refashioned several of his paintings as frescoes to decorate the walls of a casino in Knokke-le-Zoute in Belgium.

Magritte: Day and Night (Henri de Gerlache, 2009)

One of the most fascinating documentaries about the artist was made in collaboration with the Magritte Museum in Brussels. Its premise is that an actor (Charlie Dupont)—who sometimes also seems to be the filmmaker—is preparing for his role as René Magritte. This causes him to review the painter's life and to travel to various places where he lived (Brussels and Paris), studied (the Brussels Royal Academy of Art), and exhibited (the Museum of Modern Art, the Menil Collection, and the Pompidou Center). We also see the actor in his production trailer (replete with monographs on the artist), as well as on the "Stage Magritte." Early in the film, he proclaims, "What a joy for an actor to play Magritte!" and states that his goal is to understand the "colorful character tucked beneath the bowler hat."

While the actor's voice renders the primary narration, at times we hear Magritte himself. For instance, at one point the artist says, "I've always dreamed of bringing together the different components of . . . mystery," and at another he asserts, "All visible things hide visible things." Additionally, the actor conducts a series of interviews with curators, artists, models, critics, scholars, and relatives of one of Magritte's champions, Alexander Lolas. The most captivating of these is that conducted with Duane Michals, the photographer who visited Magritte in Brussels a year before his death to create a series of unique and provocative images. Like many others, Michals comments on the dissonance between Magritte's bizarre imagination and the quotidian nature of his life—having lunch at a regular time each day followed by a nap on his couch (fully clothed in his ubiquitous suit and tie). Michals tells us that one of the artist's favorite television shows was the Western *Bonanza* (1959–73), and we are not surprised when later movie footage depicts Magritte trying on a ten-gallon hat in Houston, where he traveled for an exhibition.

The documentary contains motion-picture footage authored by Magritte. For instance, we see him with Georgette visiting European capitals (Rome, Venice, Pisa) during the period (late in his life) of his greatest international success. We also watch numerous more self-conscious home movies (mostly shot in black and white with a few in color) that include images of:

A glass of water placed on an umbrella (mimicking his canvas *Hegel's Holiday* [1958])

Magritte pouring water onto an umbrella

Another man pouring water on several umbrellas

Georgette changing hats

A faux firing squad aimed at three women which reminds us of the presence of rifles in several of Magritte's paintings (e.g., *The Hunters at the Edge of Night* [1928] and *The Survivor* [1950]).

Magritte holding his head as though in pain

Magritte making faces at the camera (like early cinema's "facial contortion" films)

Magritte assuming strange positions

Magritte in a pointed helmet (which riffs on an illustration of his depicting Erich von Stroheim, *Homage to Erich von Stroheim* [1957])

Georgette holding a painting of her face in front of her face (mimicking his canvases of landscape paintings that block out real landscapes, as in *The Human Condition* [1933]; see figure 8.1)

Georgette apparently taking a real apple from a painting of an apple

Shrouded people (mimicking Magritte's canvas *The Lovers* [1928]; figures 2.1 and 2.2)

Georgette holding a sign that reads *Fin* (The end)

A posterior view of a man in a bowler hat (like the oblique point of view in *Not to Be Reproduced* [1937]; see figure 12.5)

Georgette in a bowler hat

A parade of people

People dancing

Magritte: Day and Night is also arresting for the way it not only displays Magritte's work but also creatively adapts it for the screen in a manner consonant with the artist's sensibility. One shot, for instance, splits the screen between a Magrittian cloud-filled blue sky and a shot of the actor walking down a Parisian street. A second conjoins an image of the actor on a Parisian bridge with an image of Magritte's painting *Homesickness* (1941).

A third links footage of the river in which Magritte's mother drowned with his morose canvas—*The Musings of a Solitary Walker*—seen as reflective of this trauma (figure 2.3). A fourth intermixes an image of Magritte's painting *Carte Blanche*, which portrays a woman riding through the woods, with footage of a real forest. A fifth merges a shot of a chessboard with Magritte's *Checkmate* (1926), in which a man holds a gun to his head against a background of black and white squares.

At other points, the filmmaker juxtaposes photographic shots of Magritte with some of his paintings, making clear the parallels between them—as in a rearview image of Magritte conjoined with one of his canvases that takes a similar perspective. Moreover, in filming the places where Magritte lived, the movie offers us a detailed sense of the ambience of his various homes. Thus, we enter his childhood residence in Lessines and view many of its architectural details. At one point, the filmmaker links a picture of Magritte standing by the building's fireplace with one of the actor perhaps at the same spot.

Finally, throughout the film, various assertions are made about Magritte—the person and the creator—by the actor or those he interviews. Thus we learn: that Magritte did not seek to be an "artist" but rather a simple workingman; that while in Paris he kept his distance from the French Surrealist circle,

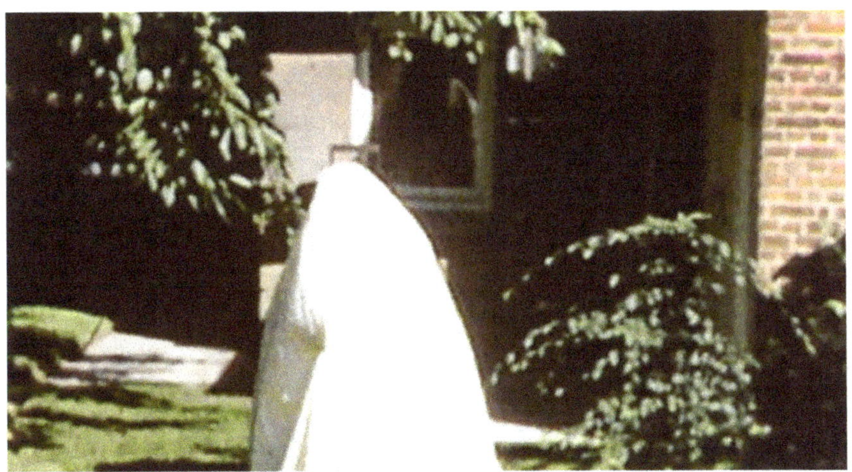

FIGURE 2.1. In this Magritte home movie, the shrouded characters imitate those in his painting *The Lovers*.

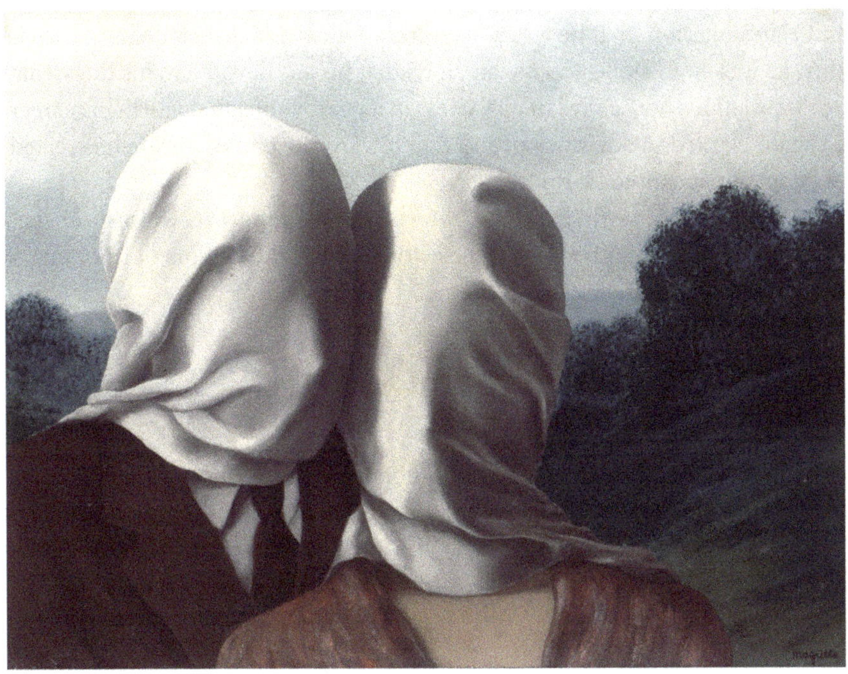

FIGURE 2.2. *The Lovers* (*Les amants*) (1928)

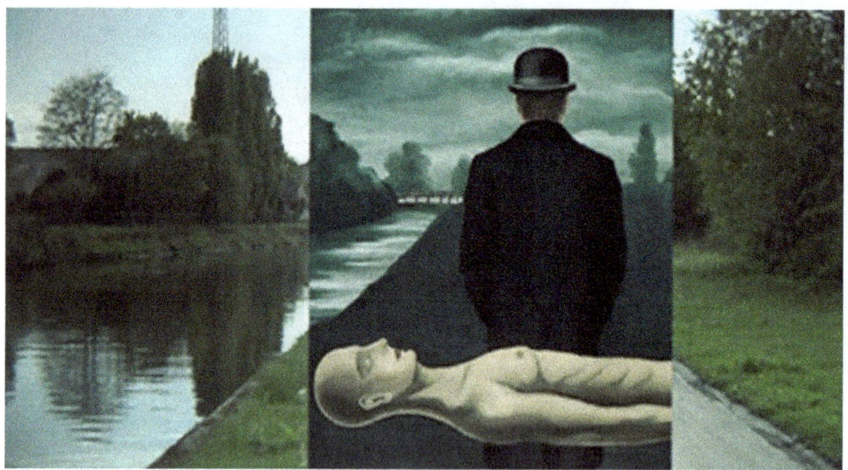

FIGURE 2.3. This image from *Magritte: Day and Night* (Gerlache, 2009) intermixes a shot of a real river with Magritte's *The Musings of a Solitary Walker* (1926).

which viewed him as too bourgeois; that he loved the stories of Nick Carter and Nat Pinkerton; that he was a "conjurer of ideas"; that, despite his conviviality, he was often alone and melancholy; that he was devoted to his dogs; that he rarely left his house save to play chess in a nearby cafe; that late in his career he again worked in advertising; and that toward the end of his life he created work mainly meant to be sold.

Despite such information and the visuals to support it, we suspect that we have not truly plumbed (what the actor deems) "the enigma of [the] man," leaving Magritte as deliciously puzzling as his canvases.

Magritte e il cinema . . . Chapeau! (René Magritte, 1956–60)

Not an art documentary but a work containing three silent amateur films, *Magritte el il cinema . . . Chapeau!* provides works made by the artist between 1956 and 1960. They are presented on a disc that accompanied the publication of Marcella Biserni's book of the same title.[3] They will be discussed individually—first by summarizing and then by commenting upon them.

Paul Colinet (October 1956–March 1957)

Paul Colinet has three segments involving Paul Colinet, a Belgian poet, friend, and colleague of Magritte. In the first segment, Colinet sits at a table, spills sugar cubes on it, then takes notes in a small notebook. Seen from another angle, he removes a decorative vase from the floor and puts a sugar cube in it. In the second segment, after kneeling behind a chair, Colinet pours water from a pitcher into a stemmed glass and plays around with it, eventually returning the water to the pitcher. The segment ends with Colinet clapping. In the third segment, he wears a false mustache and holds a baton that resembles one a magician might carry. He plays around with the glass and pitcher, then uncovers a pointed helmet on the table (which bears an eagle insignia) and puts it on. Later, he takes it off and crouches behind the table. The film ends with Colinet rolling his eyes.

Clearly, *Paul Colinet* relishes the nonsensical. There seems to be no purpose to arranging sugar cubes on a table and even less to take notes on so doing. Similarly, there is nothing very interesting about the everyday act of pouring water into a glass and absolutely no reason to clap for having done so. When Colinet wears a fake mustache and carries a baton (while again playing with the pitcher and glass), he suggests a magician who might utilize such objects in his act (perhaps magically having the water pour from one vessel to another). As we know, Magritte was a fan of screen magic. The helmet is clearly a German one that Magritte has referenced in his drawing *Homage to Erich von Stroheim*.[4]

The Antillean Dessert (April 1957), with Irène Hamoir and Louis Scutenaire

In *The Antillean Dessert*, Surrealist poet Louis Scutenaire appears with a napkin in his collar eating at a table; he wipes his mouth, drinks, and belches. He then folds his arms, leans back and closes his eyes. Irène Hamoir, a Surrealist novelist, clears the table, shrugs, picks up a banana peel, and shakes it around. In close-up, she is seen chewing something. In reverse motion, she spits out pieces of the banana and "reconstitutes" it. Finally, she brings the banana to Scutenaire who eats it.

If *Paul Colinet* alludes to magic, *The Antillean Dessert* makes a clear reference to it. Not only does the film highlight a banana (whose peel on the floor was the stuff of slapstick comedy), but it utilizes the type of reverse motion that was popular in early trick films.

Tuba (Interior) (November 21, 1960), with René Magritte, Georgette Magritte, Irène Hamoir, Louis Scutenaire, Nicole Desclin, Suzi Gablik, and Alan Schmeer

Tuba, considerably longer than the other amateur movies, begins with a sleeping woman (presumably Irène Hamoir) holding a red half mask. She awakens and puts it on, then takes a tuba from under the bedsheets and blows on it. In

Magritte's use of the mask as a prop, we recognize a trope from such works as *The Intelligence* (1946), *The Sage's Carnival* (1947) (see figure 13.2), and *The Married Priest* (1960). Similarly, in utilizing the tuba, we think of such paintings as *The Discovery of Fire* (1934–35).

As seen from the rear, another woman (presumably Georgette Magritte) looks into a mirror and removes her red knit cap. She opens a closet door, discovers a tuba inside, puts the hat on the floor with the instrument, and closes the door. We next see a man (presumably Louis Scutenaire) wearing a dress and sitting in a chair as a third woman (presumably Suzi Gablik) walks over to him and puts a red hat on his head. The man peels and eats a banana, as Georgette rings a bell.

The man brings a pitcher and basin near Georgette's feet and pours water into the vessel, as though a servant responding to her call for a foot bath. Another man (presumably Alan Schmeer) peels a banana and eats it. Scutenaire then drapes a white sheet over a seated woman's lap (presumably that of Nicole Desclin); she wears a red mask. When the sheet is lifted, we find a tuba on the floor.

We next see Declin wearing a red mask, writing at a table. She dips her pen into ink, spills some on the paper, and smears it with her fingers.

As the camera pans left, we see two people kissing—shrouded in white sheets, as in Magritte's painting *The Lovers* (see figure 2.2). A pan down reveals that they are both wearing skirts and women's shoes.

In the next segment, several women are shown reading and exchanging books. The camera pans to an armoire as Scutenaire picks up a tuba and then cuts to a shot of Magritte working on a canvas that depicts the sky, a bell, and a curtain (probably *Mona Lisa* [1960]; figure 2.4). While Magritte is not looking, Scutenaire steals the canvas. When Magritte turns around and finds the painting gone, he looks shocked. Scutenaire puts the painting in the armoire, but when Magritte opens it, he finds only a tuba. He takes the instrument out, stands it on its bell, and ponders it. In the next shot, Magritte wears the red mask (figure 2.5) and, in the one following, the tuba "wears" it. Next we see Scutenaire holding the red hat and crying. As the film ends, several people are shown laughing and dancing while the tuba rests on the floor.

Tuba essentially stars three items that are found in many Magritte canvases: a tuba, a mask, and a white shroud. He renders all of them in illogical or unconventional ways—locating the tuba under bedsheets; having it substitute for a painting in a closet; having the mask worn not only by people but by a musical instrument; having the shroud cover lovers who turn out to be female. Beyond that, there are the usual surprising, absurd, or magical touches: a cross-dressing man, a woman smearing ink on a piece of paper, people eating

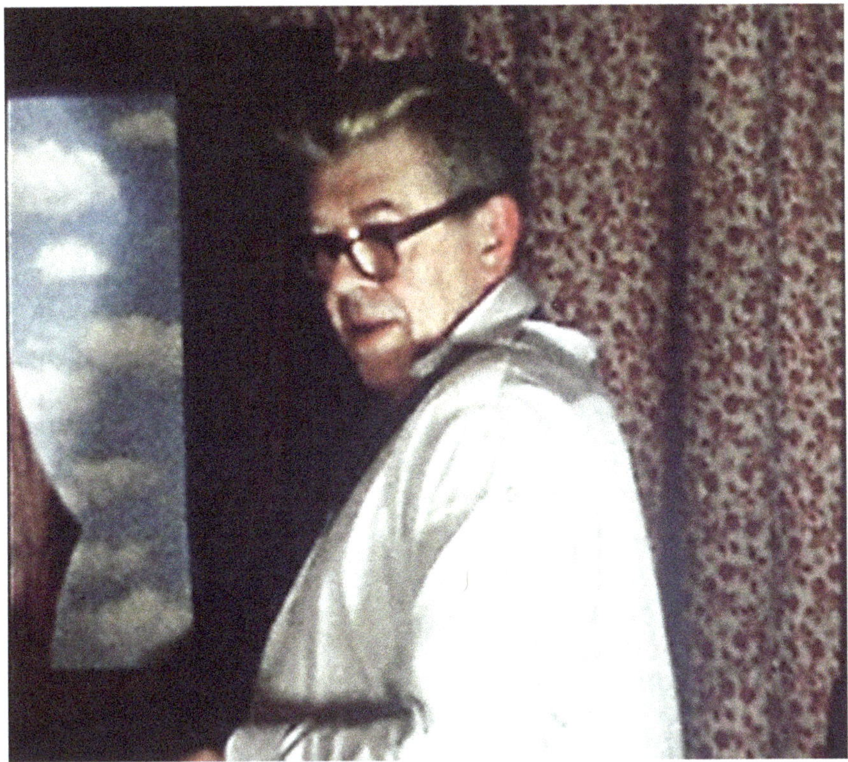

FIGURE 2.4. In this shot from a home movie, Magritte stands by what appears to be his *Mona Lisa* (1960) painting.

bananas, a man who cries for no reason, and objects that materialize then disappear. Finally, Magritte himself is featured in the film as an artist (working on *Mona Lisa*) who cannot keep track of his canvas.

René Magritte (David Wheatley, 1979, color and black-and-white)

David Wheatley made *René Magritte* for the BBC's *Omnibus* series while he was still a student. Without doubt, it is one of the more creative and innovative art documentaries about the painter. This is because it combines a variety of modes: live-action dramatization, movie clips, images of paintings and photographs, and animated sequences. All are accompanied by a voice-over that stands in for Magritte himself, speaking words that seem to have been excerpted from his interviews or publications.

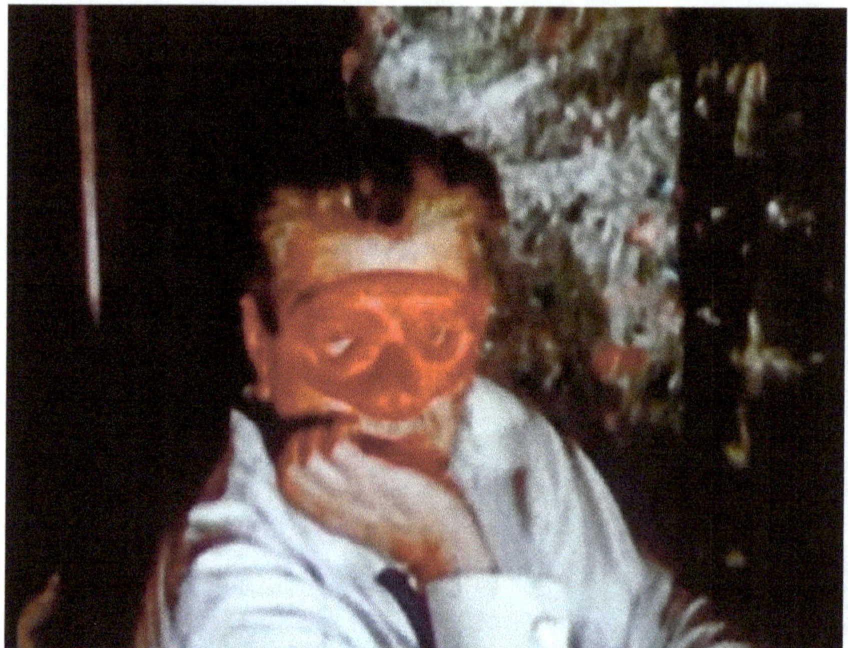

FIGURE 2.5. Magritte wears a red mask (a frequent object depicted in his paintings) in *Tuba*, one of his home movies.

The dramatized sequences follow benchmarks in the artist's life (but not necessarily in a chronological order), including:

- The night when (as a child) the balloonist landed on the roof of Magritte's home and "filled him with a sense of mystery"
- His art school experience (whereby he "developed a distrust of established art and artists")
- His observation of a painter at work (who "seemed to be performing magic")
- His discovery of Futurism (a "new form of painting")
- The suicide of his mother when he was a teen (after which "death forever remained a mystery")
- His childhood moviegoing (which evinced an "appetite for mystery, horror, and violence")
- His second encounter with Georgette, which led to their marriage
- His work at a wallpaper factory

- His discovery of the work of De Chirico (which would influence him greatly)
- His move to Paris in 1927 to join the Surrealist circle
- His return to Brussels (disillusioned with the group)
- His post–World War II neo-Impressionist turn (which critics deemed his "nasty period")
- Resumption of his signature Surrealist style

In general, the film's imagery (be it paintings, photographs, or live-action footage) is keyed to the biographical moment being reenacted. Thus, when we learn that Magritte discovered Futurism, we are shown a series of relevant Modernist canvases (including Marcel Duchamp's *Nude Descending a Staircase* [1912]). When Magritte speaks of using established paintings as models to be revised, we see Édouard Manet's *The Balcony* (1868), which the former transformed into *Perspective: Manet's Balcony* (1950).

Similarly, when the suicide of Magritte's mother is referenced, we see his painting *The Musings of a Solitary Walker*, which depicts a river and a corpse. Likewise, when we view a dramatization of the young Magritte sitting in a movie theater, we are presented with clips from *Fantômas* (1913–14) and its remake *Judex* (1963) (discussed in chapter 13), as well as *Nosferatu* (1922) and several French avant-garde films.

Often, Magritte's words, rendered in voice-over narration, communicate his artistic philosophy and are illustrated with relevant works. Thus, as he talks of being fascinated by the "unexpected relationships between objects," we see his canvas *Personal Values* (1952) (see figure 20.13), with its bizarre juxtaposition of a huge comb with a tiny bed. Later, when he observes that "by changing [an object's] name the object can be seen freshly," we view *The Treachery of Images* (1929) (see figure 7.1), with its famous declaration, "Ceci n'est pas une pipe."

Especially intriguing and novel, however, are the sequences that Wheatley animates or combines imagery within the frame. This begins with one of the first shots of the film in which the actor playing the adult Magritte tips his decapitated head. This is mirrored by a later shot in which Magritte's head pops out of the seat of a chair. Likewise, after the sequence in which the balloonist lands on Magritte's roof, we see an eye with that figure matted into its iris.

At the moment when Magritte asserts his discovery that "life could be transformed," we observe the chandelier in his apartment inexplicably rock back and forth, and the objects on his table move on their own accord. Later, in imitation of paintings, like *The Unexpected Answer* (1933), in which a door is marred by a cutout, we see a piece of a door fall away.

Among the other animated sequences in the film is a female bust dripping blood and opening its eyes—a version of the painting *Memory* (1948) (see figure 10.2). Similarly, mimicking the painting *The Portrait* (1935), we see an animated sequence in which a piece of ham on a plate opens up to reveal an eyeball at its center. Finally, referencing the canvas *The Red Model* (1935), we see a real pair of feet painted as though they were shoes, toes wiggling. Thus, Wheatley manages in his film to instruct us about Magritte's life and aesthetic while simultaneously utilizing cinematic special effects to creatively approximate the artist's vision and style.

It is interesting to note that some eight years after making *Magritte*, David Wheatley shot a feature fiction film, *The Magic Toyshop* (1987), adapted from a 1967 novel of the same name by Angela Carter (who also wrote the movie's screenplay). While it would be a stretch to call *The Magic Toyshop* an homage to Magritte, it certainly has interesting ties to the artist's vision—such that a reviewer called the film a "natural progression" from Wheatley's art documentary.[5] Also, critics of Carter's literary work have connected her fictional world view to that of Magritte's.[6]

The Magic Toyshop concerns three British upper-class children being looked after by a housekeeper who suddenly learn that their parents have died while travelling. They are whisked off to the home of their uncle Philip (Tom Bell), significantly a bowler-hatted man who runs a toy shop.

He turns out to be a cold, mean, tyrannical person who controls everyone in his household (his mute wife, Margaret [Patricia Kerrigan], and her two brothers). He makes the children work in the shop for their lodging.

Our perspective on the narrative is linked to one of the children—Melanie (Caroline Milmoe), a sixteen-year-old girl on the verge of sexual maturity who falls in love with Margaret's brother Finn (Kilian McKenna) while living in her uncle's home. She finds a hole in the wall of her bedroom through which she observes strange goings-on in the house, reminding of us of Magritte's peephole imagery in *The Spy* (1928) (see figure 5.1) (and especially of *Painted Object: The Eye* [1936 or 1937], in which a woman's eye is seen through a circular opening).

The film evokes Magritte's sensibility in its blended mixture of fantasy and reality. Every now and then, Philip puts on a puppet show in the shop for members of the family. His stage is surrounded by the kind of red curtains that Magritte loved (discussed in chapter 17), and in one image they look much like those in *La belle captive* (1967) (see figure 3.2) since they are suddenly positioned in the outside world. One of Uncle Philip's productions is "Living Statues" and involves an artist putting finishing touches on a white female statue—one that resembles those in some of Magritte's canvases. What is peculiar about the show is that one cannot tell whether the puppets are artificial or real people, and credits indicate that at least one is played by a human. Later on, Philip requires Melanie to perform with a huge avian puppet in a sadistic version of Leda and the Swan, further mixing up animate and inanimate beings. Moreover, at several points, puppets are dismembered or decapitated, again reminding us of Magritte's iconography (discussed in chapter 16).

Throughout the film, magical things occur. Early on, when the housekeeper enters Melanie's room after the latter has learned of her parents' demise, the room is strangely filled with feathers. Moreover, at the toy shop, puppets come to life, a dog jumps into a painting of itself, a room is suddenly transformed into a beach, people walk through a stage set on to the real world, a fiddle plays by itself, Aunt Margaret suddenly speaks and becomes an otherworldly being, and Uncle Philip is turned into a huge wooden puppet and burned in effigy.

While *The Magic Toyshop* is not an outright tribute to Magritte, it would seem that Wheatley chose a novel to adapt to film that was compatible with the artist's taste for the Surreal. Furthermore, the movie demonstrates that Wheatley learned his lessons from making his prior documentary on the artist.

In this chapter, I have primarily considered two types of works, art documentaries and amateur movies, some of which overlap. The art documentaries about Magritte range from fairly standard ones to those that involve some creative dramatization. While most present their visual material (images of Magritte, his family, his cohorts, his artwork) in conventional ways, others utilize the powers of cinema (matting, superimposition, montage, animation, etc.) to attempt to approximate some of Magritte's experimental techniques. All of them offer useful biographical information about the artist as well as critical insights into his method.

Magritte's amateur movies, featuring his wife, friends, and members of the Belgian Surrealist circle, were made in the late 1950s and early 1960s. Some of these are included in the art documentaries (as part of narrating Magritte's life and practice). But others appear on a separate disc.

This home movie footage comprises a treasure trove of images and provides insight into how Magritte imagined utilizing the cinema during the brief period in which he toyed with it. On one level, the material (with its comic turns and nonsenical episodes) reveals his continuing love of silent film comedy. On another, however, it demonstrates that he conceived of film as a medium with which to transpose the iconography of his paintings (tubas, masks, shrouds, water glasses, umbrellas, apples, helmets), rather than one that could offer its own inventive equivalences for the strangeness of his art. Thus, with few exceptions (e.g., his use of reverse motion), he did not consider tapping the formal elements of cinema (shot distance, editing, special effects, camera movement, etc.) to translate the bizarre sensibility of his canvases into a new medium (even though, as I have argued, his pictorial style already invokes film). His home movies remain too "literal," giving him little reason to continue with his experimentation. Though we might wish that he had, his onscreen imagery is, in fact, better suited to the static metaphysics of painting. Perhaps this is the reason that he soon abandoned his career as a cineaste—realizing that painting was his true métier.

3

HONORING THE ARTIST

Cinematic Tributes to Magritte

> To be a surrealist means barring from your mind all remembrance of what you have seen, and being always on the lookout for what has never been.
>
> René Magritte[1]

THERE HAVE BEEN very few films made (save amateur ones posted on YouTube) that, in an extended fashion, constitute homages to René Magritte—a surprising fact given the cinematic nature of his oeuvre. In this chapter, I discuss works that have, which run the gamut of experimental film, art film, mainstream film, music video, and web-based creation.

Homage to Magritte (Anita Thatcher, 1974)

Anita Thatcher's *Homage to Magritte* (1974) makes its tribute to the artist clear in its very title. Shot in 16 mm color, it is only ten minutes long and even today does not seem to be available in digital format. Its status as film qua film is significant, since all the special effects utilized in it to construct a Magrittian alternate reality likely had to be accomplished by laborious optical printing or in-camera trickery. Utilizing the abstract, short film format, Thatcher creates a variety of beautiful but anomalous tableaux—employing dissonances of both the aural and visual kind to evoke Magritte's uncanny universe.

In the film's first segment, someone seen from the rear (the pose of many of Magritte's subjects) walks toward a window, and the sound of the person's steps are synchronized to the movements. Within short order, however, we hear footsteps without seeing the person any longer—an audiovisual incongruity. Here Thatcher takes advantage of the acoustic dimension of cinema for a bizarre touch, an element unavailable to Magritte.

The next section draws on techniques of matting. Initially, we view the surface of water as we hear liquid sounds. At some point a frame within the frame appears, and sometimes the movement of the water within it is at odds with the larger image (either static vs. moving, or flowing in a different direction). Soon, however, the acoustic dimension ceases entirely, and water fills the entire screen. Ultimately, a picture of an egg yolk appears embedded in the internal frame; it is surrounded by water, as though frying on its surface. The two images (egg and water) have as little connection to each other as the train and fireplace in Magritte's canvas *Time Transfixed* (1938) (see figure 20.2). On the other hand, both water and eggs appear as part of Magritte's iconography (the former in *The Seducer* [1953] and the latter in *Elective Affinities* [1933]).

The tableau that follows plays games with a mirror, a favored object in Magritte's iconography (as in *Not to Be Reproduced* [1937]; see figure 12.5). On the wall of a room, a mirror reflects a window toward which a woman walks while humming. At first, the looking glass shows her properly. Soon, however, the temporality of the mirror's view is at odds with the action we witness outside of its purview. At one point, it shows the woman when she is not there, and later it fails to reflect a vase of dried flowers that sits on the sill.

Certainly, Thatcher's use of the time-based aspects of the cinematic medium (and its potential for disorientation) draws on the spirit, if not the letter, of Magritte's work. Furthermore, in Thatcher's play with a reflective surface, we are reminded of the title of one of Magritte's most famous paintings, *The False Mirror* (1929)—depicted on the cover of this volume. We also think of André Bazin's notion that the film image is like a mirror "the tin foil of which retains the image."[2]

Subsequent segments of the film concentrate on an ocean scene. At first, we see a fully realist image of the sky and sea separated by the horizon line. By the third iteration, however, such relative "normalcy" is abandoned, as the top section depicts sand; the middle, waves; and the bottom, sky. Here, in particular, we might think of Magritte's *The Song of the Storm* (1937), which locates clouds on the beach, disrupting the usual hierarchy of nature. In Thatcher's fourth iteration, this arrangement is scrambled again, with sand on the top, sky in the middle, and sea on the bottom.

The final sequence of the film depicts a woman arranging flowers by a window while humming (what seems to be) Joni Mitchell's "Both Sides Now"—a title that might characterize the paradoxical sense of much of Magritte's oeuvre. Through the window, we see the sky outside—but it is strangely enlarged so that the clouds look too big. Soon the view miraculously changes to a sunset and then to the solar system, followed by an immense eye and then a close-up of the woman's face—as though the window were transformed into a movie screen (figure 3.1). Finally, a shot of the sky is superimposed over the entire frame as the film ends. Here, of course, we discern the play with scale so rampant in Magritte's work, as when an apple or flower fills a chamber (in *The Listening Room* [1952] or *The Tomb of Wrestlers* [1960]) or when a huge comb and match populate a room in *Personal Values* (1952) (see figure 20.13). We also identify Magritte's fixation on the sky, as when he superimposes it over the face of Napoleon in *The Future of Statues* (1937).

In sum, although Thatcher, in her desire to honor Magritte, does not mimic any precise canvas (as do some of the makers of art documentaries), she skillfully exploits some of his privileged images—eye, sea, sky, egg, and beach. By sectioning the film frame, she is also able to ignore the laws of the

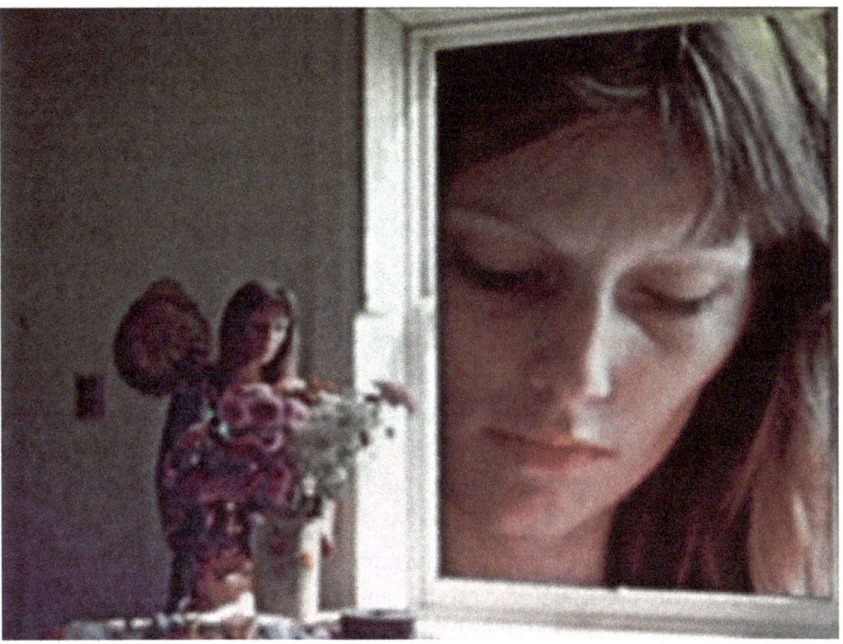

FIGURE 3.1. Imitating the artist's play with scale, Thatcher depicts a huge face outside a window in *Homage to Magritte* (1974).

natural world, as Magritte does when he paints floating boulders in *The Castle in the Pyrenees* (1959) (see figure 14.3). Moreover, Thatcher toys with proportion and dimension in the views she grants us through a window, yet another preferred site for the projection of Magritte's imagination, as in *The Human Condition* (1933) (see figure 8.1). Finally, by using elements of cinema unavailable to a painter (duration and sound), Thatcher extends Magritte's sensibility into another medium.

La belle captive (Alain Robbe-Grillet, 1983)

Alain Robbe-Grillet's film *La belle captive* (1983) is named for Magritte's series of paintings (done between 1931 and 1967) and is thus a clear homage to the artist (figure 3.2). It is only the director's second color film, a necessity for any work invoking Magritte's rich palette. *La belle captive* was released eight years after Robbe-Grillet published a picto-roman of the same title.[3] The latter is a novel illustrated with seventy-seven Magritte reproductions—a fascinating work of literary-pictorial intermediality. As Ben Stoltzfus points out, the ties between the two artists are clear since both "devalue the real in favor of the imaginary," commingle "the visible and the invisible," and "draw curtains" on the world.[4]

The relationships between word and image are clear in the novel, with paintings often inserted following their invocation through language. The opening lines of the volume reads: "It begins with a stone falling, in the silence, vertically, immobile."[5] (Of course, the notion of an immobile fall is an impossibility.) Significantly, on the novel's facing page is a reproduction of Magritte's *The Castle in the Pyrenees* (see figure 14.3), in which a huge boulder (on top of which sits a citadel) hovers in the sky. There is another passage that describes a "murdered mannequin . . . lying on the long wooden, white-enamel table,"[6] and this is accompanied by Magritte's *The Murderer Threatened* (1927), portraying a dead person laid out on a chaise. On one page of the novel, there is mention of a "flesh-colored rose" with a "blushing heart."[7] Taking up two of the following pages is a huge reproduction of Magritte's *The Tomb of the Wrestlers*, which depicts an oversized rose filling a room. Later on, the novel's narrator looks at the palm of his hand and, on the page that follows, is the image of *The Dark Suspicion* (1928), a Magritte painting that shows a man doing just that. Similarly, the novel's narrator speaks of a "small shiny key in the keyhole,"[8] which is illustrated on the same page with Magritte's *The Devil's Smile* (1966), displaying a parallel iconography.

While Robbe-Grillet's novel and film have the same title and both are influenced by Magritte, the stories told in each bear little resemblance to each

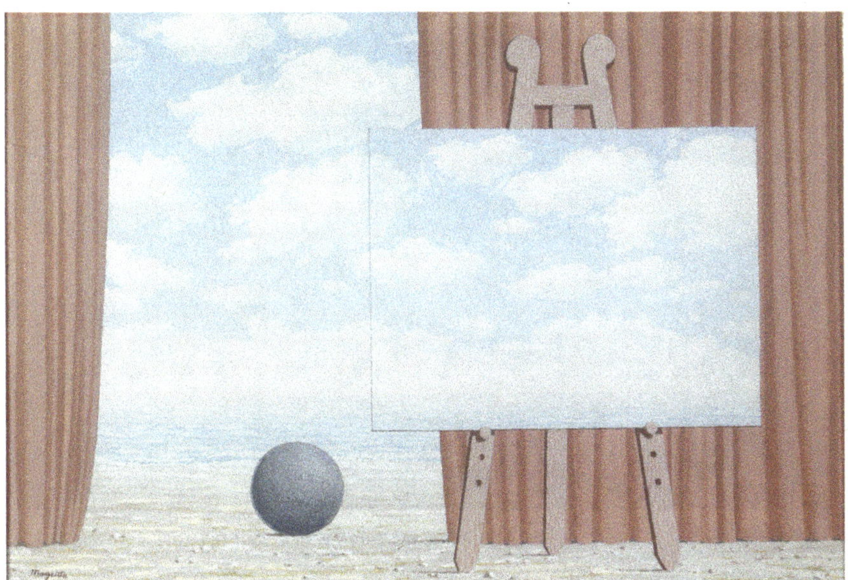

FIGURE 3.2. *La belle captive* (1967)

other, aside from their being equally bizarre and oneiric. In writing about the film, Roch C. Smith points out a few direct citations of the book in the motion picture: the brown suitcase depicted on the novel's cover (that references several Magritte paintings)[9] reappears in the movie on the back of a bicycle and in a closet; and the book itself can be glimpsed on a shelf in the latter.[10]

Part jumbled and erotic detective film, *La belle captive* offers no coherent narrative but follows Walter Naime (Daniel Mesguich), a man who works for some mysterious "organization" whose director (Sara Zeitgeist [Cyrielle Clair], seen repeatedly riding a motorcycle) orders him to deliver a letter to Comte Henri de Corinthe.

While driving to the appointed location, he comes across an injured young woman lying in the road (Gabrielle Lazure), her hands bound in chains. He recognizes her as the same girl with whom he had danced earlier in the evening at a bar. Though she had refused to tell him her name, he later learns that she is Marie-Ange van de Reeves—the fiancée of the Count. To get help for her, he stops at a mansion that is populated by strange men dressed in black (evocative of Stanley Kubrick's *Eyes Wide Shut* [1999]). A doctor ushers the couple into a bedroom and ominously locks the door behind them. The woman astoundingly revives and begins to make vigorous love to Walter in a vampiristic fashion (biting his neck). On the wall behind the bed is a painting

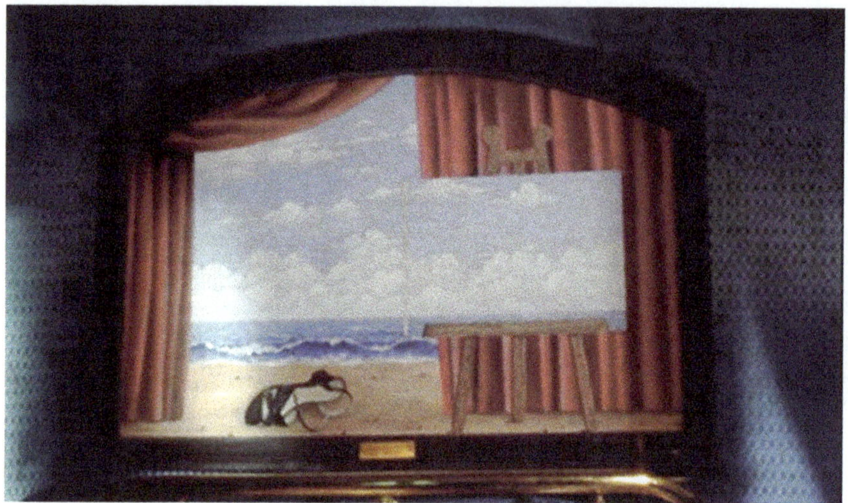

FIGURE 3.3. An altered version of Magritte's *La belle captive* (1967) hangs on a wall in Robbe-Grillet's 1983 film of the same name.

that constitutes an altered version of Magritte's 1967 *La belle captive* (figure 3.3). As Lisa K. Broad notes, it "appears throughout the film and serves as the key to its quantum or labyrinthine temporal structure."[11]

The rest of the drama recounts Walter's nightmarish journey (and he frequently questions if he is dreaming). Throughout, Marie-Ange appears and disappears in various bizarre incarnations (alive and dead, bound and unbound, injured on the road, dancing by the sea, back in his bed, in framed portraits, etc.). Some of these scenes take the form of flashbacks; others, of visions. At times, Walter also pops up in Sara's bedroom, as though the two were a couple. Other puzzling events transpire. When he arrives at the Count's dwelling, he learns that the man (who looks just like him) is dead. Furthermore, after tracking down Marie-Ange's spiritualist father (who claims that his daughter died years ago), he allows the man to attach electrodes to his head, forcing him to dream (figure 3.4). The apparatus resembles the kind of metallic headgear that a character is made to wear in *Eternal Sunshine of the Spotless Mind* (2004) to wipe his mind of memories. (That film receives further treatment in chapter 10.) Toward the end of the film, several episodes involve a group of armed men capturing Walter, tying him to a pole, and readying him for execution—perhaps for the murder of Marie-Ange or the Count—a "crime" for which an inspector has pursued him throughout the film (shades of Detective Juve in the *Fantômas* serials).

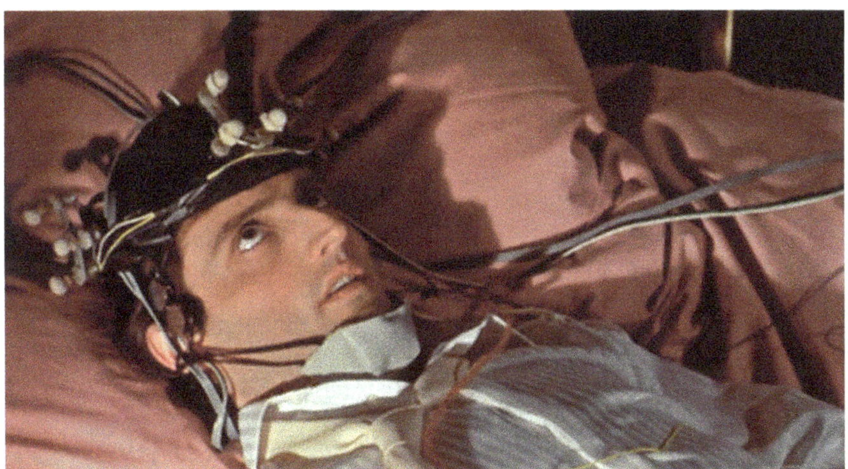

FIGURE 3.4. Walter (Daniel Mesguich) wears a helmet in *La belle captive* (Robbe-Grillet, 1983) that forces him to dream.

Already in the nature of the film's narrative, we see certain parallels to Magritte (as well as to Surrealism in general). While most of the images in Robbe-Grillet's movie are highly realistic (as are the painter's), the world that they reveal is entirely fantastic. The drama's time frame is ambiguous, as events seem to repeat themselves and it is difficult to ascertain which episodes precede or follow others. (Early on, for instance, Marie-Ange even says, "Time doesn't exist for me").

Its spatiality is equally compromised. Many sequences are staged to seem entirely synthetic (e.g., those of Sara riding on her motorcycle, people dancing in a bar, or an episode in a cemetery with excessive fog). A bedroom that looks normal in one shot is suddenly covered with pages of newsprint in the next. Moreover, when Walter explores the house next door to the Count's, he discovers rooms that are identical to those in the Count's residence. This sense of déjà vu is augmented by the fact that Robbe-Grillet evidently used the same building for all scenes in the film, simply altering the decor.[12] Sounds carry over from one space into another (e.g., bird sounds on the beach are heard in a bedroom). Furthermore, with a single cut, characters are whisked from one locale to another without any explanation of the geographical transition.

There is also the theme of the double in the film: Walter and the Count seem identical, and the former is told that there is a second woman who is often mistaken for Marie-Ange. As we will see (particularly in chapter 16),

Magritte often "multiplies" figures in his canvases, most notably the omnipresent "man in the bowler hat." We find this especially in a scene from *La belle captive*, in which a group of men peer through a window at Marie-Ange on the floor (figure 3.5)—also raising issues of voyeurism. Clearly, this image bears parallels to Magritte's *The Month of the Grape Harvest* (1959) (figure 3.6).

Furthermore, in the skeletal detective/secret agent tale that forms the basis of the narrative, we detect echoes of Magritte's love of Feuillade crime serials, as well as Nick Carter and Nat Pinkerton stories. Significantly, Walter wears a cliché trench coat and fedora throughout the film, and his thoughts are rendered in the kind of internal voice-over that is common in film noir. Finally, there is the movie's fixation on Woman—part femme fatale and part object of desire—a familiar and contradictory trope in Surrealist art. There is even a nod to perverse sexuality in the film (notably foot fetishism) in its concern with Marie-Ange's lost and bloodied shoe.

But clearly, the most vital homage to Magritte lies in Robbe-Grillet's repeated reference to the painter's *La belle captive* series. The film opens with an acknowledgment of it in the form of a picture frame with an enclosed transparent pane positioned by the ocean; through it, we watch the waves roll (figure 3.7). Later in the film, there is another nod to transparency when we see Walter through a canvas posed on an easel on the beach. (These images are also relevant to the discussion of the film *A Draughtsman's Contract* [1982] in chapter 8.)

The second specific citation of Magritte's *La belle captive* is a verbal one: the strange men that Walter encounters in the house at which he stops call Marie-Ange a "beautiful captive" and offer to buy her from him. The third one occurs after the couple is ushered into a bedroom, and the film cuts to a picture frame and red curtains positioned by the sea. The fourth reference is an image of the same thing, but this time the camera moves through the frame to find the curtains freestanding on the beach. The fifth reference is a shot already mentioned—an altered version of Magritte's painting on the wall, labeled "*La belle captive* after René Magritte." The sixth instance involves another shot of the painting. The seventh time a version of Magritte's painting appears, it is on a postcard that Walter finds in the home of the Count. Following that, there are repeated images of Marie-Ange dancing on the beach in a white, sheer gown, framed by red curtains reminiscent of those in Magritte's canvas. Toward the end of the film, we return to the image that opened it—a framed transparent picture posed on an easel by the sea.

Beyond specific references to Magritte's *La belle captive*, there are other intimations of the artist. In several shots, we see empty picture frames reminding

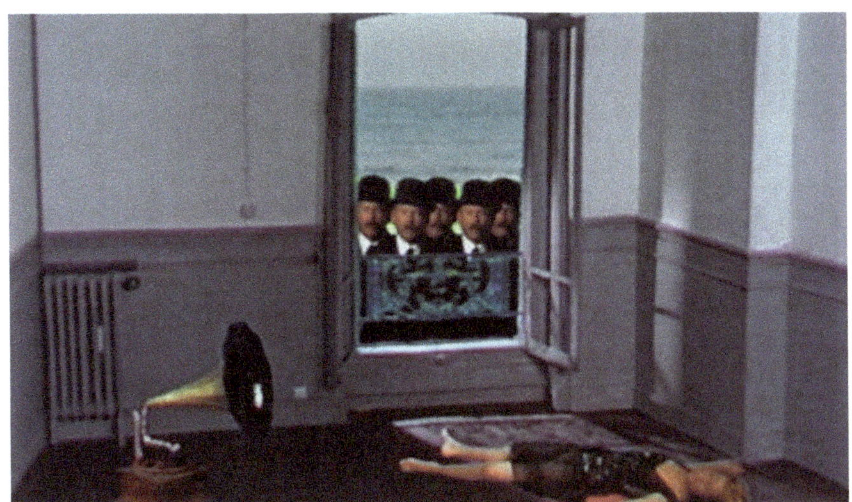

FIGURE 3.5. Men stare through a window at Marie-Ange (Gabrielle Lazure) in *La belle captive* (Robbe-Grillet, 1983), reminding us of those in Magritte's *The Month of the Grape Harvest* (1959).

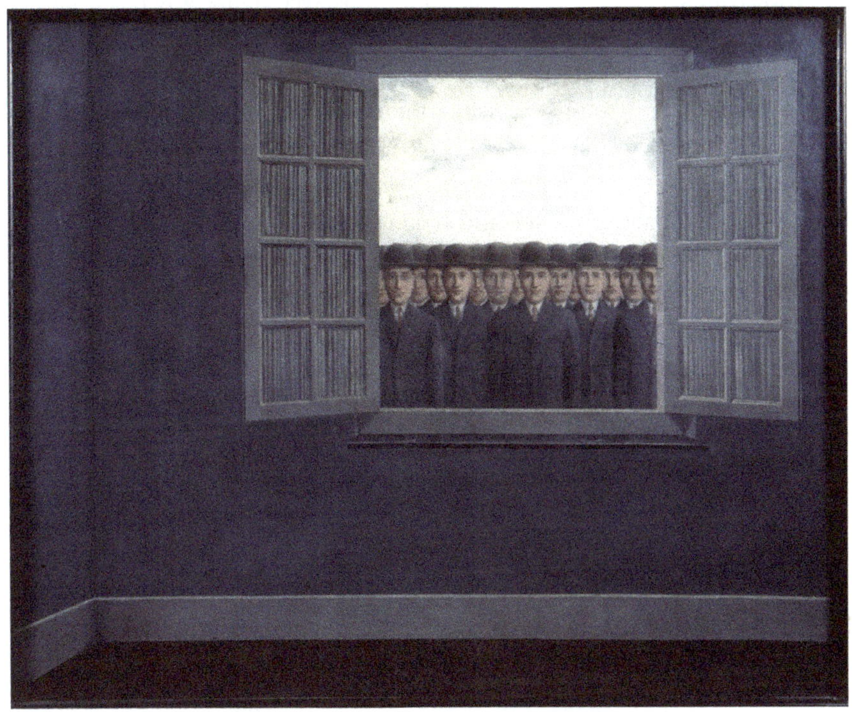

FIGURE 3.6. *The Month of the Grape Harvest* (*Le moi des vendanges*) (1959)

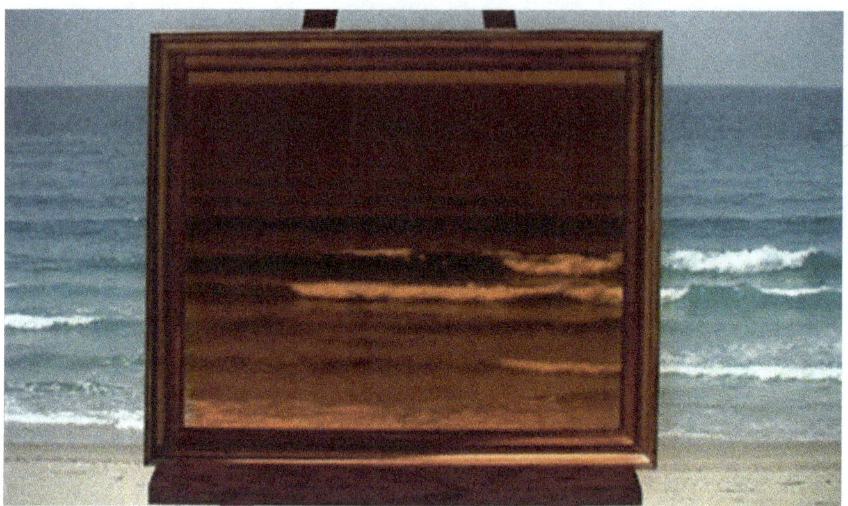

FIGURE 3.7. A transparent picture frame is posed by the ocean in Robbe-Grillet's *La belle captive* (1983), recalling canvases of the same name painted by Magritte.

us of Magritte's 1934 canvas of the same thing (see figure 9.1, *Blood-letting* [1938 or 1939]). Moreover, both in the Count's home and in his neighbor's, there are pictures of the sky with clouds—a repeated icon in Magritte's oeuvre. Furthermore, in the Count's mansion, there is a white bust of a female head, reminding us of Magritte's *Memory* (1948) (see figure 10.2).

Additionally, at one point, Walter's interior monologue speaks of billowing waves, a painter's easel, and red curtains—all elements of Magritte's pictorial vocabulary. Finally, when attempts are made to kill Walter, it is by firing squad, reminding us of Magritte's numerous paintings depicting guns (e.g., *Universal Gravitation* [1943], *The Survivor* [1950] *and Hunters at the Edge of Night* [1928]). Furthermore, in one such image, Robbe-Grillet juxtaposes his shot of Walter with Édouard Manet's *The Execution of Maximilian* (1867–69).

It is telling that the painting Robbe-Grillet chose to honor Magritte (*La belle captive*) is one that includes a picture frame and curtains. Clearly, the former invokes the issue of artistic representation as well as that which encases it. The latter, of course, draws attention to the element of theatricality in both life and on the stage—a quality that Robbe-Grillet heightens in his hyperbolic and self-reflexive drama. As discussed in chapter 19, the drapes that figure prominently in Magritte's work can also be seen to suggest those of the old-fashioned movie theater.

But ultimately, interpretations of Magritte's painting and Robbe-Grillet's movie are left unresolved. Significantly, Walter's voice-over narration speaks to this issue. At one point while he is driving, the camera cuts to a shot of heavy, half-drawn theater curtains as he wonders where they are from and what they are doing there. Then, after questioning whether he is in a dream, he thinks: "One feels it means something—something important—but one doesn't know what."

We might say the same thing about both versions of *La belle captive*—painting and film.

René and Georgette Magritte with Their Dog in the Park (Joan Logue, 1984)

"René and Georgette Magritte with Their Dog after the War" is a song written by Paul Simon in 1981 and recorded in 1983 on his album *Hearts and Bones*. In 1984, a color music video of the song (directed by Joan Logue) was also released. As its title makes clear, the song and video are homages to Magritte and his wife. Both forms were evidently inspired by photographs of the couple taken by Lothar Wolleh in the 1960s. The video, however, does not use actual footage of René and Georgette; rather the couple is dramatized by others (most likely Paul Simon and his then wife, Carrie Fisher).

The video begins with what looks like a mobile Cinerama screen (much like the image in Magritte's *The Memoirs of a Saint* [1960], discussed in chapter 19; see figure 19.2). On it are projected moving images of a man, woman, and dog walking in the park. Soon the screen spins around and becomes a keyhole matte, as the lyrics speak of the couple returning to their hotel suite after a stroll. Clearly, in the keyhole configuration is a reference to the theme of voyeurism in Magritte's work (discussed in chapter 5). As the words speak of dancing, we see seven tiny sepia images of a couple waltzing around. Significantly, drawing on Simon's own musical roots, the song imagines the Magrittes moving to the tunes of early rock-and-roll groups: the Penguins, the Moonglows, the Orioles, and the Five Satins. Of course, this is highly unlikely as the real couple's musical taste would have been different.

A page-turning wipe (made up of a Magrittian blue sky) takes us to footage of René and Georgette walking along an urban sidewalk (which the lyrics imagine as Christopher Street in New York City). It has them stopping at a men's store where they see mannequins "that brought tears to their immigrant eyes." In this allusion, Simon is invoking the stilted, affectless quality of so many of the personages Magritte portrays in his canvases as well as to his images of statues and busts.

After a puzzle-piece wipe, the video cuts to an image of blue sky with a man in a bowler hat, center frame, back turned to us, holding a globe. His positioning is familiar to us from Magritte's paintings; often an individual's face is hidden from the viewer (discussed further in chapter 13). Soon the image collapses into the shape of an eye per Magritte's *The False Mirror* (pictured on the cover of this volume). In the iris is matted footage of a couple in the park with their dog. Against trapezoidal images of the blue sky, the picture of a couple on a mattress floats by as the lyrics talk of the Magrittes falling asleep side by side.

Soon a picture of a bureau appears. On its surface lie glasses, sunglasses, keys, and a wallet. One of the dresser drawers opens to show a high-angle shot of a dinner party as the song mentions the Magrittes dining with the "power elite." Once more the old rock-and-roll groups are invoked as black-and-white photographs of them float by. After a while, an image of a man in a bowler hat appears. It then dissolves into a mock-up of Magritte's painting *The Pilgrim* (1966), in which a decapitated man is accompanied by his own separated head. The face of the latter is that of Paul Simon, literally positioning himself within one of the artist's canvases (figure 3.8).

The song is a heartfelt tribute to the love that Simon assumes existed between Magritte and his wife. Significantly, the album on which it appeared was produced in the year that Simon married Carrie Fisher. Merging his own persona with that of the painter's, Simon imagines the couple responding to classic American rock-and-roll as sung by black male groups in the 1950s and 1960s.

The video, however, goes beyond the song, to create visual tropes reminiscent of those of Magritte (clearly an artist beloved by Simon): the blue sky, the keyhole matte, the eyeball, multiplied imagery, mannequins, everyday objects (like glasses or keys), and the man in the bowler hat. On some level, Simon sees himself as one of Magritte's "everymen"—as is evident in the last image of the video in which his own face is substituted for one of Magritte's stone-faced and opaque "doubles."

The Thomas Crown Affair (John McTiernan, 1999)

While the films discussed thus far fall into the art or experimental film mode, there is one commercial work that involves a cursory homage to Magritte. The 1999 version of *The Thomas Crown Affair* is a remake of a movie by the same name made in 1968 by Norman Jewison. While the original concerned a bank

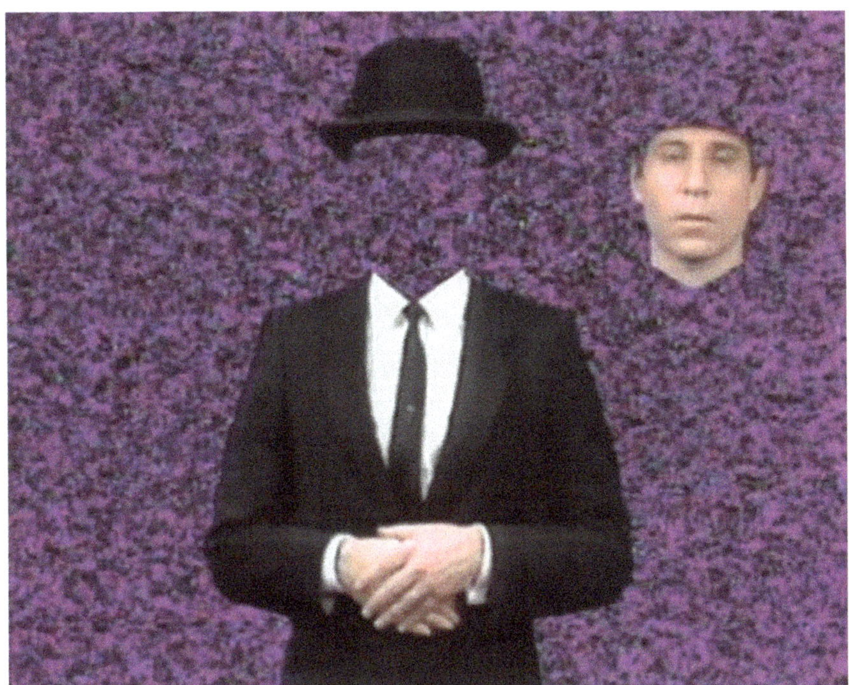

FIGURE 3.8. In this shot from *René and Georgette Magritte with their Dog in the Park* (Logue, 1984), Paul Simon mimics Magritte's painting *The Pilgrim* (1966).

robbery, the later film transposes the theft to the art world. The plot of the movie is as follows:

> Bored billionaire Thomas Crown (Pierce Brosnan) decides to entertain himself by stealing a Monet from a reputed museum. When Catherine Banning (Rene Russo), an investigator for the museum's insurance company, takes an interest in Crown, a complicated back-and-forth game with romantic undertones begins between them. In an attempt to find out where Banning's loyalties lie, Crown returns the painting and essentially turns himself in, hoping that Banning's feelings for him will lead to an escape.[13]

What is interesting about the movie is that on several occasions Magritte's *The Son of Man* (1964), which pictures a bowler-hatted man with an apple in front of his face, is featured in scenes taking place at the museum, a major locale within the narrative (figure 3.9). At first, we see it only on a banner that advertises the museum or a particular exhibit. But later, the painting takes a more central

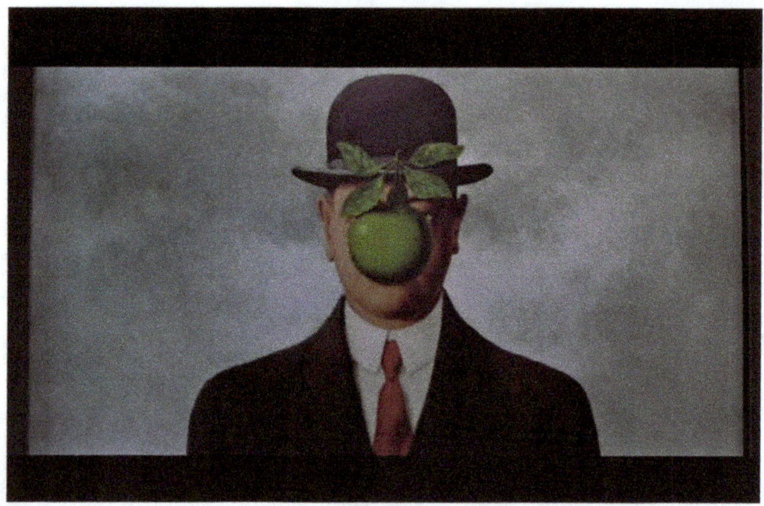

FIGURE 3.9. In *The Thomas Crown Affair* (McTiernan, 1999), there is a museum sequence in which Magritte's painting *The Son of Man* (1964) is featured.

role when Banning and Crown spend an evening together at the museum and she wryly pauses before the painting and calls it a portrait of him.

Toward the end of the narrative Magritte's canvas is highlighted once more when Crown returns to the museum (cognizant that the police are watching him), dons a bowler hat, and moves through the crowd of people. While this seems a silly move (as his headgear easily identifies him), it soon becomes obvious that he has arranged for numerous bowler-hatted men to circulate in the melee, thereby confusing the cops. Catching on to Crown's ruse, one of the detectives peers at *The Son of Man* on a gallery wall. When the police apprehend one of the Crown doubles, his briefcase flies open and countless reproductions of *The Son of Man* fall to the floor—mirroring the plethora of real bowler-hatted men.

So the question arises as to why the film may have singled out Magritte's *Son of Man* to foreground. On one level, the canvas's obfuscated face tends to represent the cagey and hard-to-read Crown, which is why Banning deems it a "portrait" of him. Furthermore, given that the artist's bowler-hatted man has been seen as a representation of the bourgeois everyman, it makes a good costume for Crown's surrogates, since each of them can be easily mistaken for the other, as all are interchangeable. This is also the sense we get when the multitude of Magritte reproductions fall to the floor.

Web-Based Creations

While conventionally distributed films that pay tribute to Magritte are few and far between, if one searches the web, one finds countless works that people have posted that seek to do this—similar to "mash-ups" of famous movies. Looking exclusively on YouTube, I found that such works (of wildly varying quality) fall into a few categories and I will discuss a representative one in each group. The totality of such postings are too numerous to mention, and many are not worthy of discussion. In the process, however, I discovered the existence of Magritte-themed children books, operas, and ballets—indicating the artist's continuing popularity with the public.

Live-Action Re-creations

The live-action re-creations are quite amateur and poor attempts to translate some Magritte painting into a real-world setting. A favored painting for such re-creations is *The Lovers* (1928) (see figure 2.2)—one that Magritte himself, as we have seen, had reenacted for one of his home movies. One video posting, for example, is a thirty-four-second work by Ana López González (2016) that quite simply poses a man and a woman (dressed and shrouded like the couple in the canvas) in front of a blank background resembling the painting. They embrace, kiss, and we cut to a close-up of the man's hand passionately grabbing the woman's red dress. He leaves the scene and she remains as the video concludes.[14]

Three-Dimensional and Virtual-Reality Attempts to "Enter" a Magritte Painting

Step Inside: René Magritte's "Le groupe silencieux" is a one-and-a-half-minute video produced by Christie's auction house in 2018. It focuses on a painting from 1926 (*The Silent Group*) and allows us to "enter" it as a three-dimensional space.[15] The iconography of *Le groupe silencieux* is quite abstract but involves the following objects set inside a pink room: a wooden cutout of a human silhouette, a curtain, a cube decorated with images of eyes, an empty picture frame, a canvas depicting foliage, and a doorway through which we see the edge of a castle. After viewing the painting on a wall, we move into it and through the doorway pictured in the background to the castle and a waterfall. We then circulate around various objects in the room as some are animated (e.g., the curtain blows). At the end of the video we exit pictorial space and again view the framed canvas on the wall.

GIFs

Magritte Animation by Joel Remy (2016) is a series of GIFs created from numerous Magritte paintings.[16] As popularly understood, GIFs are looped video clips that endlessly repeat themselves. In animating *Attempting the Impossible* (1928) (see figure 6.1), for example, the artist depicted on the canvas continually paints and unpaints his model, while in the animation of *The Six Elements* (1929) (see figure 20.5), images in each of the many frames come alive (e.g., the bells in the lower-right corner move up and down repeatedly). Similarly, in the animation of *The Double Secret* (1927) (see figure 14.1), the face of a man (initially torn from his skull) repeatedly moves back and forth to close or open the gap.

Animations/Transformations of One Painting

Referencing one of Magritte's most famous paintings, Nathaniel Holt's *Magritte "False Mirror" Video Interpretation* (2014) is a thirty-five-second work focusing on a real person's eyeball. Initially it is matted with a moving image of the sky and a large black pupil (as per Magritte).[17] Soon, however, the space inside the iris fills with documentary footage of social horrors: starving children, piled dead bodies, Nazi concentration camps, factory explosions, and so on. The video ends by returning to the opening image.

Animations/Transformations of Numerous Paintings

This Is Not a Film (2003) is a short (three-and-a-half minute) animated movie by James Kelly.[18] To an initial soundtrack of repetitive electronic music, the film presents a series of moving images based upon several Magritte paintings. Often, however, the iconography is transformed. For example, an early image is derived from Magritte's *The Murderer Threatened*, yet while the original canvas has a picture in the background, Kelly's shows an opening in the wall with the ocean and a crescent moon revealed.

The mise-en-scène from this Magritte painting recurs throughout the film. In a later iteration, the flesh-toned woman who lies on a chaise in Magritte's work becomes a white statue-like figure who is bleeding from her head. A man enters the room and places a red rose on her body. Later, the statue woman is overlaid with a blue tone on her bodice and flesh tone on her lower body. In these sequences, Kelly combines many of Magritte's paintings or tropes. The red rose is, of course, a familiar icon in his work, most famously in *The Tomb of the Wrestlers*, in which it fills a room. White female statuary appears in *The Light of Coincidences* (1933) and a bleeding statuary bust in *Memory* (see figure 10.2). Finally, an image of a sky-tinted nude is the subject of *Black Magic* (1934).

Other Magritte paintings are also referenced in the film—for instance, *Golconda* (1953), in which bowler-hatted men seem to rain down from the sky. In Kelly's work, we periodically see men's legs falling into the frame, and eventually we witness them in full-body mode descending onto a bridge, one familiar to us from Magritte's *Homesickness* (1941).

Another recurrent image in the film is derived from Magritte's *On the Threshold of Freedom* (1930), a work in which a room is covered, wall to wall, with sectional paintings. In Kelly's film, the image is changed. Instead of being divided into four panels, we see six, and the images contained within them are different (e.g., an apple and a rose—both iconographic elements of Magritte's work). But the framed sections also contain a full painting by Magritte, *Personal Values* (1952) (see figure 20.13), in which a room (furnished with an armoire and a bed) contains oversized items like a comb, glass, shaving brush, and bar of soap. At a later point in the film, a man walks into the room and opens the armoire.

A few more animated Magritte paintings are noteworthy in the film. At one point, a man closes the kind of sky-tinted windowpane that we find in *The Field Glass* (1963). In another sequence, a door (with a curious cutout) reminiscent of the one in *The Unexpected Answer* (1933) closes. Finally, in another episode, a birdcage with an egg in it (referencing *Elective Affinities*) swings on a hinge.

Beyond this, the film is peppered with additional iconographic elements associated with Magritte: bells, blue sky, the ocean, masks, ambiguously lit street scenes, and even Fantômas.

4

THE BELGIAN SURREALIST CINEMATIC AVANT-GARDE

> I could say that I am Fantômas in a way.
>
> René Magritte[1]

As a resident of Brussels, René Magritte did not work in an artistic vacuum. Rather, as mentioned earlier, he was part of a broader Belgian Surrealist group. Patricia Allmer and Hilde van Gelder note, however, that these individuals have been marginalized in the critical literature in comparison to the more dominant French wing of the movement.[2]

Belgian Surrealism was born in 1924 (the same year as André Breton published *The Surrealist Manifesto*), with the emergence of the journal *Correspondence*, which consisted of a series of one-page tracts—often critiquing the French Surrealists.[3] At that time, Magritte was more affiliated with Dadaism, and in 1925 he and E. L. T. Mesens published the periodical *Osophage*. Eventually, however, the two artistic camps merged under the banner of Surrealism. Ties were also established with their Parisian counterparts, and they cooperated "on special issues of *Variétés* in 1929, *Documents* in 1934, and the collective work *Violette Nozières* in 1933 which brought together Bréton, [René] Char, [Salvador] Dalí, [Paul] Éluard, Mesens, [Max] Ernst, [Jean] Arp, and Magritte."[4]

Filmmakers were also part of the broader Belgian Surrealist group; of particular interest (in relation to the work of Magritte) are Ernst Moerman and Henri Storck.

Monsieur Fantômas (Ernst Moerman,1937)

Openly billing itself as "a Surrealist film," *Monsieur Fantômas*, a short movie directed by Ernst Moerman, definitely lives up to that claim. As Moerman once stated, the universe of Surrealism is "a world where nothing is impossible, and where a miracle is the shortest route from uncertainty to mystery."[5] Though it has a musical score, it proceeds much like a silent black-and-white movie and seems to be set in that antique era. This is not surprising since, as the title indicates, the film harks back to the *Fantômas* serials of the teens—a favorite of Magritte's—as is clear from this chapter's epigraph. Though its narrative makes little sense, it seems to bear a self-reflexive element. Early on, we see a woman on the beach incongruously typing on a machine set on a small pedestal. We later see a page that mentions Fantômas and "chapters." When we return to the woman several subsequent times, she is typing in the ocean (nearly covered with water), and ultimately we see a typed page floating in the waves.

Whether or not she is an authorial stand-in, the film proceeds as an episode of the *Fantômas* saga. Our hero first appears in a familiar stance, as though lifted from a movie poster, masked and posing above the city on a building roof. In other scenes, we find him in his signature black bodysuit. The film has almost no plot. Fantômas searches for the woman he loves (Elvire) and eventually kills her. Detective Juve investigates and tracks him down, sentencing him to death. As soldiers fire a cannon at him (odder than a firing squad), he magically disappears and Juve and his cohorts are left wrestling with one another. As the film closes, nuns and priests dance around the column at which Fantômas stood for his failed execution. This is not the only joke at the Catholic Church's expense. At one point, a nun opens a door to a confessional and finds a priest wearing women's bloomers while powdering his face.

What is interesting about the film (aside from its tribute to a hero of a bygone cinematic era), is the bizarre and numerous Surrealist tropes that pepper it. Fantômas, for instance, finds Elvire lying in a pool of swamp water, wearing what looks like a nightgown or bridal outfit (reminiscent of Magritte's mother's drowning). As he pledges his love, he reads lines from Paul Éluard's poetry collection *The Capital of Pain* (1926): "Your tomb and my fall eternalize my life." Later, they walk to the beach with Elvire wearing another strange costume.

Outlandish things are found there as well, for instance, a tailor's dummy, a cello, an easel next to a dead bird, footprints in the sand that end in a series of shoes, Juve soaking in a bathtub on the shore, and his compatriots discussing the case with him—their bodies buried in the sand and only their heads protruding. They wear bowler hats—a Magritte icon as early as 1926 in *The Musings of a Solitary Walker*.

There are other Surrealist images in the work that call up specific paintings by Magritte. While one might argue that these are simply derivative tropes and not artistic tributes, there is one shot that directly references Magritte—indicating that his shadow hovers over the entire enterprise. Toward the end of the film, we see a painter working at an easel as a woman (ostensibly his subject) leans against a white brick wall.[6] Eventually, we get a shot of the painting he is completing (figure 4.1), and it is Magritte's *Rape* (1935) (see figure 16.3—a disturbing canvas, discussed in chapter 16, that depicts a female torso in which the breasts serve as eyes, the belly button as nose, and the pubis as mouth).

Given this citation, it is possible to see much of the film's iconography as related to that of Magritte—the best known of the Belgian Surrealists and an artist who had already had a one-man show in Brussels in 1927 and, by 1936, a similar one in New York City. Here we think of a doorframe that stands in the middle of the beach surrounded by open space. Rather than walk around it, Fantômas and Elvire open it and walk through it. As early as *The Scars of Memory* (1926 or 1927), Magritte had begun his fascination with doors, including a canvas depicting a freestanding one (as in *Monsieur Fantômas*). In 1933, he painted *The Unexpected Answer* in which a closed door, rather than blocking-off space, has a large cutout in its center through which people can move. Thus, like the door in the film, it serves no purpose. At the time that *Monsieur Fantômas* was made, it is also possible that Magritte was working on *The Poison* (1938 or 1939), in which a door opens on to a beach.

Moerman milks one more joke from the doorframe on the sand. When Juve and his assistants approach it, they knock on it and look through the peephole rather than simply bypass it (simultaneously echoing Magritte's interest in voyeurism). One of the men then goes in search of a key and finds a huge one. Rather than trying to open the door with it, however, the men use it as a battering ram to knock the door down (figure 4.2). Given the size of the key, it is interesting to note that by this time Magritte had already begun to play with scale. *The Giantess* (1931) (see figure 10.5) depicts an oversized naked woman who towers over a man in the foreground and a sofa in the background. The canvas also portrays a door in the room in which she stands, but she seems too large to pass through it.

There are yet other intimations of Magritte in the film. At one point, Fantômas and Elvire walk on the beach and begin to argue when she asks him to remove his mask. Suddenly the two are shown roped together struggling to

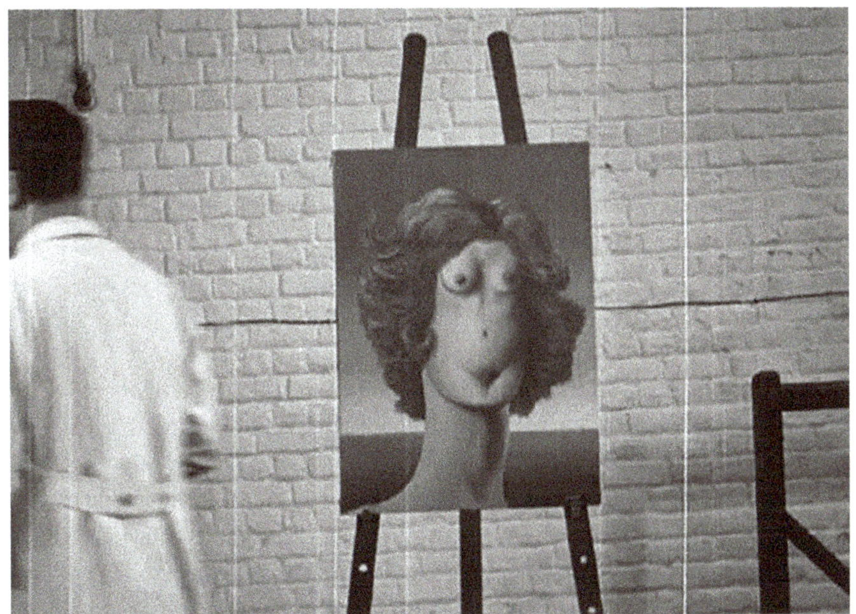

FIGURE 4.1. In Moerman's *Monsieur Fantômas* (1937), an image of Magritte's painting *Rape* (1935) appears.

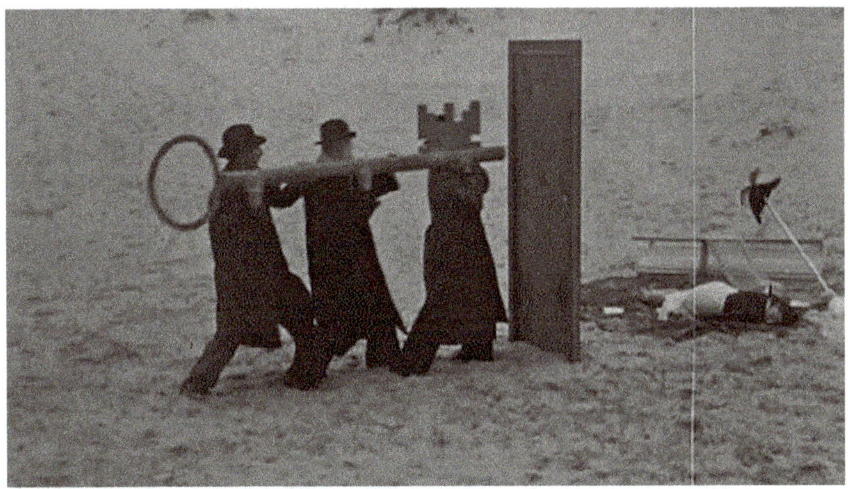

FIGURE 4.2. Moerman's *Monsieur Fantômas* (1937) involves a play with scale (here a key) and unmoored objects (here a door) worthy of Magritte.

get free of each other, and we are reminded of Magritte's *Titanic Days* (1928) (see figure 18.3), in which a man and a woman seem sutured together, thrashing around in order to tear themselves apart. Finally, two of the objects Magritte depicts in *The Interpretation of Dreams* (1930) and mislabels linguistically appear in *Monsieur Fantômas*. Juve finds a woman's black high-heeled shoe in the sand (also a featured object in Alain Robbe-Grillet's *La belle captive* [1983]) and all the detectives wear bowler hats.

Pour les beaux yeux (Henri Storck, 1929)

Another important filmmaker of the Belgian avant-garde was Henri Storck, who in the late 1920s made some experimental films but became known primarily for his documentary work. Storck's *Pour les beaux yeux* is a relatively plotless movie whose iconography focuses upon the image of an artificial eyeball. In the beginning of the film, a man sitting outdoors looks down and finds a glass eyeball on the ground. He picks it up, takes it home, places it in a box, and tries unsuccessfully to mail it. At another point, we see a one-eyed man go to buy an artificial eyeball. He purchases one and inserts it into his eye socket. Eyes are important in other shots of the film: close-ups of a woman's face, as well as those of various masks. Furthermore, at one point, a man places a glass eyeball on a large pedestal, which we see from an overhead point of view. At

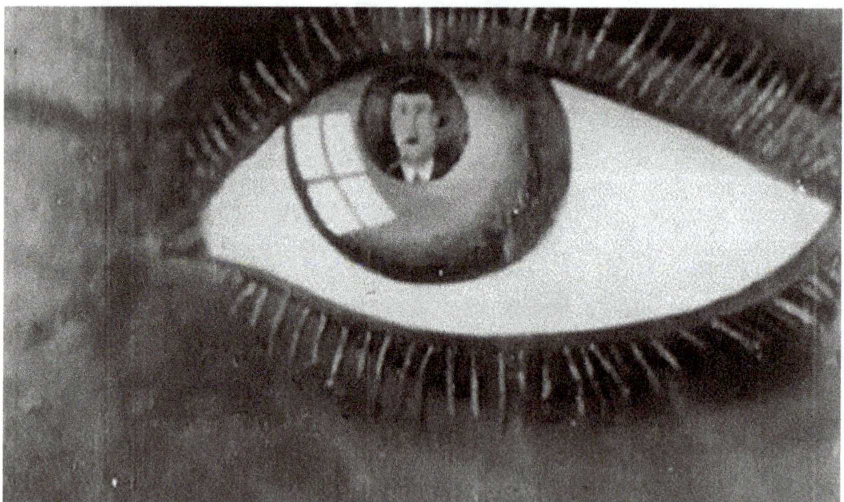

FIGURE 4.3. Storck's *Pour les beaux yeux* (1929) features eyeballs evocative of those in Magritte's painting *The False Mirror* from the same year.

various moments in the film, a huge close-up of a fake eyeball appears and in its pupil is an image of man's face (figure 4.3).

While some commentators have seen the film's obsession with eyes as derived from Salvador Dalí and Luis Buñuel's *Un chien andalou*—made a year earlier[7]—I would like to raise the possibility that the movie might also relate to a painting by Magritte. As already noted, *The False Mirror* (1929) (a work that would become world-famous and appears on the cover of this volume) depicts a massive eyeball whose iris contains a picture of the sky (much as the pupil of an eye in *Pour les beaux yeux* contains a man's portrait). Is it possible that Storck knew of this canvas and tipped his hat to it? Possibly since both men traveled in Belgian Surrealist circles.

2

RESONANCES OF MAGRITTE IN FILM HISTORY, THEORY, AND PRACTICE

5

VOYEURISM AND THE GAZE

> Sometimes an image can seriously accuse the viewer.
>
> René Magritte[1]

MAGRITTE'S *THE SPY* (1928) is a rather simple painting on the visual level (figure 5.1). On the right side of the canvas we see a well-dressed man peering through a keyhole in a door. On the left side, we see a head of a woman suspended in a black void. The implication is that he is looking at her. There is a spatial disjunction in the painting. While the man is seen in profile, the woman is viewed frontally. While a good portion of the man's torso is represented, the woman seems almost decapitated. While the canvas seems to represent continuous space, a white line separates it into two regions, which may or may not align. So the closer you look the more ambiguous the scene becomes.

But it is not these aspects of the work that are salient to our investigation. Rather, it is the emphatic focus on voyeurism. Of course, the title *The Spy* has an obvious link to the scene depicted and is lacking the enigmatic quality of those for so many of Magritte's works. From one perspective, the title highlights the artist's well-known love of the detective genre—including the *Fantômas*, Nick Carter, and Nat Pinkerton series. From another, however, the canvas is a treatise on the issue of scopophilia—the pleasure (often sexual) realized from looking at someone who is unaware of your gaze. Here the straight white line makes the distinction between seer and seen abundantly clear—a boundary that cannot be breached without ruining the effect.

Certainly, the issue of vision, in general, is central to the history of film theory, practice, and criticism as is the subject of voyeurism. And, in this

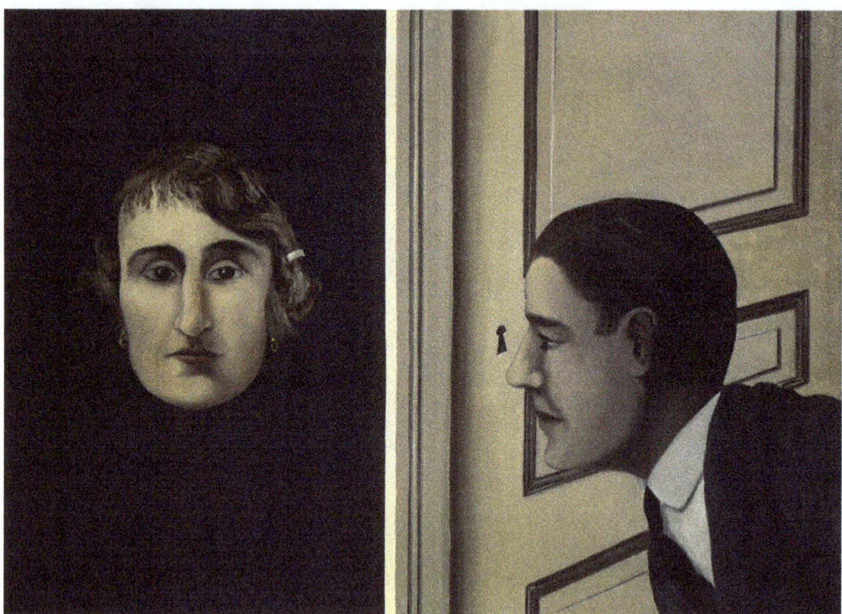

FIGURE 5.1. *The Spy* (*L'espion*) (1928)

respect, Magritte's oeuvre shares this concern. There can be no painting that so emphatically highlights the topic as *The False Mirror* (shown on the cover of this book), a picture of a huge eyeball, which he painted in 1929. The eye takes in the world (signified by the sky in the iris). Its giant size also seems to auger mass surveillance, a task handled today by closed circuit videography. Interestingly, some have seen the painting as the source of the long-standing CBS television logo. Coming close to *The False Mirror* is *The Difficult Crossing* (1926), in which a man's head consists entirely of an eyeball—emphasizing that vision is the preeminent sensory mode of modern times. But beyond those works, the eye pops up in other Magritte paintings in most unexpected situations—for instance, in the middle of a slice of ham in *The Portrait* (1935), which creates a comic Surrealist juxtaposition of food and body part. It also appears in *Homage to Shakespeare* (1963)—atop a piece of wood that is similar in shape to one positioned behind the man in *The Difficult Crossing*.

In contemplating Magritte's iconographic focus on the eyeball, we cannot help but recall signal moments in film history that utilize the same imagery: Dziga Vertov's superimposition of the eyeball on the camera lens in *Man with a Movie Camera*, and Luis Buñuel and Salvador Dalí's slicing of the eyeball in *Un chien andalou*—both from 1929—the same year as *The False Mirror*. If we go back even further in film history, we might also consider Georges Méliès's *A Trip to the Moon* (1902), in which a rocket lands on the eyeball of that extraterrestrial body. (These three images are pictured on the cover of this volume.)

But the specific question of voyeurism (that Magritte raises in *The Spy*) has particular relevance to cinema and the development of film theory. For Stanley Cavell in *The World Viewed*, the wonder of movies is tied to the spectator's disconnection from events on the screen and to her sense of being able to see a world that can never look back or make demands on her (or, as Magritte's epigraph implies, "accuse" her). "How do movies reproduce the world magically?" he asks. "Not by literally presenting us with the world, but by permitting us to view it unseen. This is not a wish for power over creation (as Pygmalion's was), but a wish not to need power, not to have to bear its burdens."[2] Laura Mulvey asserts much the same point in her canonical essay "Visual Pleasure and Narrative Cinema." As she notes, "The mass of mainstream film . . . portray a hermetically sealed world which unwinds magically indifferent to the presence of the audience, producing for them a sense of separation and playing on their voyeuristic phantasy. Moreover, the extreme contrast between the darkness in the audience . . . and the brilliance of the . . . screen helps to promote the illusion of voyeuristic separation."[3] While Cavell does not treat the question of voyeurism from a psychoanalytic or gendered perspective, Mulvey does. Here, drawing on Freud, she sees the stance as a particularly male-oriented phenomenon, with the object of sight a female—hence the familiar notion of the peeping Tom. Clearly, Magritte's characterizations in *The Spy* conform to this model. Furthermore, Mulvey invests the masculine perspective with a sense of consummate power. As she comments, in film (as in the broader culture) Woman is the image and Man the bearer of the look.[4] For Mulvey, the cinema (whose instrument of articulation is the camera) is particularly well suited to voyeuristic discourse, and the fact that its history has been largely authored by men only adds to its aptness for voyeurism. Mulvey points to classical Hollywood cinema for her examples—for instance, Josef von Sternberg's intense and fetishistic visualization of Marlene Dietrich in a canonical group of films.[5]

While, in general, Magritte's painting *The Spy* has relevance to cinema's inherent voyeurism, it has even more specific ties to a series of films from the silent era—ones that foreshadow the painting by envisioning people looking through keyholes. Here one thinks of such works as *The Peeping Tom* (1897), *Through the Key-Hole in the Door* (1900), *What Is Seen through the Keyhole* (1901), *A Search for the Evidence* (1903), and *The Boarding House Bathroom* (1905).

The Peeping Tom starts with a man wearing an apron (probably a workman) on an upper floor of a boardinghouse. He looks through the keyhole of one door and sees a woman making up her face (figure 5.2). When he peers through a second door, he views a woman divesting herself of falsies, dentures, and finally a wig—revealing that she is actually a man. Through the third door, he sees a large woman and a small man drinking and embracing. When he spies through the fourth door, however, a man emerges and beats him up.

A Search for the Evidence follows a similar pattern—though it positions a female in the role of the viewer. She is not, however, a voyeur but, as we surmise, a woman whose mate is cheating on her—which explains the gender switch. The film begins in the hall of a rooming house. A man and woman enter, and immediately the woman bends down and peers through the peephole of a door. What she sees (a man in a nightshirt walking a fussy baby) is framed in a keyhole matte. She next moves on to another door and looks within, and what we view (once more in a keyhole matte) is a slapstick scene of a blind man trying to change a lightbulb in a chandelier. She then peers inside a third door, and the keyhole matte reveals a doctor and nurse tending to a sick girl in bed. In looking at the fourth door, the keyhole matte frames a group of men playing cards, and inside the fifth door is a woman getting ready for bed. Moving on to the sixth door, the keyhole matte discloses a man and his lady friend smooching and drinking. The woman indicates to her male companion (most likely a detective—or private "eye") that this is the scene she has sought. The detective breaks into the room, and the wronged woman

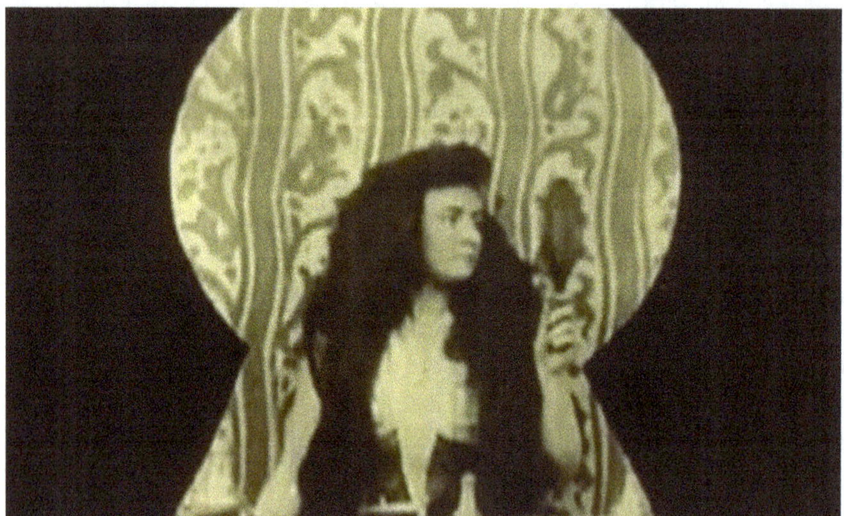

FIGURE 5.2. A peephole view from *Peeping Tom* (1897) reveals a woman in a room.

scolds her mate while throwing his lover down on the floor. The film ends with the jilted woman in tears.

A far more sophisticated version of this narrative occurs in a film, *The Blood of a Poet* (1932), which Magritte would likely have seen a few years after he painted *The Spy*. It was written and directed by Jean Cocteau—an artist who worked at the fringes of the French Surrealist movement. One section of this avant-garde film is set at the Hôtel des Folies Dramatiques—a fantasy space that the protagonist (the Artist) has entered by going through a mirror. (Interestingly, there was a Théâtre des Folies-Dramatiques, which opened in Paris in 1832 for staging melodramas.)

What we see on the screen is a corridor with many doors—exactly like the one in *The Peeping Tom* or *A Search for the Evidence*. At first a man wearing a suit and hat enters; he knocks on a door, gets no answer, and leaves the scene. In dress and demeanor, he is reminiscent of the detective in the 1903 film. Then the Artist (Enrique Riveros) arrives, bare chested and wearing pants rolled up to his knees. He makes his way through the space (strangely clinging to the wall) and kneels to investigate each portal through its keyhole (figure 5.3). Thus, in the film, a man is once more the voyeur. But what he finds behind the doors is far stranger than in the earlier "primitive" films.

At the first door, he sees a Mexican man shot (in slow motion) by a series of rifles aimed at him. (Here we recall the presence of guns in several Magritte paintings [e.g., *The Survivor*, 1950]). The footage is then reversed, and the man revives. At the second door, the scene through a keyhole matte reveals a shadow of someone cleaning an opium pipe; smoke faintly rises and fills the air. At the next door, we get only a reverse shot of the Artist's eye (framed in a keyhole matte). We never actually see what is in the chamber. In this image, we are reminded of another Magritte work *Painted Object: The Eye* (1936 or 1937), which depicts someone's eye framed in a circular matte (which could be a hole in a wall). Interestingly here, however, Magritte inverts the typical gendered paradigm and shows us a woman looking. Gazing through the keyhole of the next door, the Artist sees a young girl being scolded and whipped by a stern old woman dressed in black and, at the next door, an animated scene of a hermaphrodite seated on a chaise before a rotating spiral wheel (reminiscent of Marcel Duchamp's *Rotary Demisphere* [1925]). In front of some doors, shoes have been left (ostensibly for polishing). Often, they signal who is in the room; for instance, ballet slippers (which cannot really be polished) have been placed before the door of the room in which the little girl is being punished. Here we recall another Magritte painting *The Red Model* (1935), in which shoes merge with the feet within them. At the end of the sequence, a disembodied arm

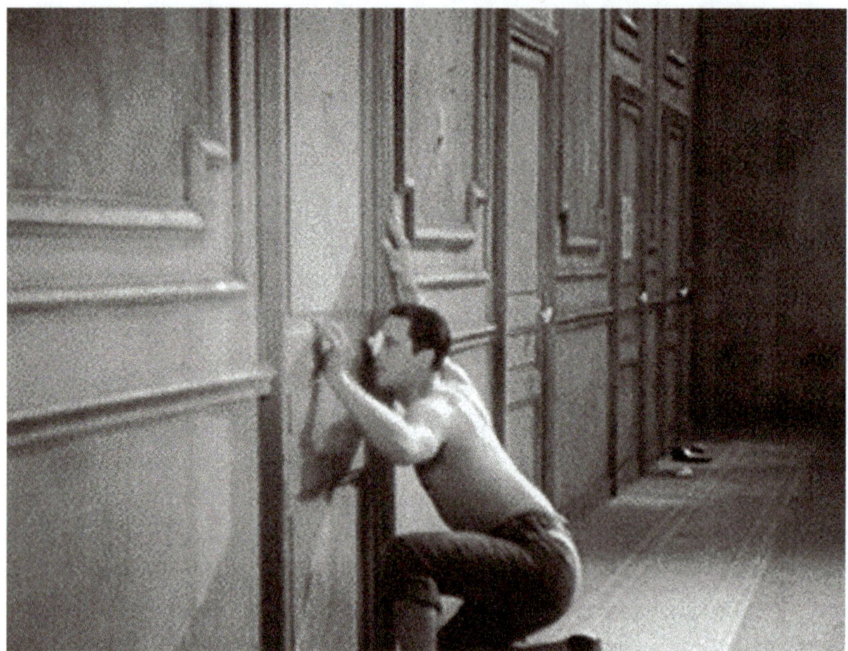

FIGURE 5.3. The Artist looks through a keyhole in *The Blood of a Poet* (1932).

hands the Artist a gun, and he shoots himself in the head. Magritte remained fascinated by the keyhole until late in his career. *The Devil's Smile* (1966) portrays a "close-up" of a doorframe in which we see a keyhole surrounded by an oval brass plate. In the center of it is the key itself—which, ironically, blocks the view of what is inside and does us no good.

The important point here is that in numerous paintings Magritte focuses upon what has come to be regarded as cinema's "original sin"—voyeurism. The primitive movies that we have discussed precede Magritte's *The Spy* and may well have formed an influence on it through his engagement with silent cinema. Cocteau's experimental film postdates Magritte's canvas but may have responded to the same set of early films. Regardless, the theme of vision—so central to the cinema—becomes a parallel obsession in the annals of Modernist art.

6

FICTIONAL VERSUS REAL PERSONS AND SPACES

> The finished picture is a surprise, and its creator is the first to be surprised.
>
> René Magritte[1]

Attempting the Impossible (1928) is one painting by Magritte whose title actually makes sense (figure 6.1). What we see is a man (an artist) who holds a brush and palette in his hands and what appears to be a real woman standing naked before him. We soon notice, however, that part of her right arm is missing and that it is this spot at which the artist's brush is aimed. Clearly, we are to believe that he is in the act of painting or constructing her body part. Obviously, this is unfeasible and "surprising" (to echo Magritte's words above). Were the woman positioned as a figure on a canvas, his actions would make sense. But here they do not, given an actual woman posed before him.

In portraying this scene, Magritte is foregrounding the illusionism of representational art and the viewer's (and perhaps the artist's) oft-mistaken notion that the subjects painted are real. He may also be highlighting the artist's desire to control flesh-and-blood persons like he does those created in his work; and it seems no accident that, as with other of Magritte's canvases, the individual shown is a woman—here, based on his wife, Georgette. Beyond this, as a Surrealist, Magritte participates in the movement's obsessive figuration of the female as the supreme object of desire for the male—one that he repeatedly imagines in his art.

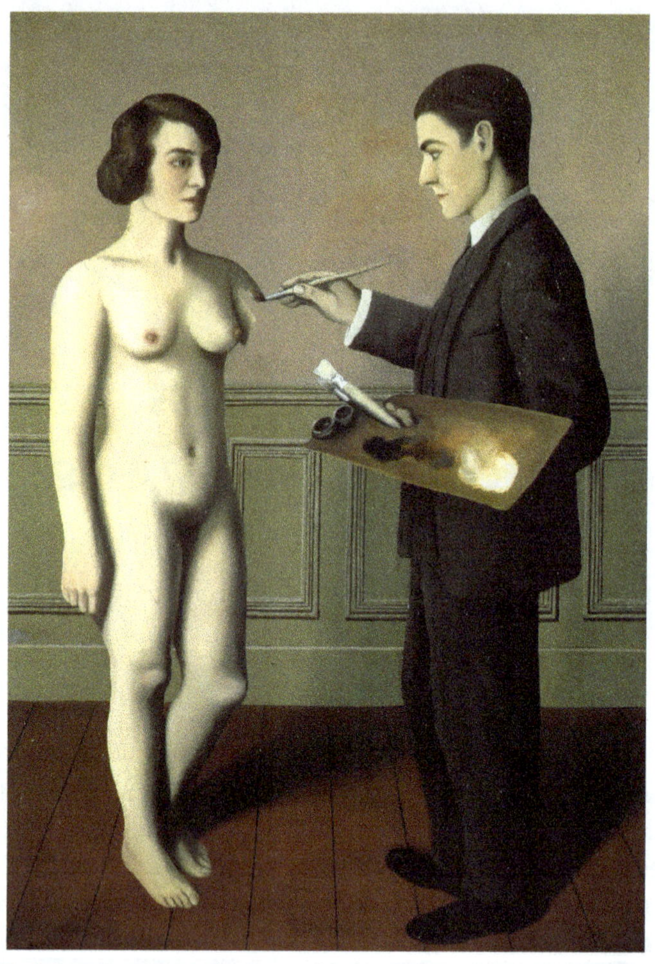

FIGURE 6.1. *Attempting the Impossible* (*La tentative d'impossible*/*The Impossible Attempt*) (1928)

To make matters more interesting, a photograph exists in which Magritte is depicted posed as though he were actually painting Georgette; called *Love*, it is a 1928 snapshot of Magritte and his wife re-creating the scene from *Attempting the Impossible*.[2] This is not an isolated instance of Magritte transferring tableaux from his artwork to the photographic medium. He did so, as we have seen, in many of his home movies. There are also additional photographs in which Magritte sits in front of the canvas *Attempting the Impossible*—further mixing up real and representational space—and drawing on the photographic medium to do so. (He took a similar confusing photograph of himself painting

Clairvoyance [1936], which is a self-portrait of him painting a picture.) In several of these instances, we face the trope of infinite regression.

If we turn to the cinema, we realize that from its earliest days, the medium has also been consumed with questions of illusionism, and the muddle of real and fictional characters and spaces, and this may have been an influence on Magritte's art. Given that Magritte's youth coincided with the cinema's silent era, it is not unlikely that some of what he saw influenced him. Most closely paralleling Magritte's work is Georges Méliès's, of whom Magritte was a fan, and for this reason I give his films significant attention (and do so again in chapter 16).

At the turn of the last century, Méliès produced a series of trick films that focused on either painters or sculptors. In *The Mysterious Portrait* (1899), we first see a large empty picture frame through which we view a door. Méliès soon raises a curtain behind it, revealing that the door was simply part of a painted backdrop—a fictional versus real space. Suddenly the scene behind the picture frame is transformed to a medieval town. Next, Méliès puts a painted canvas into the frame and sets a stool on its lower edge. The frame goes black and dissolves to what looks like a painting of Méliès seated on a stool. After a few moments, the painting "comes to life"—tangling real and pictorial spaces. In *Drawing Lesson* (1903), a magician creates a female "statue" that is actually played by a live woman. Pupils come into the scene and begin to draw it, but when the statue moves, they are shocked.

In *The Hilarious Posters* (1907), Méliès takes on yet another form—advertisements. A series of individual posters are hung on a gate to create a multiframe collage; some policemen stand and talk in front of it. Soon the figures in the pictures come alive and begin to interact with one another. When a bourgeois man passes by, they all throw things at him, and when the cops return, they douse them with flour. Eventually, the ad posters fall on the policemen, and actual people are revealed behind the gate—the very characters who populated the prints. Ultimately, the advertising block is restored, and people jump through its paper surface.

In *Delirium in a Studio* (1907), a woman lies within a picture frame and is mysteriously turned into a painting (a reversal of the action in *Hilarious Posters*). And finally, in *A Tricky Painter's Fate* (1908), an artist (with easel, canvas, and toolbox) sneaks onto the sleeping car of a train after it has unloaded its passengers at the station. To prevent others from coming into his car, he puts up numerous pictures in the train windows to fool people and deter them from entering: one is of a woman with babies, two are of people smoking, and another is of a man holding his head in apparent horror.

Eventually, people catch on to the ruse, chase the painter, and smash a canvas over his head.

But the cinema also created narratives that were self-reflexive about film (vs. the pictorial arts)—again underscoring tensions between real and artificial people and places. In *Uncle Josh and the Moving Picture Show* (Edwin Porter, 1902), a rural hayseed sits in a movie theater watching the Edison projecting kinetoscope. The first short film he sees, "Parisian Dancer," depicts a dancer lifting her skirt and high kicking. Josh leaps from his seat onto the stage and dances with her, mistaking the female screen image for a real human being. When later a film called "Country Couple" is projected (showing a man and woman embracing and kissing), Josh gets so excited that he tears down the screen in his endeavor to enter the filmic terrain. Certainly here the protagonist "attempts the impossible" but, unlike Magritte's artist, fails to succeed. Actually, *Uncle Josh* was a "remake" of a 1901 British film by R. W. Paul, demonstrating how popular this scenario must have been.

Oddly enough, another "remake" of this type of film emerged some six decades later in a scene from Jean-Luc Godard's *Les Carabiniers* (1963). It occurs when one of the two soldier protagonists sees his first movie. Michel-Ange (Patrice Moullet) takes a seat in a darkened theater and looks at the screen. The initial film that he sees is a modern rendition of the Lumière brothers' *The Arrival of a Train* (1895), and like the mythical credulous spectator, he hides his eyes in fear. The second film he watches is an update of the Lumières' *Feeding the Baby* (1895). Michel-Ange smiles and laughs at the title character, especially when the child throws down his plate and his father douses him with whipped cream. The third film is a remake of *After the Ball, the Bath* (1897) by Georges Méliès, in which a woman undresses and gets ready to bathe. As she does so, Michel-Ange stares lasciviously at her and rises from his seat. When she is entirely nude and gets into the tub, he approaches the movie screen. After trying to jump into the picture and caress her two-dimensional body, he finally rips down the screen only to reveal the theater wall behind it.

There is another but very different famous silent film that entails a misperception of real and fictive people and spaces. In Buster Keaton's *Sherlock Jr.* (1924), a projectionist (played by Keaton) falls asleep and dreams that the movie he is showing stars characters from his life, including his girlfriend and his rival. Furthermore, he imagines himself (within the screen narrative) in the guise of a heroic detective who solves a mystery, catches a criminal, and gets the girl—all things he struggles with in reality. In a pivotal shot of the film, Buster leaves the projection booth, walks down the auditorium aisle, and enters the movie screen.

A contemporary film that draws on all these earlier texts is Woody Allen's *The Purple Rose of Cairo* (1985) and, in so doing, echoes Magritte's canvas. Set in the American Depression, the film recounts the story of Cecilia (Mia Farrow), the wife of an unemployed ne'er-do-well (Danny Aiello), who abuses her. While she supports them both by working in a diner, he hangs out with his friends gambling; furthermore, he is having an affair with another woman. To drown her sorrows, Cecilia frequently attends movies at the small town's one theater, the Jewel. There she often sees the same film numerous times, including one titled "The Purple Rose of Cairo."[3] While we never see the complete film, we do see numerous scenes, many of them repeated over and over, and we gain an understanding of the genre to which the movie belongs.

It is a spot-on imitation of a 1930s exotic adventure film. (Interestingly, as Cecilia enters the theater one time, we see a poster on the wall for a similar but real film, *Clive of India* [Richard Boleslawski, 1935], starring Ronald Colman). "The Purple Rose" (the film within a film) is set partly in Egypt, where explorer Tom Baxter (Jeff Daniels) has gone on an archaeological mission, and partly in upscale and cosmopolitan Manhattan, where he parties with a wealthy set of socialites. Baxter has met the New York City sophisticates in an Egyptian tomb—he, the expert, and they, the tourists. Baxter introduces himself as an "explorer and adventurer"—as though these were standard occupations. The New Yorkers have gone to Egypt because they are bored with "cocktail parties, opening nights, and weekends at the races" and crave voyaging to some "exotic and romantic" place. On a whim, Baxter decides to return with the group to Manhattan where he is entertained at a tony Art Deco apartment and an Art Moderne nightclub.

On one occasion, however, as we and Cecilia watch a scene replay of "The Purple Rose" in the Jewel, Baxter looks out (beyond the frame of the screen) to the audience and catches Cecilia's eye (breaking the fourth wall). Nonplussed, she turns around, looking for an explanation, then faces the screen and asks him whether he is looking at her. He says yes and confesses that he has noticed her there before. Eventually, he plunges out of cinematic space and into the theater, grabbing Cecilia, and whisking her away (figure 6.2). Suddenly, the rest of the cast of "The Purple Rose" break character and complain about the actor's exit, wondering what they are supposed to do now (as though the movie is a live performance). The audience of the Jewel Theater screams in horror.

As we follow Cecilia and Baxter on the streets of the town, we realize that although the latter has exited "The Purple Rose," he is still the character he has played—since he has no other existence. He believes, for instance, that his prop money is real and gets into trouble when he tries to use it to pay for

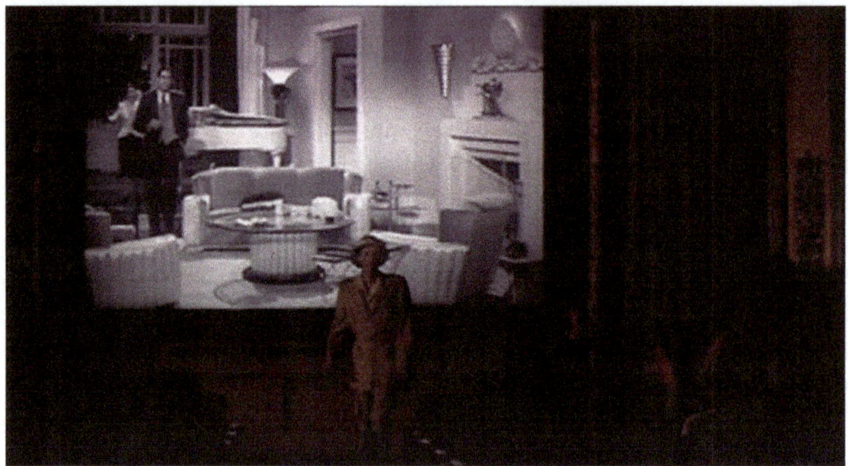

FIGURE 6.2. The movie character Tom Baxter (Jeff Daniels) walks off the screen in *The Purple Rose of Cairo* (Allen, 1985).

a meal in a restaurant. Given that in "The Purple Rose," he plays an earnest, heroic guy (having been "written that way"), he acts the part with Cecilia with whom he has "fallen in love." Since her real life is awful and her husband a brute, Cecilia enjoys her imaginary lover's attentions. Ultimately, in a reverse of the action we have previously seen, Baxter coaxes Cecilia to accompany him to the Jewel and enter the realm of "The Purple Rose"—allowing her to experience the glamorous world it portrays. She does so, and we see her transformed into a black-and-white figure relishing a chic night on the town.

Here we recall that (like Magritte and Georgette), Woody Allen and Mia Farrow were a couple at the time. While Allen had already turned Farrow into a cinematic icon by virtue of her role in *The Purple Rose*, by placing her inside a film within a film, he further underscores the confusion between actual person and artistic subject. Hence, she is abstracted on two levels. Georgette as well became a Modernist celebrity through her figuration in the work of her husband while remaining his wife in real life.

Eventually, the actor who plays Baxter—Gil Shepherd (a role also filled by Jeff Daniels)—comes to Cecilia's town in order to convince her to reject Baxter's advances and force his character to return to the movie. Shepherd is horrified by tabloid reports about the situation and fears for his career. He tricks Cecilia by pretending to adore her and promising to take her to Hollywood. Cecilia convinces Baxter to return to the screen, but Shepherd flees town, leaving her in the lurch. At the end of the film, we find her crying in the movie theater while watching Fred Astaire and Ginger Rogers dance—no better off than she was before.

But what does *The Purple Rose of Cairo* have to do with *Attempting the Impossible*? I would argue that just as, in the painting, the man mistakes a real person for the subject of his art (or alternately fantasizes that the subject of his art is real)—Allen's film allows for the possibility of a screen character coming to life. While on the surface, the film proposes Baxter as the desiring subject, his exit from "The Purple Rose" is equally propelled by Cecilia's longing for a romantic love object—so multivalent desire is at the film's core. Moreover, in *The Purple Rose*, we have dual versions of Tom Baxter—both played by the same individual. One is the character from the film within a film while the other is the actor who has created him—both seen, on one occasion, as populating the same space simultaneously. In a nod to the reproducibility of art in the age of mechanical reproduction, we learn that all over the country, Tom Baxters are escaping from film prints. Similarly, in the photograph of Magritte posing in front of his canvas *Attempting the Impossible*, we have two versions of the artist—the real and the representational.

There is a further similarity between *The Purple Rose* and Magritte's work. As we have seen, Baxter moves beyond the plane of the movie screen to emerge into the theater. Thus, the screen functions both as a flat depiction of a scene and a three-dimensional space that can be traversed into another. Here we recall Magritte's *The Key to the Fields* (1936) (figure 6.3), which shows us something similar. A window in a room reveals a landscape outside. But its pane has cracked, and surprisingly, the pieces that have fallen to the floor in front of it portray the exterior landscape—as though the view had been transferred to the transparent glass. Thus, the windowpane (with its faux images) bears some resemblance to a movie screen (which has often been likened to a "window onto the world"). In Magritte's glass shards (imprinted with pictures of the landscape), we think of André Bazin's notion of photography as inscribing a "decal" of reality onto celluloid. When Magritte's window fragments hit the floor, like Baxter, they seem to have escaped their "frame" and entered the three dimensional "real" world before them.

While *The Purple Rose of Cairo* is the most elegant treatment of the split between real and imaginary persons, other films raise similar questions and thus bear a relation to the work of Magritte. *American Splendor* (Shari Springer Berman and Robert Pulcini, 2003) is an innovative biopic about Harvey Pekar, an author of a series of graphic novels. To accomplish its experimentation, the film employs various means of representation. On one level, it presents us with comic book images of Pekar as drawn by numerous artists—since Pekar

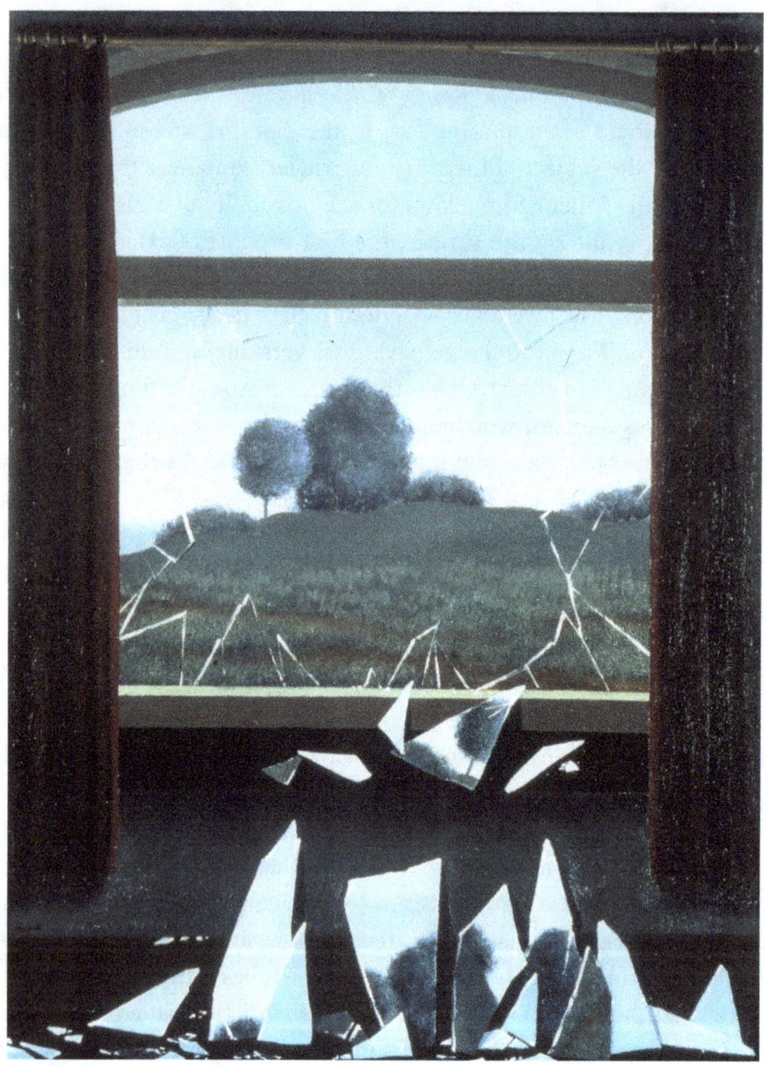

FIGURE 6.3. *The Key to the Fields* (*The Key of the Fields*) (1936)

only writes the text for his publications. In each edition, he looks completely different—a point that is voiced in the narrative when his future wife travels to meet him and does not know which "version" of him to expect. Here the film's use of drawings is particularly resonant, given Magritte's status as a graphic artist.

Beyond the diverse cartoon incarnations of Pekar, an actor (Paul Giamatti) plays him on screen, and sometimes we see him in real space while at other times within a cartoon landscape—and occasionally in a merger of the two. Here again, we might think of the photograph that Magritte had taken of him sitting in front of *Attempting the Impossible* palette in hand—present both in imaginary and in real space.

But the conundrums of real versus fictional persons and spaces does not stop here since the film also introduces us to the *actual* Harvey Pekar who is often seen (in documentary fashion) in a rather abstract white studio surrounded by some of the objects that play a role in the narrative. In addition, we see the actual Pekar within comic-book frames, making the play of identities even more complex. Finally, we view him (in documentary fashion) at his actual office retirement party, surrounded by other people in his life who have been "tripled" within the narrative (as themselves, as played by actors, and as cartoon figures).

But the sequence of the film that is most reminiscent of *The Purple Rose* and the enigmatic work of Magritte is the one in which the fictional Harvey (Giamatti) is positioned as it were on a blank page that gets sequentially drawn to depict a room. Suddenly, however, we find Harvey outside on a real street. In a shot that follows, however, Harvey steps through a cartoon window (that has a photograph of the street matted within it) into the comic-strip room—seamlessly navigating the transition from three-dimensional to two-dimensional space (figure 6.4).

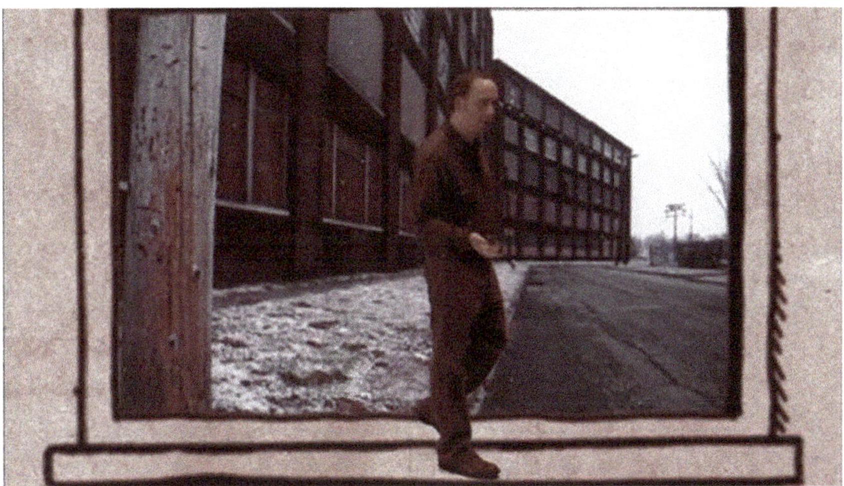

FIGURE 6.4. The fictional Harvey Pekar (Paul Giamatti) is often photographically set within a graphic cartoon world in *American Splendor* (Berman and Pulcini, 2003).

To summarize, in silent film works like *Uncle Josh* or *Sherlock Jr.* and contemporary movies like *The Purple Rose of Cairo* or *American Splendor*, filmmakers play with the purposeful confusion between real and fictional persons as well as physical and illusory space—force fields that cinematic technique makes possible. While the earlier films may well have been an influence on Magritte, the latter ones reflect the cinema's shared and ongoing concerns with the type of conceptual paradoxes that animated the artist's oeuvre.

7

WORD VERSUS IMAGE

> If a picture could be explained in words, words would suffice, and the picture would be superfluous.
>
> René Magritte[1]

UNDOUBTEDLY, ONE OF the most famous paintings by Magritte is *The Treachery of Images* (1929) (figure 7.1), a work that has been endlessly analyzed for its perplexing discourse of word and image. By one reading, of course, the painting is pointing out that what we see on the canvas is not a pipe but a *picture* of a pipe—thus stressing the distance between the objective world and its pictorial representative (no matter how realistic). On another level, Magritte is also demonstrating the arbitrary nature of the linguistic sign, which is essentially random. While the image of the pipe (according, at least, to the system of American philosopher Charles Sanders Peirce) is an *icon* (since it resembles the smoking device), the word *pipe* is a *symbol* since it bears no similarity to the object in question. In another language, say, German, the word would be *Pfeife*. And we can imagine that the English word for it might well have been *spoon*.

Magritte himself makes this very point in a series of other paintings titled *The Interpretation of Dreams*, created over many years. In these, the objects he depicts are "mislabeled" with the wrong words (simultaneously a dig at psychoanalysis). Hence, in the 1927 version, a leaf is identified as "the table," while in the 1930 version a picture of a shoe is labeled "the moon." Similarly, in the 1935 iteration (with the words in English instead of French), a horse's head is tagged "the door." *Phantom Landscape* (1928) represents a variation on

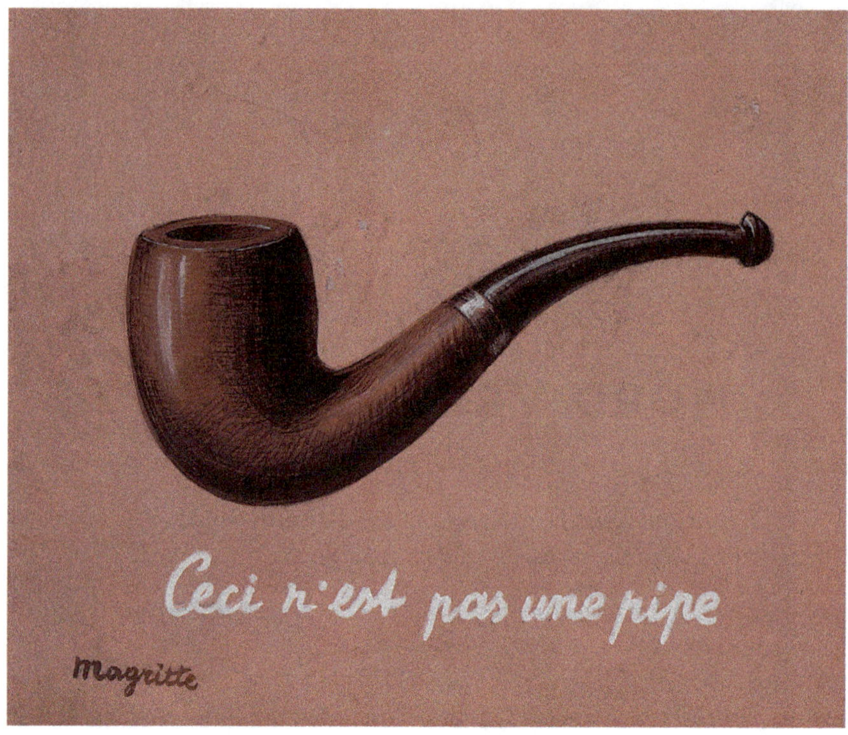

FIGURE 7.1. *The Treachery of Images* (*La trahison des images*) (1929)

the theme. Instead of multiple objects presented on the canvas, there is only one—a portrait of a women. Over her face is written "mountain." While the viewer may search for hidden meaning in these verbal/visual discrepancies, her efforts will not be rewarded. The labels seem as arbitrary as the nature of language itself. To make matters even more confusing, in certain paintings (those from 1927 and 1935) some of the pictures are properly characterized: thus, an image of a sponge is labeled "sponge" and the picture of a valise is labeled "valise." Strangely, the fact that they are properly matched throws us off course. As this chapter's epigraph makes apparent, all these strategies derive from Magritte's skepticism of language in general and particularly of the ability of words to describe or interpret art.

In truth, Magritte's major treatise on the tension between the pictorial and linguistic realms came not in the form of a painting, but in an illustrated essay. In "Words and Images," published in the journal *La révolution surréaliste* in 1929,[2] Magritte offers a series of propositions on the subject. In one (which shows a leaf labeled "canon"), Magritte opines that no word is so attached to an object that one cannot find a better one for it. In another (which depicts a drawing of the sun), he states that sometimes a picture can take the place of a word (reminding us of today's use of emojis).[3]

There is also the question of the titles that Magritte affixes to his paintings, which have received a great deal of attention, with numerous interviewers asking him to comment on them. Of course, he refuses, stating, "The titles of pictures are not explanations, and pictures are not illustrations of titles. The relationship between title and picture is poetic."[4] He goes even further: "A poetic title is not a scrap of information" and has "nothing to teach us."[5] Rather, it must "surprise us and enchant us."[6] Finally, he selects (or has his compatriots select) particular titles in order to subvert the viewer's intellectualization. As he remarks, "The titles are chosen to prevent my pictures from being placed in a reassuring region in which the mechanical functioning of the mind would place them, in order to underestimate their significance. Titles must be an additional protection to discourage all attempts to reduce poetry to a pointless game."[7] Michel Foucault puts it another way, stating that titles in Magritte's work "play an ambiguous role: supporting pegs and yet termites that gnaw and weaken."[8]

Nonetheless, on occasion, Magritte has spoken about the titles of specific paintings—not exactly elucidating them but offering some resonant thoughts. Of *The Discovery of Fire* (1934–35), for instance, which depicts a flaming tuba, he notes, "This amazing discovery of fire. Thanks to the friction of two bodies together, suggestive of the physical mechanism of pleasure."[9] Of course, his words do not unpack the puzzling iconography of the picture. Similarly, of the canvas *Raminagrobis* (1946), which portrays a cat sitting on railroad tracks, Magritte says, "The cat still exists in the twentieth century. The legend bursts into modern life." What legend? we might ask, still perplexed by the imagery. The point is that more than other Modernist artists, Magritte is committed to the collision of word and image. While it is true that other painters of his era have included language in their canvases (e.g., Pablo Picasso's use of newsprint in *Bottle of Vieux Marc, Glass, Guitar and Newspaper* [1913]), none of his era employed it so vigorously or conceptually as Magritte.

Of course, some theorists have argued for the inherent parallels between language and image. In some languages, for instance, words are, in fact, pictures. The Egyptian hieroglyph for the term *worship* resembles a person praying.[10] The same obtains for many Asian languages. As Will Eisner remarks, "In the development of Chinese and Japanese pictographs, a welding of pure visual imagery and a uniform derivative symbol took place. Ultimately, the visual image became secondary . . . marking the transition from pictographs to characters." Certainly, this is what led filmmaker Sergei Eisenstein to liken the roots of the Japanese ideogram to filmic montage.[11]

But theorists have gone even further in comparing verbal and visual elements of writing, arguing that all language has a pictorial base. As Anne-Marie Martin states, "Writing was born from the image, and whatever the system of writing, whether ideographic or alphabetic, its effectiveness comes from the fact that it is an image."[12] W. J. T. Mitchell agrees: "Writing, in its physical, graphic form, is an inseparable suturing of the visual and the verbal, the 'imagetext' incarnate"[13]—a term that seems especially applicable to a strain of Magritte's oeuvre.

One might also argue that typography lends a potentially pictorial quality to all printed words. Serif fonts, for instance, are those with decorative accents on the end of alphabetic characters—originating in the brushstrokes used for creating early typefaces, eventually becoming standard. Notoriously, the Bauhaus movement (requiring form to follow function) favored sans-serif typography, since it was believed to be more practical and legible. More recently, Steven Heller and Karen Pomeroy remarked on how the perception of word and image has been seen to overlap. As they note, "The traditional notion that text was to be read (a linear, encoded, left-brained activity) and images were to be seen (a holistic, experimental, right-brained activity) was questioned. Text became cross-functional . . . moving into the realm of the illustrative . . . atmospheric, or expressive. Similarly, images could be 'read,' sequenced, and combined to form more complex information patterns."[14] Not surprisingly, one of the earliest contemporary textbooks for film analysis was titled *How to Read a Film*.[15]

When it comes to dramatic cinema, however, the melding of printed word and image has rarely equaled the style of Magritte. For the most part, visible language has been used in a conventional manner—for titles, intertitles, subtitles, credits, plot exposition, or insert shots. Its reflexive use in relation to the image has been largely absent (save in works like Jean-Luc Godard's *A Married Woman* [1964] in which it plays a pivotal role in the form of billboards, signs, or magazine print). Perhaps this is because on screen, the image of an object (like a pipe) is far more convincing than that which Magritte painted—making it all the easier for the spectator to fall for the illusion of its reality (this aided by the darkened movie theater vs. the lighted museum gallery). Thus, in a traditional movie, the viewer is far more likely to think that a pipe "is" a pipe than when seen on a canvas.

Of course, avant-garde filmmakers have often countered the medium's inherent verisimilitude, and some have done so by self-consciously juxtaposing word and image. One such artist is Hollis Frampton. His 1970 film, *Zorns Lemma*, constitutes what critic Scott MacDonald has deemed "a phantasmagoria of . . . language." The work's title refers to a proposition in set theory, that branch of mathematics that studies groups of objects. (For example, in this book, my "set" is filmic texts related to the art of Magritte). In *Zorns Lemma*, the primary "objects" collected are: (1) letters of the Roman alphabet, (2) images containing words beginning with those letters, and (3) seemingly random footage that sequentially replaces those depicted in group two.

More specifically, the film involves a series of one-minute, handheld, live-action shots of words (generally located on New York City signs), arranged from *A* to *Z*. (Here we recall that critic Alistair Sooke once compared some of Magritte's canvases to shop signs.)[16] When each run-through of the alphabet is complete, there is a minute of black leader as separation; then the process resumes with a series of new "environmental words,"[17] which seem almost to be written on the screen (figure 7.2). There is some variation in how the words are captured. While most appear on advertising, street, or traffic signs, some are written as graffiti or appear superimposed by Frampton over a wordless live-action shot. Others are part of paper collages constructed by him. In one case (*xylophone*), we watch a word being "unwritten" (as the shot is printed in reverse motion).

Eventually, we notice that some shots of alphabetized signage are replaced by other wordless footage. For instance, when we come to *X*, a shot of a blazing fire is substituted. From that point on, each time we return to *X*, we see the same image of flames. Gradually, many other letters are replaced: instead of *Q*, we see steam escaping from a sidewalk grill; instead of *J*, a man painting a wall; and instead of *Y*, a pan shot of tall weeds.

There are numerous word/image conundrums in the film that remind us of the work of Magritte. When we see a sign that reads "whale," we do not see the animal represented by the word—but merely its linguistic symbol. Furthermore, the moving images that replace the letters do not necessary remind us of a word starting with that letter—so their choice seems as arbitrary as language itself.

But another aspect of *Zorns Lemma* is relevant to Magritte's work—spectator response. It has often been noted that a sense of play permeates Magritte's art—with the viewer urged to puzzle out the relationship of a painting's title to its content, the meaning encapsulated in its Surreal mise-en-scène, or the connection between the words and objects on the canvas. This is not to say that one can win the game, as Magritte allows no real solution.

While it is expected that the viewer of *Zorns Lemma* already knows how to read and does not need a review of the alphabet, she is forced continually to

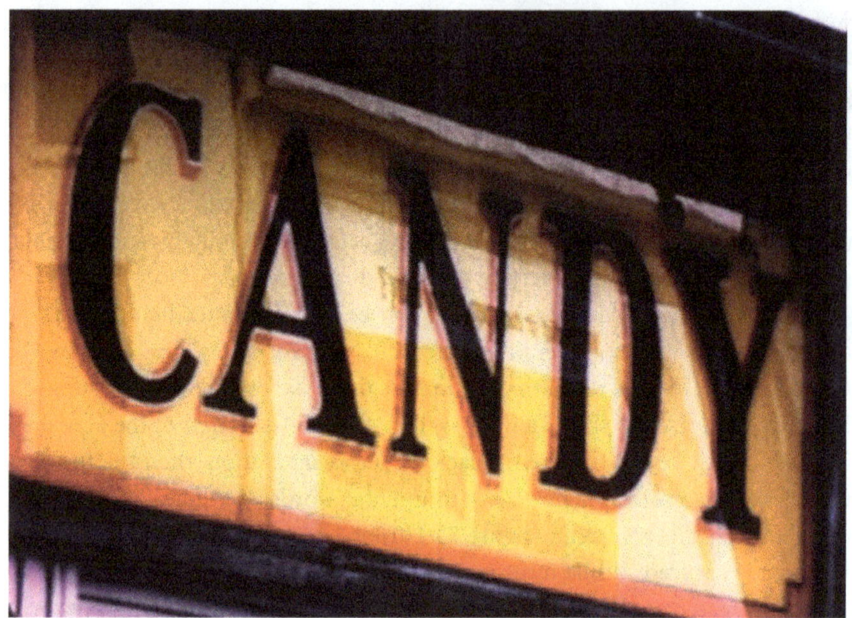

FIGURE 7.2. A photographed word on signage (standing for alphabet letter *C*) in Frampton's *Zorns Lemma* (1970)

silently recite her *ABC*'s as the signage shots go by, trying to keep track of their order. Then, as words are replaced by seemingly indiscriminate images (a child on a swing, a man walking around a city block, construction workers digging a hole), the viewer is impelled to notice what letter they stand for. This becomes a bit like playing the childhood board game Memory, and there is certainly a ludic element here.[18] Beyond reciting the alphabet and identifying the letters for which replacement shots substitute, we sometimes try to make sense of the order of the words depicted onscreen. When a sign for "member" follows the one for "limp," we get the joke, as we do when "hive" comes before "itch," or "bore" before "college." But often there is no such logic. On the other hand, sometimes the words have obvious relevance to the film we are watching, as when we discern signs reading "cinema" and "movie." Similarly, the letter *A* is replaced by a shot of someone turning the pages of a book—referring us back to issues of reading and writing.

In many ways, *Zorns Lemma* was ahead of its times in relation to art criticism (as was the work of Magritte). It was only around the period of *Zorns Lemma*'s release that the question of semiotics came into prominence in film studies, with the publication of Peter Wollen's *Signs and Meaning in the*

Cinema[19] and the translation of Christian Metz's *Film Language: A Semiotics of the Cinema* in 1974.[20] In fact, the title of Wollen's book could be used as a wry alternative for *Zorns Lemma* since Frampton photographs store "signs" while dealing theoretically with the nature of both verbal and visual "signs." In his book, Wollen draws upon Peirce's discursive concepts—which also included the notion of the index—a sign that has an "existential bond" to that which it represents (e.g., a footprint that testifies to the fact that an individual once stepped there).[21] Clearly, cinema is the indexical medium par excellence, and as previously noted, André Bazin saw its imagery as a kind of decal or transfer of reality onto celluloid.[22]

In *Zorns Lemma*, we have all three kinds of Peircean signs—often at once—while Magritte had recourse to only two—the symbolic and iconic. The signage words we see in the film (e.g., "joint" or "eat") are symbolic. On the other hand, they appear as moving picture images that are simultaneously indexical. Furthermore, the shots are iconic in that they resemble the objects originally photographed (while having a status different from them). As we watch *Zorns Lemma*, we must be aware of these blended but contradictory layers as we must be cognizant of the difference between the worded and wordless shots (e.g., those of signage, and those of "pure" action [like beans falling into a container]).

In creating a word/image mix in *Zorns Lemma*, Frampton (like Magritte) counters what he sees as a "logophobia" in the rhetoric of the contemporary visual arts. Frampton regrets the art world's continued rejection of language. As he states, "Only the poetics of the title escaped inquisition, for a time"—and we have seen how masterfully Magritte simultaneously exploits and disrupts this fact.[23] Frampton warns that "to ostracize the word is disingenuous" and conceals a "fear of the word—and the source of that fear: that language, in every culture . . . is . . . an expanding arena of power, claiming for itself and its wielders all that it can seize, and relinquishing, nothing."[24] Perhaps it was a desire to reject this power that led Magritte to annihilate the meaning of words and attach to them to pictures that they fail to signify.

(nostalgia) (1971) is a second Frampton film with ties to the word/image conundrums in Magritte's art, although here language comes to us acoustically rather than visually (a platform unavailable to the painter). It features a series of black-and-white photos taken (or collected) by Frampton in New York City during the period in which he practiced that art. Each one is placed on a hot plate and soon begins to burn, then disintegrate into ashes. Here we think of the fact that, in *Zorns Lemma*, one shot constituted a reverse-action image of a man writing. As that shot depicted the "unwriting" of a word, so *(nostalgia)*'s shots portray the "unmaking" of photographs.

A male voice (ostensibly Frampton's but actually filmmaker Michael Snow's) is heard on the soundtrack relating personal information about the photographs: what constitutes their subject, when and where they were shot, and what other events attended their production. The only problem is that voice and image are "out of step" (in a manner that parallels Magritte's uncoupling words from their signified). As we hear the narrator give an account of one photograph, we watch another (which does not "match up" with the aural portrayal). It is only when the next photograph arrives on screen that we realize that *it* relates retroactively to the description the man has previously uttered. So our mind literally works at cross-purposes.

If *The Treachery of Images* instructs us that what we see is "not a pipe," *(nostalgia)* continually teaches us that what we see is not what is described. For instance, as we view a photograph of artist Carl Andre, we hear an account of a snapshot of Frampton. So we might label the image of Andre "Ceci n'est pas Hollis Frampton." Thus, in viewing the film, the spectator is playfully challenged to make sense of the scrambled audiovisual sensorium.

The film is also about pictorial versus linguistic discourse, and the paradoxes that can arise from their clash—clearly, a favored topic for Magritte as well. As Frampton notes, *(nostalgia)* "is mostly about words and the kind of relationship words can have to images." He continues, "My first interest in images probably had something to do with what *clouds of words* could rise out of them."[25] Here his celestial metaphor seems evocative of Magritte's painting *Palace of the Curtains III* (1928–29), which counterpoises a framed image of a cloudy sky with a similarly shaped frame containing the word that denotes it. There is a final aspect of *(nostalgia)* that is suggestive of Magritte's work. Many of the painter's canvases, as we have already seen, portray something burning—for instance, *The Ladder of Fire* (1938 or 1939), *La belle captive* (1949), or *The Discovery of Fire* (1934–35). What is humorous (and counterintuitive) about the first painting is that while some of the items depicted are highly flammable (crumbled paper), others are not (a key), so the latter's combustibility is impossible. Here *(nostalgia)*'s destruction of photographs on a hotplate comes to mind. While it is true that each photograph burns (printed as it is on paper), in some sense, its image is indestructible. First of all, in the age of mechanical reproduction, a photograph can be "resurrected" at any time by printing a duplicate. Second, in *(nostalgia)*, the photograph's obliteration has been recorded on film, giving it a second life (which allows us to return to the original). So its annihilation has been a sham (much like that of Magritte's burning key or tuba), and the joke is on us.

There is a third film by Frampton with relevance to the work of Magritte—*Poetic Justice* (1972). Here the link is to the works by the painter that completely substitute word for image—denying us the pleasure of a picture. In *The Empty Mask* (1928), we see an irregularly shaped frame with four sections. In one is written the word "sky"; in another, "human body (or forest)"; in a third, "curtain"; and in a fourth, "house facade." Nowhere do we see a depiction of any of the items linguistically tagged—though, of course, these things are portrayed in numerous other Magritte canvases. Here words alone must suffice.

We face a similar situation of aggressive sensory deprivation in Magritte's *The Living Mirror* (1928) in which words denoting "person breaking out in laughter," "horizon," "cries of birds," and "armoire" are contained in amorphous "blobs." Once more, no pictures are supplied. The only images we have are those of the written words themselves. Furthermore, there is an irony in the painting's allusion to sounds like the "cries of birds" since it is impossible for such a work to ever communicate them. Of such "blob" canvases, Foucault states: "An object in a painting is a volume organized and tinted so that its shape is immediately recognizable and need not be named . . . [In these works] Magritte elides the object's form and superimposes the name directly upon the mass."[26]

Poetic Justice is the Frampton work most reminiscent of these Magritte paintings. In it, he pens a "faux" screenplay (really a Modernist parody thereof) that he never intends to dramatize or shoot. He then films each page of the script as a separate shot—without ever showing us the images imagined by the written discourse. Hence, *Poetic Justice* consists mostly of pictures of words—a literal movie of a screenplay.

Aside from successive sheets of paper and the words inscribed upon them, the only object we regularly see in *Poetic Justice* is a table that holds the pages of a screenplay, a coffee cup, and a cactus plant (figure 7.3). Interestingly, Frampton also released *Poetic Justice* as a flip-book—a volume that animates the printed page as one riffles through it, thus blurring the distinction between cinema and printed text.

But the film is far more complex than this.[27] First, while refusing to visualize the events implied on the printed page (e.g., "a zoom shot of a lilac seen outside a window," "a hand picking up a photograph," "a couple making love in bed"), *Poetic Justice* depends on the fact that the spectator will attempt to visualize them—thus highlighting the active mental role of the viewer in watching films (or the reader in processing text). Essentially, as we watch *Poetic Justice* on the screen, we simultaneously try to run the movie it describes in our

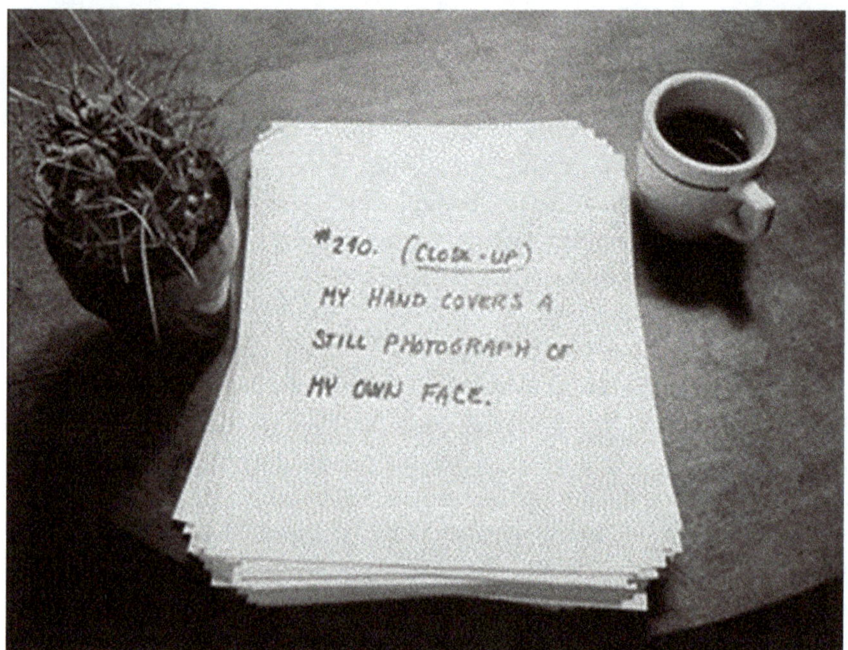

FIGURE 7.3. Pages from a screenplay (posed on a table with a cactus and coffee cup) constitute the total imagery of Frampton's *Poetic Justice* (1972).

heads, creating cognitive overload. In a similar fashion, in both Magritte's *The Empty Mask* and *The Living Mirror*, the viewer of the paintings may attempt to visualize the objects or persons denoted by the words—all to no avail.

Second, there are moments of *Poetic Justice* when the film we are watching and the one imagined in the screenplay overlap and intersect, as when shot 4 describes "A small table below a window. A potted cactus. A coffee cup"—the very things we are seeing.[28] The four "tableaux" of which the screenplay is composed involve a love story (and perhaps a love triangle)—the favored subject of mainstream cinema from its earliest days till the present. As Bruce Jenkins has noted, the film described in *Poetic Justice* (which itself is without sound) is also lacking auditory cues and hence may be an homage to the silent cinema (the word *tableau* seems antique and was commonly used in that era).[29] Of course, Magritte's canvases are always silent, which lends the Frampton film a further connection to the artist's work—this despite the fact that Magritte ironically alludes to sound in *The Living Mirror*.

Third, despite the interior narrative mimicking the standard love story, bizarre occurrences (worthy of Magritte) are noted in the script. Thus, as the couple makes love in bed, strange things are seen outside an open window: eggs hatching baby turtles (shot 176), grizzled drovers herding sheep (shot 175), or a crystal of pure nicotine (shot 165). Here, of course, Frampton is hailing both Surrealist fantasy and the possibility of cinema to use special effects (like matting) to render hallucinatory apparitions—precisely the technique employed by Anita Thatcher in the scenes depicted out the window in *Homage to Magritte* (1974).

Fourth, unlike traditional cinema, which attempts to erase the producer from audience consciousness (to make the spectator feel that she is watching an unstaged occurrence), *Poetic Justice* underscores the act of filming and the role of the filmmaker in the script itself. Thus, already in shot 7 we get the following text: "My hand places a color photograph of your face on a table." Later, in shot 179, we read, "Bedroom. Love Making. Outside the window, I am aiming a camera." The use of the pronouns "my" and "I," and the fact that some situations involve forms of image-making, leads us to believe that this narrator/character is the director surrogate—usually an invisible participant in screen drama. A later shot (239) mentions "a still photograph of my own face"—thus "embodying" and revealing more about the phantom cinematographer. Here we think of Magritte's *Clairvoyance* (1936) (see figure 20.15), which pictures an artist painting, as well as other works by Magritte that foreground the creator figure. As we have seen, in *Attempting the Impossible* (1928) (see figure 6.1), an artist paints a live woman instead of a canvas.

Other "characters" within the screenplay in *Poetic Justice* (designated as "you" and "your lover") are said to have cameras or photographs in their hands—though the use of the second person also, of course, hails the film spectator. Again, the act of viewing is important to Magritte's concerns. While he does not often directly depict observers—although he does in *The Spy* (1928) (see figure 5.1) and *The Month of the Grape Harvest* (1959) (see figure 3.6)—as we have seen, he has numerous paintings of eyes, most famously in *The False Mirror* (1929), depicted on the cover of this volume.

At the end of the film its self-reflexivity and conundrums become even more vertiginous. Shot 237 tells us, "Your lover's hand is holding a still photograph of my hand writing this text." Shot 238 then says, "Your lover's hand is holding a still photograph of myself, filming these pages." Hence, both the writing of the screenplay and its transfer to cinema are embedded in the film script itself.

The final shot of the film is an unexpected one—that of what looks like a rubber glove dropping onto a blank page—the only real filmed action in the movie. In the glove, we get an object that potentially touches the author's hand

and, in a humorous, unromantic, and corporeal fashion, stands in for it. Use of the glove seems more self-conscious when we realize that Frampton was also a photographer who may have had to use it in developing film. Furthermore, it reminds us of a Surrealist painting by Giorgio de Chirico (*The Song of Love* [1914]) in which a glove hangs on a wall next to a sculpted bust. Here we recall that Magritte deemed De Chirico (and that painting specifically) as one of his major creative inspirations—and we recognize in its depiction of a ball and statue, objects that would become emblematic in Magritte's work. Furthermore, in one of Magritte's film scenarios from the 1930s, he imagines a situation with some similarities to *Poetic Justice*. A man sits at a table writing, whereupon a glove drops down onto its surface.[30]

As stated earlier, the voice we hear narrating the photographs in *(nostalgia)* is that of Michael Snow, a Canadian artist and colleague of Frampton's. In Snow's film, *So Is This* (1982), he adopts the imagistic minimalism of *Poetic Justice* and takes it one step further while continuing the Magrittian tradition of word/image play. Essentially, the film is like an animated version of a book. Each frame presents a single word which, when edited together with others, creates sentences. The manner in which words appear varies. Most are shown as white on black, but sometimes colored flares illuminate the frame; also the size of the font shifts for different words. Sometimes scale has no relation to the term (e.g., when "and" appears in huge lettering). But other times it does, as when "big" is shown in large format. Furthermore, the time allotted to each shot differs—sometimes in line with the meaning of the term. For instance, when "length" appears on screen (as part of the sentence "One of the interests of this system is that each word can be held on the screen for a specific length of time"), it remains there for a full minute (much longer than most)—creating word/image dissonance. (Here we are also reminded of Magritte's play with scale in such works as *Personal Values* [1952]; see figure 20.13).

Furthermore, as Snow himself makes clear, much of the text articulated in the film has the kind of ambiguity and irony found in Magritte's canvas *The Treachery of Images*. After a sentence proclaims there will be a French version of the film (a fact that would have pleased Magritte), words assert:

> Le titre de ce film sera: Ceci est le titre de ce film. Ça fait penser l'auteur au tableau bien connu de Magritte: Ceci n'est pas une pipe. C'est vrai ici aussi. L'auteur aime beaucoup le mot "ceci."
>
> [The title of this film will be: This is the title of this film. This *makes the author think of the well-known painting of Magritte: This is not a pipe.*

> *It's true here as well.* The author very much loves the word "this."] (my emphasis)

Clearly, here he directly hails the Belgian artist.

That Snow loves the word *this* is apparent in the following passage from the opening of the film:

> This/is/the/title/of/this/film./The/rest/of/the/film/will/look/just/like/this./
>
> This/as/they/say/is/the/signifier.

About it, critic Justin Remes remarks: "There is an inescapable and unresolved ambiguity in these sentences. For example, when the film asserts that 'this . . . is/the/signifier,' we are left wondering *what* is the signifier, exactly? The word *this*? The language Snow is using? The medium of film? Or perhaps all of the above?"

Beyond confusing us, Snow tells comical lies in the film (much as Magritte is untruthful when he identifies a woman as a mountain). At one point, a sentence states that the film will last two hours (a seemingly impossible duration for the viewer to endure), while, in fact, it runs for forty-nine minutes (for some, still unbearable). At another moment, the film promises that it will be "personal" and "confessional," which it is not (at least in the conventional sense of those terms). Finally, he alerts us that the film will never say "shit," which, of course, it does by making that statement.

Snow also engages in visual/verbal puns. He refers ironically to the act of apprehending his film as "light reading," a term that generally signifies entertaining literature but here also denotes reading words illuminated by light. At one point, he refers to his experimental film as "a shot in the dark," which usually means something with an unknown effect, but here alludes to watching the film in a darkened theater. Magritte was also a punster. The title of his painting *Evening Falls* (1964) renders a joke based on two senses of the word *fall*. The canvas depicts a windowpane that has broken and released shards onto the floor. But, curiously, the image of the outside scene (a landscape at dusk) is imprinted on the broken fragments. Thus, evening "falls" (occurs) at the moment that the windowpane "falls" (drops). There is also a kind of wordplay in the title of Magritte's painting *Castle in the Pyrenees* (1959), which tropes on a French phrase "a castle in Spain" (which is similar to the English expression "a castle in the air")—meaning an impossible locale.[31]

Finally, there is an interesting tension between Snow's use of words in *So Is This* that have no pictorial equivalent ("possible," "essentially," and "however"), and words that do but whose visualization we are denied seeing ("lips," "flower," or "cave"). Of course, when the term "screen" appears before us, we realize that it signifies precisely what we are seeing—adding a level of reflexivity to the text. Moreover, when it does materialize, it is framed in a rectangle of light embedded within the larger film frame—as though the shot was created by projecting the image and refilming it.

In sum, when it comes to the use of language in painting during the era of high Modernism, René Magritte is the dominant practitioner—one who led the way for later uses of language in art in the work of Roy Lichtenstein, Andy Warhol, Ed Ruscha, Robert Indiana, and Barbara Kruger. Within the film world, this discourse has been less prominent, given the narrative and pictorial thrust of conventional movies. However, in the experimental work of Hollis Frampton and Michael Snow, we discover not only the Magrittian "treachery of images" but the "treachery of words." Beyond that, following the nod of the painter, we encounter the "treachery of word/image aggregations."

8

PICTURES AND LANDSCAPES

> *Trompe l'oeil* allows me to give the painted image the expression of depth of the visible world . . . because my painting has to resemble the world in order to evoke its mystery.
>
> René Magritte[1]

SOME OF MAGRITTE'S most celebrated works depict what seems to be a canvas in front of a window whose subject (a landscape) appears to block out the exact same scene as the painted representation. Here we think of Magritte's statement that "what one sees on an object is another hidden object."[2]

Generally, there are slight clues that reveal that what we are viewing in front of the window is, in fact, an opaque rather than a transparent surface (the latter always being a possibility—though not a favored critical construal). In *The Human Condition* (1933) (figure 8.1), for instance, part of the artwork hangs over the window curtain on the left, indicating its status as a picture. Since the overlap is so slight and easy to miss (as is the white line that indicates the depth of the canvas), there is an element of trompe l'oeil to the work—by which beholders may think that they are simply looking through a transparent window rather than also viewing a painting. Magritte's interest in trompe l'oeil effects is obvious from his statement in the chapter epigraph.

As is the case with so much of Magritte's imagery, there are multiple variations on the same theme. In *The Human Condition* (1935), the illusion is only partial since the canvas extends way beyond the arched doorway. Alternatively, in *The Call of Peaks* (1943), neither a doorway nor a window marks a separation between interior and exterior worlds, though a curtain on the right

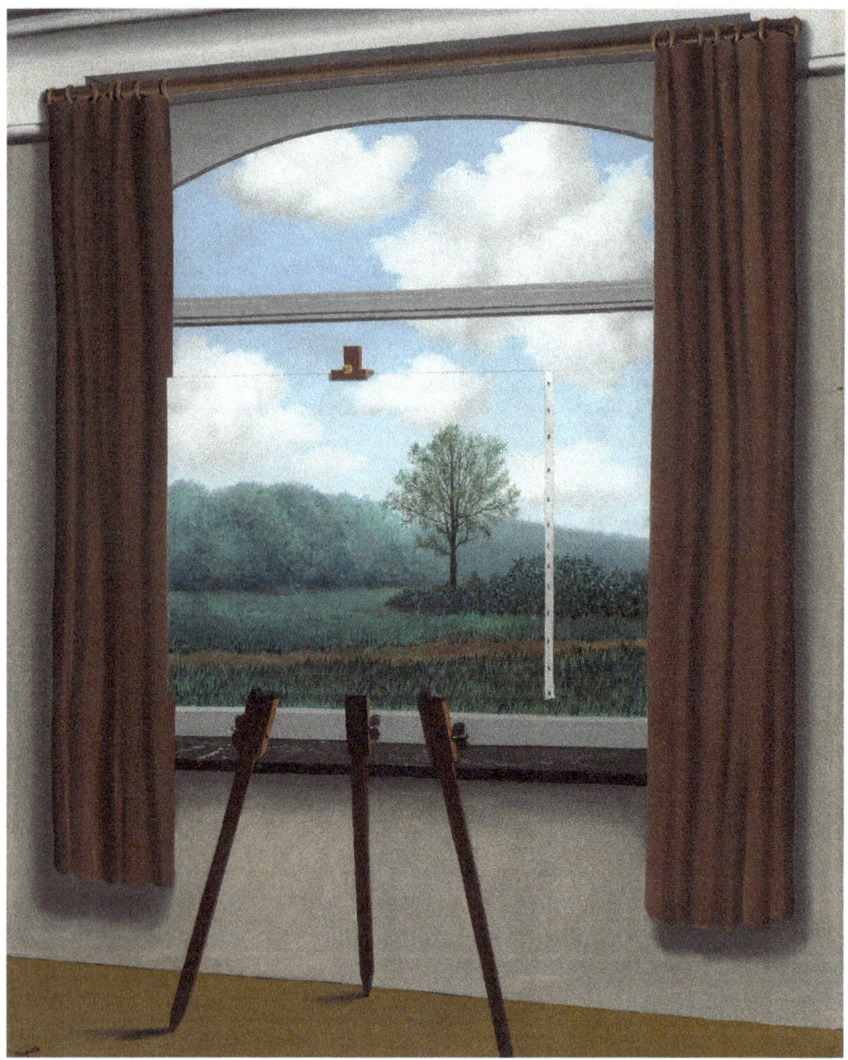

FIGURE 8.1. *The Human Condition* (*La condition humaine*) (1933)

and some flooring seems to indicate that there is one. Since the rectangular slab on the easel does not overlap anything, we may imagine that is it not a painted canvas but transparent glass.

But the paintings with which I am most concerned are those in which a picture frame is located *entirely in the outside world*. Such a scene occurs in Magritte's *La belle captive* (1949), where it is situated on a beach. Once more there is a clue or "tell" that demonstrates that the frame is not empty, since what is in it reflects the burning tuba. The surface, however, could be transparent glass, as that would catch the light as well. There is yet another variation on the motif. In a 1931 version of Magritte's *La belle captive* (figure 8.2), an easel stands in a bucolic field. On it there is a rectangular panel—a fact that we know from our view of its left side, which indicates thickness. While we assume that the easel holds a painting (since its match to the landscape is the kind of paradox that Magritte enjoys), it could be a transparent pane through which we are viewing the scene behind it. Of course, in all these artworks Magritte is playing with the painterly illusion of realism—which is, ostensibly, so great that the representation may not be easily distinguished from its source. Again, this is a variation on the technique of trompe l'oeil whereby an illustration is intended to create the impression of a three-dimensional object.

Of the two readings I have proposed for the 1931 version of *La belle captive*, I prefer the one that sees the item on the easel as transparent. Most interesting is the fact that, as noted in chapter 3, in Alain Robbe-Grillet's 1983 film of the same name (in which he pays homage to one iteration of Magritte's *La belle captive*), the movie opens with a frame that encloses transparent (though tinted) glass posed by the sea (see figure 3.7). We know that it is transparent because through it we can see waves flowing toward and away from the shore.

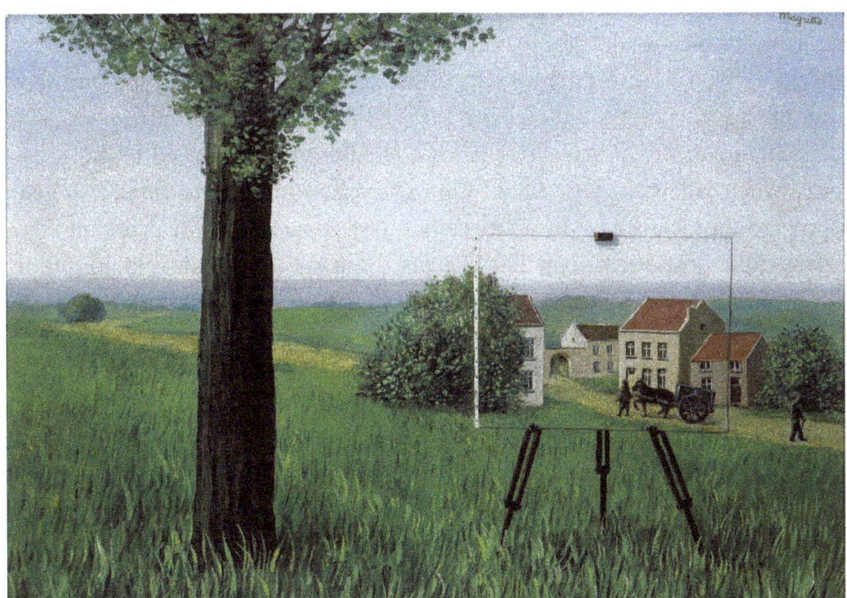

FIGURE 8.2. *La belle captive* (1931)

This notion of transparency resonates with another film: Peter Greenaway's *The Draughtsman's Contract* (1982). While I examine the movie's connection to Magritte, most critics have discussed it in conjunction with artists like Georges de La Tour or Thomas Gainsborough—owing to the overall look of the work, its setting in the seventeenth century, and its vintage mise-en-scène.[3]

The Draughtsman's Contract takes place in rural England and concerns an artist, Mr. Neville (Anthony Higgins), who is hired by Mrs. Virginia Herbert (Janet Suzman) to sketch twelve drawings of her absent husband's estate. The lecherous draftsman agrees to do so only on the condition that Mrs. Herbert be available to him sexually whenever he wishes—a contractual obligation to which she assents. Later, her daughter, Mrs. Sarah Talmann (Anne-Louise Lambert), who is childless and unhappily married, blackmails Mr. Neville into providing for her erotic (and perhaps reproductive) needs as well. Eventually, Mr. Herbert is found dead and a mystery surrounds his demise—with various theories circulating as to who is the perpetrator. Furthermore, Mr. Talmann learns of his wife's infidelity and discovers certain clues in Neville's drawings that point to the affair (e.g., a ladder leaning against his spouse's window). As the drama closes, Neville is attacked by Talmann and his associates. They burn out his eyes, destroy his drawings, and beat him to death.

What is most interesting about the film (from the vantage point of Magritte's paintings) is the tool that Mr. Neville uses to plan his drawings. It consists of an empty rectangular frame (adjustable as to its distance from the subject) through which he can envision his future canvas. It is divided by wire into four smaller rectangles—allowing Neville to focus on particular aspects of a scene (figure 8.3). There is also a second smaller frame attached to the apparatus which facilitates the visualization of even more minute details.[4] Often, we regard the grounds of the estate through this device, and the resultant view is later juxtaposed with Neville's sketch of the selfsame vista—highlighting the connection between the scene and its pictorial representation, which are identical save for color. That their views are alike is emphasized by the fact that we sometimes see on the drawings the grid marks that the draftsman has transferred from his tool to the paper (as we see grid or graph paper marks on some of Magritte's studies for future paintings—e.g., *Study for l'embellie* [1942]). Thus, his work is characterized by precise realism. Furthermore, to emphasize the parallels between the apparatus view and the static drawing, in these sequences, the camera is stationary.

Neville's device is intriguing in several ways—one cinematic and the other Magrittian. First as we see it sectioning reality into a rectangle, we are

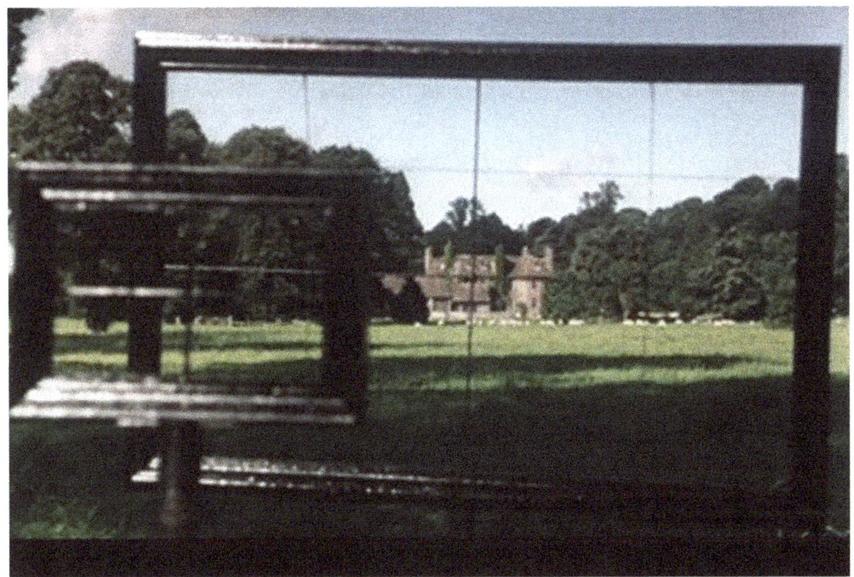

FIGURE 8.3. In *The Draughtsman's Contract* (Greenaway, 1982), painter Neville (Anthony Higgins) uses a frame with wire grids to analyze the landscape as preparation for painting it.

conscious that the motion-picture camera does the same thing. The fact, however, that we see *beyond* Neville's device to the wider landscape reminds us of André Bazin's insight that the film image presents us less with a frame than a mask that only temporarily obscures what lies beyond its borders—a space that remains potential.[5]

Second, in the positioning of Neville's apparatus on the Herbert estate (affording us framed "pictures" of the property), we find reverberations of Magritte's versions of *La belle captive*. The one from 1931 places an artist's easel in a field—as does Neville. The 1937 canvas locates a frame (which resembles Neville's gadget) on the beach. While Neville's frame is empty (save the wires), Magritte's may contain a painting or, as I conjecture, a transparent pane through which the scene behind is visible. Clearly, the latter reading would constitute a closer match to Neville's apparatus.

There are further elements in *The Draughtsman's Contract* that emphasize self-reflexivity in a manner reminiscent of Magritte. In interior shots of the mansion, we see numerous windows (a favored Magritte icon), and some are divided with mullions that echo the apparatus grid. Sometimes Neville's hand is shown while drawing, and here we are reminded of Magritte paintings that depict the artist at work (e.g., *Clairvoyance* [1936]; see figure 20.15, and *Attempting the Impossible* [1928]; see figure 6.1). In fact, the hand is Greenaway's, and furthermore he sketched all the drawings attributed to Neville in the film.[6]

Extending the film's self-consciousness, at one point Neville comments on paintings in the mansion, noting how narratives can be embedded within them—just as they are within his own work. He also duplicitously claims that he "tries hard never to distort or dissemble" in his work, and on some level this is true. He is more a copyist than an inspired artist in the Romantic sense. As Leon Steinmetz puts it, Neville "is everything Mr. Greenaway is not."[7] In a contradictory statement, however, Neville asserts that his drawings are "redolent of mystery." (Furthermore, other people find "allegorical meanings" in his sketches, underscoring how realism can veil obscure significations.) This tension between verisimilitude and enigma pervades Magritte's work as well, since through scale, juxtaposition, and lighting he invests his realistic images with a strange and curious aura—at least from the viewer's perspective. Magritte, however, would deny that his canvases contain secret univalent meanings to be revealed.

Periodically in *The Draughtsman's Contract*, there is a quasi-Surrealist touch (evocative of Magritte's and Jean Cocteau's uncanny statues).[8] Intermittently, a strange character appears skulking around the estate. He is covered (or, more precisely, camouflaged) with an opaque gray-green metallic tint, and it is unclear whether people see him and (if they do) whether they know that he is "alive" and not a sculpture.

Thus, *The Draughtsman's Contract* echoes the work of Magritte in several ways: in the film's "confusion" of reality with its pictorial representation, in its focus on the nature of the frame, in its insistence that the realist work can evoke mysteries, and in its depiction of the artist at work. While, to my knowledge, no critic has written in depth about the ties between *The Draughtsman's Contract* and Magritte, at least one has commented on more general links between Greenaway's oeuvre and the painter. In *Being Naked Playing Dead*, Alan Wood remarks on the two artists' shared interest in wordplay. Beyond that, he finds that the "the look of the twilight exteriors in *A Zed & Two Noughts* [1985] owes something to Magritte's night/day painting, *L'Empire de Lumières*."[9] Though not referencing *The Draughtsman's Contract*, he mentions something that is relevant to it: Magritte (like Greenaway) is an "artist who uses grids, often of boxes containing objects" (as in *Obsession* [1927]).[10] Finally, in noting the filmmaker's "insistence on artifice," Woods asserts that Magritte's "interest in . . . illusion . . . in metaphor and literalism . . . is clearly of crucial importance to Greenaway."[11]

There is one other film that sparks associations to the type of Magritte paintings that we have been discussing, and it is of a more experimental bent than *The Draughtsman's Contract*, involving no narrative at all. It is a short film by avant-garde cineaste J. J. Murphy, *Sky Blue Water Light Sign* (1972) (figure 8.4). It begins with what looks like a colorful long shot of a landscape with flowing water and trees in the foreground. Accompanying the image we hear the sound of a gurgling brook. The camera slowly pans from left to right past other foliage, and we eventually see a campground with smoke rising from a fire. We continue to pan past a waterfall and soon the scene fades to black. We notice that the quality of the image is rather poor—in low resolution—as though a "dupe" of an original print, or shot off a television screen.

In fact, what we have been looking at (without realizing it) is an animated ad sign for Hamm's beer—the realistic effect augmented by sound. Like Magritte's canvases positioned in front of windows, we have not realized that what we are looking at is an artificial picture versus the actual world itself. The only hint of this (unless one is familiar with the advertisement) comes in the credits, which thank Hamm's Brewery.

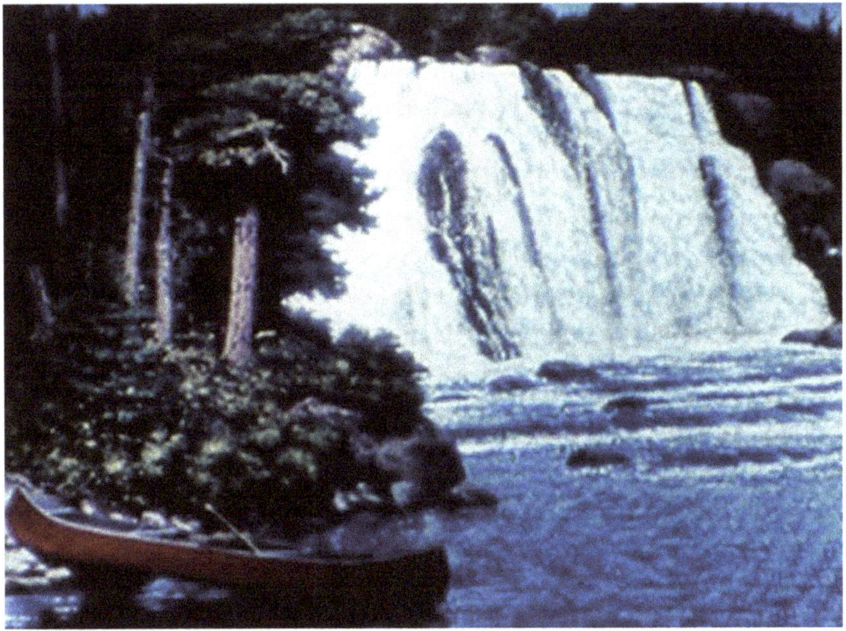

FIGURE 8.4. This highly realistic landscape scene in Murphy's *Sky Blue Water Light Sign* (1972) is actually an animated sign for Hamm's beer.

9

EMPTY FRAMES AND X-RAY VISION

> Don't search for hidden meanings in my paintings. What is behind my paintings is the wall.
>
> René Magritte[1]

As discussed in chapter 6, in the silent film *Uncle Josh and the Moving Picture Show* (Edwin Porter, 1902), when the naive spectator tries to join the action of the movie, he inadvertently tears down the screen to reveal nothing but a black theater wall behind it—letting us know that the cinema frame was always, on one level, "empty." Magritte's painting *The Blood-letting* (1938 or 1939) (figure 9.1) has interesting resonances of this work on several planes. On one, an alternative version of its title (*The Empty Picture Frame*) points to the fact that there seems to be no painting within the frame that Magritte depicts, and hence it is devoid of art. But, of course, it is not truly empty, as we see within its borders red bricks that presumably stand behind the plaster gallery wall. Here we think of Magritte's statement in this chapter's epigraph, which attests to his hostility toward interpreting what is "behind" his work. But there is also a Magrittian paradox to the painting, since if you look closely, you see a gap between it and the wall—signaling that what is within the frame might actually be a representation of bricks. But at first glance, the canvas seems to give us X-ray vision—an impossibility in the normal museum setting. It is this reading that I will privilege in my discussion—given that X-rays have ties to photography and the cinema.

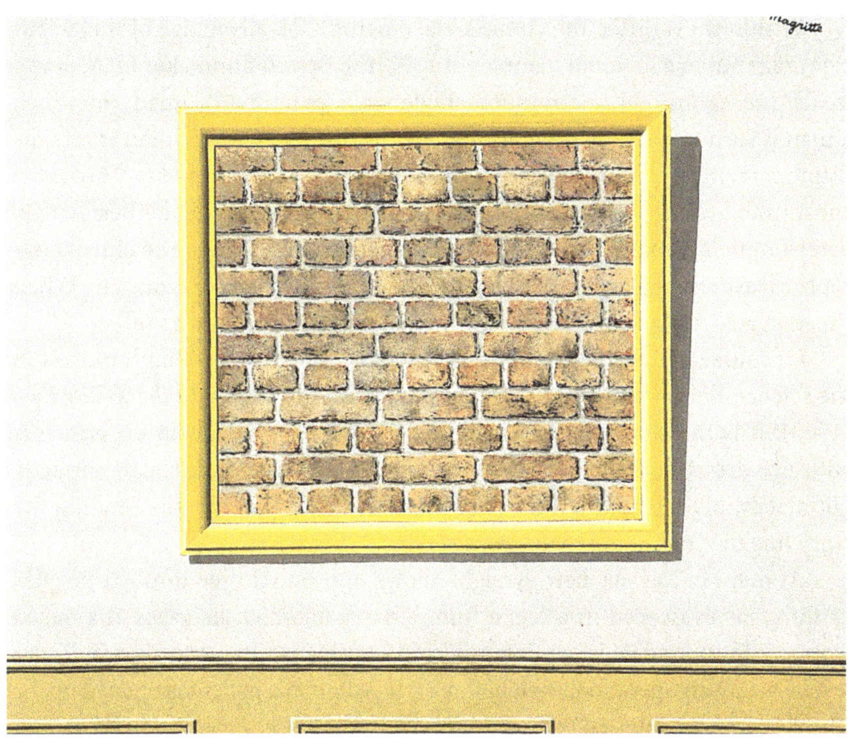

FIGURE 9.1. *The Blood-letting* (*La saignée*) (1938 or 1939)

As defined on a basic level, X-rays are a form of electromagnetic radiation that can be used to take images of living beings as well as objects. What is amazing about the process is that it reveals what is inside the body or item in question—a fact that would interest Magritte whose art often erased the boundaries between interior and exterior. For our purposes, it is crucial that the X-ray process produces a *visual image on film* (almost like an analog photograph)—which links it to the medium of cinema. And, as we know, it was not long before the static X-ray picture (usually said to have debuted in 1895—the same year as the movies) was followed by X-ray cinematography.

Clearly, one of the major uses for the new X-ray technology was in medicine and science, and significantly, in 1897 the first X-ray motion-picture film (depicting a frog leg in motion) was produced by Scottish physician John Macintyre.[2] Some frames from it were published in the *Archives of Skiagraphy* in the same year,[3] and an excerpt of one of his X-ray films can now be seen on YouTube (as posted by the National Library of Scotland).[4]

Within short order, the commercial cinema took advantage of this scientific craze but in a fictional manner. In 1897, the British filmmaker G. A. Smith made *The X-Rays*—a one-minute, single-shot "primitive" comedy in which a man is seen to court a young woman. As he does so, another man enters the frame carrying a camera labeled "X-rays" and aims it at the couple. Through a substitution trick, they are both replaced by faux skeletons. Nonetheless, they carry on their romance, which lends it a maudlin tone. When the cinematographer leaves the scene, the couple returns to their natural clothed state. When the man gets fresh, however, his lady friend slaps him and walks off.

Of course, much later in film history there were feature-length movies in the science-fiction mode like Roger Corman's *X: The Man with the X-Ray Eyes* (1963). It is the story of Dr. James Xavier (Ray Milland), who experiments with eye drops that alter his vision, allowing him to look through surfaces. Ultimately, his research wreaks havoc on his life and on others—lending the story line the traditional mad scientist bent.

At first Dr. Xavier's new eyesight allows him only to see through people's clothing (as evidenced in a scene from a party in which he gazes at a naked woman). But the effect is "cumulative," and later his vision proceeds to a deeper level. During an operation, even before an incision on a patient is opened up, he sees the woman's internal organs. In this shot, the viscera seem to be "real," but in later sequences, when Dr. Xavier's looks through people's bodies, we see only graphic diagrams of their innards. Significantly, echoing Magritte's *The Bloodletting*, at one point the doctor looks through a wall, which reveals the construction elements within it (e.g., joists) (figure 9.2). The point is that, once again, a Magritte painting highlights a particular scientific process of visualization that has strong connections to cinema history as well as to its camera-eye.

The other captivating aspect of Magritte's canvas is, of course, the apparent emptiness of the picture frame (assuming one reads it as providing a look through the wall). The artist utilizes the same trope in two other works, both from 1928. In *The Perfect Image*, a woman looks at an empty picture frame on the wall (the title seeming an ironic comment on art). In *The Delights of the Landscape*, an empty frame is propped against a black wall next to a rifle; a label on the frame reads "Landscape"—a clear joke—or a comment on whether or not a word can stand in for an image.

When it comes to cinema, as we have seen, there is a direct citation of Magritte's vacant picture frames in Alain Robbe-Grillet's 1983 *La belle captive* (an out-and-out homage to the artist)—where one hangs on the wall of a room. But a more interesting meditation on the subject occurs in Hollis Frampton's structural film *Special Effects* (1972).

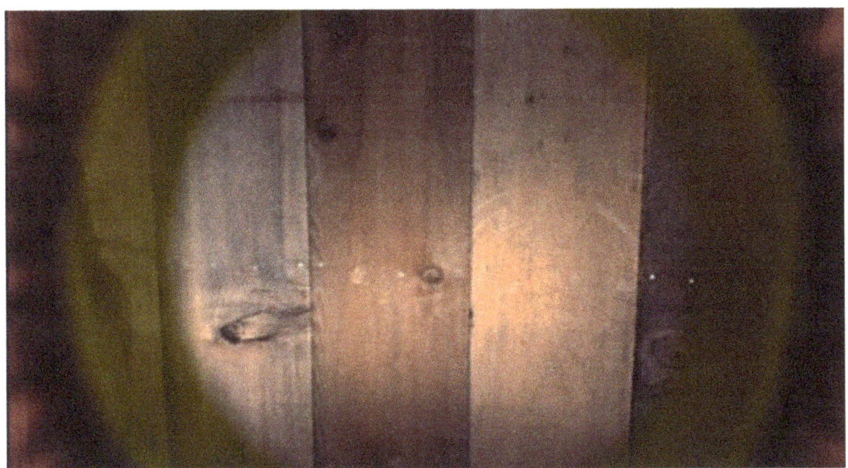

FIGURE 9.2. In this shot from *The Man with the X-Ray Eyes* (1963), the protagonist is able to look through a wall and see the joists within it.

Unlike Robbe-Grillet's movie, Frampton's has no narrative or action, and rather than being concerned with a picture frame, he is interested in the cinema frame itself. For the ten minutes that the work lasts, we see a graphic representation of an empty rectangular film frame (drawn with a broken perforated white line against a black background) accompanied by an electronic soundtrack that mimics a repeated and distorted descending scale (figure 9.3). According to Frampton, he wanted some audio accompaniment to his visualization because one's view of the film frame is always "tempered . . . by the breath, tremor, heartbeat of the perceiver."[5] No images or events enter the frame in *Special Effects*, lending the title a mockery that Magritte would have valued.

The white frame within a frame jumps around (providing the film's only "action") since Frampton shot it with a handheld camera, using a telephoto lens that exaggerated his shaking. Clearly, this adds a human element to the voided scene. Frampton creates this barren iconography in order to emphasize that no matter what spectators view onscreen, they are always watching through their minds' eye—which processes, distorts, or augments that information. As he states, "The frame itself . . . divides what is present to consciousness from what is absolutely elsewhere." He advises the viewer to "people this given space . . . with images of your own devising."[6] Perhaps that is why the frame is perforated—implying a certain permeability.

Beyond conceiving the film frame as a "kind of synonym for consciousness," Frampton aims in *Special Effects* to "affirm and honor [it] . . . [b]ecause

FIGURE 9.3. Frampton's *Special Effects* (1972) consists entirely of a perforated empty frame (within the larger film frame).

so much of what we know now, so much of our experience is something that comes to us through that frame." Here he gives the example of having only seen the Egyptian Pyramids at the movies. Hence, for him, the film frame is simultaneously a space for imaginative play, remote documentation, and vicarious travel.

In a sense, filmmaker Ernie Gehr takes the Magrittian empty frame one step further. In his 1970 work *History*, even Frampton's minimalist graphic frame within a frame is eliminated, and what we see onscreen is entirely vacated of all legible static or moving pictures. In fact, what we are actually watching are the black-and-white grains of the film strip's emulsion as they twinkle. To make the film, Gehr "held black fabric in front of a movie camera without a lens ('its image-forming device'), using a light to illuminate the cloth." Thus, according to critic Jonas Mekas, *History* comes closest "to being nothing but the reality of the film materials and tools themselves."[7]

In a sense, what Gehr accomplishes in *History* is to provide a figurative brand of X-ray vision, cutting through the facade of cinema (that which is photographically rendered) to view its "brick wall"—the celluloid surface itself.

10

MINDSCREENS

> I believe the mind likes the unknown—that is, what is not within the bounds of knowledge, since the meaning of the mind itself is unknown.
>
> René Magritte[1]

IN 1949, MAGRITTE created a poster for the second Film and Fine Arts World Festival of Belgium (figure 10.1). The very focus of the event is interesting in terms of the project of this book, since it seeks to position cinema within the broader visual arts. What is especially intriguing about the poster is that it situates a woman's head between two screens—one behind her (ostensibly a movie screen) and one in a location identified with her mind. Furthermore, the woman's eyes are closed (or she is blind)—which highlights her internal vision (or consciousness). Finally, there is nothing pictured on either screen—both remain "spotless" as it were. Significantly, the arts festival for which the poster was created takes place in Knokke-le-Zoute, a venue that, in the 1950s, Magritte was commissioned to decorate with his frescoes.

Scholarly work on Magritte's art has made note of its relevance to questions of human consciousness. In *Mental Space*, analyst Salomon Resnik examines psychological illness, drawing on his experiences with patients. Significantly, he frequently uses the work of Magritte to demonstrate some anomalous psychic state.[2] In one instance, he mentions *The Blood-letting* (1938 or 1939) (see figure 9.1) as a means of portraying how mentally ill people feel vacant.[3] Similarly, he refers to *Fortune Telling* (1938 or 1939), which portrays a cloud seeping into a room, in order to conceive the stultifying fog that obscures some

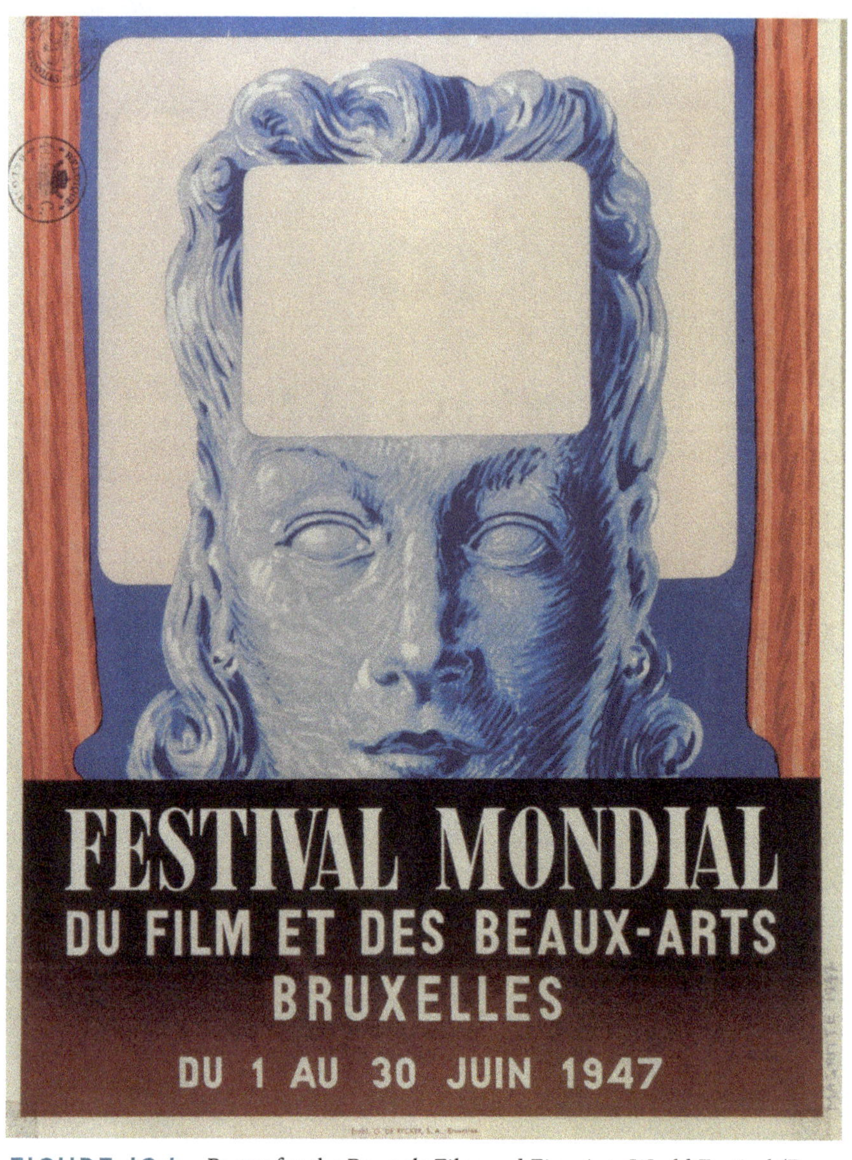

FIGURE 10.1. Poster for the Brussels Film and Fine Arts World Festival (Brussels International Festival of Film and Fine Arts, Exhibition Poster) (1949)

patients' minds. He considers his job as an analyst to "contain the bloating cloud and make the air easier to breathe."[4] He asserts that psychosis involves a person's move from a three-dimensional to a two-dimensional universe and references Magritte's *The False Mirror* (1929)—pictured on the cover of this volume—which communicates an ambiguous dialectic of space and confuses external and internal realms. As he notes, "Mirror reflection is passive, dead but a reflection in an eye penetrates inside."[5] Yet another Magritte canvas in which he sees the mental dialectic of interiority versus exteriority is *Euclid's Promenades* (1955)— one of Magritte's canvases that positions a painting before a window.[6] Thus, for him, the work of Magritte is a perfect text since "psychoanalysis is a quest for the internal world that is in inevitable conflict with the external world while at the same time striving to interact with it."[7] In Magritte's *Castle in the Pyrenees* (1959) (see figure 14.3), which depicts a boulder in the sky, Resnik locates a perfect illustration of a patient's mental syndrome that involves feeling as though a huge rock were floating above her head.[8] And in *Evening Falls* (1964), he sees an objectification of how patients often feel "two contrary instinctual drives" at once.[9]

Taking a similar approach to Resnik, Ellen Handler Spitz in *Museums of the Mind*, investigates Magritte's work from a psychoanalytic perspective, noting how he represents broad "intrapsychic conflicts in visual terms."[10] So, for example, his canvases stage "a battle between mind and body, memory and desire"[11] as well as the "splitting of subject and object."[12] At certain points, she has recourse to Magritte's biography and the traumatic impact that the suicide of his mother had on him when he was a teen. Here she notes a discourse in his paintings of mothers abandoning children as seen in his pictures of birds and eggs.[13] Spitz also discusses the psychic effects of his pictures on their viewers noting that they "are not easy to look at, despite their wit. Their absurdity stings."[14] She adds: "When we gaze at a Magritte, it returns that gaze; it bites us back."[15] Furthermore, she remarks on how through "destabiliz[ing] our visual environment," his canvases make us "feel insecure."[16] Like Resnik, she relates Magritte's work to experiences of her patients. Thus, in discussing the artist's "radical elimination of the face" (discussed in chapter 13) and his discourse of "concealment and revelation," she speaks of a "posttraumatic patient who . . . sought symbolic invisibility as a result of the particular trauma she had suffered."[17] Essentially, because of their extraordinary power, Magritte's paintings enter the museums of our mind, places "where images from the past are preserved in an inner cache or treasure trove from which none of us, artist or otherwise, can escape."[18]

Magritte himself was opposed to psychoanalytic exegeses of his work, which, of course, has not prevented scholars from employing them. As he asserts,

"Psychoanalysis is not qualified to analyse my painting."[19] This is so because "no one in his right mind believes that psychoanalysis could elucidate the world's mystery. . . . Psychoanalysis has nothing to tell us about works of art that evoke the mystery of the world."[20] Unlike his fellow Surrealists, neither does Magritte privilege the oneiric state for artistic inspiration (though the word *dream* does appear in several titles of his works).[21] As he remarks, "I have never dreamt of pictures to be painted. The world doesn't come into my sleep as a dream. I cannot 'see' a picture unless I am fully awake, and have, moreover, perfect presence of mind. I do not have the presence of mind when I am asleep."[22] Neither is he interested in the unconscious. As he notes, "I manage very well without believing in the necessity of an unconscious activity."[23] This is not to say, however, that Magritte was unconcerned with human consciousness (or what he refers to in the chapter epigraph as the "mind"). Rather, he was consumed by it, despite the fact that he found it to be a realm of the "unknown." As he once stated, "It is impossible for us to have anything but the mental universe," and by this he meant "everything we can perceive through the senses, reason, imagination, intuition [or] instincts."[24] Furthermore, the title of a series of his works is *Memory* (figure 10.2)—depicting a female statuary head—again invoking the cerebral realm.

A film that resonates with Magritte's poster for the second Film and Fine Arts World Festival of Belgium is *The Eternal Sunshine of the Spotless Mind* (2004), directed by Michel Gondry and written by Charlie Kaufman. The highly enigmatic narrative tells the story of a rather depressed and affectless young man, Joel (Jim Carrey), who meets an artsy and bohemian young woman, Clementine (Kate Winslet), with whom he falls in love. She is impulsive and adventurous and seems to prod him out of his rut.

Their relationship, however, soon sours, and as it deteriorates, Joel learns of a letter sent to a friend by Lacuna, an organization that wipes bad memories from people's minds. Its contents reveal something alarming—that Clementine has had her recollections of Joel (and his acquaintances) erased. Here we recall that Magritte's female bust in *Memory* is bleeding—a sign of mental pain.

Devastated by Clementine's treachery, Joel visits Lacuna and requests the same treatment for his remembrances of Clementine. For his next session, he is told to bring along objects that remind him of her. Thus, he collects such ordinary items as a mug, a photo album, and a letter. However, like the everyday objects pictured in Magritte's paintings (an umbrella, birdcage, egg or door), these are invested with extraordinary associational power.

For Joel to undergo the memory erasure procedure that he desires, attendants attach a metal helmet to his head while he sleeps and reprogram his thoughts (much the same thing as happens to Walter in Robbe-Grillet's *La*

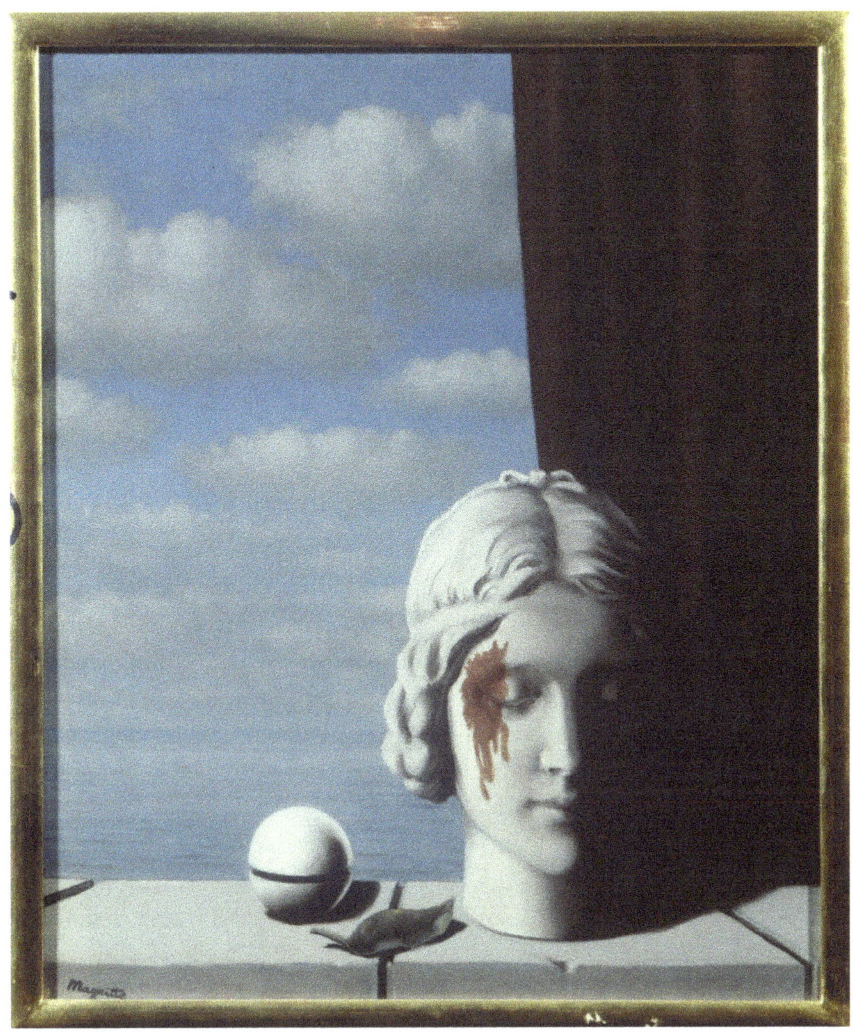

FIGURE 10.2. *Memory* (1948)

belle captive [1983]). As they do so, we see alternating scenes of technicians performing their tasks and images from Joel's mind. Here we are reminded of Magritte's painting *The Pleasure Principle* (1937), which depicts a man's head replaced by some electric force. Clearly, the procedure to which Joel submits is meant to decrease his pain and increase his pleasure.

Most of Joel's induced reminiscences picture him with Clementine, and one, in particular, portrays the couple with their faces blurred (figure 10.3).

This image is evocative of Magritte's *The Lovers* (1928) (see figure 2.2), in which a couple embraces with heads covered in fabric, blinding them to each other's existence. Other shots in the film portray individuals with faces that are literally shrouded.

Some of Joel's memories pertain to his youth. In one reverie, he appears as an adult of childlike proportions hiding under a huge kitchen table. In another, he reaches for a gigantic refrigerator. And in a third, both he and Clementine bathe in a kitchen sink. In a fourth, a real-sized Clementine (imagined as a childhood neighbor) and a miniature Joel appear within the same frame (figure 10.4), reminding us of the impossible relative sizes of a woman and man in Magritte's *The Giantess* (1931) (figure 10.5). In terms of scale, these images also evoke other Magritte paintings in which objects are oversized for the space that contains them (e.g., *Personal Values* [1952]) (see figure 20.13).

Obviously, in playing with scale in the images described above, the film is also manipulating time, merging Joel's present (signified by his adult body) and past (signified by his childhood scale) in the same shots. In one particular Magritte painting temporal boundaries are also crossed in a bizarre way. *The Mathematical Mind* (1936 or 1937) (at one point called *Maternity*) depicts a large figure with a bald baby-like head dressed in an adult woman's clothes—already an anomaly. But, beyond that, the figure holds what size wise seems to be an infant but one that bears an adult woman's head with mature features and long hair. Clearly, temporality is entirely befuddled here as well as the proper roles of mother and child.

Aside from a play with dimension, there are several bizarre scenes in *Eternal Sunshine* in which anomalous situations are portrayed—be it a bed located on a beach or rain falling inside an apartment. Here we think of such fanciful Magritte paintings as *Golconda* (1953) (in which men fall from the sky) or *Heartstring* (1960) (in which a cloud fills a wineglass).

In other sequences, persons or things disappear from the screen for no apparent reason—visually imitating the act of forgetting. As Joel recollects a day when he and Clementine ran through Grand Central Station to catch a train, the people in the hall are erased one by one. In another scene, shop signs inexplicably vanish as Joel passes by them. In these "disappearing acts," we are reminded of Magritte's *Man with a Newspaper* (1928) (see figure 20.4), in which the person depicted in the first frame is absent from the subsequent three (the frames themselves being reminiscent of a film strip).

But perhaps the most Magrittian image of all in *Eternal Sunshine* occurs in a recollected scene that takes place in Joel's living room as he and Clementine sit on the couch, eating Chinese food and watching television. Suddenly

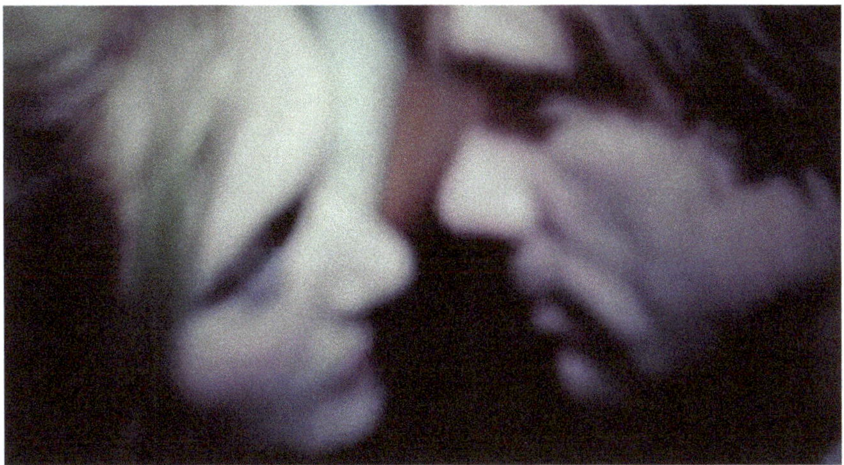

FIGURE 10.3. The faces of Joel (Jim Carrey) and Clementine (Kate Winslet) are blurred in *Eternal Sunshine of the Spotless Mind* (Gondry, 2004), echoing Magritte's shrouded couple in *The Lovers* (1928).

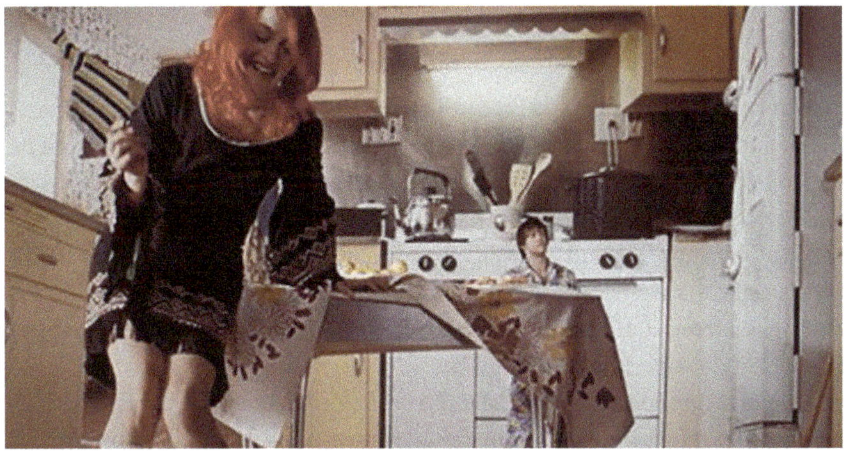

FIGURE 10.4. A miniature Joel (Jim Carrey) as a child is paired with a full-sized Clementine (Kate Winslet) in a recollected scene in Gondry's *Eternal Sunshine of the Spotless Mind* (2004), reminiscent of Magritte's play with scale in *The Giantess* (1931).

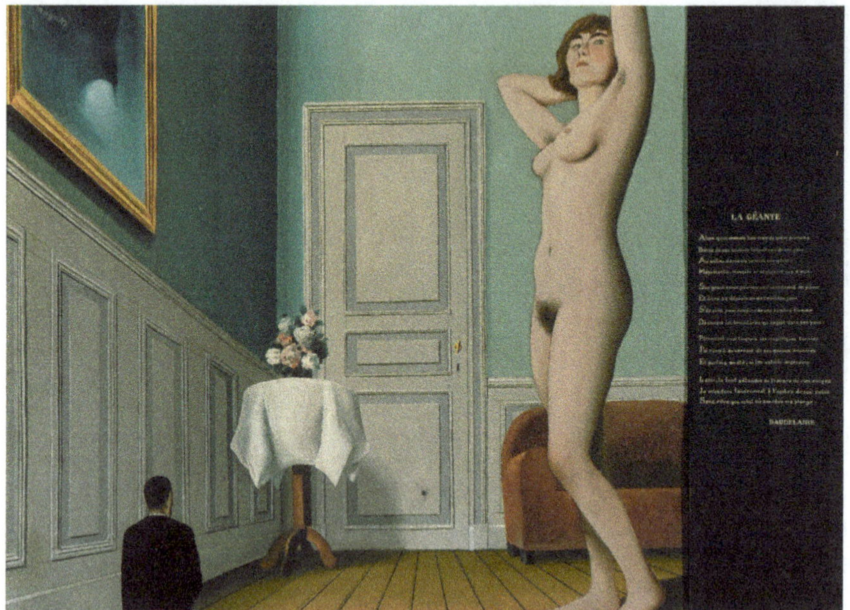

FIGURE 10.5. *The Giantess* (*La géante*) (1931)

Joel looks nonplussed and walks to the television, which strangely broadcasts Clementine back on the couch. Then Joel stands behind the television, and its screen depicts the part of his body hidden by the television, with the take-out food container discernible in his hands (as though the screen were transparent). In this shot, we find an equivalent for Magritte's *Carte Blanche* (1965), which depicts a woman on horseback riding through the woods. While it is clear that a tree should have obscured our view of her, she is nonetheless visible, as though superimposed upon it.

There is one additional image in *Eternal Sunshine* that sparks associations to Magritte. At various points in the narrative, we see Joel in bed (with or without Clementine), and as part of the ensemble of sheets, we see a pillowcase covered in a pattern of blue sky and white clouds—much like the background of so many Magritte canvases and the entire subject of works like *The Curse* (1931, and 1936 or 1937).

A final thought-provoking aspect of *Eternal Sunshine* is its brand of self-reflexivity. Many theorists have seen parallels between the cinema and human consciousness, most notably Hugo Munsterberg, writing in 1916. For example, he viewed the cinematic flashback as mimicking memory—a theme important to Gondry's film. As he notes, "The cut-back may have many variations and serve many purposes. But the one which we face here is psychologically the most interesting. We have really an objectivation of our memory function. . . . [Here] we must recognize the mental act of remembering."[25] More broadly, Munsterberg asserts that cinema often "obeys the laws of the mind rather than those of the outer world."[26] Decades later, Bruce Kawin, in examining Modernist film, utilizes the term "mindscreen" to underscore the similarities between the movies and consciousness.

Clearly, *Eternal Sunshine* takes advantage of that comparison—even incorporating within it images of the brain (ostensibly garnered by Lacuna), as well as utilizing editing and special effects to simulate the erasure of memories from one's awareness. Furthermore, in one sequence portraying Joel's recollections, he and Clementine go to the movies—cementing the connection between the film's focus on consciousness and film. Magritte, too, in his 1949 poster, establishes a parallel between cinematic and mental space—depicting a literal mindscreen. Each space is a kind of tabula rasa—ready to be inscribed by an artist or the vagaries of life.

11

PETRIFICATION, HORROR, AND FANTASY

Stones reveal the perfection of their existence.

René Magritte[1]

IN THE LATE 1940s, René Magritte began a series of paintings with a common theme involving the petrification of organic matter—which some have called his "stone age" works.[2] In certain cases, the images involve people and by extension their clothing, as in *The Song of Violet*, *Intimate Journal*, *The Magic Potion* (all from 1951), and *The Horns of Desire* (1960). In other cases, petrification applies to Magritte's familiar cross-species creatures (discussed in chapter 15), as in *The Wonders of Nature* (1953) (figure 11.3). Elsewhere the rock beings that Magritte imagines are animals, most notably, birds—as in *The Flavour of Tears* (1948), *The Wasted Footstep* (1950), *The Fickleness of the Heart* (1950), *The Domain of Arnheim* (1952), *The Secret Agreement* (1962 or 1963), *The Idol* (1965), or *The Connivance* (1965). In one work, ironically named *The Fountain of Youth* (1957), a stone bird forms a part of a tablet on the ground that looks much like a gravestone (imprinted with "Coblenz," a city largely destroyed in World War II). Finally, Magritte also paints petrified fruit, as in *Memory of a Journey* or *The Pledge* (both from 1950) or *The Great Table* (1962 or 1963), focusing upon his beloved apples.

But what can we say about these strange pictures? First, they are rather horrific despite, as the chapter epigraph indicates, the fact that Magritte sees perfection in stones. Second, and most obvious, in multiple ways they reveal

Magritte's love of the paradoxical. Clearly, there are profound differences between organic and nonorganic materials—between people, animals, comestibles, and stones—and to mix them up is rather comical. In the case of Magritte's petrified birds, there is an additional absurdity, since they are creatures that fly, entirely defying the earth-bound weight of rocks.

However, the most crucial distinction between animate and inanimate beings is that the former can be "alive," and, when dead, they generally decay, not petrify. So, in a sense, the portrayal of organic subjects as boulders seems an assault on the messiness of death and an attempt at eternal preservation. On one level, this theme may be tied to the traumatic suicide of Magritte's mother when he was a teen. On another, however, given the dates that these paintings were produced (the late 1940s through the early 1950s), they may relate to the shock of World War II and the desire to be protected from further destruction, especially after the Hiroshima and Nagasaki bombings in which people were burned to cinder. As Magritte once said, "The present reeks of . . . the atom bomb."[3] So, ironically, his stone age paintings may not only refer back to ancient times but to the future of the atomic age as well. Magritte evidently considered the state of petrification as dreadful. According to Abraham Hammacher, he "did not regard [it] as a process, but as a kind of catastrophe, like that at Pompeii, when lava transfixed the world and brought all movement to a halt."[4]

But what is the relevance of these paintings to the cinema? Once more, there are both theoretical and material answers to the question.

Film Theory

Taking the former issue first, one cannot help but relate Magritte's effort toward challenging death through petrification to the famous "mummy complex" discussed by film theorist André Bazin. In his seminal essay, "The Ontology of the Photographic Image," Bazin examined motion pictures and still photography (the latter being cinema's predecessor), concluding, "If the plastic arts were put under psychoanalysis, the practice of embalming the dead might turn out to be a fundamental factor in their creation."[5] Thus, he conceives the cinema as an art "aimed against death" by seeking "survival" through "the continued existence of the corporeal body."[6] Hence, the medium promises a "preservation of life by a representation of life" in the screen image.[7]

Of course, the cinema can preserve not only the static image of a living organism but also its movement over time (something that Magritte's canvases were unable to do). In this respect, there is another fascinating resonance between film and the artist's stone age paintings. If we were looking for the rhetorical equivalent of petrification in motion pictures, it would take the form of the freeze frame, "an optical effect . . . in which a single frame . . . is reprinted in a continuous series, which when shown gives the effect of a still photograph."[8] Through this technique, both time and movement are arrested and life, itself, seems to hang in the balance. Significantly, numerous films in which characters risk or face death end on such an image—for example, *Thelma and Louise* (Ridley Scott, 1991) when the women drive their car into the Grand Canyon.

But there have been experimental films that openly play with the shift between motion and stasis. Most notable is Dziga Vertov's *Man with a Movie Camera* (1929), which presents a sequence involving people being driven down a Moscow street in a horse-drawn carriage. Periodically, Vertov freezes a frame, stopping the action for a while. Here the effect is employed not to signal mortality but to announce, self-reflexively, the power of cinema to capture and investigate the activities of daily life. Nonetheless, Vertov's analysis occurs when the image is "petrified"—like a dead insect pinned to an entomologist's board.

In a book whose subtitle is *Stillness and the Moving Image*, Laura Mulvey theorizes the freeze frame.[9] If Jean-Luc Godard once claimed that cinema was "truth 24 times a second," Mulvey revises his aphorism to read "death 24 times a second." This is because "throughout the history of cinema, the stilled image has been contained within the creative preserve of the film-maker, always accessible on the editing table and always transferable into a freeze frame on the screen."[10] Once utilized, this "freezing of reality . . . marks a transition from the animate to the inanimate, from life to death."[11] She continues, "As stillness intrudes into movement, the image freezes into the 'stop of death.'"[12]

While generally the freeze frame has been used for brief moments of screen time, the still photograph has been employed more thoroughly in cinema and functions as another means of "petrifying" the moving image. Moreover, it has often been associated with mortality in the film narratives in which it is contained. In Michelangelo Antonioni's *Blow Up* (1966), which takes photography as its subject, a snapshot forms the basis of the film's enigma. Significantly, it is one that may reveal a murder (possibly a corpse hidden in the trees of a park). While Ingmar Bergman's *Persona* (1966) is not about photography, photographs are extremely important in the film. The drama concerns an actress who has had a mental breakdown and refuses to speak. At one point, she gazes at a disturbing photograph that depicts a Jewish child being rounded up by the Nazis to face extinction in a concentration camp. It seems to symbolize her horror with the world. Furthermore, in the abstract opening sequence of the film, after seeing what appear to be several cadavers, a young boy lying on a morgue table suddenly comes alive and puts his hand up to a large screen on which still images of two women's faces appear. Certainly, here again, the photograph is associated with death.

Film Practice

Experimental Film

There are other films, however, in which photographs function as a major formal element. We have already discussed Hollis Frampton's *(nostalgia)* (1971) in another context, but it is equally relevant to the theme of petrification. As noted, it features a series of black-and-white snapshots taken (or collected) by Frampton in New York City. Hence, it is an autobiographical work in which Frampton's memories and the bodies of those people he has known are conserved photographically. However, in a paradoxical move that Magritte would have enjoyed, each photograph is placed on a hot plate where it burns, flames, and disintegrates. Thus, while Magritte turns to the solidity of stone for petrification, Frampton's photographic mode is fragile and perishable. Of course, a photograph can always be reprinted, thus reviving its conservatory function.

But perhaps the most famous film entirely based on photography is Chris Marker's *La jetée* (1962), a *ciné-roman* made later than Magritte's stone age paintings but a work that also issues from the immediate post–World War II era. It is an abstract film that simultaneously looks at the past (Auschwitz, Hiroshima, the German occupation of France), at the present (Algeria, the Cuban missile crisis, the Cold War), and the apocalyptic future (the nuclear age). If it has a "plot" at all (as articulated by voice-over narration and static images), it concerns a man who has a persistent childhood memory of having spotted a woman at Orly Airport during a scene of violence.

Eventually, Paris is destroyed in a third world war, and the man is imprisoned in an underground Nazi-like concentration camp in which scientists experiment on his mind. They cause him to regress in time and meet the woman with whom he has been obsessed. At one point, the two stroll through a park, and later, through a natural history museum. In another encounter (occurring before they visit the natural history museum), the couple pass a series of outdoor statues; several depict the bodies of female subjects and one portrays a male head. These are important objects because they serve as totems against death—human subjects that can never die.[13] As Emmanuel Levinas once stated, "Every artwork is, in the end, a statue—a stoppage of time, or rather its delay itself."[14] Unlike the peculiar stone age figures in Magritte's oeuvre (petrified birds or leaves), the statues in *La jetée* are familiar human ones from the realm of art.

While Magritte did not often depict statues, he did so occasionally, as in *When the Hour Strikes* (1964–65) which portrays a female body with head, arms and lower legs missing (as though ravaged by time). However, one of his most notable series of works (mentioned earlier) is *Memory* (1948) (see figure 10.2), which portray a sculpture of a female head. Curiously, however, the statue bleeds—thus foregrounding the incompatibility of life and death. Furthermore, in one version, next to it is a bird's nest containing eggs, which promise a forthcoming birth. A final element of the picture (the setting sun) conversely signals endings rather than beginnings. So, although Magritte paints a "normal" subject, it bears all the contradictions of his stone age figures.

The Light of Coincidences (1933) pictures a statue of a woman contained in a framed shadow box. Here the sculpture is not bleeding but shows a similar vulnerability since its head and arms are missing. Significantly, it is illuminated by a candle that we know will eventually be extinguished (much like the setting sun in one iteration of *Memory*).

In all these statue paintings by Magritte we are again reminded of Jean Cocteau's *The Blood of a Poet* (1932), in which a statue of a woman comes to life (a movement in the opposite direction of Magritte's petrification), only to return to its original state later on (figure 11.1). While it is destroyed in the beginning of the film, it is reanimated toward the end of the drama.

But the Magritte work that most announces the sculptural paradox of life and death is *The Future of Statues* (1932–37)–a three-dimensional reproduction of Napoleon Bonaparte's death mask. Distracting from its casting of Napoleon's features, however, is a surface that is covered by sky and clouds. Helmutt Wohl cites this work as evidence of Modernism's refusal to create traditional, transcendent monuments. As he writes, "The liberation of memory from its embodiment in material form is the theme of . . . *The Future of Statues*. . . . With eyes closed and lips lightly parted, the emperor dreams of his transfiguration. . . . Magritte puts into question . . . the validity in our time of casting memory and commemoration in the physical, palpable form of monuments . . . regardless of their style."[15]

In considering statues in Magritte's oeuvre as well as in *La jetée*, we also need to ponder a contemporaneous nonfiction film codirected by Marker, Alain Resnais, and Ghislain Cloquetby. *Statues Also Die* (1953) is a documentary about African art (and the negative effects of colonialism upon it). Its

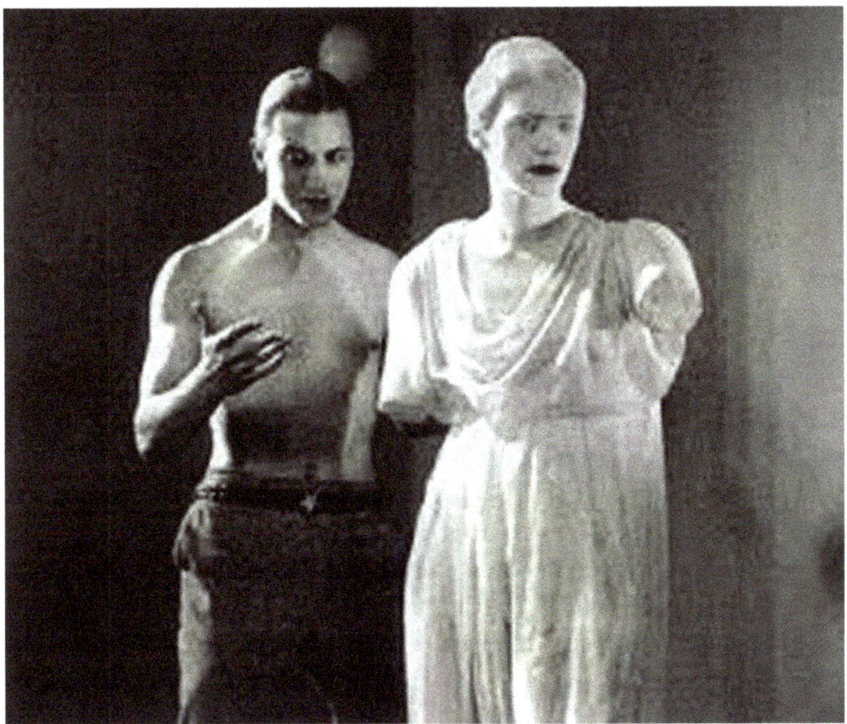

FIGURE 11.1. The Artist stands by a female statue in Cocteau's *The Blood of a Poet* (1932).

soundtrack consists of a spoken text conceived by the same individual who composed the one for *La jetée*: Jean Négroni. Combined with aestheticized shots of African sculpture is anthropological footage of the continent: people dancing, preparing food, weaving, boating, and crafting modern souvenirs. Interestingly, the film's opening narration immediately raises the issue of mortality as tied to sculpture: "When men die, they enter history. When statues die, they enter into art. This botany of death is called culture. That's because the society of statues is mortal. One day, their faces of stone crumble and fall to earth. A civilization leaves behind itself these mutilated traces." Thus, death haunts not only the object but the people who produced it. In the case of African sculpture, the situation is more complex—as the dominance of the white man has transformed and degraded the art.

In *La jetée,* aside from backsliding into the past, the protagonist time-travels into the future where he encounters strange humanoid beings. At the end of the film, he returns to the scene of his recurrent memory and chases after the woman at Orly, only to be shot by camp guards who cause his death. Some critics have read the film's puzzling narrative as the impossible story of a man remembering his own demise.

La jetée has been thoroughly and copiously analyzed over the years, and I will not rehearse its various exegeses. Rather, I will highlight only the issues pertinent to my discussion of Magritte. Certainly, the film—like *(nostalgia)*—connects the use of static photographs to the past, memory, and death. But there is another aspect that has particular relevance to Magritte—the scene taking place in the museum. Significantly, it is a zoological institution replete with exhibits of myriad embalmed or stuffed creatures: birds, mammals, and fish. Here we should note that, previously in the film, Marker has shown us living creatures—birds, cats, and farm animals grazing in a field—as though to emphasize the difference between animate and inanimate states. On the other hand, in the same sequence, he also includes footage of a cemetery. In keeping with the latter image, it seems significant that it is through a rather "morbid" museum that the man and woman wander at the moment of their temporal reunion (one that will end in the man's execution).

The point is that the postmortem beings they encounter there are as close to being "petrified" as any we can imagine, and thus bear comparison to the granite ones in Magritte's paintings. If such a scene took place in another film, it might not be provocative, but in *La jetée*, it is embedded in a work that underscores photography's ability to "embalm the dead," thus foregrounding the ontology of the cinematic medium.

But cinema's relation to mortality goes beyond the elements already discussed. There is also the fact that for the past decade film scholars and cultural pundits have been declaring the "death of film" itself, based on the decline of celluloid and its replacement by digital reproduction and streaming (a "virtual" experience of movies). Thus, perhaps, we should think of the antiquated film medium as having become as "petrified" as Magritte's painted subjects.

However, if we consider film qua film (i.e., the actual film strip), we find that the medium ages more like a living thing than an inert object—slowly decomposing. The enigmatic beauty of such a process has been captured in works like *Lyrical Nitrate* (Peter Delpeut, 1991), and *Decasia* (2002, Bill Morrison), which conjoin surviving (but moldering) fragments from lost silent movies into a formal whole, creating a mournful but stunning collage. As we learned in *(nostalgia)*, though photography is meant to "petrify" its object, its very substance is subject to the forces it means to control.

The Art Film

Another French film (this time a feature) with subtle overtones of Magritte's petrification series is *Les visiteurs du soir*, directed by Marcel Carné in 1942 during the Nazi occupation. While, on the one hand, it seems devoid of political allegory (especially since it is set in 1585), Michael Atkinson sees it as resonant with cultural overtones: "To viewers . . . this return to the all-or-nothing medieval courtly love tradition was stone-cold liberation, courageous and indisputably native, all about resisting evil machinations with only the fierce devotion of an enraptured spirit."[16] (Of course, his use of the term "stone-cold" is suggestive here—though meant in a completely different sense than one pertaining to Magritte's art.)

Les visiteurs du soir is a strange slow-paced movie with a fantastical narrative transpiring in the Middle Ages. It concerns two envoys sent by the devil to a castle—Giles (Alain Cuny) and Dominique (Arletty). They are posing as minstrels, and Dominique is initially dressed as a young man. They are welcomed at court by the baron (Fernand Ledoux), and they perform for him and his guests. Almost immediately, however, Giles falls in love with the baron's daughter, Anne (Marie Déa), who is engaged to Renaud (Marcel Herrand). Renaud, however, is enamored with Dominique (who later appears in female clothing), but she also flirts with the baron who still mourns the death of his wife. In some respects, the story resembles Shakespeare's *A Midsummer Night's Dream* (1595–96) and words like "magical" and "marvelous" pepper the dialogue.

As an emissary of the devil, Giles can perform feats of prestidigitation—like making a trained bear appear as a gift for a poor entertainer who has been ejected from the castle or turning Anne's homely maid beautiful. Furthermore, during a dance party at the castle, he and Dominique freeze the celebrants in place, whereupon Giles walks off with Anne, and Dominique (now dressed as a woman) pairs with Renaud. When the two couples return, the dance resumes with no one the wiser for the interruption. So here we have an intimation of the petrification process particular to the cinema (though it is ultimately reversed).

While Dominique is a cold seductress who plays with the affections of both Renaud and the baron, Giles falls madly in love with Anne who returns his affection. Clearly, she has found her fiancé heartless and wanting. When she speaks to him of her dreams, he calls them "dangerous and useless" and claims to never dream himself. Giles, on the other hand, converses with Anne with words filled with the discourse of passion ("To me you are all the love in the world")—so much so that they seem cliché or a parody of French cinema dialogue of the era. Eventually, he confesses that he serves the devil and that she only loves him because of Mephistopheles's ruses. When Giles is found in Anne's bedroom, he is taken away by guards and chained in a dungeon.

At about the same time, a mysterious visitor (dressed all in black) appears at the castle and asks for the baron's hospitality. We soon realize that he is the devil (Jules Berry), who has come to check up on his minions. Eventually, he strikes a bargain with Anne to release Giles (if she stays with him), but he strips the latter of his memories, including those of his love for Anne.

The devil is an antic, comic figure who, like Giles and Dominique, can perform tricks. (Here we think of early magic films like *The Red Specter* [Segundo de Chomón, 1907], in which the magician takes the form of the devil.) At one point, he even states, "I am not a bad devil." He can transport people from one place to another at will. Thus, he transfers himself, Giles, and Anne to a fountain and drops a stone into a pool of water. Magically, on its surface (as on a movie screen), it shows a duel taking place between the baron and Renaud, who fight over Dominique; blood stains the image as the latter expires.

In the film's final scene, Anne and Giles again meet at the fountain, and because he cannot remember her, Giles repeats the dialogue he uttered when they first declared their love. The devil appears on horseback and orders Anne to leave Giles, but the latter (whose memory has been miraculously restored) responds, "Nothing can separate us now." The devil threatens to turn them both to stone and does so as we watch successive images of their gradual petrification (figure 11.2). The devil is nonplussed when, instead of the "deathly silence" that he anticipates, he hears the beating of a single heart emanate from the statue (a bodily sound that we have also heard on the soundtrack of *La jetée*). He tries to destroy the monument but fails as the film comes to a close. Interestingly, in terms of the final image of petrification, numerous reviewers of the film critiqued the movie for being "static."[17]

In *Les visiteurs du soir*, the process of petrification constitutes a testimony to love. Giles rejects his service to the devil for his devotion to Anne, and she embraces death and the risk of damnation to remain with him. This theme seems especially "French," and derivative of Surrealism's obsession with "the obscure object of desire." These are motifs with which Magritte would have been familiar, and they surface in many of his works, especially those that focus on the female image. In *Black Magic* (1945), a title alluding to the devil, a woman's body (his wife, Georgette's) is half-corporeal and half-ethereal (covered with sky and clouds), bespeaking the enchantment associated with sexual love.

But, in particular, *Les visiteurs du soir* conjures up one of Magritte's stone age paintings. *The Wonders of Nature* (figure 11.3) portrays a petrified couple apparently locked in an embrace. As one writer puts it, this canvas "illustrates

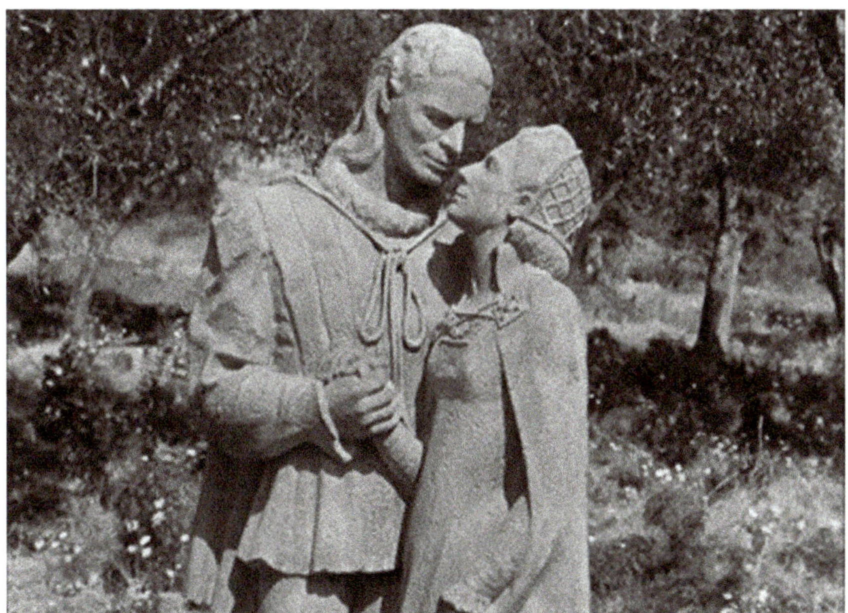

FIGURE 11.2. The lovers, Anne (Marie Déa) and Giles (Alain Cuny), gradually petrify into a statue in Carné's *Les visiteurs du soir* (1942).

fully Magritte's poetic sensibility . . . [by] depicting two fish-headed lovers apparently joined in song."[18] Here we note that Giles is a troubadour and often sings of his love for Anne. Similarly, as Magritte's paintings blur the border between life and death, so does the statue in *Les visiteurs du soir* with its animate heart that continues to beat. In this image, we also think again of Magritte's *Memory* (see figure 10.2), with its bleeding statue—another indication of the confusion of life and death. Once more, *Les visiteurs du soir* (with its erasure and restoration of Giles's memory reminiscent of *Eternal Sunshine of the Spotless Mind* [2004]) engages the theme of consciousness. As Michelle Bolduc remarks, the sculpture at the end of the film "expresses a lamentation, even a mournful memory that combines past, present and future."[19]

Beyond this, as Danièle Gasiglia-Lasteur has noted that with its supernatural aura, *Les visiteurs du soir* "creates a medieval world that is '*rêve*' [dream] rather than reconstructed."[20] Similarly, Edward Baron Turk (who deems the work a "dreamlike fantasy") remarks on how the spectator might "construe the entire film as the unfolding of a dream." Linking dream to petrification, he notes how, in the film's opening scenes, Gilles and Dominique ride through "rugged crags [and] petrified lava flows."[21]

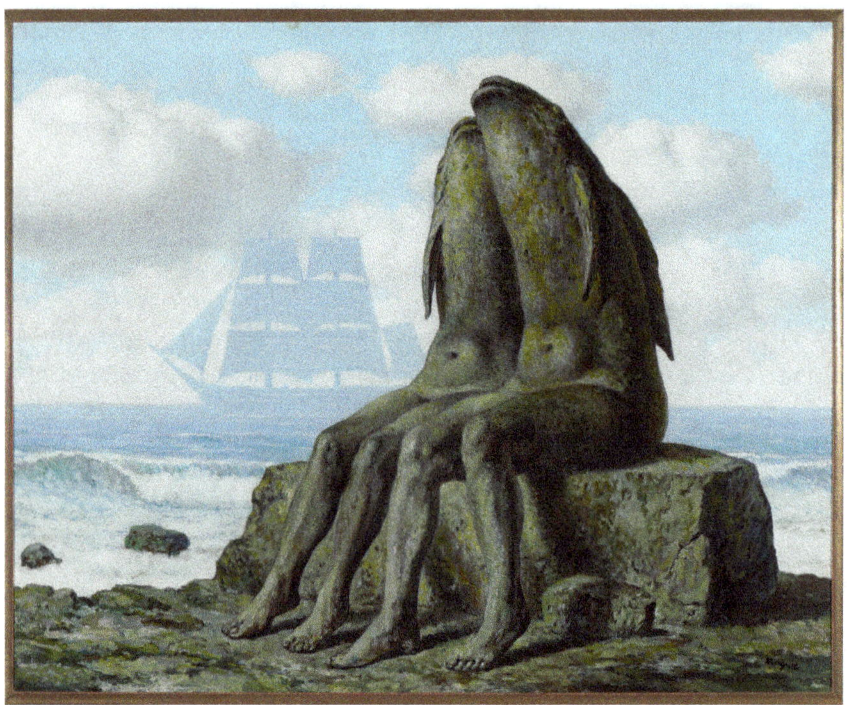

FIGURE 11.3. *The Wonders of Nature* (*Les merveilles de la nature*) (1953)

Here we cannot help but recall Magritte's painting *The Art of Conversation* (1950) with its fossilized word *rêve* (dream) spelled out—representing the ultimate sign of human death as the demise of the imagination.[22]

The Horror Film

On a more literal level than represented in the art film, we find a group of works (several from the 1950s, the height of Magritte's production of his petrification series), that narrativize the process of humans turning into stone. It is no surprise that these often fall into the horror genre—and here we recall that the term *petrify* also means to scare and that one can be "scared to death."

Clearly, Magritte did not invent the notion of organisms turning to stone; rather, the trope has long been a part of legend and fairy tale. Most notable is the Greek myth of the Gorgon, a tale of three sisters named Stheno (strength), Euryale (wide leaping), and Medusa (ruler or queen). They are "ugly monsters with huge wings, sharp fangs and claws, and bodies covered with dragonlike scales. They had horrible grins, staring eyes, and writhing snakes for hair.

Their gaze was so terrifying that anyone who looked upon them immediately turned to stone. Two of the Gorgons, Stheno and Euryale, were immortal, but Medusa was not. In one of the more famous Greek myths, the hero Perseus kills and beheads her with help from Athena."[23]

The Gorgon (Terence Fisher, 1964) is a British Technicolor film that updates this legend and sets it in the fictional European village of Vandorf at the turn of the twentieth century. It was produced by the Hammer studio—known for releasing B movies in Gothic and horror genres. The poster for the film plays with the double sense of the word *petrify*.

The drama involves a series of mysterious murders that take place in the town. While various inquests rule the deaths murders or suicides, a physician, Dr. Namaroff (Peter Cushing), and his assistant, Carla (Barbara Shelley), know that the victims have died from petrification at the hands of a strange creature that haunts a nearby castle. The audience becomes aware of this mode of death when a woman's corpse is brought to the doctor's office. We first see her brittle finger break off and fall to the floor, and a later shot reveals her stone body (figure 11.4). The perverse spirit that haunts the town is named Megaera, which is actually one of the Furies in Greek mythology and not a Gorgon. She is unleashed whenever there is a full moon, and we repeatedly get shots of the night sky reminiscent of the one that opens *Un chien andalou* (1929).

When artist Bruno Heitz (Jeremy Longhurst), the lover of the deceased woman, turns up dead as well, his demise is made to look like a suicide, but his family members have their doubts. His father (Michael Goodliffe) comes to Vandorf to investigate. However, when he wanders into the deserted castle (at the center of which is a broken statue), he catches a glimpse of a female figure and is turned to stone.

Once more, Dr. Namaroff fakes the death certificate and lists the cause as "heart failure." When Paul Heitz (Richard Pasco) arrives to continue the family's inquiry, he unearths his father's tomb and finds him petrified. In his search to discover the truth, Paul is assisted by Professor Karl Meister (Christopher Lee) and, in the process, falls in love with Carla. Paul, too, rambles into the castle one night and sights the phantom but views her image indirectly in a mirror—a fact that saves him from petrification. Here the film taps into the legend of Perseus, who was able to decapitate Medusa by looking at her reflection in his shield (rather than gazing straight at her). The professor helps Paul to realize that Megaera inhabits the body of Carla. When Paul is attacked by the specter, the professor rescues him by severing its head. As if by magic, her face gradually turns to that of Carla.

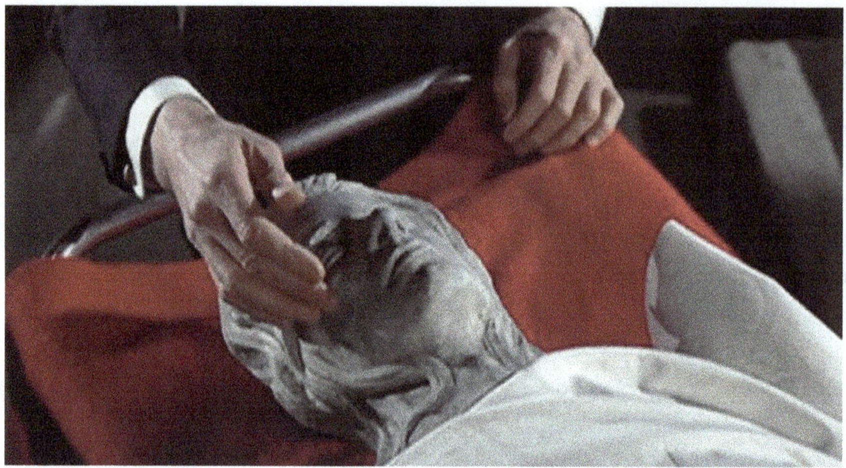

FIGURE 11.4. A petrified female corpse is brought to a doctor's office in *The Gorgon* (Fisher, 1964).

The Man Who Turned to Stone (1957), directed by Lászlo Kardos for Columbia Pictures, is an earlier horror film on the same theme. It is another B movie, though shot in black and white. The drama is set at the La Salle Detention Home for Girls—a prison residence for young women. Repeatedly during the night, inmates hear screams and subsequently notice an alarming number of deaths in their population. The institution is an oppressive one, run with a stern hand by Dr. Murdock (Victor Jory) and Mrs. Ford (Ann Doran), assisted by a thug named Eric (Friedrich von Ledebur) who resembles Dr. Frankenstein's monster. The only sympathetic staff member is the social worker, Carol Adams (Charlotte Austin), who listens to the women's complaints and grows suspicious herself. A coroner's inquest into one of the deaths is attended by psychiatrist Dr. Rogers (William Hudson), who vows to investigate the mysterious events. We eventually learn that Murdock and Ford (along with Mr. Cooper [Paul Cavanagh] and other prison personnel) are conducting experiments within a laboratory by which they submerge female inmates in a tub of liquid and, through some electric process, transfer the women's life force to individuals on the verge of death—thus allowing them to preternaturally extend their existence. We see this action performed on Eric, who, when in need of the procedure, takes on a hardened appearance—achieved filmically (on the cheap) through ample use of dark, shadowed makeup. We learn, however, that his coarsened look is the first stage of petrification by which the experimental subject would turn to stone and expire.

At one point, Cooper confesses to Rogers that he is 220 years old and asks Rogers to take a scissors to try to stab him. When Rogers does so, he is unable to make an incision, and the scissors make a metallic clang when hitting Cooper's skin. Later, when Rogers searches through the detention home's basement, he comes upon the "stone" corpse of Cooper. Alarmed, he accidentally tips it over, causing it to make a heavy thud on the floor—unlike the sound of flesh. Significantly, a later scene in which Rogers goes to find Cooper's hidden diary (which explains the history of the experiment) takes place in a rocky locale, as if to emphasize the zombies' material nature. As is usual with such mainstream narratives, by the end the villains have been vanquished, the women rescued, and the home destroyed; in addition, a romantic relationship has blossomed between Rogers and Adams.

Finally, it is interesting that Rogers's first hint that something is amiss at the home comes in reference to art. When he admires a painting hung over the fireplace in the institution's living room, Cooper tells him that is by Rembrandt. When Rogers inquires how such a valuable work made its way to a prison, Cooper says that he purchased it at a bargain price hundreds of years ago. When Rogers is taken aback by this statement, Cooper "corrects" himself and says it was in "1950." Significantly, the canvas is a portrait—a form that memorializes an individual and "preserves" him from death. As though to emphasize the point, the mantel includes a number of stone or porcelain figures and busts.

The Monolith Monsters (1957), directed by John Sherwood for Universal International, is a black-and-white B movie that crosses the boundaries between horror and science fiction. While the "monsters" in the title point to the former, the film's prologue intimates the latter. Throughout the narrative, it will hover between the two generic poles.

As the movie opens, we see a painterly star-lit sky. A comet shoots through it and Earth moves closer toward us. A booming male voice intones that comets hurtling through space are generally destroyed in the process. If they make it to Earth and strike land, a crater is formed, and we are shown images of such pits in the desert. As we see a meteor explode, the voice-over becomes more mystical and foreboding, mentioning how meteors issue from "infinity" and leave a "strange calling card." With their substances "unknown," they "lie dormant" on earth, just "waiting."

The drama is set in the small California town of San Angelo, where a federal geologist, Ben Gilbert (Phil Harvey), drives through the desert and notices a group of strange black rocks on the sand.

He brings one back to his office and confesses to the local newspaper publisher, Martin Cochrane (Les Tremayne), that he has no idea what it is.

That night, a storm hits town, and through an open window in Ben's office, water soaks the rock. When Dave Miller (Grant Williams), Ben's supervisor, looks for him the next morning, he finds Ben's office in disarray—covered with copious odd rocks. Ben is dead, apparently having been petrified.

Meanwhile, Dave's girlfriend, Cathy Barrett (Lola Albright), a teacher, has taken some students on a field trip into the desert. A young girl, Ginny Simpson (Linda Scheley), takes one of the peculiar rocks home with her. When Dave learns of this, he is concerned, and the next day visits the Simpson farm, only to find the buildings destroyed and the land covered with rocks. While Ginny's parents are dead, she survives, but as a shot of her darkened hand reveals, she is turning to stone. She is taken to a medical center and put in an iron lung. Other townspeople (and even a dog) who have come in contact with the rocks also succumb to petrification.

Much of the remaining drama involves Dave and his former professor, Arthur Flanders (Trevor Bardette), attempting to learn what "activates" the rocks—since, in some circumstances, they pose no danger. As Flanders opines, they have "been gathering secrets of time and space for billions of years." When a fragment of a rock falls into Dave's office sink (into which he later pours coffee), it steams and expands. The men conclude that water initiates its heinous transformation. They analyze the rock's mineral composition and realize that it is made of silica that it leaches from the soil. They hypothesize that it robs humans of the silicon that keeps their skin flexible. They confirm their discovery by injecting Ginny with the substance and watching her recover.

Unfortunately, another storm hits town and Dave and Flanders realize that this will set the meteorites off. They return to the desert and we view myriad shots of the pyramidal geodes rising from land into the air (like skyscrapers) until they become so heavy that they fall and break into pieces. As Dave remarks, "San Angelo will [soon] look more like a petrified forest than a town." While recommending to police that the population be evacuated, the men search for the key to arresting the growth and proliferation of the rocks. They soon realize that salt will accomplish this and engineer a complex solution to the meteor disaster.

Given that *The Monolith Monsters* is a low-budget film, its special effects are especially "creaky." In sequences in which the boulders topple over near Dave's car or at the edge of town, one can see the "seam" that connects two matted scenes, and there is often an accompanying vibration in one of them that reveals the split. Similarly, in closer shots of the meteorites crashing into houses, the use of models is painfully obvious.

To summarize, I have shown how Magritte's interest in petrification (as seen in his stone age pictures from the 1950s) has reverberations in film theory in terms of the medium's "mummification" of the image, as well as its recourse to freeze frames and its inclusion of still photographic images. I have also demonstrated how the issue of petrification (understood metaphorically) inserts itself into experimental films like *The Blood of a Poet*, *La jetée*, *Statues Also Die*, and *(nostalgia)*. Furthermore, I have noted how the theme appears in an important French art film made during World War II, *Les visiteurs du soir*. Finally, I have demonstrated that the discourse of petrification also emerges in numerous American horror films of the post–World War II era, the period in which Magritte created his stone age series.

Given that so many of the works in question date from this epoch (both painterly and cinematic), it is tempting to see the theme as relevant to the fear of the atomic age, with its capability for reducing the human form to a burnt, petrified mass—much like the remains of Pompeii cited by Abraham Hammacher in his discussion of Magritte. Furthermore, in *The Monster Monolith*'s placement of a calcified girl in an iron lung (another image of petrification), we get intimations of a second post–World War II scourge—the polio epidemic.

12

ANIMATION

An object may be ridiculous or not.

René Magritte[1]

ON ONE LEVEL, film animation would seem to be a likely genre in which to find parallels to painting, given its graphic nature. And, of course, there has been a historic tradition of animated experimental films. Here one thinks of the work of Hans Richter and Viking Eggeling in the 1920s (e.g., *Rhythmus 21* [1921] or *Symphonie diagonale* [1924]), with its black-and-white geometric imagery. Similarly, one considers the colorful representational films of Lotte Reiniger from the same era like *The Adventures of Prince Achmed* (1926), which drew on the lineage of Asian silhouette puppetry. This European tradition continued in future decades with work by artists like Peter Kubelka (e.g., *Adebar* [1957]), which took representational forms and reduced them to black-and-white abstractions. In the 1950s, some American filmmakers emerged to forge links between animation and painting. Prominent among them was Robert Breer who in such experimental movies as *Blazes* (1961) rendered an onscreen version of Abstract Expressionism. As computer technology became available (first analog, then digital), filmmakers like John Whitney began to pioneer its possibilities for film art, as in such groundbreaking works as *Arabesque* (1976) with its curvilinear ballet of forms.

While there is an established history to this cinematic form, few works in this mode have ever taken advantage of the possible relationships between animation and the work of Magritte. I will consider some that may be imagined to have done so—though no direct linkage is asserted.

Commercial Cinema

In *The Unsilvered Screen*, Van Norris writes about the appropriation of Surrealism into mainstream American cartoons.[2] One film that he cites in passing is *Porky in Wackyland* (1938), directed by Robert Clampett for Warner Bros. It is a black-and-white movie about Porky's hunt for the elusive Dodo bird in Africa in order to collect a reward. While Norris does not analyze the film, there are elements of its imagery that, in their nod to Surrealism, have a decidedly Magrittian sense.

In examining the cartoon, however, one must keep in mind that it is a *popular* work aimed at a *mass audience*, so its parallels with experimental Surrealism can only go so far. Furthermore, cartoons are *comic* works filled with, to borrow Magritte's term from this chapter's epigraph, "ridiculous objects" as well as beings (often aimed at the child audience) and therefore must mute the disturbing aspects of the movement's concerns in favor of the absurdist ones.

In viewing the film, we first notice its use of print text in the image. In numerous shots, for instance, the nonsense word "Foo" appears (figure 12.1). And in one other shot, a sign for "Hello" is presented upside down. Beyond linguistic confusion, the film also partakes in verbal/visual puns. In one shot, hangars dangle from a tree as though riffing on the term "clothes tree." In another, a suitcase that appears to be sprouting from a tree is labeled "tree trunk." Interestingly, the bizarre tree limbs bear sheet music instead of leaves, which reminds us of Magritte's painting *The Lost Jockey* (1926) (see figure 20.1) in which tree-like bilboquets are decorated with musical notation. Significantly, by the time *Porky in Wackyland* was made, Magritte had produced a great many paintings that utilized language in both a nonsensical and witty fashion—for example, *Plant with Word* (1929), in which a plant is depicted with the label "cannon."

The film contains yet other tropes reminiscent of Magritte's humorous iconography. A fish in Wackyland has an anchor attached to it, ridiculous for an animal known for floating effortlessly through water. Similarly, another fish holds up an umbrella, as though afraid of getting wet. Here we might consider Magritte's *Hegel's Holiday* (1958), which absurdly positions a glass of water on top of an umbrella, or *Elective Affinities* (1933), a painting of a birdcage that contains an egg—surely not an object that is in danger of escaping. Of course, there is a second joke here: that the egg precedes the birth of the bird, the proper subject of captivity.

In yet another shot, Porky tries to open a door that is not attached to any building but is simply freestanding on the ground. Here we are reminded of Magritte's *The Scars of Memory* (1926 or 1927), one of his first studies of unmoored

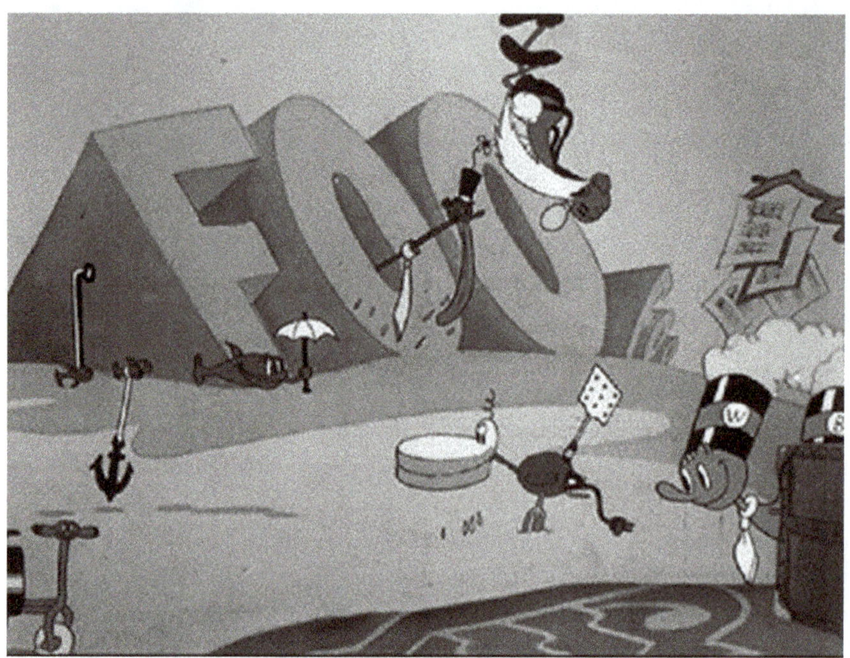

FIGURE 12.1. There is much use of nonsense words in Clampett's *Porky in Wackyland* (1938), reminding us of Magritte's irreverence toward language.

doors, or *Victory* (1939) (see figure 20.11). There are other variations on unmoored objects in *Porky in Wackyland.* A window and a swing are suspended in midair, as is a barred gate behind which a prisoner is "trapped" (figure 12.2).

As a side note, in another cartoon (*The Screwy Truant* [1945] by Tex Avery), there is a nonsensical play with doors in a chase between the Screwy Squirrel and a dog. Doors appear to open and close on the floor as well as on the ceiling, and when one of the animals tries to open a door positioned correctly (on a wall), he finds only a wall of bricks behind it with a sign: "Imagine that, no door!"[3] In this image, we are also reminded of Magritte's *The Bloodletting* (1938 or 1939 [see figure 9.1]), in which a painting-less frame hung in a gallery reveals a just brick wall.

By the 1930s, Magritte had also painted some hybrid beings—like the human-fish combinates in *Collective Invention* (1934) (see figure 15.1)—discussed further in chapter 15. Wackyland is populated by such bizarre beings, as seen by the merging of cat and dog into one animal. Even some of Wackyland's curious residents (like a rubbery three-headed creature) are reminiscent of beings conceived by Magritte—as in *The Acrobat's Exercises* (1928).

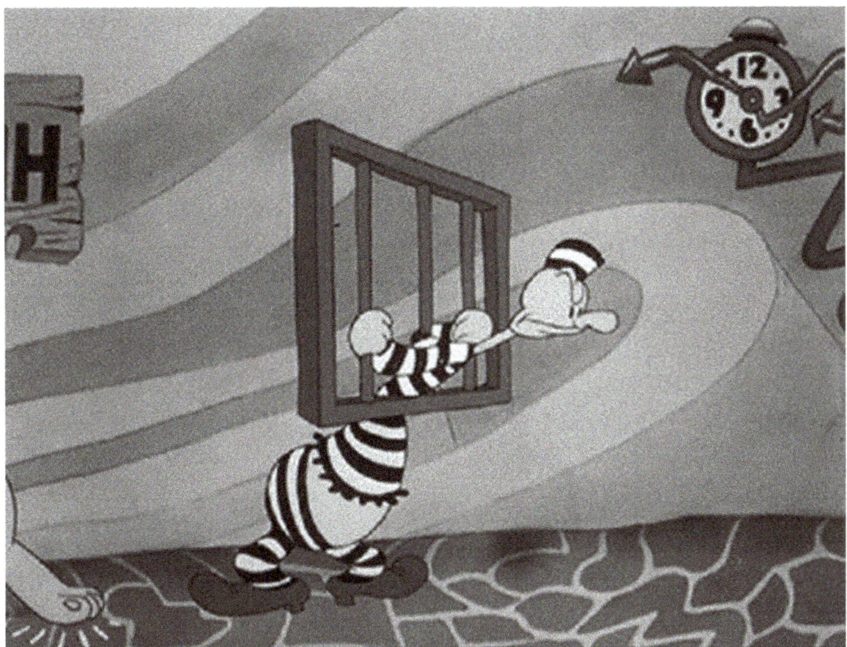

FIGURE 12.2. Like many of Magritte's unmoored objects, prison bars in *Porky in Wackyland* (Clampett, 1938) are not tethered to the ground.

One sequence in *Porky in Wackyland* even jokes with trompe l'oeil—the confusion between painted illusion and reality—much as Magritte had done in *The Human Condition* (1933) (see figure 8.1) and *Key to the Fields* (1936) (see figure 6.3). In that scene, the Dodo (chased by Porky) comes upon what looks like a cliff. We think he will have to jump, but instead he rolls up the landscape in front of him as though it were a theatrical backdrop—thereby changing it to flat terrain and solving his problem.

Finally, if one examines Magritte's output prior to the making of the Clampett film, we find a few paintings that seem consonant with the mise-en-scène of Wackyland—among them *The Oasis* (1926) (with its table in the midst of a landscape and its clouds within trees) and *The Roof of the World* (1926) (with its vein-covered mountains and its swiss cheese topography). We can only imagine the fun that Porky would have in navigating these geographies.

But most relevant to animation are Magritte's paintings from his so-called *vache* (cow) period—also called his nasty period (1947–48)—which have a decidedly cartoonish sensibility to them, with saturated color influenced by the Fauve movement. Evidently, in 1948, Magritte was invited to mount his first one-man Parisian show at the Galerie du Faubourg. By this time, however, he was resentful of the fact that it had taken so long for him to win recognition in France. In a rebellious act, he experimented with a brash new style for the exhibition—one that would be roundly rejected. According to Bernard Marcadé, the paintings treaded "a line between vulgarity and coarseness," and what characterized them was "their garish tones, their exuberant, grotesque and caricatured subjects, all executed rapidly and casually in the name of a freedom from aesthetic and moral injunctions and prescriptions."[4] This is evident in such works as *The Triumphal March* (1947), *The Pictorial Content* (1947), *The Ellipsis* (1948) (figure 12.3), and *Pom'po pom'po pon po pon* (1948).

Interestingly, *Porky in Wackyland* was later remade into the Technicolor *Dough for the Do-Do* (1949), a version that pays direct homage to Salvador Dalí (not Magritte)—with its desert setting, ancient columns and ruins, skeleton bones, and melting watches.

Although in the contemporary animation literature, there continue to be few references to Magritte, Dani Cavallaro, in a book on the Japanese director Hayao Miyazaki, mentions in passing similarities between the floating islands in *Laputa: Castle in the Sky* (1986) and Magritte's *The Castle of the Pyrenees* (1959) (see figure 14.3). However, Cavallaro fails to note an additional parallel between an image in the Miyazaki film and Magritte's *Almayer's Folly* (1951); both involve apparently organic material (with roots dangling) hovering in the sky. Furthermore, in discussing Miyazaki's later film, *Porco rosso* (1992), Cavallaro finds that its protagonist (a pig-man) bears some resemblance to the hybrid creature in Magritte's *A Stroke of Luck* (1945), discussed in chapter 15.[5]

I have mentioned only a few classic American cartoons—those suggested incidentally in passing in the literature on Magritte. But one suspects that if one surveyed the larger history of cartoons (American, European, and Asian), there might be found a huge number of parallels to Magritte's work—articulated in a comic rather than unsettling tone.

Independent/Experimental Cinema

While Warner Bros. cartoons like *Porky in Wackyland* were light cinematic fare that transformed Surrealist tropes into zany comedy, the animation created by Czech filmmaker Jan Švankmajer is experimental and Modernist and therefore more consonant with the movement's sensibility.

Švankmajer is a Surrealist cineaste who combines live action, claymation, pixilation, puppetry, and stop motion within his highly varied work. Born

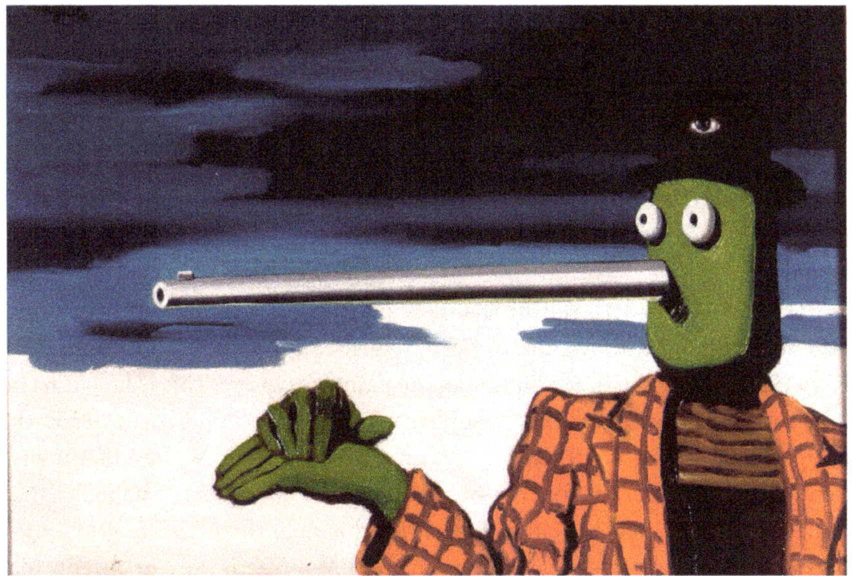

FIGURE 12.3. *The Ellipsis* (*L'ellipse*/*The Ellipse*) (1948)

in Prague in 1934, he studied at the College of Applied Arts and later in the Department of Puppetry at the Prague Academy of Performing Arts. His films are avant-garde in form and content, and he has made both short subjects (e.g., *Flora* [1989]) and features such as *Alice* (1988)—the latter a version of *Alice in Wonderland*. Like Magritte, he is a fan of Edgar Allan Poe and has adapted some of the latter's stories for the screen (e.g., *The Pendulum, The Pit and Hope* [1983]).

Many of Švankmajer works are somber and haunting. In *Dimensions of Dialogue* (1982), two claymation figures (male and female) continually decompose or get buried in mounds of clay. Finally, they attack each other and claw at their mate's eyes, face, and other body parts. In these bleak scenarios, we may be reminded of similarly gloomy works by Magritte in which bodies tear apart, such as *The Double Secret* (1927) (see figure 14.1).

At other times, Švankmajer's films are lighthearted and playful. This is how one writer in the *Guardian* describes *Food* (1992). The film "follows two ravenous diners as they are ignored by the waiter: they begin eating their own clothes down to the last item of their (old) underwear. . . . [T]hen systematically they work through the crockery, cutlery and the table until the older one of them eyes the younger, a more tender diner with a certain gleam in his eye."[6] Given that the items they consume include their shoes, there is a clear homage to the comedy of Charlie Chaplin's *The Gold Rush* (1925). But *The*

Gold Rush shares another theme with *Food*—cannibalism. In the upsetting elements of Švankmajer's *Food*, we also think of Magritte's *Girl Eating a Bird [Pleasure]* (1927), in which a young woman bites into the whole feathered creature; in its more comic aspects, we think of Magritte's amusing paintings like *Night in Pisa* (1953) or *Memory of a Journey* (1950) in which a spoon or a feather stabilizes the Leaning Tower of Pisa. Furthermore, in a 1929 drawing, within a shapeless blob are printed the words "A person breaking out laughing."

Given Švankmajer's self-proclaimed association with Surrealism, it can be assumed that he knows the work of Magritte. But in one of his films, *The Flat* (1968), there is a direct citation of the painter's oeuvre. This is how Caryn James of the *New York Times* describes its illogical plot: "A man becomes trapped in a room that practically devours him. He lies on a bed that turns to sawdust, incredibly, before our eyes. His clothes are suddenly nailed to the wall. The obvious heir to Kafka's Joseph K., this man is named Josef M., and his crime is simply to exist."[7] The homage to Magritte occurs as Joseph M. looks in a mirror and twice sees views of himself that defy the logic of point of view. In one case, he regards the back of his head (figure 12.4) and, in

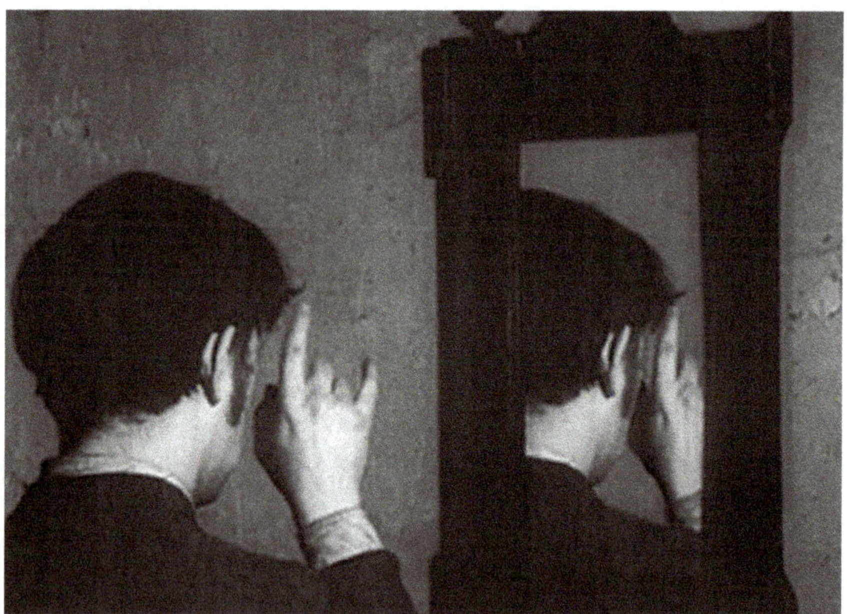

FIGURE 12.4. A man in Švankmajer's *The Flat* (1968) looks into a mirror and sees the back of his head, directly citing Magritte's *Not to Be Reproduced* (1937).

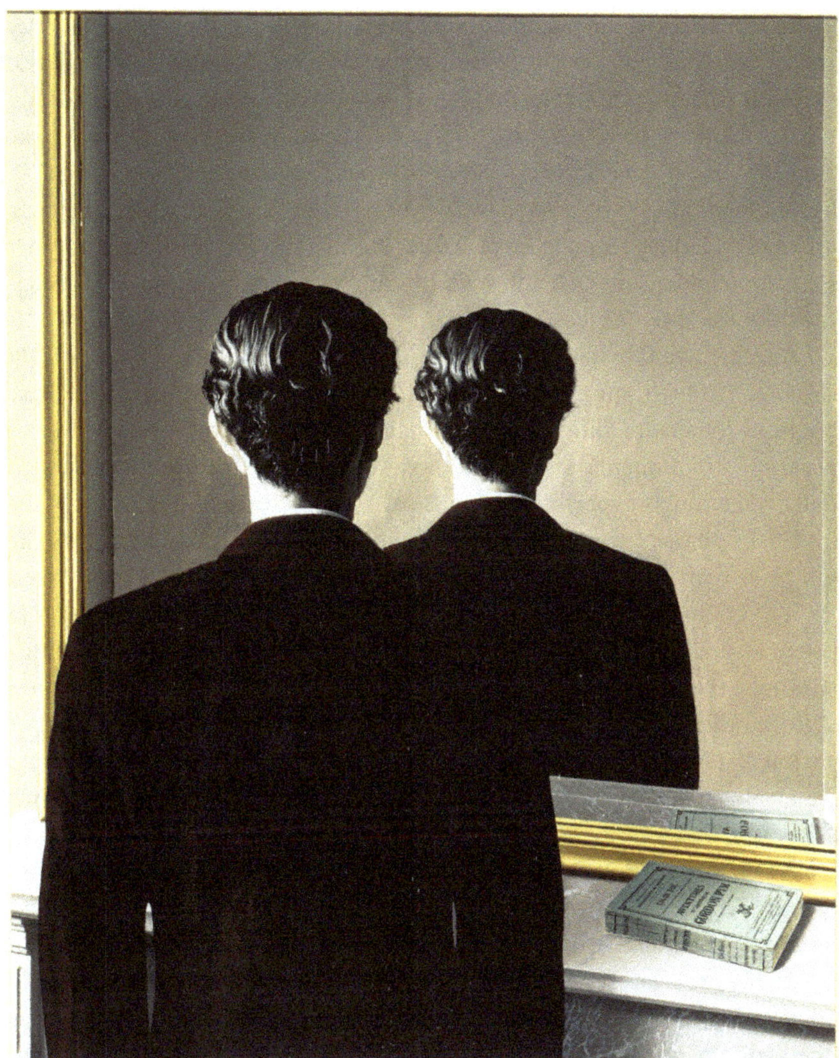

FIGURE 12.5. *Not to Be Reproduced* (*La reproduction interdite*/Portrait of Edward James) (1937)

the other, a frontal view impossible to have registered on the looking glass. The first instance quite boldly quotes Magritte's canvas *Not to Be Reproduced* (1937) (figure 12.5).

In other Švankmajer films, resonances of Magritte are less literal but still present. In *Johann Sebastian Bach* (1965), we are presented with a series of windows—a staple of Magritte's iconography. The first group that we see (as photographed from the outside of buildings) is realistic, though it frustrates our desire to peer inside. The second group, however, is more whimsical and nonsensical. In one case, the windows are removed from an edifice and stand isolated in space. Here we think of the freestanding windows in works like Magritte's *The Waking State* (1958), in which six unmoored windows hang in the sky. In another case, a window in Švankmajer's film is mounted against a brick wall—defying its purpose of presenting an open view. Similarly, another one is mounted against a blank wall. In both instances, we again recall Magritte's *The Blood-letting* (see figure 9.1).

Another Švankmajer film with intimations of Magritte is *Darkness Light Darkness* (1989) (figure 12.6). Here is how the Internet Movie Database describes its absurd plot: "A human body gradually reconstructs itself as its various component parts crowd themselves into a small room and eventually, after much experimentation, sort out which part goes where." The important phrase (from a Magrittian point of view) is "small room," as the film plays with scale in the manner of such canvases as *The Tomb of Wrestlers* (1960) and *The Listening Room* (1952), in which oversized objects (a rose or an apple) fill all the available space of a chamber. While in Magritte's paintings, the objects do not seem crammed into the room, in *Darkness Light Darkness*, the claymation man seems nearly crushed. We see another version of a Magrittian play with scale in *The Flat* when Joseph M. picks up a normal-sized glass of beer that turns into a miniature one when he puts it down.

Furthermore, in *A Quiet Week in the House* (1971), we have references to Magritte's interest in the peephole view (discussed in chapter 5), as well as to various other films that have dramatized this trope. As in *The Blood of a Poet* (1932), the protagonist of *A Quiet Week in the House* is a man who repeatedly looks through holes in doors to witness various strange occurrences on the other side. In one instance, the man sees a hanging suit jacket that, for no apparent reason, drips water.

There are also intimations in Švankmajer's films of some of Magritte's most favored objects. One such element is the rock, which appears in a number of the painter's works, including *The Glass Key* (1959).[8] Certainly, these are not common iconographic components of art, unless depicted as part of a landscape. Yet Švankmajer's *A Game with Stones* (1965) consists entirely of rocks. In some shots, a stone is simply pictured. But in others, it is linked, absurdly, to some incompatible object. Hence, a wall clock drops rocks into a bucket each time it chimes the hour. Similarly, a plumbing pipe incongruously seems to emit stones, as though it were blowing bubbles. Finally, in the

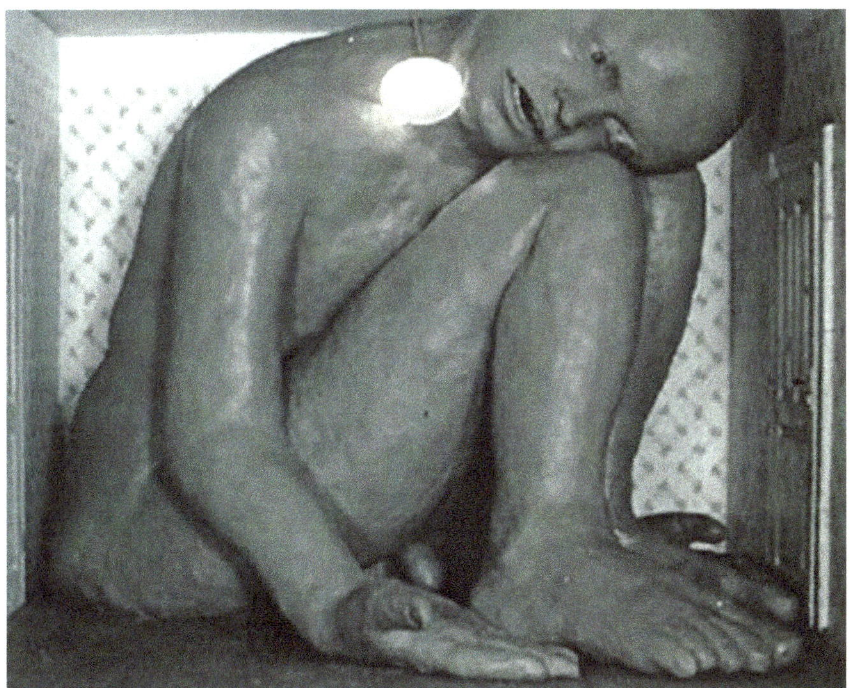

FIGURE 12.6. In *Darkness Light Darkness* (Švankmajer, 1989), an oversized human figure is squeezed into a tiny room, similar to the apple in Magritte's *The Listening Room* (1952).

same work, Švankmajer makes a more whimsical use of rocks by forming them into fossilized creatures that echo Magritte's interest in human and animal petrification.

Other Magrittian moments are more random and fleeting in Švankmajer's movies. In *Historia naturae* (1967), which catalogs various species in different biological classes (birds, reptiles, fish, mammals, simians, etc.), an image reveals two birds in a cage (the latter an object that Magritte often includes in his canvases). The next shot, however, shows the cage with a bird skeleton in it. The paradoxical quality of this image reminds us of Magritte's *Elective Affinities* in which a birdcage houses an egg. By showing a skeleton, Švankmajer pictures something that follows a bird's death, while Magritte depicts something that precedes its birth. Neither object, however, requires being caged.

Finally, in *The Flat*, there is a sequence in which a man lights a match at a gas stove, but instead of it sparking a fire, it unleashes a stream of water. Here we are reminded of the many Magritte paintings in which an article that should be nonflammable strangely bursts into flame—for example, the tuba in *La belle captive* (1947).

In Švankmajer's film, the situation is the opposite. Something flammable refuses to ignite. Clearly, Švankmajer's style, medium, tone, and iconography is quite different from Magritte's—though both men share a debt to Surrealism. Nonetheless, if one carefully peruses the Czech filmmaker's oeuvre, one finds passing intimations of the painter's sensibility that inform and deepen one's view of the work.

13

FACES AND MASKS

> In a recent painting, I have shown an apple in front of a person's face. At least it partially hides the face. . . . This process occurs endlessly. Each thing we see hides another, we always want to see what is being hidden by what we see.
>
> René Magritte[1]

THE FACE IS an iconic element of Magritte's art. However, unlike conventional painters, his versions of it are always strange or obfuscating in myriad different ways. In *The Pilgrim* and *The Road to Damascus* (both 1966), for instance, the face is separated from the rest of the body, hanging in midair. Similarly, in other works, elements of the head (noses, ears, eyes) are stranded in space without any unifying structure to support them. Here one thinks of *The White Race* (1937) or *Every Day* (1966). But perhaps Magritte's most favored perspective on the face is to *block it* in some fashion, as revealed in this chapter's epigraph. In certain works, he paints an individual with his back to the viewer (often one of his bowler-hatted men), as in *Pandora's Box* (1951), *The Siren's Song* (1952), *The Great Century* (1954), *The Schoolmaster* (1955), *Double Vision* (1957), *The Intimate Friend* (1958), *The Orphan Boy* (1958), and *Decalomania* (1966).

There is also an entire series of paintings in which objects (a bird, an apple, or a bouquet) are bizarrely positioned in front of the subject's face, obstructing the spectator's view of it. This is the case in *The Man in the Bowler Hat*, *The Son of Man* (discussed in chapter 3), and *The Great War* (all from 1964). Interestingly, as we have seen in chapter 2, in one of Magritte's "home movies," his wife, Georgette, holds a painting of herself in front of her face—simultaneously blocking it and calling attention to it.

Employing a parallel theme, Magritte in *The Invention of Life* (1928) covers one of his figures with a cloth. Likewise, in *The Lovers* (1928) (see figure 2.2), he conceals the heads of both of his subjects with sheets—perhaps creating a cynical statement on romance. He uses a similar motif in *The Central Story* (1928), in which fabric obscures a woman's visage.

Clearly, in all these examples, Magritte is creating uncanny scenarios as well as denying the viewer access to the subject. Beyond that, some have seen his shrouded figures as referring back to the death of his mother, who was pulled from a river with her face covered by her nightgown.

Certainly the paintings discussed are not technically "portraits," since that term generally signifies a work that reproduces the likeness of an *actual* person. Interestingly, however, critic Richard Brilliant has seen at least one of Magritte's creations as a veiled self-portrait—*Bauci's Landscape* (1966) (figure 13.1)—this despite its being nearly "faceless." While Magritte did render some traditional portraits, many were not. When he executed one of patron Edward James in *Not to Be Reproduced* (1937) (see figure 12.5), he did so with the subject's back to the viewer.[2] The one he created of Rena Schitz in 1937 depicts a female head and hand resting on a rectangular block.[3] In many such portraits, even while the face is painted realistically, the background is peculiar. In one of Thérèse Lambert from 1956, it consists of leaves the size of trees and a tiny person on horseback.

Even in painting "fictional" portraits, however, artists often not only strive to present a visible and realistic external image of an individual (a farmer, an aristocrat, a prostitute, etc.) but also to convey something of the character's inner life.[4] This is the same goal as portraiture which, as Shearer West has noted, is "about both body and soul."[5] In particular, the face has had a special role in this genre of painting, and West talks about individuals who pioneered the field of physiognomy (like Johann Caspar Lavater), advancing "the idea that the face reveals the soul."[6]

Of course, photography and cinema provided new tools for analyzing, categorizing, and appreciating facial expression. Here one need only think of a work like *The Passion of Joan of Arc* (1928), which almost entirely comprises facial close-ups. Early film theorist, Béla Balázs called this type of shot a "silent soliloquy" that revealed a person's "inner drama."[7] Even when an actor's expression was ambiguous, he viewed it as "a sort of physiognomic chord [through which] a variety of feelings, passions and thoughts are synthesized in the play of the features as an adequate expression of the multiplicity of the

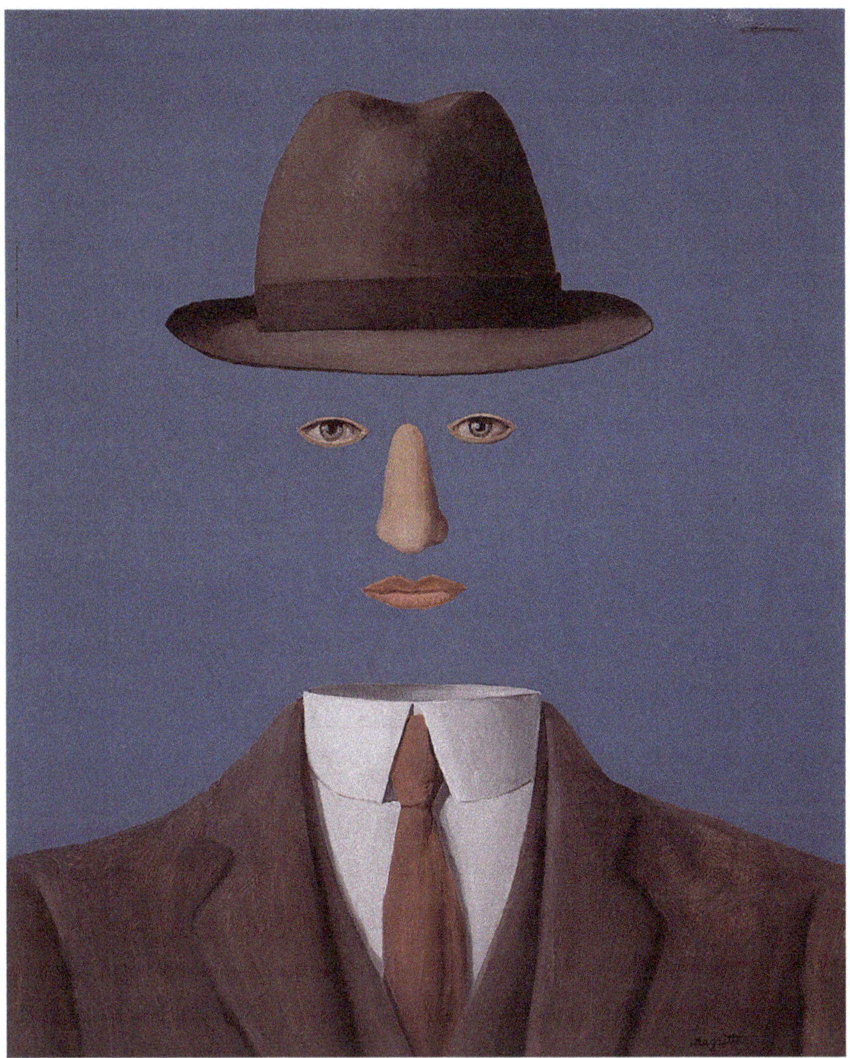

FIGURE 13.1. *Bauci's Landscape* (*Le paysage de Bauci*) (1966)

human soul."[8] As Jacques Aumont demonstrates, a similar point of view was evident as early as 1916, in writings of Hugo Munsterberg.[9]

The face continued to have a prominent place in film criticism, with some writers waxing poetic on the countenance of certain stars, such as Roland Barthes on the face of Garbo.[10] In recent years, there has been a spate of books entirely devoted to the topic. As Noa Steimatsky writes in *The Face on Film*: "Even if not named as such, the face is operative in a great deal of film criticism and theory, and it reasserts itself with the tides of cinematic practice."[11] Furthermore, she claims that the face on screen is "both a compelling iconographic and discursive nexus and a way of seeing, a critical lens, a mode of thought."[12] Nonetheless, she admits that "even for iconophiles and cinephiles, the visuality of the face is, in fact, equivocal. While we take it to be the most nuanced register of an inner life, the face is also sensed as a barrier."[13] Other recent books on the subject are also skeptical about the power of the photographed human countenance. Therese Davis's *The Face on the Screen: Questions of Death, Recognition and Public Memory* argues that the face in contemporary media (talking heads, star photos, images of the dead) has become so ubiquitous that it is often banal. Furthermore, the authentic human face "has been eclipsed by the spectacle of computer-generated effects, such as morphing."[14]

Thus, in the contemporary era, notions of the meaning of the face have changed, and the face is seen as far less transparently revelatory of an individual's persona than in the past. As filmmaker Eric Rohmer once asked: "Doesn't a troubled face betray some interior emotion? Yes, it is a sign, but an arbitrary sign, as it denies the powers of falsity and greatly shrinks the limits of the invisible world to which it proudly refers."[15] Paul Coates's *Screening the Face*, a book about the face in film, shares Rohmer's sense that the human countenance is highly ambiguous and often "masks" an alternate persona than that which its surface seems to project.[16]

In this regard, Hans Belting's *Face and Mask: A Double History* is especially useful, as it sees the human visage as not entirely individual but instead constructed by social forces.[17] In claiming this, Belting draws upon the work of Émile Durkheim, who conceived the self as partially a performed cultural role.[18] Thus, for Belting, a "person is the actor of his own face."[19] Here Brilliant's thoughts on Magritte's *Bauci's Landscape* are telling. As he notes: "The artist's metaphysical concept addresses the process of becoming a person rather than the attainment of a fixed state of being. This allows Magritte to comment on the way in which identity is given to a person from the outside and to modify the conception of a visible likeness, so long tied to the idea of portraiture."[20] Belting also points out how there is no analysis of the face without a discussion of the mask. We must, he says, "accept face and mask as a single theme in the organizing principle of a 'history of the face,' and not view these concepts in sharp contrast to one another."[21] Thus, he sees facial communication as both disclosing and obscuring. As he asserts, "The expressive achievement of the living face lies as much in its ability to show and proclaim as in its ability to conceal and deceive."[22]

Clearly, in Magritte's use of objects to hide the face, he is questioning the truth-value of gazing at (and deciphering) the human countenance. However, in certain works, he goes beyond this to portray subjects wearing actual masks. Thus, he takes a metaphor utilized by theorists of the face and turns it into a physical object. In *The Intelligence* (1946), masks are worn by men who resemble criminals. And in *The Married Priest* (1960), as a joke, they appear on two apples—objects that have no eyes and can never display a personality. Furthermore, in *The Sage's Carnival* (1947) (figure 13.2), one appears on a beautiful, young naked damsel—seemingly a contradiction in terms. Of course, there is also Magritte's love of Fantômas, a mask-wearing villain.

Beyond speaking figuratively about masks, Belting also "investigates material ones." As he comments, "Face and mask can each be understood as an image that appears on a surface, whether that surface be natural skin or an imitation made from some inert material."[23] Speaking of the type of mask depicted in Magritte's paintings, he notes, "The half mask, which leaves a portion of the face visible, demonstrates the fluid transition between face and mask."[24]

It is interesting that Belting briefly references film in his discussion of facial expression, but not by citing Balázs, Munsterberg, or the close-up. Rather, he mentions Lev Kuleshov's well-known editing "effect." As he writes, the director proved that "one could produce facial expression with montage alone."[25] Famously, of course, Kuleshov utilized the same expressionless facial close-up of the actor Ivan Mosjoukine juxtaposed with shots of various things (e.g., a bowl of soup, a girl in a coffin, a woman on a divan). In each case, viewers imagined that Mosjoukine was expressing different emotions—hunger, grief, or desire, respectively. Here we think of Eisenstein's critique of Balázs for "forgetting the scissors" in his discussion of the role of the face in film.[26]

In Magritte's fascination with masks we are also reminded of another film theorist—André Bazin, who conceived the film frame not as a window onto the world but as a "mask" that blotted out everything beyond its borders while, simultaneously, leaving access to those realms through a slight camera movement. As he writes: "The screen is not a frame like that of a picture but a mask which allows only a part of the action to be seen. When a character moves off screen, we accept the fact that he is out of sight, but he continues to exist in his own capacity at some other place in the decor which is hidden from us."[27] Clearly, this is a *different* sense of the term *mask* than that which Magritte employed, and it only makes sense as a comparison between the "porous" film frame and the fixed frame of a painting that borders on nothing but the gallery wall. Neither does it involve masking in Magritte's bodily sense. Nonetheless, it

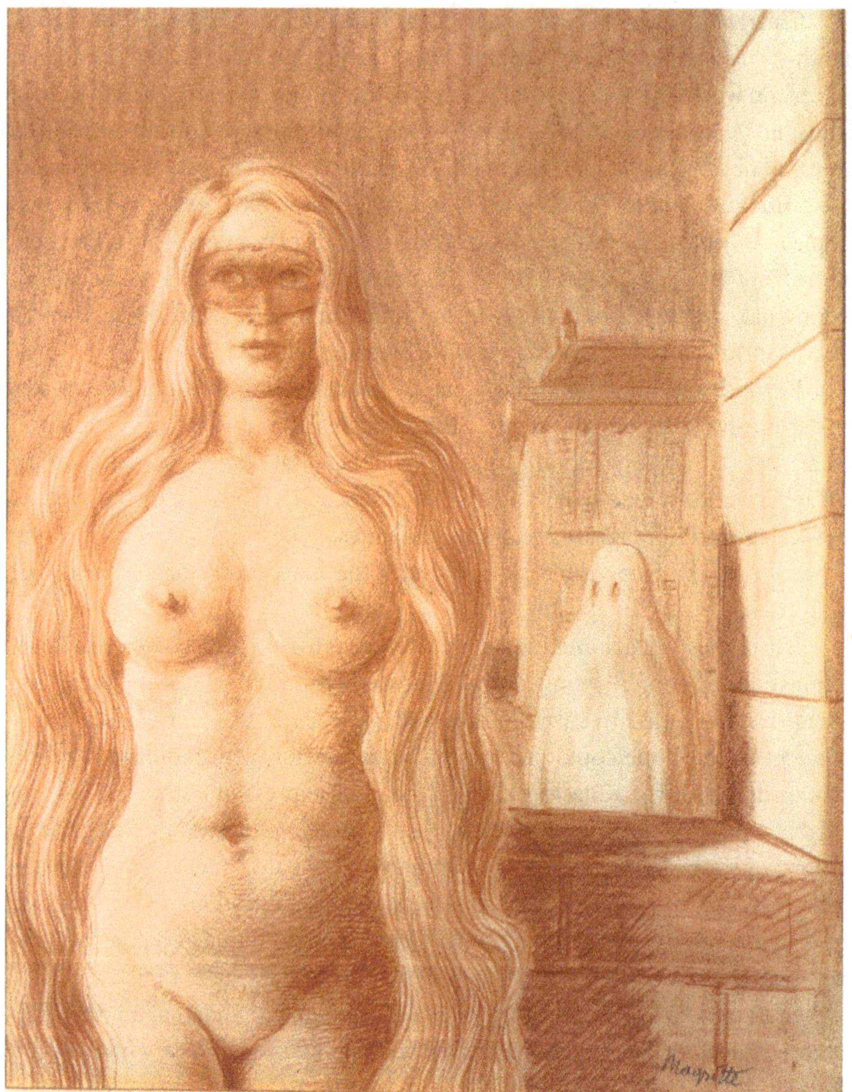

FIGURE 13.2. *The Sage's Carnival* (*Le carnaval du sage*) (1947)

does connote a tension between that which is visible and not, as well as invoke the discourse of film theory.

Several other paintings by Magritte on the subject of the face are more disturbing than the ones already noted. In *He Is Not Speaking* (1926), a plaster mask is posed before a woman's face. While her eyes are open, the mask's are closed, which makes it seem like a molded death mask. Here, of course, we are reminded of Magritte's *The Future of Statues* (1937), a literal death mask of Napoleon. In *The Face of a Genius* (1926), we have what appears to be the identical mask as in *He Is Not Speaking*, now standing alone, with parts of it dissected to reveal Magritte's familiar bilboquet.

Significantly, Magritte also used the mask as icon in his commercial advertising work, as is evident in graphics for the fashion house Maison Norine (from 1924 and 1925), in which the mask functions either as part of an outfit or background.[28] Furthermore, he employed it in several of his amateur movies. As stated earlier, in *Tuba* a woman dons a red mask as she lies in bed. In a later shot, Magritte himself wears it (see figure 2.5). In another amateur film image (not previously discussed), Magritte reclines with his eyes closed in a bed (next to a white bloodstained plaster female bust) as a series of grotesquely masked people file by.

The mask has a long history in cinema as an aspect of costume and narrative. Sometimes it has had a rather innocuous or even joyful valence, as when characters attend a masked ball. This is certainly the case in Cecil B. DeMille's *Madam Satan* (1930), in which a jilted wife goes to a party incognito and attracts her unknowing husband. Here her jeweled mask and risqué outfit make her sexy and alluring in a way that she has not seemed before.

A more emphatic and resonant use of the mask occurs in Max Ophüls's *Le plaisir* (1952), an "anthology" film that combines three short stories by Guy de Maupassant through the voice-over of a narrator (Jean Servais) who tells the tales and stands in for the author. The first narrative is fittingly titled "The Mask" and takes place at a dance hall. Utilizing Ophüls's signature moving camera, the opening sequence communicates both the energy of the frenetic dancers as well as that of the apparatus itself, creating a mood of gaiety and vivaciousness. Sprinting into the group comes a man that the staff knows as Monsieur Ambroise (Paul Azaïs). He enthusiastically joins in the dancing, spinning around with his partner at great speed. We immediately notice something strange about his face, which has a white, plastic appearance to it and an expression that does not change. Underscoring this, the narrator tells us that he looked like a figure from a wax museum—adding a sense of the uncanny to an otherwise realistic narrative. Soon the man collapses, and a doctor (who is at the ball) is asked to examine him. To do so, the physician (Claude Dauphin) must cut away the man's tight clothing and remove what is shown to be a facial mask (figure 13.3). When the latter is detached, the visage of an old man is disclosed. The doctor takes him home and learns from his wife that the man was a lothario and bon vivant in his youth and that he now tries to recapture that experience by attending dances while masquerading as a young dandy. At various points in the narrative, we see the mask again (on a seat in a carriage, hung on a chair in the man's home), and it seems almost like a decapitated head.

Clearly, this tale concerns the tragedy of aging as well as the pain that comes to those who do not accept its progress. But, in utilizing the mask as a way of signaling this issue, the film adds a disturbing and Surreal element. Beyond that, it draws upon a symbol used by Magritte to announce the gap between surface and interior, between human appearance and psychological depth. While the other two stories in the film do not utilize the figure of the mask, they both deal with hypocrisy (or "two facedness"). "The House of Tellier" concerns a brothel to which a town's upstanding male citizens secretly go on a regular basis. "The Model" relates the story of an artist who seduces a beautiful young woman and then, inexplicably, loses interest in her, thus highlighting the duplicity of love.

But the cinematic use of masks most relevant to Magritte's eerie canvases occurs in the horror film, a genre quite removed from Ophüls's romance. In *The Abominable Dr. Phibes* (Robert Fuest, 1971), for instance, the mad protagonist gives someone a decorative mask that eventually kills him by crushing his skull. In more recent years, George Romero made *Bruiser* (2000), in which a man's face is mysteriously replaced by a white mask that seems to liberate his id. While *Bruiser* is a good visual "match" for Magritte's art, it is not a successful film—entirely too obvious in its symbolism and devoid of frisson.

However, several classic horror films engage the theme of masks in a far more profound and frightful fashion. Perhaps most famous is *The Phantom of the Opera*—based on a novel by 1910 Gaston Leroux. The original movie version was made in 1925, just a year before Magritte's *The Face of a Genius* and *He Is Not Speaking* were painted. Directed by Rupert Julian, it stars Lon Chaney as Erik, the opera phantom—a ghostly recluse who lives in the basement and captures and holds hostage a lovely young singer whom he adores. When the woman first sees him, he is wearing a mask that covers the lower portion of his face. But in a shocking scene, she rips it off to reveal his deformed countenance. But there is a second mask in *The Phantom* that Erik wears when he attends a masquerade party—a scene that Julian shot in lush color. Here we are reminded of the conventional use of masks as a festive mode of playing with identity—but for Erik, it offers the only occasion for him to appear normal. Clearly, he does not have the luxury to put the mask on or take it off at will. Ironically, however, rather than sport a cheerful mask, his is skeletal—perhaps even more disturbing than the face beneath it.

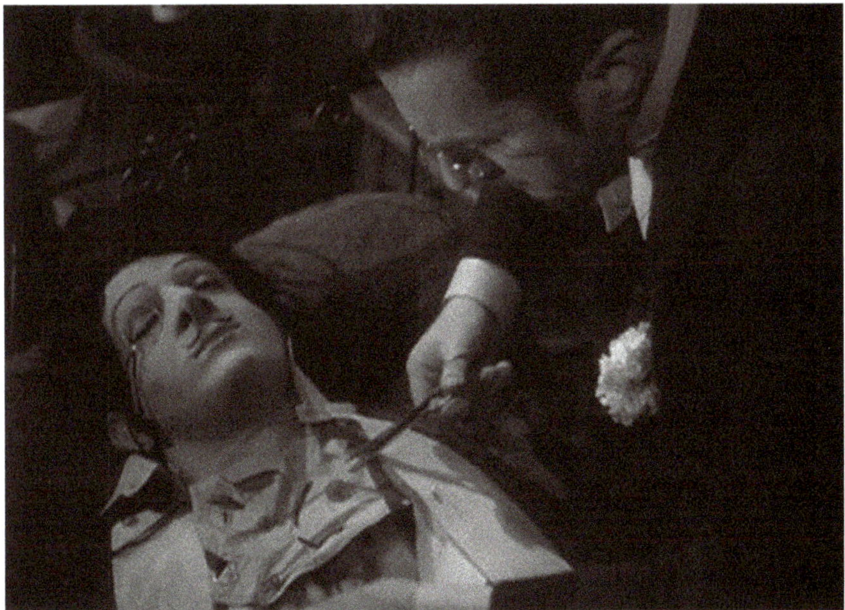

FIGURE 13.3. In *Le plaisir* (Ophüls, 1952), a doctor removes the facial mask of a dancer who has collapsed, revealing a much older man than he had appeared to be.

In Magritte's art, the mask often bears the specter of impending death. Similarly, in *The Phantom*, it hides not only disfigurement but also "mortification of the flesh" since Erik's face seems to be decaying before our eyes. He is not far from the figure of the vampire—who travels among the undead. Here Julian's style draws heavily from German Expressionism—a trend that influenced world cinema beginning with the debut of Robert Wiene's *The Cabinet of Dr. Caligari* in 1920.

But Magritte is, of course, a Surrealist, and there are two highly relevant films in that vein that also articulate a disturbing discourse of the mask—both by Georges Franju. The first is *Eyes without a Face*—made in France in 1960. Franju was highly influenced by Surrealism and, as Raymond Durgnat has noted, "is heir to Appolinaire, Cocteau and Breton."[29] Franju's earlier documentary, *Blood of the Beasts* (1949), shot in a slaughterhouse, has long been considered in the lineage of Luis Buñuel's *Land without Bread* (1933) as a work that reveals the strangeness and brutality of everyday life.

Eyes without a Face (a title that seems reminiscent of the subject of several of Magritte's canvases) tells the story of a physician, Doctor Génessier (Pierre Brasseur), who experiments with skin grafts. When his daughter, Christiane

(Edith Scob), is injured in a car accident that he has caused, he dedicates himself to surgically fixing her mutilated face. To do this, however, he requires the skin of another woman who resembles his daughter to transplant onto Christiane (thus anticipating future actual medical procedures). With the help of his assistant, Louise (Alida Valli), women are lured to his clinic, anesthetized, and operated on against their will. All the while, the doctor pretends to others that Christiane is dead.

Christiane is depressed and can bear neither for people to see her nor to view herself in a mirror. Significantly, when we first observe her, she is lying on a bed with her head buried in a pillow—barring us access to her face. To allay her daily embarrassment, she is given a white mask to wear that is molded to her features with cutouts for her eyes (figure 13.4)—somewhat similar to Georgette Magritte's act of holding up a painting of her face before her visage. As Durgnat describes it, Christiane is "flayed alive beneath her pearly mask."[30] Because the mask is not grotesque and so closely conforms to her pretty face, it has an especially uncanny aura to it—as though it were a real but pathologically opaque and unexpressive countenance. Eerily, when she speaks, her lips do not move.

But Christiane's is not the only mask in the film. During the surgeries that Dr. Génessier performs, both he and Louise both wear surgical ones—seen in tight close-ups. Furthermore, Louise has previously gone through the doctor's facial transplant operation, so ostensibly she would have once worn a mask

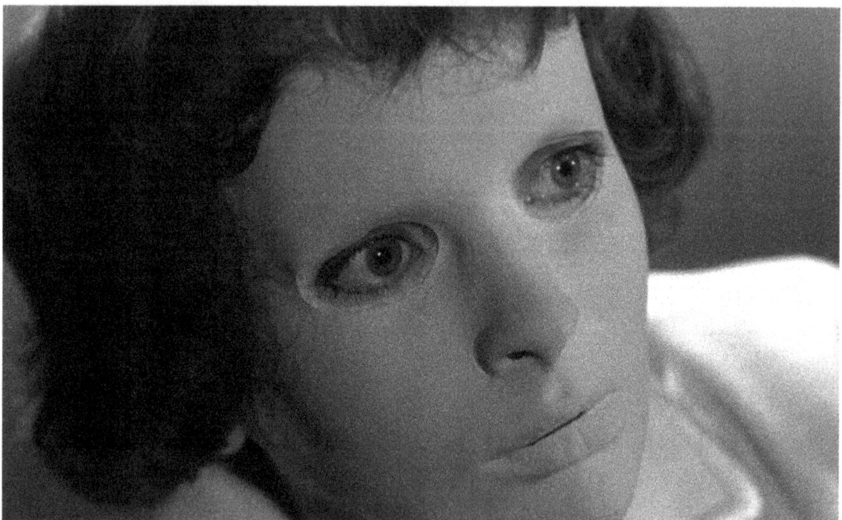

FIGURE 13.4. In *Eyes without a Face* (Franju, 1960), Christiane (Edith Scob) wears a white mask to hide her mutilated face.

like Christiane's to hide her injured face. Finally, the kidnapped woman whose face Dr. Génessier removes to transplant on Christiane is later shown with her head wrapped in mask-like bandages.

There are several especially graphic scenes in the film that reveal the horrors of Dr. Génessier's clinic. In one, we get a blurred glimpse of Christiane's real face without the mask, and at this moment *Eyes without a Face* approaches the famous scene in *The Phantom of the Opera* when Erik's true appearance is unveiled. Another one occurs after Dr. Génessier has performed a skin graft on his daughter. At first, Christiane's face looks perfectly fine, but as time progresses it seems gradually to become marred and mutilated. Here we are reminded of Magritte's *An End of Contemplation* (1927), in which a person's head seems to shred. A similar motif is also found in his painting *Polar Light* (1926–27), in which destruction affects the entire body.

But the most dreadful scene of all (and one that allegedly caused some audiences to faint) is that in which Dr. Génessier performs surgery on a woman that he has kidnapped. In great detail, we see him outline, cut, and then remove the epidermis of her face and separate it from her head (figure 13.5). Here we have the sense that, as humans, we are all born wearing masks in the form of flesh that covers our cheekbones, nose, and mouth.

Aside from a Surrealist interest in masks, there is one other detail of *Eyes without a Face* that seems reminiscent of Magritte's iconography. Dr. Génessier's

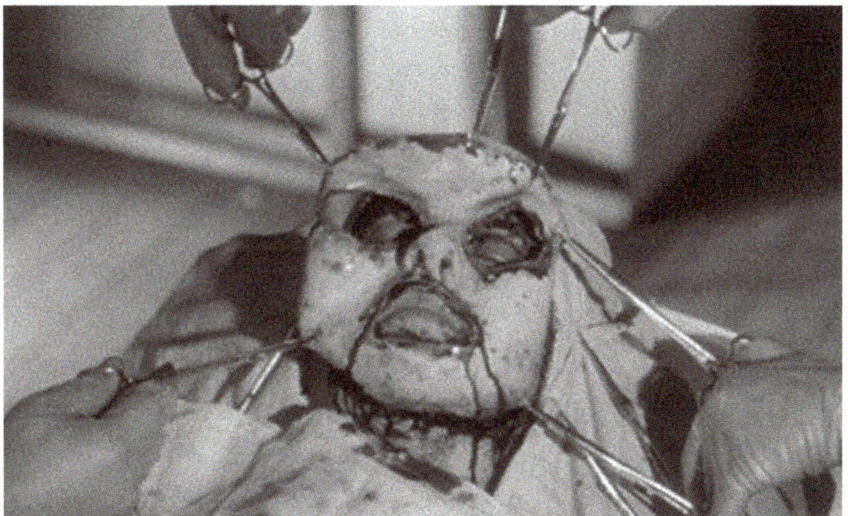

FIGURE 13.5. A surgery is performed in *Eyes without a Face* (Franju, 1960) that removes the skin from a woman's face.

clinic abounds with animals—familiar subjects in the artist's work. Dogs bark ominously offscreen throughout the film, and in a few scenes we see them confined in kennels, ready for experimental use. We also see a decorative metal birdcage in both Christiane's bedroom and the clinic basement, and it is not clear whether its inhabitants are pets or future scientific subjects. At the end of the film, after Christiane has suffered another unsuccessful skin graft, she loses all hope and begins to conceive herself as a prisoner in her home—an investigative specimen like her father's creatures. After stabbing Louise (who has procured yet another unsuspecting woman for a new operation), she frees the birds.

As we know, Magritte often included birds and cages in his image system. In *The Return* (1940), a bird made of clouds flies in the sky. In *Evening Peace* (1942), birds seem to grow from the ground like plants (while simultaneously looking like stone). In *Clairvoyance* (1936) (see figure 20.15), an artist paints a picture of a bird, and in *The Healer* (1937) a man's torso is replaced by a birdcage. Some of Magritte's paintings focus specifically on women and birds, which bring us closer to the plot of *Eyes without a Face*. In perhaps the most disquieting of all such pictures—(*Girl Eating a Bird* [*Pleasure*], 1927)—a woman eats her prey (which may still be alive), feathers and all.

But it is another series of pictures that seem closest to the Franju film. In *Black Magic*, (1934), a woman (whose upper half is tinted the color of the sky) stands with a white bird on her shoulder, and in *The Break in the Clouds* (1942), among three women seen from the rear, one holds a bird. Finally, in *Deep Waters* (1941), a lady with a white mask-like sculptural face stands next to a large bird. Her closed eyes, her dark outfit, and the black bird all have intimations of death. On some level, all of these paintings are evocative of shots from the end of *Eyes without a Face*, in which Christiane (wearing her mask) is posed with birds. They are also reminiscent of photographs of Georgette Magritte posed with birds.

Masks must have been on Franju's mind even after completing *Eyes without a Face*, because in 1963 he released *Judex*, a remake of the opening episodes of a five-hour 1916 serial by Louis Feuillade—a favorite filmmaker of Magritte. In fact, in one shot of the film, we see a detective reading a Fantômas book, reminding us of Magritte's cherished hero.

We are told early on that the name *Judex* means "the avenger," and, indeed, the plot will revolve around retribution—specifically against the banker M. Favraux (Michel Vitold), whose fortune was built on a scandal and whose selfish and cruel attitude to people has earned him lifelong enemies. In the first scene, in fact, we see a vagabond (who Favraux had promised money for silence years ago but allowed to languish in prison). This man will later prove to be an ally to Judex. The plot is ignited as soon as Favraux receives a letter from Judex threatening to kill him unless he repents and turns over his income to the sender who will share it with the banker's victims.

Judex is set in Belle Époque Paris and opens with elaborate title cards bordered by Art Nouveau graphic frames. There is an Art Nouveau telephone on Favraux's desk, and later on, the villains hide in a highly ornate Art Nouveau mansion (mirroring the use of such design in the original movie). This is significant because in a recorded interview Franju said that *Judex* was "a purely decorative film and presents itself as such," as does Art Nouveau.[31]

While masks in *Judex* are not generally as disturbing as in *Eyes without a Face*, they bear a quality of mystery and magic. Though there is no one obviously masked in the first scene of the film, there is an older man, M. Vallières (Channing Pollock), an assistant to M. Favraux, whom we immediately sense as strange looking. There is something about his head, beard, and hair which remind us of a bird. We will later learn that his present look is a disguise and that he is really Judex. But our sense of an avian quality to M. Vallières is not without import, since it will have implications for the kind of mask that Judex later wears to M. Favraux's costume party.

When Judex finally appears as himself in the film, he sports a black suit, cape, and hat, as do all his cohorts. While they are masked, Judex is often not. Like Judex, the villainess of the drama, Marie Verdier (Francine Bergé) is a bundle of disguises. She works as a governess for Favraux's granddaughter but is actually out to scam him. Furthermore, she has two names (her real one being Diana Monti). When she takes on the villainess role, she abandons her normal dress and wears a tight black bodysuit, as does her lover and fellow criminal, Morales (Théo Sarapo). Moreover, at one point in the film she camouflages herself with a nun's habit.

When she meets her demise, it is in a manner reminiscent of silent film serials. Masked and dressed in black, she hangs from the roof of a building—only to lose her grip and fall to her death. Significantly, in another nod to silent film thrillers, Judex's men crawl up the side of the building like spiders.

There are other elements of *Judex* that remind us of Magritte, including the use of a keyhole matte (when a detective that Favraux has hired spies on some maids in the house) and the quotations from *Alice in Wonderland*. Magritte, of course, titled one of his 1946 paintings after Lewis Carroll's famous book. In it, a tree masquerades as a person and seems to wear a mask made by the foliage that grows upon its trunk and circles its "eyes."

Furthermore, there is a Magrittian confusion of life and death in *Judex*: M. Favraux apparently dies and is buried only to be revived by the hero who imprisons him; similarly, his daughter, Jacqueline (Edith Scob), is tossed off a bridge and floats in the water, seemingly dead, only to be rejuvenated. Here, in particular, we recall Magritte's painting *The Musings of a Solitary Walker* (1926), which depicts a corpse and a river and has been seen to invoke the drowning death of his mother.

But, of course, the pièce de résistance of disguise in the film is the masquerade party that M. Favraux throws in honor of his twenty-year banking history as well as his daughter's engagement. Unbeknownst to him, Judex attends, wearing a frightening eagle hood (whose feathers trail gracelessly down his back) and proceeds to execute a series of incredible magic tricks that make doves appear from scarves (figure 13.6). All this is not original to the 1916 serial but is Franju's own invention. (In Judex's magic show, we recall Magritte's love of prestidigitation and of Méliès, discussed in chapter 16.) All the other guests wear elaborate masks, too (creating the kind of "human-animal hybrids" that I discuss in more detail in chapter 15). Furthermore, immediately in front of the Favraux mansion is a statue of a mythical creature with a human head and animal legs. Significantly, in speaking of Feuillade's earlier film *Fantômas* (1913), Franju discusses the hero's costume and opines that hoods "equal horror."[32] It is no less so in *Judex*.

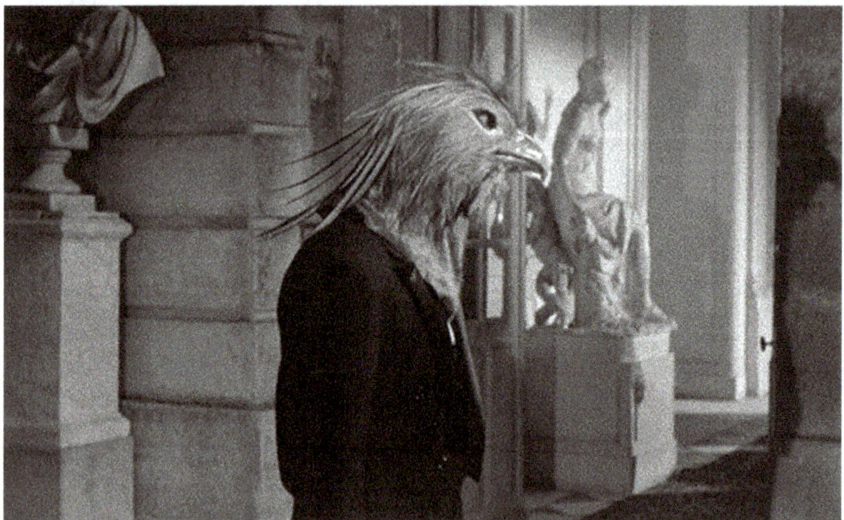

FIGURE 13.6. Judex (Channing Pollock) appears in a bird hood to attend a masquerade party in Franju's 1963 film of the same name.

Interestingly, in a filmed interview Franju speaks of his Surrealist roots and his love of painters like Max Ernst and Giorgio de Chirico.[33] He does not mention Magritte, but in his focus on magic, mystery, and masks, we cannot help but think that the two artists are profoundly simpatico.

In *Eyes without a Face*, the surgical process for which Dr. Génessier is known is called a heterograft—ostensibly the merging of one type of material with a different one. In a sense, we can see this dynamic at work in Magritte's career as well—as images move from the cinema to his canvas and back again to the screen.

14

SCIENCE FICTION

> Though the existence of gravity is proved by the laws that influence all bodies, what may trigger an aesthetic emotion seems not to exist except in man's imagination, and is created by him out of nothing.
>
> René Magritte[1]

THERE ARE INTIMATIONS of science fiction in numerous Magritte works, some menacing and others playful. Among the former is *The Double Secret* (1927) (figure 14.1), which depicts two parts of a disintegrating head. The section on the left has been sliced off the face's surface, while the one on the right shows the head's synthetic interstices as though it belonged to an android. In this figure, we are reminded of the subgenre of science-fiction film that deals with artificial humans. The uncanny thing about such creatures is that on the surface they look like people, but on the inside they are shown to be manmade. As critic Despina Kakoudaki has noted, in such movies a pivotal scene occurs when the mechanical "viscera" of the creature is revealed—a moment that may signal its imminent destruction.[2] Here we think of a scene in James Cameron's *Terminator 2: Judgment Day* (1991), in which the robot's face begins to open up (like the right head in Magritte's *The Double Secret*). An even more horrifying occurrence takes place in Alex Garland's *Ex Machina* (2015) (figure 14.2). In that movie, a humanoid automaton peels away her facial skin to uncover her mechanical innards.

All these images produce the uncanny sense that even the human epidermis functions as some kind of guise that hides a dark and mysterious interior.

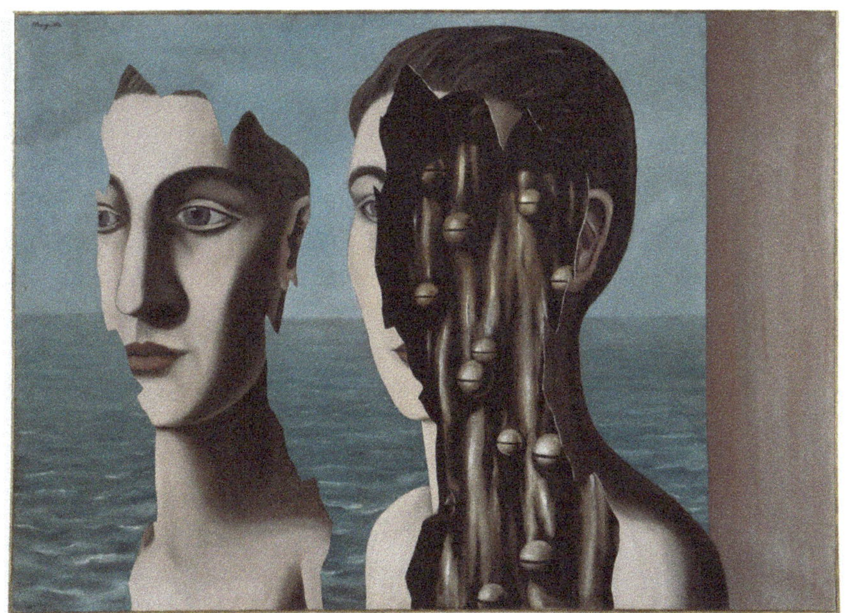

FIGURE 14.1. *The Double Secret* (*Le double secret/The Secret Double*) (1927)

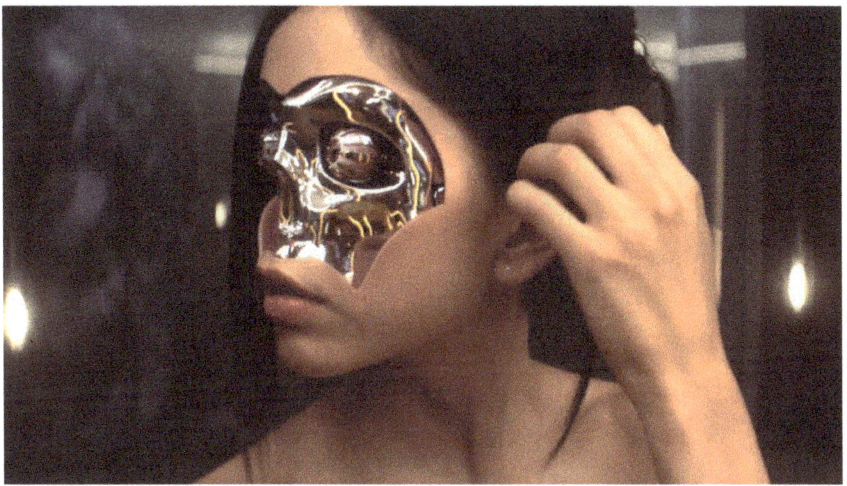

FIGURE 14.2. A humanoid robot in *Ex Machina* (Garland, 2015) tears away the "skin" from her face to reveal the mechanism inside her.

In keeping with this, there is a scene in *Ex Machina* in which one of the artificial females walks past a wall on which are hanging a series of masks used as prototypes for robot visages. She stops by one that resembles herself. In the film, after seeing so many androids that can pass for humans, a young man begins to suspect that he is a robot, too. In one shot, he tries to rip the skin away from his eye; in another, he cuts his arm to see if he bleeds.

In yet another scene, we see a series of dormant female robots hanging in a closet, as though they were pieces of clothing. Here we are reminded of Magritte's *Philosophy in the Boudoir* (1947), in which a woman's dress is draped on a hanger but has two breasts protruding; thus, it merges animate and inanimate elements (as does a pair of shoes with human toes in *The Red Model* [1935]).

While these Magritte works are rather "heavy" references to science fiction, the artist also presents "light" ones. As part of his construction of an alternative universe, he toys with the laws of nature—subverting them at will. One of the more fascinating ways in which he does this is by negating the pull of gravity. Interestingly, as the chapter epigraph reveals, he cites the latter as the complete opposite of artistic inspiration (which is unburdened rather than bogged down).

Of course, the word *gravity* has two meanings, and both are important in Magritte's oeuvre. On one level, it signifies a rule of physics regarding "the force that attracts a body toward the center of the earth, or toward any other physical body having mass." On a more metaphorical plane, however, it means "seriousness"—a frame of mind Magritte frequently contests (he once remarked, "I love subversive humour").[3] In different paintings, he draws upon one or the other sense of the term.

In *The Force of Circumstance* (1958), he engages both by comically portraying a baguette and wineglass gliding through the sky. In *The Voice of the Air* (1928) (see figure 18.1), however, oversized bells cluster in the ether like alien spacecrafts, and the effect is more disarming. Finally, in *The Active Voice* (1951), *Clear Ideas* (1958), *Castle in the Pyrenees* (1959) (figure 14.3), *The Battle of Argonne* (1959), *The Secret Agreement* (1962 or 1963), *Zeno's Arrow* (1964), and *A Sense of Reality* (1963), in which Magritte depicts free-floating boulders, the result is rather ominous given the weight of the objects represented.

Significantly, there are resonances of Magritte's untethered boulders in two recent science-fiction films that deal with outer space. In James Cameron's *Avatar* (2009), one of the geographical anomalies of the interstellar world of Pandora is its Magrittian "floating mountains" (figure 14.4) (now reproduced

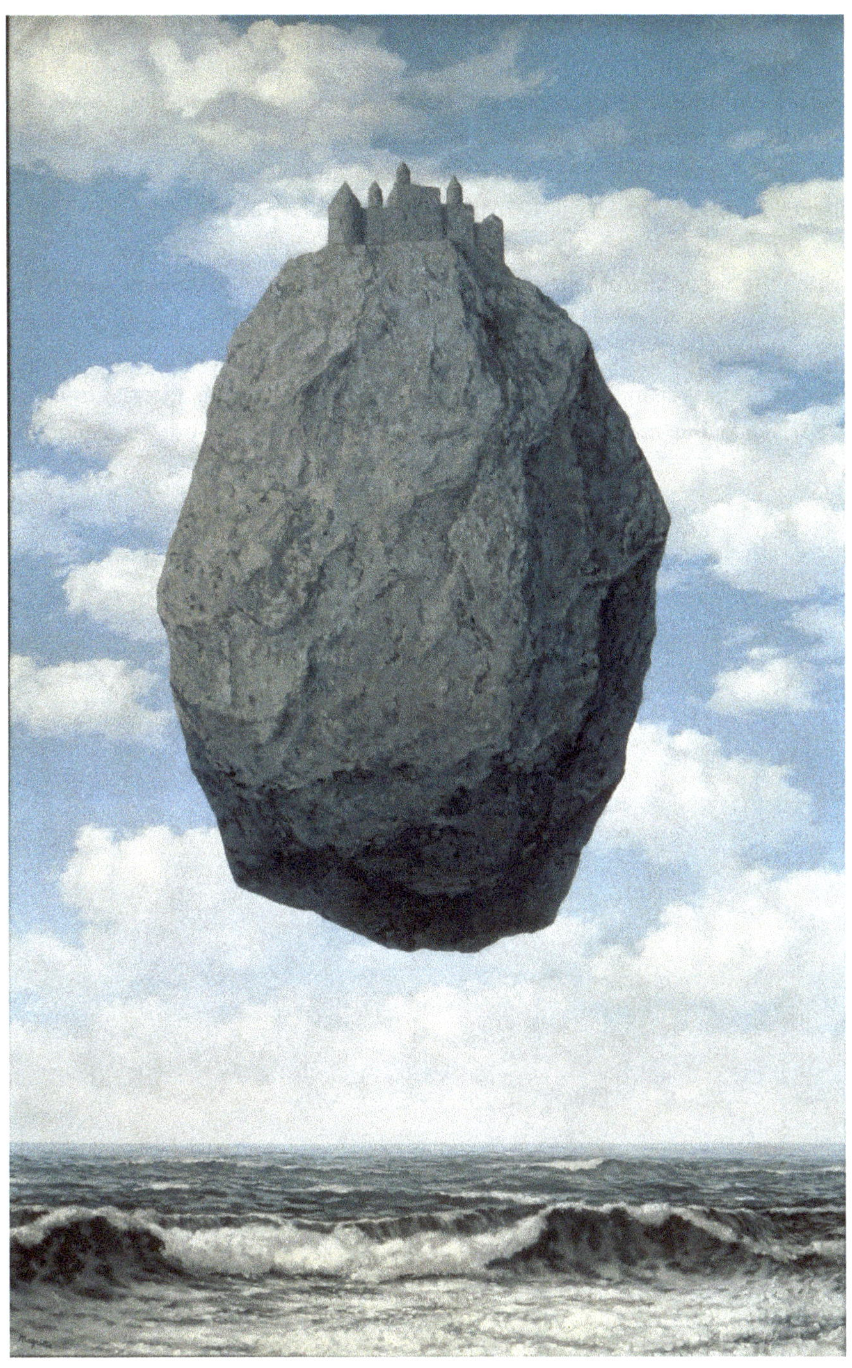

FIGURE 14.3. *Castle in the Pyrenees* (*Le château des Pyrénées*) (1959)

in three dimensions at a Disney theme park). Similarly, in Denis Villeneuve's *Arrival* (2016), the spaceship that travels near earth and hangs above it looks like a giant tumbled rock in the sky. In both works, the "alien" world is rather friendly, countering the stereotypes that circulate in such classic science-fiction films as *It Came from Outer Space* (Jack Arnold, 1953) or *Invasion of the Body Snatchers* (Don Siegel, 1956).

But science fiction is not the only cinematic genre to produce works in which the laws of nature are overthrown. When it comes to defying gravity, of course, photography (with its split-second capture of motion) has always been able to arrest things in midair. Here we might think of the well-known snapshot of Dziga Vertov leaping—an image that symbolizes his interest in camera trickery. But motion pictures have also produced such images, generally

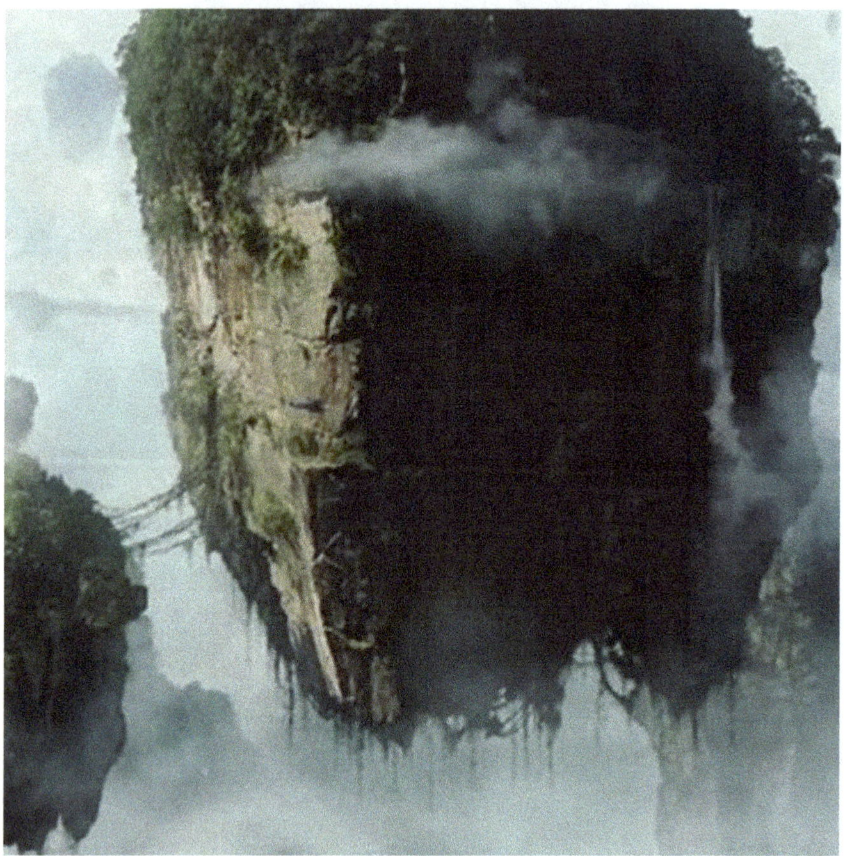

FIGURE 14.4. The celestial world of Pandora in *Avatar* (Cameron, 2009) contains floating mountains, echoing Magritte's boulders, which hover in the sky.

through the use of freeze frames (discussed in another context in chapter 11). Most famous, is the diving sequence from Leni Riefenstahl's *Olympia* (1938), which portrays athletes caught in a stage of descent. Unlike Magritte's boulders (which project a sense of weight), Riefenstahl creates the feeling that the divers are light and bird-like.

While utilizing a freeze frame is a fairly obvious means for cinema to defy gravity, some films have employed more mysterious methods. Among the strangest is the hotel sequence in Jean Cocteau's experimental work *The Blood of a Poet* (1932)—not surprising since the director traveled in Surrealist circles. As discussed in chapter 5, the Artist moves through a corridor, peering through keyholes into rooms. However, he seems to be walking unnaturally, struggling against some unseen force, and we surmise that the walls and floor of the set must not be positioned as normally as they appear. Thus, when the Artist moves along upright, he seems required to grasp onto things—as though he will fall down if he does not. Clearly, this effect was accomplished through some manipulation of the set and camera to create the illusion of movement through a bizarre but coherent space. An equally troubling moment occurs when the Artist looks into a room in which a young girl is being disciplined by an elderly woman. At one point, he sees the child "stuck" to a wall above a fireplace and, at another, attached to the ceiling. All this imagery contributes to the oneiric, hallucinatory sense of the sequence.

While in *The Blood of the Poet*, the effect of sabotaging gravity is unsettling, in the musical *Royal Wedding*, directed by Stanley Donen in 1951, it is not. In a tour de force sequence, Fred Astaire dances on a room's four walls and ceiling—all as an exuberant expression of romantic love (figure 14.5). Here Magritte's paintings *Reconnaissance without End* (1963) or *Golconda* (1953) seem more to the point as rather benign and graceful visions of weightless escapades.

In general, Magritte is obsessed with the sky and has devoted several canvases entirely to it, such as *The Curse* (1931, and 1936 or 1937). He also created works in which framed pictures of the sky hang on walls (as in *The Secret Life* [1928], *Monsieur Goulden's Drawing Room* [1928 or 1929], or *Revolution* [1935]). So it seems important that when his persons and objects break free of gravity, this is where they end up. The sky, of course, has numerous familiar cultural associations, among them heaven and the cosmos. But it can also signify the poetic domain, which requires liberation from the ballast of logic. While other Surrealists (interested in psychoanalysis) plunge downward (into the depths of the unconscious), Magritte soars upward (like an errant

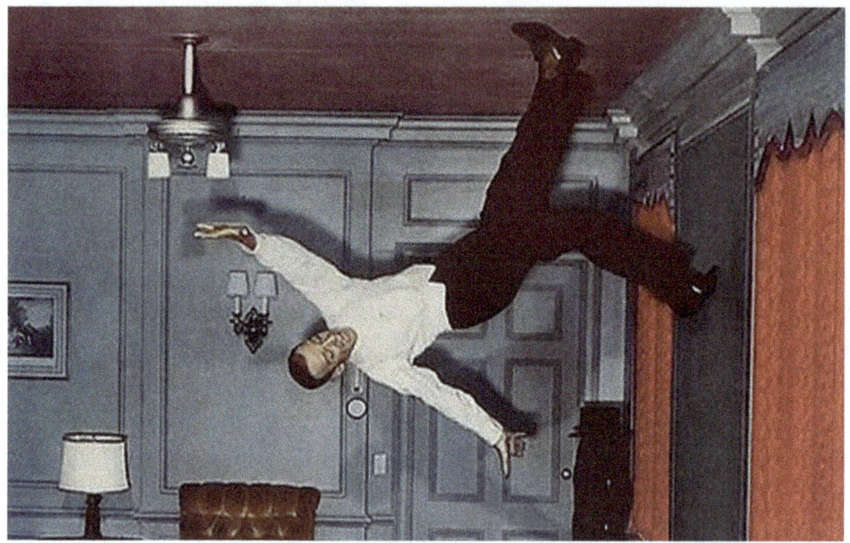

FIGURE 14.5. In this production number from *Royal Wedding* (Donen, 1951), Fred Astaire defies gravity by dancing on the walls and ceiling.

helium balloon)—not so much interested in the realm of the soul but rather the imagination.

In this respect he is perhaps like the Romantic poets. For as William Wordsworth writes in *Tintern Abbey*:

> . . . I have felt
> A presence that disturbs me with the joy
> Of elevated thoughts; a sense sublime
> Of something far more deeply interfused

He locates this in:

> . . . the light of setting suns
> And the round ocean, and the living air,
> And the blue sky in the mind of man[4]

Of course, with the phrase "the blue sky in the mind of man," we think of Magritte's *The False Mirror* (1929) pictured on the cover of this volume. While on one level, the eyeball can be seen simply to reflect the sky, on another, perhaps it allows us, figuratively, to see the sky in the person's consciousness. As

W. J. Lillyman has noted, post-Romantic sensibility tended to see the celestial realm less positively and viewed it as signifying the universe's indifference to people. Here he cites a line from Louis MacNeice's "Refugees" in which the poet warns, ". . . do not trust the sky, the blue that looks so candid / Is non-committal, frigid as a harlot's eye."[5] Perhaps both senses of the firmament (as comforting or frightful) are represented in Magritte's canvases, which often hover between the two opposing poles.

15

HUMAN-ANIMAL HYBRIDS

> An inner force develops [the work of art] from the inside outwards, like a fetus. The work of art will see the light of day, like the child, when its organism is complete.
>
> René Magritte[1]

Clearly, part of the Surrealist aesthetic involved impossible and unsettling juxtapositions—be it a pocket watch melting in the desert, as in Salvador Dalí's *The Persistence of Memory* (1931), or the crustacean telephone receiver in his *Lobster Telephone* (1936). In a similar fashion, Magritte paints *Love Disarmed* (1935), in which hair grows out of a pair of shoes.

Sometimes, however, Surrealist artists created juxtapositions within the selfsame object or figure. This is a method employed by Magritte when he designed uncanny "hybrids." One instance of this is found in his painting *Discovery* (1927), in which he combines human flesh with the grain of wood.

Also provocative are Magritte's gender-bending paintings in which he merges males and females; in *Titanic Days* (1928) (see figure 18.3), for example, masculine and feminine parts of a single human being seem to be warring with each other (alternatively, as seen in chapter 18, the painting can be read more aggressively as an attempted assault on a woman by a man).

But some of his more interesting amalgams occur when Magritte intermixes human and other species. Often this process is rather indirect as when in *The Uncertainty Principle* (1944) (see figure 20.12) he sketches a woman who projects a bird shadow on the wall—implying that she is a composite of the two. Clearly, in the work's title, Magritte is playing on physicist Werner

Heisenberg's 1927 uncertainty principle, which asserts that one can never simultaneously know the exact position and the exact speed of an object. While that kind of uncertainty does not apply to the sketch, doubt looms over the precise species of the figure portrayed. While it is not clear that Magritte had any real interest in science, it has been noted that "Surrealism emerged in France during probably the most momentous period in the history of physics" and had an effect on the work of some of his compatriots like André Breton.[2] As for uncertainty, there is also a degree of this in Magritte's *Present* (1938 or 1939), which again utilizes an avian subject, but in this case the bird is dressed in a man's jacket, lending it a human touch.

However, there is nothing indirect about his canvas *A Stroke of Luck* (1945), in which a pig's head sits atop a human's body, or a 1944 untitled drawing in which a woman's torso is topped off with a horse's head, or *Aladdin's Lamp* (1954), in which a suited man has an ape face. Here we think of the chapter epigraph and Magritte's comparing the work of art to a developing fetus, but in these works the organism "birthed" is a form of unnatural progeny.

Magritte's favored animal for this kind of concoction is the fish. In *Collective Invention* (1934) (figure 15.1), a humanoid fish is beached on the shore, and its legs look more female than male (but without engaging the romantic mermaid trope). And in *The Old Gunner* (1947), a fish again has human legs, one of which seems to be prosthetic. In *The Wonders of Nature* (1953) (see figure 11.3 and the discussion in chapter 11), two fish-human figures sit on a rock while seeming to turn into stone. Here, judging by their legs, both may be male. Though Magritte is no Expressionist, and the beauty of his paintings tend to minimize the aura of the grotesque, his visions are nonetheless both literally and metaphorically monstrous.

There are numerous movies that resonate with Magritte's iconography of hideous interspecies creatures. In chapter 13, I discussed *Judex* (Georges Franju, 1963), whose central locale, an estate, is guarded by an animal statue with a human head. The film imagines another human-animal hybrid when the hero appears in a frightening eagle hood that makes him seem part avian, and the other guests are dressed as birds or insects.

However, there are movies in which the theme of animal-human contagion is far more prominent, and here the seminal work is *The Island of Lost Souls* (1932), a horror film directed by Erle C. Kenton for Paramount Pictures, which was based on an 1896 novel by H. G. Wells, *The Island of Doctor Moreau*. In large part, the book's publication was fueled by a campaign in Great Britain against animal vivisection since the plot involves Dr. Moreau's crafting of human-beast combinations through surgical means conducted in a House

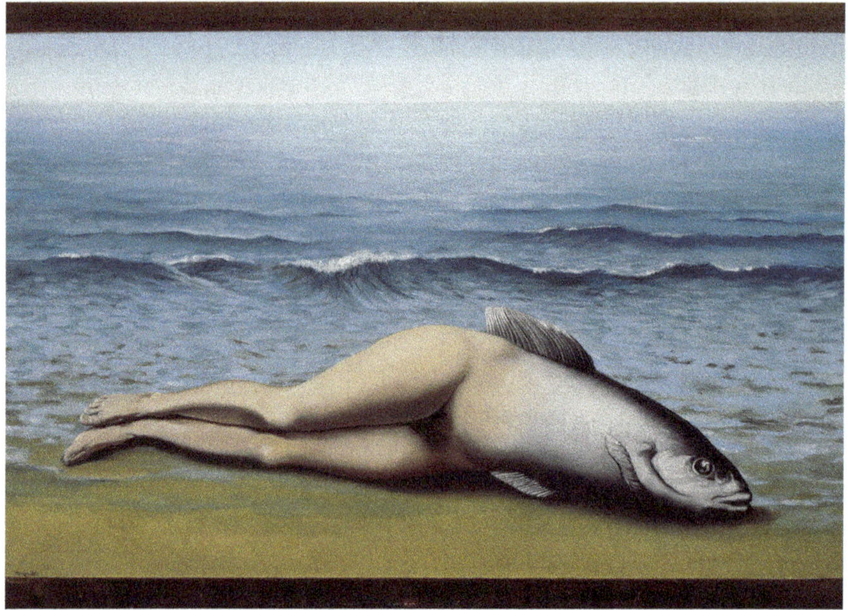

FIGURE 15.1. *Collective Invention* (*L'invention collective*) (1934)

of Pain. The film, however, has no such higher purpose and, instead, wallows in the shock of such corporeal admixtures.

The Island of Lost Souls tells the story of Edward Parker (Richard Arlen), who is shipwrecked and picked up by a passing vessel, so the film has the seaside setting so common in Magritte's canvases that depict hybrid species. (Here we think again of the artist's *The Wonders of Nature* with its sailing ship depicted in the background.) But rather than take Parker to the port that he requests, the ship captain leaves him off on a mysterious island to which he is delivering a cargo of animals. Once there (accompanied by an island resident named Montgomery [Arthur Hohl]), Parker notices that the "natives" are exceedingly strange looking (figure 15.2). Given racist Western notions of the primitive at the time (as alien "other"), he simply accepts this impression as fact.

Parker is taken to the home of Dr. Moreau (Charles Laughton), where he learns that Moreau is conducting biological and zoological "research." Specifically, his work entails surgical experiments that transform animals into quasi-human form—ostensibly doing away with thousands of centuries of evolution. His creatures are ruled by a "native" called the Sayer of the Law (Bela Lugosi), who keeps the hordes in check. When thoughts of violence begin to take hold,

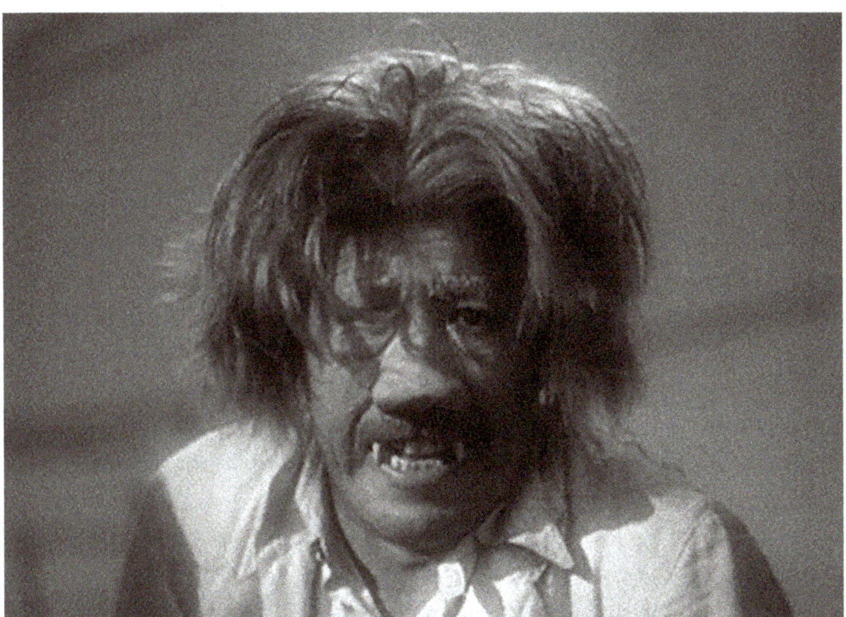

FIGURE 15.2. One of the "natives" in *The Island of Lost Souls* (Kenton, 1932) who has been experimented on by Dr. Moreau

drawing on their base animal instincts, he encourages them to ask "Are we not men?"—a query that calms them down and appeals to their "higher" nature. The most convincing of Moreau's experimental subjects is the Panther Woman (Kathleen Burke), a sexy beauty who Parker first believes is human. However, when he looks at her hands, he sees that they are claw-like, and he realizes that she, too, is a freak. Eventually, Parker's fiancée and a sailor companion arrive at Moreau's island to rescue him, and at the end of the picture, all three escape.

In certain ways, the character of Dr. Moreau bears parallels to an artist, since he speaks of letting his "imagination run fantastically ahead" in designing his new organic "handiwork." On some level, human-animal hybrids have a long history in modern art—but each movement brought to the conception a different valence. For Art Nouveau, the human involved was generally a lovely woman and the animal a beautiful creature—like the dragonfly—as in René Lalique's famous brooch (1897–98). Though a bit strange, there is nothing really threatening about such a piece; rather, it combines two gorgeous beings into one—hence its function as an expensive piece of jewelry.

While, on some level, the style and look of *The Island of Lost Souls* has ties to German Expressionism—with its dark lighting and mad scientist theme (as in Robert Wiene's *The Cabinet of Dr. Caligari* [1920])—an argument can be made that its links to Surrealism are stronger, given its weird collocations. When one considers the representation of animals in Expressionism (or in the Blau Reiter movement, which preceded it), one thinks immediately of Franz Marc's horses; but these are stunning creatures that stay comfortably within their own genus (as in *Blue Horse with Rainbow* [1913]). The same applies to Erich Heckel's woodcut *White Horse* (1912). When animals in Expressionism are represented in a grotesque fashion, it often has to do with the carnage of World War I, as in *Destroyed Battery*, a lithograph by Otto Heffner (1914). Where we occasionally find macabre images of human-animal fusions is in the work of George Grosz. For instance, in an untitled watercolor of 1927, a nude flapper kisses a repulsive pig-man. But Grosz's intent was largely political and satirical—a critique of Weimer culture. As a MoMa description of the picture states, "It is one of many farcical caricatures of sexually available women and boorishly lewd men Grosz made during the 1910s and 1920s."

Thus, Magritte's combinations of humans and animals seem to stand apart in the annals of Modernist art and bear a Surrealist sense of wry but troubling amalgamation. It is for this reason that I cite them in relation to *The Island of Lost Souls*. There have, of course, been numerous remakes of this film—one in 1977 and another in 1996 (both given Wells's original title *The Island of Dr. Moreau*)—but the 1932 film is the only one to be made within Magritte's lifetime and thus seems most relevant.[3]

Clearly, beyond Expressionist painting, *The Island of Lost Souls* sparks other associations in the history of horror (especially to fairy tales—with their frog princes and bestial suitors). But these stories are works of literature and not primarily visual texts (though they have often been illustrated when published). Significantly, however, if one considers the transposition of the genre to film, it is yet another Surrealist work that comes to mind—Jean Cocteau's *Beauty and the Beast* (1946), whose protagonist seems an heir to one of Dr. Moreau's zoological fabrications. Like Magritte's hybrid creatures, the Beast is not as threatening as those in the 1932 film, and the audience is meant to sympathize with him. But he is no less weird—pointing to a shared Surrealist skepticism about rigid classification and a love of category confusion.

Within the contemporary era, the genre of human-animal horror film has periodically reared its head. One such instance is the film *Splice* (Vincenzo Natali, 2009), a forgettable science-fiction movie that tells the tale of two scientists who experiment with creating blends of animal species in order to harvest proteins to cure numerous diseases. Eventually, of course, they are tempted to develop a human-animal hybrid. When they do so, they create one that grows up to be part woman, bird, reptile, and amphibian (figure 15.3). At first, the creature seems rather sweet and harmless, almost like a pet. But eventually she becomes violent, shifts her gender to male, and rapes the female scientist. At the end of the narrative, the latter is pregnant—awaiting the birth of yet another monstrous Rosemary's baby.

Interestingly, during the opening credits of the film, which depict semi-transparent tissues through which we can see intertwining venous and arterial vessels, we are reminded of Magritte's *Blood of the World* (1927), which seems to depict some veined biological matter. A. M. Hammacher sees this canvas as indicative of the artist's urge to create "invented organisms . . . and forms only indirectly and ambiguously related to reality." Moreover, for Hammacher, it seems to portray "organisms resembling legs and arms which lack their extremities and have been skinned, like those in pictures of anatomical lessons."[4]

Ironically, the most interesting aspect of the film may be its title, *Splice*. On the one hand, this term clearly relates to the notion of gene splicing, which

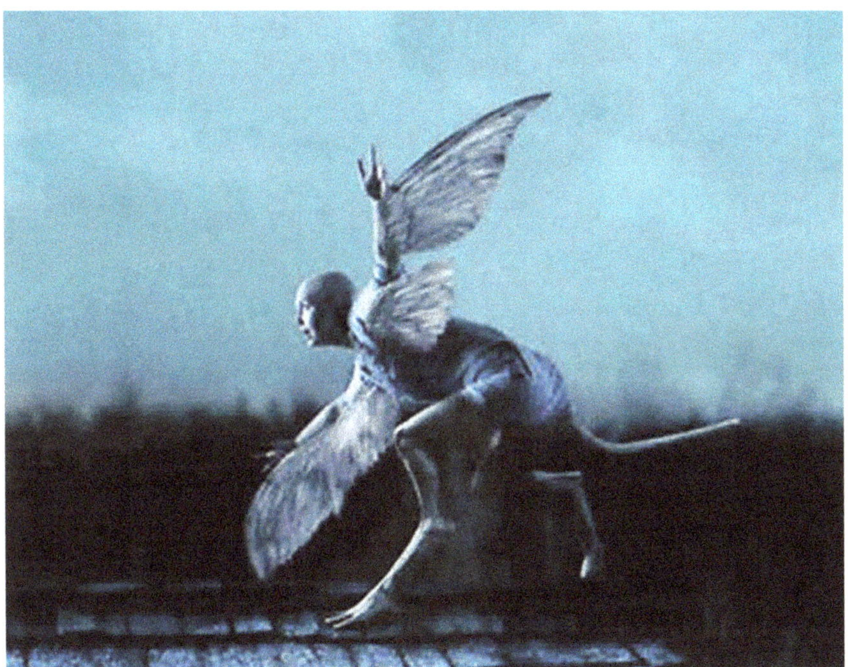

FIGURE 15.3. The human-animal hybrid in *Splice* (Natali, 2009)

allows scientists to design new DNA sequences that intermix material from two different species. But the term also has a meaning in the discourse of cinema—although an antiquated one—of editing together two sections of a film strip in order to create new spatiotemporal relations.

The point is that the cinema, with its editing capacities and its special effects, now bolstered through CGI, has always had the ability to take the kind of human-animal hybrids that Magritte fashioned in pictorial media and translate them to the movie screen while lending them an even greater aura of bizarre realism.

16

MAGIC

Dismemberment and Decapitation

> The art of painting . . . seemed to me to be vaguely magical and the painter gifted with superior powers.
>
> René Magritte[1]

IN CHAPTER 2, I mentioned Magritte's love of magic. In this regard, he shared an interest consonant with many other Surrealists. Fittingly, a 2014 exhibition at the Art Institute of Chicago was called *Magritte and the Magic of the Surrealists.*

Magritte made many statements about magic, including the one in this chapter's epigraph, where he identified it with the artist's lofty talents. At another point, he spoke of seeking a "magical conception of the world" and elsewhere noted that "magical art imitates the enchanted world-that is the universe itself."[2] Furthermore, the titles of several of his paintings (ranging from the 1920s to the 1950s) make this fascination with the marvelous clear: *The Magician's Accomplices* (1926), *The Magician* (1951) (figure 16.1), and *Black Magic* (1934 and 1945). Significantly, of the latter (which depicts a female nude whose upper body is tinted blue), Magritte once said: "It is an act of black magic to turn a woman's flesh into the sky."[3] The imagery of two of these paintings most suggests prestidigitation. *The Magician* depicts a four-handed man eating at a table—hinting at the sleight of hand required by such professionals. *The Magician's Assistant* seems to portray a disappearing act involving women sliding mysteriously in or out of tubes. Given

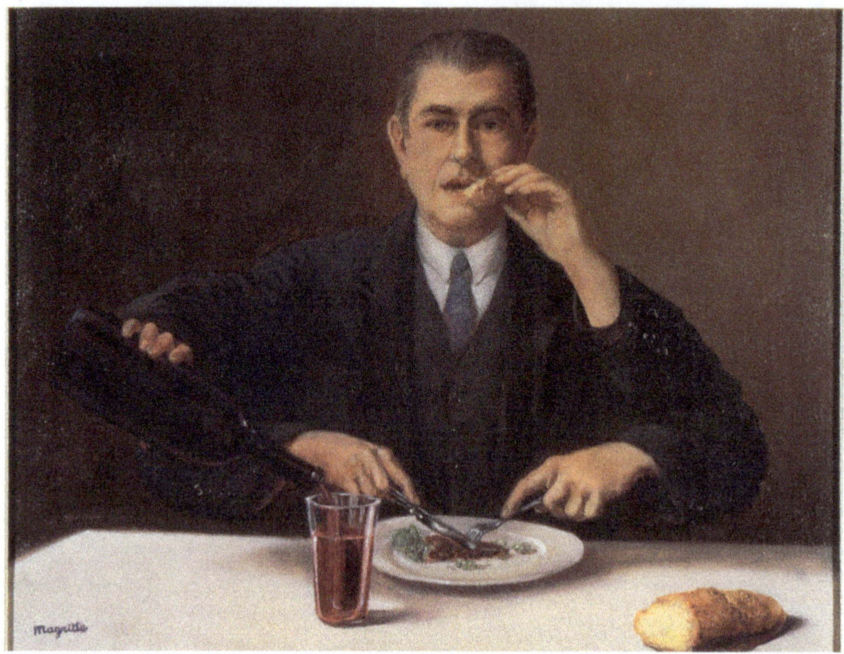

FIGURE 16.1. *The Magician* (*Le sorcier/The Sorcerer, Self-Portrait with Four Arms*) (1951)

Magritte's clear interest in magic, I pursue associations between his work and the early trick films of Georges Méliès, whose oeuvre the artist was sure to know.[4] Because of the potential import of this comparison, I devote considerable space to discussing Méliès's films.

Significantly, in Magritte's *The Magician* we have an allusion either to time lapse photography or to cinematic superimposition—the latter a favored Mélièsian trick. Moreover, Magritte compared artists to prestidigitators. As he observed: "When the investigations of the magician and the artist render the universe *enchanting*, they seem to me to be guided by a feeling of new-found freedom."[5] Interestingly, one version of *The Magician*'s title deems it a "self-portrait." Furthermore, in Magritte's essay "Surrealism in the Sunshine" (1946), he imagines Alice (ostensibly Lewis Carroll's character) "playing with a little rabbit," at which point "Méliès . . . popped up out of the blue." As Magritte continues, "The golden age, which we refuse to locate in the abstract future, from now on brings enchantment within the confines of our lives."[6]

In examining Magritte's ties to Méliès, we will concentrate on two of their shared themes: decapitation and duplication. These tropes are highlighted in

Noam Elcott's book *Artificial Darkness: An Obscure History of Modern Art and Media*, which includes a chapter titled "The Black Art of Georges Méliès."[7] There he explores the director's use of the black screen as a background for creating magical effects (like the subsequent utilization of green screen in television and the movies). "Méliès's mastery of the black screen," states Elcott, "situated him . . . at the dawn of twentieth-century special effects and narrative film."[8]

Dismemberment/Decapitation

A discourse of decapitation is present in several of Magritte's paintings, including *The Conqueror*, in which a man's head is replaced by a piece of wood; *The Explorer's Return*, in which a headless figure has a pipe emerging from its neck; *The Shooting Gallery*, in which a man's head hangs from the ceiling (all 1926); and *The Silence of Smiling* (1928), which depicts four decapitated heads. In *The Pilgrim* (1966), a man's head floats in midair, separated from his hat and torso like three puzzle pieces that might eventually fit back together, and in *Gem-Stones* (1967) a man's and a bird's head are positioned on a block of wood. Finally, there is a version of *The Lovers* (1928), in which a decapitated male head kisses a fully embodied woman. A comic twist upon the motif is seen in *The Idea* (1966), in which an apple substitutes for a man's head.

While these paintings all involve male subjects, others represent women. *The Midnight Marriage* (1926), for instance, depicts a severed male head (its face turned away from the viewer) positioned on a table that holds a second hollowed-out female head (or wig stand) on a shelf below. More emphatic in its reference to women is *The Double Reality* (1936) (figure 16.2), which portrays two decapitated female heads, one right side up and the other upside down, hanging on a wall. There is also *The Two Sisters* (1925), which portrays two female heads on stands. On the one hand, they look like sculptures; on the other, the open eyes of the left-hand piece make it look decidedly real. Similarly, in *Georgette* (1935)—strangely titled for Magritte's wife—two women's heads appear (minus any bodies), one full face and the other in profile. One also thinks of Magritte's multiframe painting *The Eternally Obvious* (1930), which dissects the nude female body into five discontinuous parts, including the head. Finally, one of his advertising graphics also smacks of decapitation. Drawn for Brussels' Maison Norine, it depicts a headless female mannequin with wooden arms and a wooden rod emerging from her neck.

Clearly, all such imagery is highly unsettling and seeks to disquiet the spectator, but those of female decapitation have a special resonance. For Sigmund

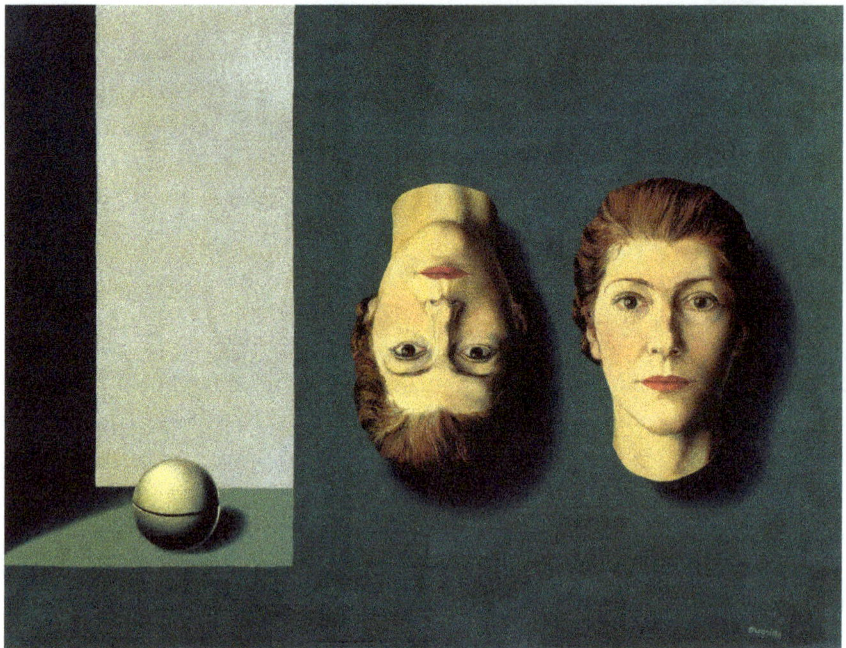

FIGURE 16.2. *The Double Reality* (1936)

Freud, of course (as per his 1922 essay "Medusa's Head"), such imagery signals both the male fear of castration and of the female genitals, which announce such a possibility.[9] Perhaps the Magritte painting that most solicits this reading is *Rape* (1935) (figure 16.3). It shows a headless female body, topped by flowing hair, arranged to propose itself as a face—with the breasts as eyes, the belly button as nose, and the genitals as mouth (shades of the vagina dentata). So the head is simultaneously there and not there.

While many other Magritte paintings of women can be criticized for their idealization of the female as Surrealism's "obscure object of desire" (e.g., *Flowers of Evil* [1946] or *Freedom of Mind* [1948]), *Rape* has incurred the wrath of feminist critics for other reasons. (In titling the painting *Rape*, of course, Magritte seems to acknowledge its implicit gender violence.) Robin Adèle Greeley,[10] for instance, criticizes it for implicitly denying the woman language. As she writes, "She no longer speaks with words. If she speaks at all it is through her sexual anatomy." Likewise, Susan Gubar opines that the painting denies woman personhood and agency. As she notes, "When the female is simultaneously decapitated and recapitated by her sexual organs, the face that was supposed to be a window to the soul embodies a sexuality that is less related to

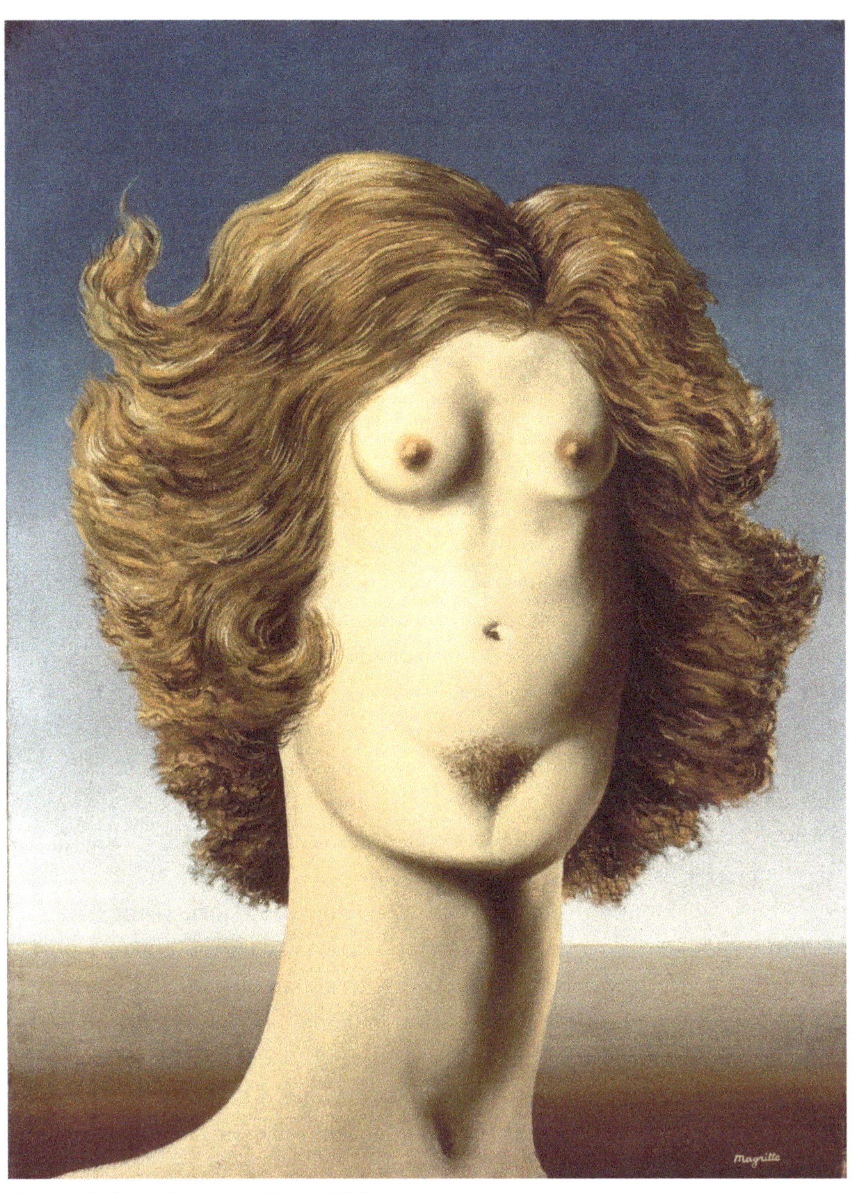

FIGURE 16.3. *Rape* (*Le viol/The Rape*) (1935)

pleasure than to dominance."[11] While, on the one hand, *Rape* obviously sexualizes woman, ironically it also erases the female erotic body by turning it into a head—thus, dissolving the threat of castration implied by the female genitals.

A Freudian reading of decapitation seems highly relevant to another Surrealist painter who employed such iconography—Salvador Dalí. Here is how one writer describes his oeuvre: "Dislocated body parts . . . began to appear in his work when the artist was in his early 20s. Later productions feature sprawling, limbless, decapitated bodies. . . . In the grotesque 1934 *The Spectre of Sex Appeal*, a small boy stares up at a naked female body without a head."[12] Certainly the oedipal stance of the tiny male child peering up at the huge (read: maternal) female figure smacks of the very syndrome that Freud elaborates. Finally, Georges Bataille, a literary figure on the fringes of Surrealism (loathed by André Breton), founded a secret society, Acéphale, whose symbol was a headless man. So the theme of decapitation was "in the air" in the circles in which Magritte traveled.

Turning to Méliès, as stated, the filmmaker employed the black screen as a primary tool for trick effects. His first cinematic engagement of it was, significantly, to produce the illusion of decapitation. *The Four Troublesome Heads* (1898) starts with a magician (Méliès) standing between two white tables against a black background. He removes his head and places it on a table to his right. Miraculously, another head reappears on his shoulders, and the disembodied one looks at it, astonished. Méliès then removes his head two more times—placing one on the table to his right and the other on the table to his left. He then grabs a banjo and begins to play as the three dismembered heads sing along. Apparently displeased with their voices, he thrusts the banjo at the two heads on his right making them disappear. He disposes of his own head for a final time, grabs the remaining decapitated head, and attaches it to his torso. Thus, he ends the film as the coherent body with which he began it. While the function of dismemberment in this trick film is more to amaze and amuse than to shock, there persists something disconcerting about the its imagery—a trope that Magritte and other Surrealists employ with a much darker spin.

Elcott also focuses on a similar Méliès film. *Man with a Rubber Head* (1901) (figure 16.4) takes place in a workroom in which a man takes a small head (that of Méliès) out of a box and puts it on a stand. When the man removes his wig, we recognize him as Méliès. He takes a large bellows and attaches it to a tube running from the stand; he pumps it until the head grows extremely large (reminding us of Magritte's *The Art of Living* [1967]). He then lets the air out of the tube, and the head progressively becomes tinier. He ushers another man into the workshop who proceeds to overpump the head so that it explodes in a puff of smoke. In this film and another, *Tit for Tat* (1904), in which Méliès places his head in a glass box on a stand, we find a similar iconography to Magritte's *Midnight Marriage* with its two heads on a table.

Elcott mentions in passing two other Méliès films involving black screen decapitation: *The Cook's Revenge* (1900) and *The Mysterious Knight* (1899), the latter being the only one of the group involving a female head (interestingly created through a drawing rather than taken from a live woman). Strangely, Elcott does not foreground *Decapitation in Turkey* (also known as *The Terrible Turkish Executioner* [1904]), a rather famous Méliès's trick film. The scene is set at an exotic marketplace, where four prisoners are dragged. A man puts a plank with holes over the men's heads, and another man with a huge sword decapitates them in one fell swoop. The heads (now dummy props) fall on the floor and the headless men sit down. The dummy heads are placed in a barrel. Suddenly one of the heads (this time a real, animated one) emerges from the barrel and places itself on a prisoner's torso, recapitating him. That man then takes the other heads out of the barrel and puts them on his three compatriots. The prisoners then grab the swordsman and cut his torso in half

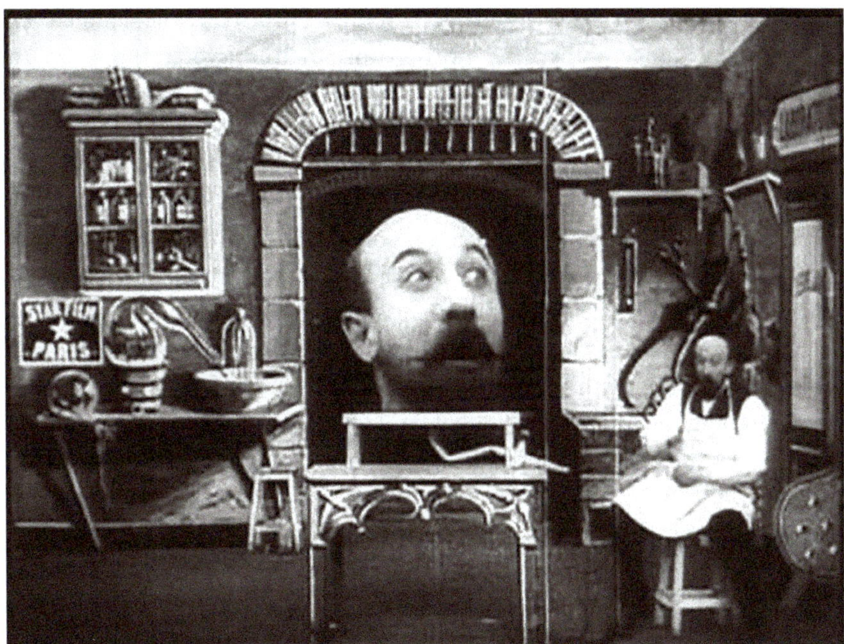

FIGURE 16.4. In Méliés's *Man with a Rubber Head* (1901), a decapitated head is blown up to giant size.

(dismemberment, if not decapitation). The criminals run off, and the swordsman manages to reconstitute himself.

While to the modern viewer scenes of decapitation in both the work of Magritte and Méliès seem arcane and fantastic, to the painter and the filmmaker they were a fact of life. In both Belgium and France, the guillotine was used for executions, which often took place in public and drew significant crowds. In Belgium, we know of such an execution taking place as late as 1918; Magritte would have been twenty years old.[13] In France, the guillotine remained in use until 1977—so it would have been a method of execution for all Méliès's life.[14]

Hence, while Freud envisioned decapitation as an oedipal mental fantasy experienced by the male, for some in the nineteenth and twentieth centuries, "losing one's head" was a distinct possibility. Perhaps (if only unconsciously) the reality of this haunted the work of Magritte and of Méliès before him.

Duplication

In addition to painting canvases that imagine decapitation, Magritte created ones in which people were duplicated. Thus, in one trope something is lost, and in the other, something is gained. Although, for instance, he doubled the figure of Paul Nougé in his 1927 "portrait" of him, the favored individual to be multiplied was the so-called man in a bowler hat—a figure that populates much of Magritte's work. Perhaps his earliest use of it was in *The Musings of the Solitary Walker* (1926), where, with his back to the viewer, the man walks away from a corpse.

We have already noted the appearance of a decapitated "man in the bowler hat" in *The Pilgrim*, where, as usual, he is a middle-aged gentleman, sporting a deadpan expression. Many critics have seen this figure as representative of the typical bourgeois citizen, and some have viewed him as a stand-in for Magritte who led a rather conventional life. Sandra Zalman, for instance, in her preface to Magritte's writings, said that he "looked like a small-town banker."[15]

In *Golconda* (1953), a series of bowler-hatted men rain down from the heavens, while in *The Masterpiece or Mysteries of the Horizon* (1955) three of them stand beneath a sky containing several partial moons. In *The Month of the Grape Harvest* (1959) (see figure 3.6), the men ominously peer into the window of a house, and in *Reconnaissance without End* (1963) two of them amble through the sky. Much of the uncanny effect of these paintings arises from the endless reproduction of a single individual who, traditionally, has been seen to be entirely unique. Even now, with cloning a scientific possibility,

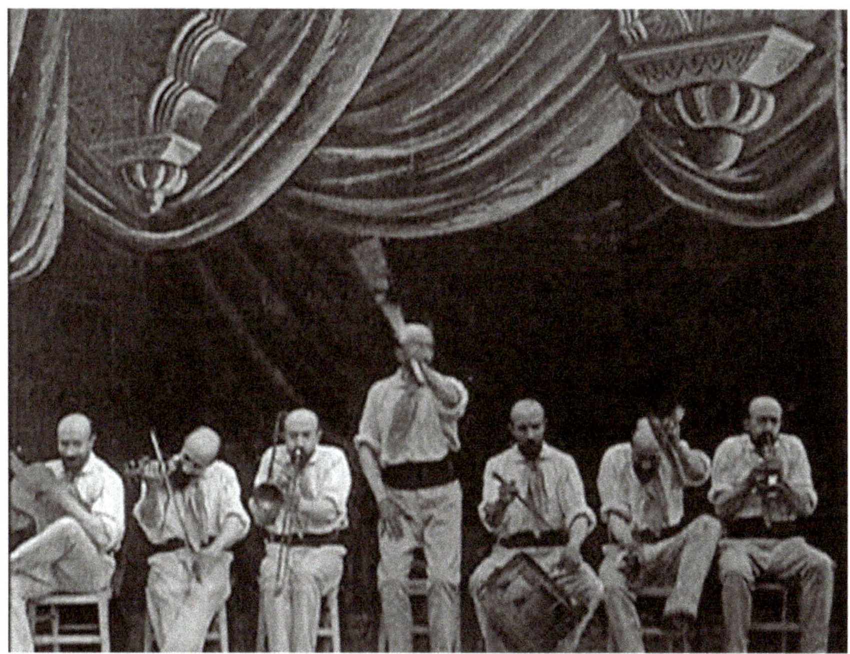

FIGURE 16.5. In Méliés's *One Man Band* (1900) the magician/filmmaker is duplicated numerous times until he constitutes the entire musical group.

there are ethical prohibitions against using the process. Furthermore, the emotionless and vapid countenances of the men seem to deny them personhood as well.

Once more, we find early manifestations of such human multiplication in the work of Méliès, and usually it is the magician/director himself who is reproduced—relevant, if we see "the man in the bowler hat" as a Magritte doppelganger. Again, Elcott highlights several of these films. *One Man Band* (1900) (figure 16.5) begins with Méliès onstage against a black background, with seven chairs positioned in the foreground. Moving screen right to left, he sits down on each chair, duplicating himself with every seating. Each self-incarnation holds a different instrument, which they eventually play with Méliès conducting. Finally, one by one, each Méliès folds back into another until only the conductor remains.

In *An Impossible Balancing Feat* (1902), Méliès stands onstage with a chair. Soon, miraculously, three other incarnations of him appear, as though born from his body (like Eve from Adam's rib). One of them balances on the magician's head, and the other two on his outstretched arms. They do somersaults until they are all balancing on their heads. Suddenly, they disappear, and Méliès is left waving two flags.

The Triple Conjurer and the Living Head (1900) hits the jackpot by entailing both decapitation and duplication. It starts with Méliès onstage, whereupon he doubles himself. His doppelganger takes out a female dummy head that soon becomes a living one. (This is a rare instance of an allusion to female decapitation in Méliès, but here it is a toy head rather than a real one, as in the films about men.) The second Méliès turns the female head into a fully embodied live woman. Suddenly, a man in a prince's clothing appears and makes the woman disappear. The two Méliès run off the stage and the prince reveals himself to be a third incarnation of the magician/director.

The Melomaniac (1903) also involves both decapitation and duplication. It opens with Méliès (holding a giant treble clef) leading a group of chorines onstage; each woman holds a piece of paper and a stick. Méliès throws the treble clef above him onto one of five wires strung across the stage (like lines on musical composition paper). He then flings up one of the sticks to the wires as though to mark the end of a musical bar. He takes off his head and tosses it up so that it lands on one of the wires and resembles a note. He does so five more times. He then takes sticks from the women and lobs them up to complete the musical signs.

We might imagine that the duplicated worlds of Méliès and Magritte come together through the film-related medium of photography. It does so many decades later by the intervention of a third artist—photographer Duane Michals, who visited Magritte in 1965. At that time, he produced a series of images picturing the painter wearing a bowler hat—indicating the autobiographical nature of such haberdashery in Magritte's paintings. Significantly, in several of the photographs, Michals multiplies the body of Magritte, utilizing superimposition, matting, or optical printing. So here, like Méliès in his movies, Magritte is multiplied photographically along with the hat that adorns his Everyman in so many of his canonical paintings.

As mentioned earlier, from a twenty-first-century perspective, Magritte's fascination with human duplication takes on a particular slant—given that we are now in the era of cloning (creating "an animal or plant in a laboratory that is an exact copy of another using the original animal's or plant's DNA").[16] Thus, in a sense, Magritte's ubiquitous men in bowler hats can be seen as clones, and in this respect, the artist has been prescient.

It is worth noting that we have recently seen a spate of international films in which cloning functions as a major aspect of the narrative—aided by the possibilities of CGI, which make reproducing actors on screen quite simple. One of the first was the comedy *Multiplicity* (Harold Ramis, 1996), in which an overworked contractor, who has little time for his wife and family, takes advantage of an offer to have himself reproduced. The rest of the films in this category, however, veer toward science fiction. *The 6th Day* (Roger Spottiswoode, 2000) concerns a man who encounters a duplicate of himself and learns of a conspiracy by which clones will take over the world. In *Star Wars: Episode II, Attack of the Clones* (George Lucas, 2002), Anakin Skywalker discovers a secret clone army crafted for the Jedi. In the French film, *À ton image* (Aruna Villiers, 2004), a woman, unable to have children, decides to clone herself in order to become a mother. *The Island* (Michael Bay, 2005) tells the complex tale of a future community that believes that all the world is contaminated save a particular island. Those who go there, however, are merely clones of other individuals and will be used for organ harvesting or surrogate parenthood. The British film *Moon* (Duncan Jones, 2009) tells the story of an astronaut who has spent three years in space. Toward the end of his stint, while out in his lunar rover, he crashes the vehicle. When he awakens, he finds a duplicate of himself as well as a facility in which hundreds of his doppelgangers are hibernating—all part of a plan to economize on the cost of training new astronauts. In the Canadian television series *Orphan Black* (Graeme Manson and John Fawcett, 2013–17), a woman sequentially assumes the identity of her various clones. Finally, in *The Reconstruction of William Zero* (Dan Bush, 2014), a man awakens and is told that he has had an accident. He remembers nothing of his earlier life but is tended to by a man introduced as his twin brother. Eventually the amnesiac learns that he is a clone of the man who is caring for him.

In all but the comedy *Multiplicity*, clones have an unsettling and perverse aura about them. This is also the case in Magritte's clone paintings—especially *The Month of the Grape Harvest*, in which multitudes of bowler-hatted men spy on an apartment, or in *Golconda*, in which they seem to be invading the earth. While drawing upon the rich literary history of the doppelganger, Magritte translates it to the less familiar terrain of painting—simultaneously prefiguring the science of cloning and the way the cinema would harvest it for its own generic and narrative purposes.

17

WINDOWS

A window with aesthetic proportions fulfills its function little better than a false window.

René Magritte[1]

The problem of the window led to *La Condition humaine* . . . [in which] the tree in the picture hid the tree behind it, outside the room. For the viewer, the tree was simultaneously in the room in the picture and outside the room in the real landscape. That existence in two different spaces at once is like the moment existing simultaneously in the past and the present as in déjà vu.

René Magritte[2]

THROUGHOUT MAGRITTE'S CAREER, he chose windows as one of his major iconographic elements, representing them in a variety of ways. Most often, the perspective from which he viewed them was from the interior of a room.

In the most famous of these works (i.e., *The Human Condition* [1933]; see figure 8.1), discussed from a different vantage point in chapter 8, a painting is posed in front of a window and the image on it precisely aligns with the view outside. Therefore, it is unclear whether one is looking at a canvas or through glass. As the second chapter epigraph makes clear, Magritte approached the window as an intellectual "problem" to be solved—by which he meant finding a way to make it visually strange and paradoxical. As always, he favored defying conceptual barriers—be they spatial or temporal. In a variation on the theme (as in *Key to the Fields* [1936]) (see figure 6.3) previously mentioned in chapter 6, the window itself is incongruously imprinted with the external landscape, again dissolving distinctions between interior and exterior. In another iteration of the motif (as in *The Field Glass* [1963]), we view a double-paned window from inside a chamber. One of its panes is closed and depicts the sky and clouds outside. The other pane, however, is partially open, and in the gap, instead of sky, we see a black void. Further flouting logic, through the pane that is ajar we continue to see the firmament, and Magritte makes clear (by his depiction of the top corner of the window frame) that it is not emblazoned on the glass. In the last chapter, I mentioned Magritte's *The Month of the Grape Harvest* (1959) (see figure 3.6), which depicts a crowd of bowler-hatted men peering through a window, as seen from within a room. Here, of course, the specter of voyeurism is raised in addition to the discourse of outside and inside.

Occasionally, Magritte pictured external views of windows, as in *Obsession* (1927), *Summer* (1931), *The Blue Eyes* (1947), or *The Six Elements* (1929) (see figure 20.5), in which the outside of an apartment building is shown as one of multiple panels. Almost by definition, looking at a building's windows (from a street perspective) makes one wonder what is going on inside—thus, again, proposing voyeurism. The title of another work depicting the facade of a building (*The Mind's Gaze* [1946]) seems to hint at this. As Magritte once wrote, "Everyone has a private life that we can catch a glimpse of as through a window."[3]

But there are two Magritte window picture that holds special interest for cinema. In *The Stroller* (1943), we not only see the exterior of a building, but we see it through a window Alternatively, *In Praise of the Dialectic* (1937) (figure 17.1) portrays an open window (as seen from outside a building) whose interior reveals the exterior of another building, its six windows, roof, and facade visible. As in so many Magritte works, we have a spatial conundrum involving inside and outside (a type of "dialectic"). When we peer through a window on the exterior of a building, we expect to see an interior room or hall, but we do not expect to see the outside of another edifice.

From the stance of a film scholar, these Magritte works are highly suggestive of Alfred Hitchcock's *Rear Window* (1954), though in all the comparisons made between the oeuvres of Hitchcock and Magritte, I have found none that mentioned this movie (see chapter 1). *Rear Window* concerns Jeff Jeffries (James Stewart), an invalid photographer laid up at home with a broken leg who spends his time looking out his window across a courtyard into his neighbors' windows. The movie has been seen as both a treatise on scopophilia and on film editing. Furthermore, the scenes that Jeffries witnesses in his neighbors' rectangular windows have been likened to those on a film screen.

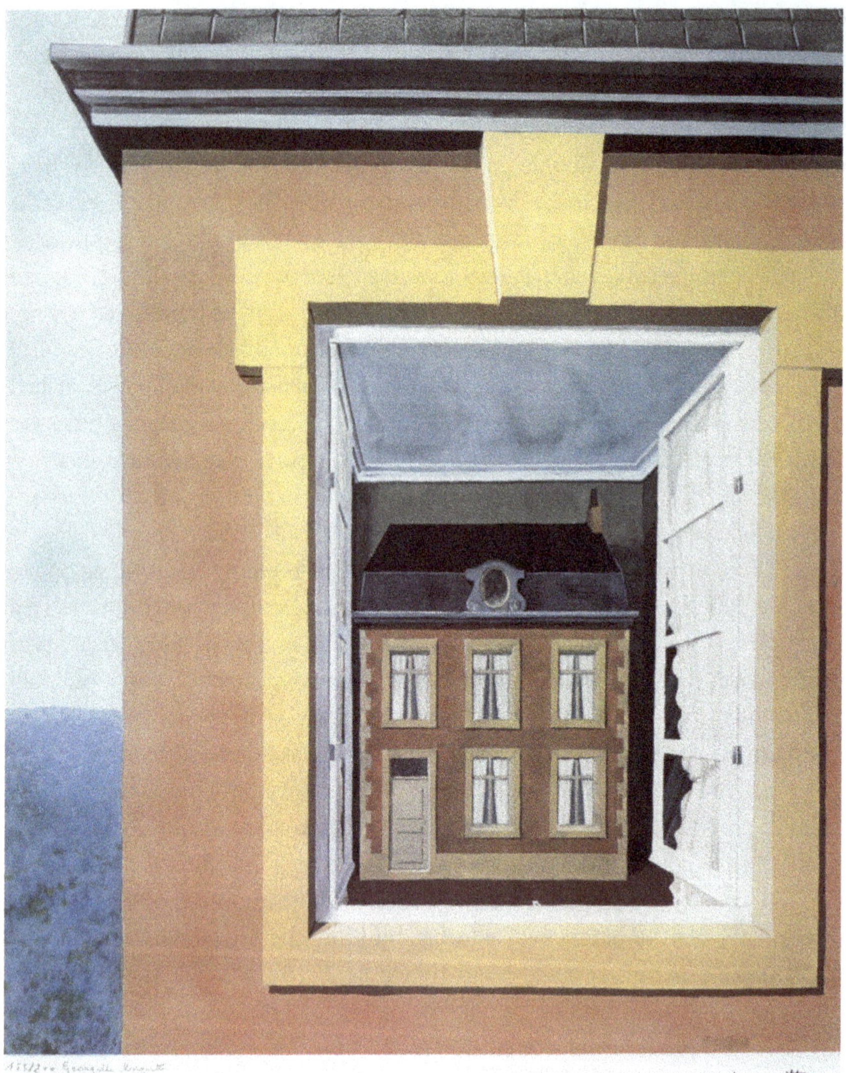

FIGURE 17.1. *In Praise of the Dialectic* (*L'éloge de la dialectique*) (1937)

The opening shot of the film is positioned from within Jeffries's apartment, looking out his window at other buildings; sequentially, three window shades rise to give us a view (figure 17.2). Gradually the camera moves partially through the window, then stops. Next, the camera explores the courtyard and pans right to left to survey the windows of individuals in the opposing residences. When the camera swings around again to Jeffries's window, it enters his quarters

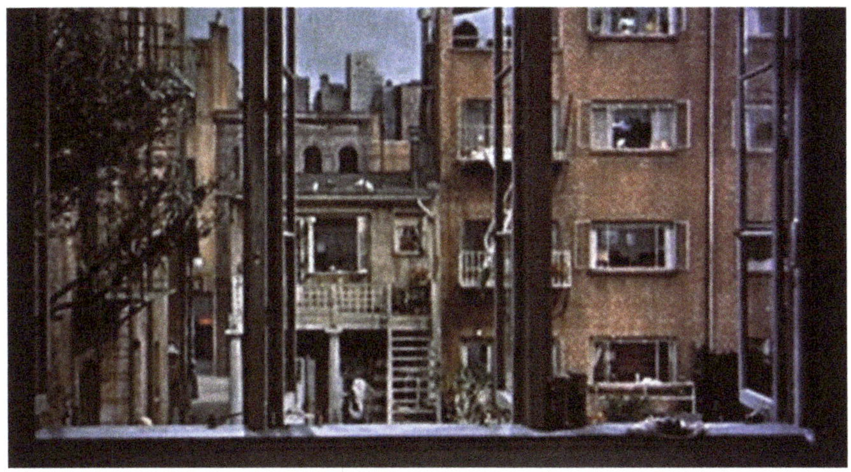

FIGURE 17.2. A view out of Jeffries's window in *Rear Window* (Hitchcock, 1954) looking at the facades of the buildings across the way.

from the outside to reveal him resting and perspiring from the summer heat. In that final camera movement, we get a sense of the first layer of Magritte's painting—a look into an apartment window from the outside. But, of course, the presence in Magritte's canvas of a second layer (another building within the first) evokes the sequence's investigation of buildings across from Jeffries's own.

Not only the opening episode, but the entire narrative of the film entails Jeffries's (and the spectators') watching scenes of characters who live across the way—primarily viewed from the protagonist's standpoint, utilizing the trope of shot/countershot. Heightening the issue of looking (a topic raised in chapter 5), Jeffries sometimes peers at his neighbors through binoculars or through a huge phallic telephoto camera lens—with his visual field represented by a fuzzy circular matte. His girlfriend, Lisa (Grace Kelly), calls his observational habit "diseased." And his visiting nurse/masseuse, Stella (Thelma Ritter), deems him a "peeping Tom" who sees "things he shouldn't." Moreover, she calls his camera a "portable keyhole," reminding us of Magritte's keyhole paintings.

Among the people Jeffries watches, there is a woman he calls Miss Lonelyhearts, who waits for a dinner date who never arrives. There is also another he deems Miss Torso, a curvaceous dancer who seems always to be entertaining beaus. He also keeps track of the activities of a sculptress, a salesman, a musician, some dog owners, and a pair of newlyweds (the only ones who keep their shades pulled).

Interestingly, there are loose parallels between Jeffries and an artist figure. He is a committed photographer-journalist who explores war zones and exotic places like Finland, Pakistan, and Kashmir. While Lisa, a rich socialite, wants him to renounce his ideals and become a commercial photographer, he refuses. Furthermore, he is opposed to marrying her and wants to hold on to his single, bohemian lifestyle. In fact, he mocks her expensive clothing, boutique sales job, meals at the Waldorf or 21, and gossip about her well-heeled friends. Stella, however, thinks that Lisa is perfect for Jeff and asks him suggestively, "Is what you want [in a woman] something you could discuss?"—hinting that his tastes are less than conventional. Additionally, every time the newlywed husband opens the window to relax and get some air, we hear his wife calling him back to bed—conceiving her as having some Amazonian sexual appetite, another reason to eschew wedlock.

While that bride may be desirous, apparently Jeffries is not, and he rebuffs most of Lisa's advances—looking out the window while she embraces him. Lisa even contemplates moving across the way in order to get his attention. Clearly, there is a theme of impotence at play here—signified by Jeffries's leg cast and inability to move. This comes out most emphatically when Lisa breaks into the salesman's apartment and Jeffries must watch powerlessly as the man returns home and aggressively confronts her. The fact is that he cannot look. Thus, sexuality in *Rear Window* is endowed with a perversity that Surrealists would have enjoyed.

Significantly, *Rear Window* is a crime film since, as part of his voyeuristic pursuits, Jeffries discovers suspicious goings-on in the salesman's apartment. He fears that the man (Lars Thorwald [Raymond Burr]) has slain his ailing wife, since the latter seems to have disappeared quite suddenly. Enlisting the help of a detective acquaintance, as well as Lisa and Stella, Jeffries ultimately helps reveal Thorwald as a killer.

Here we sense that Magritte (who was a fan of *Fantômas* films and Nat Pinkerton and Nick Carter detective stories) would have approved of the genre, and, of course, he called one canvas *The Murderer Threatened* (1927)—which could serve as a title for *Rear Window* as well. On the other hand, while Magritte loved crime narratives (which, by definition, offer us enigmas to be solved), he felt that those in his own work were different and more open ended. As he said, "The mystery in these books is a mystery with a key, finally a mystery that may have a solution. Now in my work, it's a question of an *unknowable* mystery."[4]

18

BELLS AND BELLE

> Given the difference between bourgeois thought and Surrealist thought, the latter is, of necessity, biased towards ideas of freedom.
>
> René Magritte[1]

ONE OF THE most ubiquitous images in Magritte's work is that of the bell—the kind associated with sleighs or horse teams. It appears and reappears so often that one cannot help but consider it an obsession. We see it crop up in such works as *The Flowers of the Abyss* (1928), *Pink Bells, Tattered Skies* (1930), *The Voice of the Air* (1928) (figure 18.1), *Act of Violence* (1932), *La belle captive* (1947), and *Heraclitus's Lyre* (1963).

In general, I have shied away from interpreting the symbolism in Magritte's work, but in this case it seems unavoidable. The bell, with its central slit can be read (at least on one level) as referencing the female genitalia (though Magritte positions the slash horizontally, not vertically). The association of bell and woman seems emphatic in the multiple versions of *Memory* (see figure 10.2) with its decapitated, bleeding female head positioned next to a bell. It is also present in *Act of Violence*, in which a bell is accompanied by an image of a female nude.

From the moment I began to consider the presence of bells in Magritte's oeuvre, only one film came to mind (and it did so insistently): Luis Buñuel's *Belle de Jour* (1967). Of course, for English speakers, the French title creates a homonym between *belle* and *bell*—one not available in French, for which the word for the latter term is *cloche*.

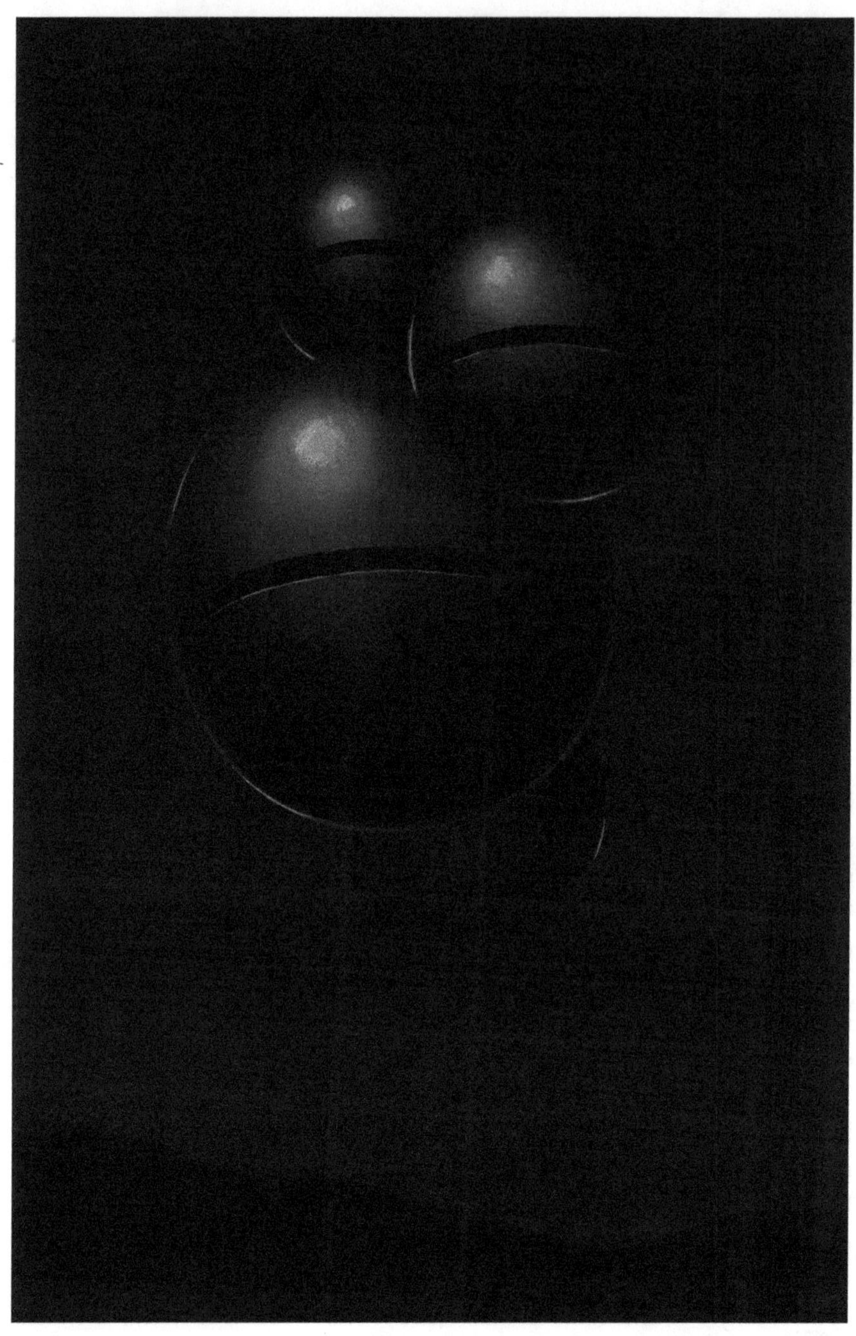

FIGURE 18.1. *The Voice of the Air* (*La voix des airs*/*The Voice of Space*) (1928)

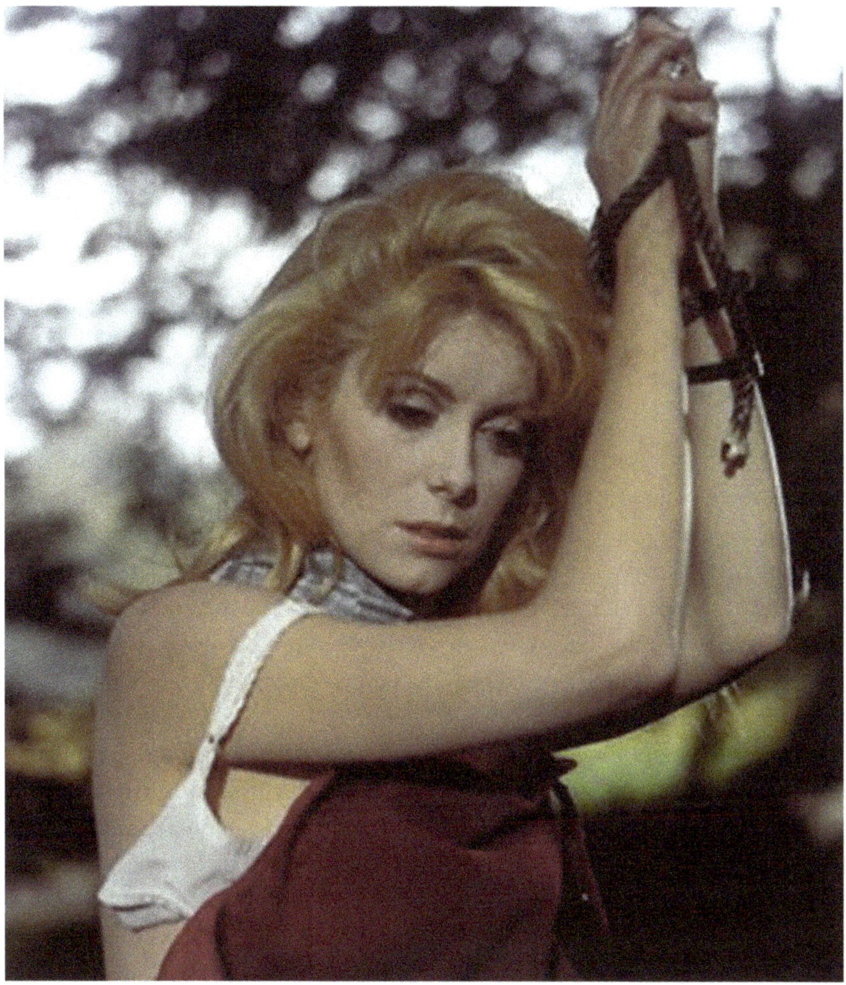

FIGURE 18.2. Séverine (Catherine Deneuve), clothing ripped and tied to a tree, in *Belle de Jour* (Buñuel, 1967)

The reason that *Belle de Jour* has resonances with Magritte's paintings is that the sound of bells (associated with horses pulling an old-fashioned carriage) can be heard at many points in the film—transposing the artist's visual iconography to the acoustic level. In fact, the opening scene starts with such an aural episode. We hear bells and see a man, Pierre (Jean Sorel), and a woman, Séverine (Catherine Deneuve), riding in a carriage through the woods, driven by several coachmen. Pierre remarks on how Séverine (whom we understand to be his wife) is "cold." Soon he commands the carriage to stop and orders her to disembark. He begins insulting her, calling her "slut" and "bitch." Then he ties her hands to a tree, rips her clothing off, and orders the men to whip her (figure 18.2). Soon he tells them, "She's yours now," meaning that they can rape her.

Suddenly the camera cuts to a bedroom, and we see Pierre asking Séverine what she is thinking, and then we realize that the previous scene has represented her fantasy. Throughout the movie, the sound of bells will be tied to visions of sadomasochism in which Woman is the victim. All are assumed to be imagined from Séverine's point of view (though, of course, they are authored by a man—Buñuel).

In the third such sequence, we hear bells as we watch a man ride in a carriage. He gets out at a cafe at which Séverine is seated and asks her to come to his home for a "religious ceremony." We next find her riding in a carriage to his estate and later see her inside, naked and covered by a black veil that falls from a crown of flowers on her head. She is ushered into a room and instructed to lie in a coffin, whereupon the man enters with a camera. (Here we recall Magritte's *Perspective: David's Madame Recamier* [1951], in which he substitutes David's woman lying on a divan with a coffin.) The man addresses her as "his beloved daughter" and claims to have "loved her too much," by which we infer that he has sexually abused her. The fantasy ends with a cut to Pierre and Séverine in their bedroom.

In a fourth fantasy sequence, we see a horse-drawn carriage but do not hear the bells. Pierre and an acquaintance, Henri Husson (Michel Piccoli), engage in a duel in the woods. Séverine is tied to a tree, blood running down her face. Pierre comes and kisses her. The final such episode occurs after Pierre has been rendered paralyzed and mute by a gunshot wound. In it, as bells ring, Pierre miraculously gets out of his wheelchair and asks Séverine whether she hears what he does. As she looks out from their apartment balcony, we see a carriage driving through the woods without any passengers.

Of course, these imaginary sequences in *Belle de Jour* do not make sense without knowing more about the plot of the film. Pierre and Séverine are an upper-class French couple, living in a Paris apartment. From the dialogue, we glean that, while Pierre loves his wife, he is frustrated by the fact that he feels that he must "force" her to engage in sex. In other words, she is erotically reticent and perhaps "frigid." Ironically, the daydreams that she has all imagine her as sexually humiliated or abused—leading us to believe that such a dynamic is the only one that excites her. Clearly, her tender husband (whom Husson characterizes as a "Boy Scout") is incapable of such an approach.

Séverine learns from a friend that one of their female acquaintances is now making extra money by turning tricks. Later, in a conversation between

Séverine and Husson, the latter talks about having frequented brothels and mentions the address of one run by a Madame Anais (Geneviève Page). As though responding to a compulsion, Séverine finds herself going there and becoming one of the madame's girls, taking on the pseudonym of Belle de Jour. In one case, a customer wants her to play the role of sadist—but she is unsuccessful in so doing. Another client, however, wants her to be harshly disciplined, a part she readily performs. The scene takes place offscreen, but we know that it has happened by the presence of blood on her sheets.

Clearly, as a Surrealist filmmaker, Buñuel is interested in revealing the underbelly of bourgeois existence, here the power of forbidden sexual desire. In the chapter epigraph, Magritte makes clear that he sees Surrealism as purposefully countering traditional morality in the name of freedom. However, there are two different ways of viewing what happens to Séverine in the film, given that her fantasies conceive her as sexually shamed or tortured. On the one hand, we might read her descent into prostitution and abjection as a liberation of her true erotic desires—ones generally suppressed in polite society. On the other hand, we might read it as a male envisioning of women as "whores" who wish (or deserve) to be punished.

But it is not only Magritte's bell paintings that are at issue here. While sadism is not a huge theme in his work, when it does appear, it often affixes to women (who are alternately idealized in other canvases). Here two works are central—*Rape* (1935) (see figure 16.3), already discussed in chapter 16, and *Titanic Days* (1928) (figure 18.3). As mentioned earlier, *Rape* shows a headless female body (already demonstrating the violence of decapitation), topped by flowing hair, arranged so as to propose itself as a face—with the breasts as eyes, the belly button as nose, and the genitals as mouth. This imagery (with its hints of Sigmund Freud's 1922 "Medusa's Head") suggests both the male fear of castration and of the female genitals, which threaten such a possibility.[2] In line with Magritte's iconography, Buñuel's conception of a frigid woman who desires castigation simultaneously removes the need for a man to confront Woman's sex organ and allows him to rebuke her for its threat.

The second relevant Magritte painting, *Titanic Days*, depicts a composite human figure. Most of it is female, but that part is being overwhelmed by another, which is male. Crucially, the female portion is naked—with her pubic hair visible. The male element (which, significantly, is clothed) can be seen as attempting to overpower the female in a manner that suggests rape. Thus, from one point of view, *Titanic Days* could stand as a painterly emblem for Séverine's fantasies in *Belle de Jour*, further linking Magritte's work to the film.

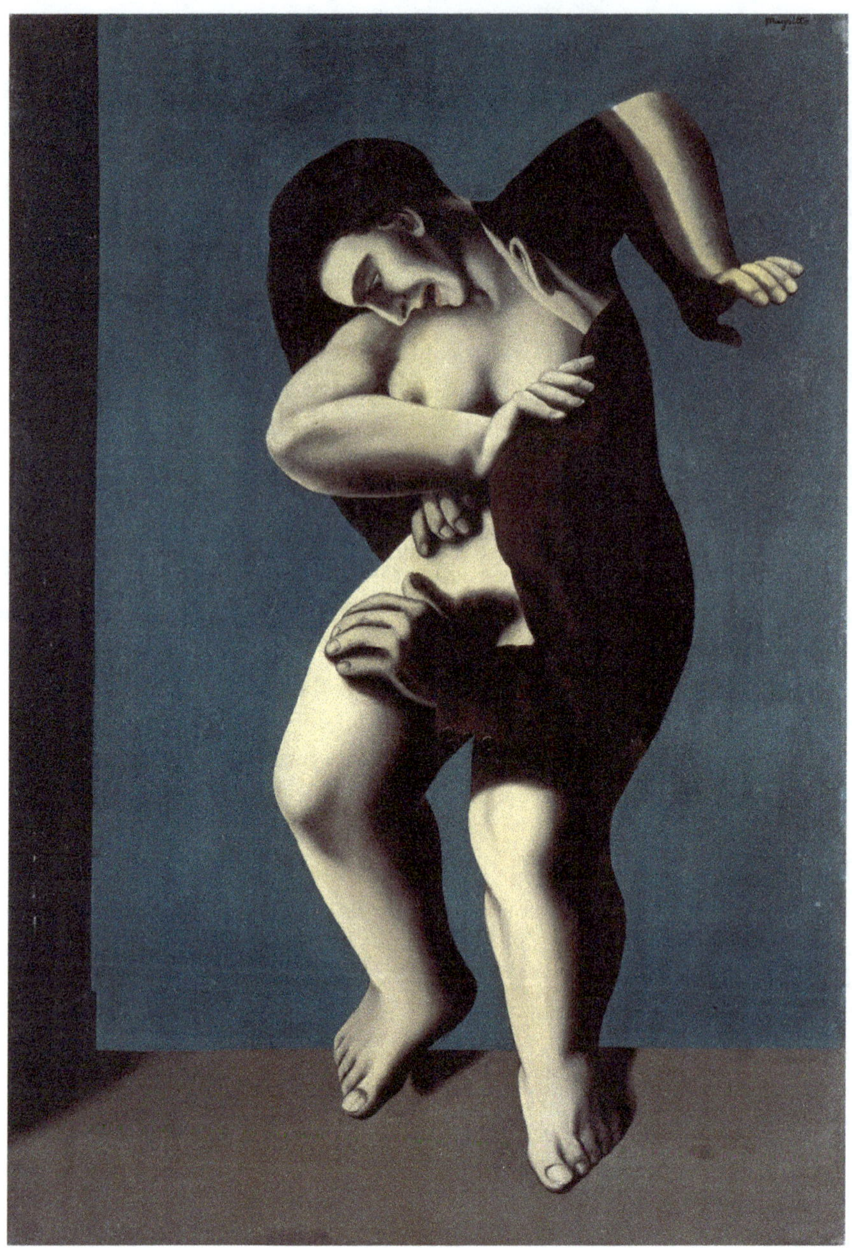

FIGURE 18.3. *Titanic Days* (*Gigantic Days/Les jours gigantesques*) (1928)

19

CURTAINS

> We are surrounded by curtains. We only perceive the world behind a curtain of semblance.
>
> René Magritte[1]

IF ONE RECALLS visiting movie theaters in the distant past, part of the ritual of how the show began was for curtains to open and reveal the screen—clearly a nod to the earlier theatrical tradition. They were often grand elements of the auditorium's decor, frequently made of plush red velvet. This is apparent in the stage design of the Oakland Paramount, a restored 1931 movie theater in California. Even though today such curtains are gone from what movie theaters survive, it is interesting to note that animations of red parting curtains are ubiquitous on YouTube, ostensibly there for people to copy and use as a prelude to their home movies or digital mash-ups.[2]

Similar curtains are present in several works by René Magritte. In some, they stand alone (as in *Coat of Arms* [1936]). But in most, they open onto the material world and not a movie screen. We have already discussed one of these, *La belle captive* (1967) (see figure 3.2) in chapter 3, which examines Alain Robbe-Grillet's 1983 film of the same name. In such paintings, the red curtain most often parts to reveal a blue sky, but different variations of this mise-en-scène occur in Magritte works—for instance, in *The Fall of the House of Usher* (1949), *Mona Lisa* (1960), and *High Society* (1962). Interestingly, Magritte once linked the sky and curtains, stating, "The sky is in the shape of a curtain because it is hiding something from us. We are surrounded by curtains."[3]

Associations between these canvases and the cinema are numerous, running from the general to the specific, focusing on either the landscape or the curtain. First, there is the ubiquity in movies of the image of the sky as either the initial or final shot of a film. Richard Linklater's *Boyhood* (2014) begins with this icon while Jacques Tati's *Playtime* (1967) and Robert Altman's *Nashville* (1975) end with it. In many ways, this shot has become a cliché—used to solve the problem of narrative commencement or closure. When in doubt, pan up to or down from the firmament.

There is also the curtain per se (rather than the scene it frames). Many people have remarked on the frequent presence of curtains in the work of David Lynch. Most interesting, perhaps, is an anonymous web posting from 2015 that focuses, in particular, on the ties between the "red room" in the original *Twin Peaks* (1990–91) television series and several of Magritte's canvases not previously mentioned in this regard (*Nocturne* [1925], *Blue Cinema* [1925], and *Memory [1948]*; see figure 10.2).[4] The author of the post also quotes Lynch as stating, "I love Magritte. He's one of my all-time favourites. I like a lot of his paintings. I just saw the Magritte show at the Museum of Modern Art in New York and I was overwhelmed by *The Menaced Assassin*. . . . It's a mysterious, beautiful thing."[5]

Responding to queries about his use of curtains, Lynch has spoken of how "there is something so incredibly cosmically magical about curtains opening and revealing a new world"—a statement that might have been uttered by Magritte.[6] Lynch also has mentioned his association of curtains with movie- or possibly theatergoing. As he notes, "I like to go into a theater, see those curtains open, and feel the lights going down. And go into a world and have an experience, knowing as little as I possibly can."[7] He says that he wants his audiences to share the same sense of wonder and confusion that he frequently has as an audience member. This is certainly the case for the spectator of his *Mulholland Drive* (2001), an enigmatic psychological thriller in which the red curtain famously appears in a bizarre scene at the Club Silencio, where a woman collapses on the stage after singing Roy Orbison's "Crying." As she does so, her vocals continue, revealing that her "live" performance has been a sham. Clearly, the issue of illusionism (so important to Magritte) is omnipresent in Lynch's scene. Significantly, a similar mise-en-scène had already appeared in Lynch's *Blue Velvet* (1986)—in a sequence of a woman (Isabella Rossellini) singing the movie's title song—marking the curtains as a recurrent (if not obsessive) aspect of the director's decor. In both instances, the red curtains materialize in mystifying movies in which reality is completely up for grabs.

Interestingly, there is a volume by Allister Mactaggart titled *The Film Paintings of David Lynch*, in which he argues that the fact that Lynch began as a painter has a profound influence on the style of his work.[8] While he sees Lynch's movies as a form of "film painting" (giving movement to the static canvas), there are precious few references in Mactaggart's book to other plastic artists and none to Magritte.

While Lynch's velvet curtains may be an homage to those that framed the old-fashioned movie screen, unlike Magritte's, they appear in a rather "normal" physical space (although nothing about the narratives that contain them is truly ordinary). There is, however, a more abstract and cinematically self-reflexive use of red theater curtains in Jean Renoir's film *The Little Theater of Jean Renoir*—a tripartite work composed of three short stories, or what Renoir deems "anecdotes." It was originally made for French television in 1970 but eventually received a theatrical release in 1975. But before we examine this film, it is well to recall how one film theorist imagined the differences between stage and screen.

For André Bazin, the singular aspect of the dramatic world is that the audience and actors exist in the same time and space, giving the latter a sense of "presence" to the former. Film (like painting) removes the human subject portrayed from the world of the beholder. Of course, in painting, the individual may be a fictional one and need not ever existed, or it may have been a real person who sat for a portrait. The cinema lies somewhere in between those two other representational forms, since, as Bazin notes, with photography, "it is no longer as certain as it was that there is no middle stage between presence and absence." While the individual depicted onscreen is removed from the viewer's current universe, he or she (at least in live-action films) did exist in the past and was recorded by the camera. What is special about film (that painting cannot rival) is that the subject's image is indexical and thereby testifies to his or her existence in a previous world. As Bazin notes, movies make "a molding of the object as it exists in time and, furthermore, makes an imprint of the duration of the object."[9]

In valorizing the cinematic close-up, however, Bazin wonders, "What we lose by way of direct witness do we not recapture thanks to the artificial proximity provided by photographic enlargement?"[10] Here we might sense parallels with painting which, through portraiture, can give us a more a proximate and intimate view of an individual than can the stage. Of course, as seen in chapter 13, Magritte purposely refuses to take advantage of this possibility by depicting duplicate beings or "clones," or ones whose faces are often obscured or turned away from the viewer.

For Bazin, another way that cinema differs from theater is in terms of spectator identification. As he remarks, "The characters on the screen are quite naturally objects of identification, while those on the stage are, rather, objects of mental opposition because their real presence gives them an objective reality and to transpose them into beings in an imaginary world the will of the spectator has to intervene actively . . . to transform their physical reality into an abstraction."[11] According to this logic, painting would be similar to cinema in that, when an individual is represented, it is already an abstraction—thereby facilitating identification. Of course, Magritte frustrates the beholder by denying his subjects a sense of humanity.

Bazin also sees a difference between cinema and theater in the relation of the spectator to the performance. In theater, on some level, actors are aware of an audience that is looking at them. As he notes, "The opposite is true in the cinema. Alone, hidden in a dark room, we watch through half-open blinds a spectacle that is unaware of our existence and which is part of the universe."[12] Here paintings are somewhat similar to movies in that a canvas knows not who regards it. But since Magritte highlights the act of voyeurism in so many of his works, viewers of his art are forced to think about their own spectatorship.

Elsewhere we have discussed the shared focus on objects in both painting and film, and in his consideration of drama, Bazin also makes this point. As he observes, "The human being is all-important in the theater. The drama on the Screen can exist without actors. A banging door, a leaf in the wind, waves beating on the shore can heighten the dramatic effect. . . . [I]n the theater the drama proceeds from the actor, in the cinema it goes from the decor to man."[13] Furthermore, Bazin finds the cinema liberated from the kind of space-time continuum imposed on the stage. As he comments, "Dramatic causes and effects have no longer any material limits to the eye of the camera."[14] Here again movies share something with paintings in that the latter can represent any fanciful event without being constrained by reality. This feature is especially important to works by Magritte that routinely depict a mise-en-scène at odds with actuality.

Finally, Bazin finds parallels between drama and painting by comparing stage architecture to the pictorial frame. As he notes, a theatrical set "exists by virtue of its reverse side and its absence from anything beyond, as the painting exists by virtue of its frame. Just as the picture is not to be confounded with the scene it represents and is not a window in a wall. The stage and the decor where the action unfolds constitute an aesthetic microcosm inserted perforce into the universe but essentially distinct from the Nature which surrounds." As he continues, both forms contrast, in this respect, with film: "It is not the

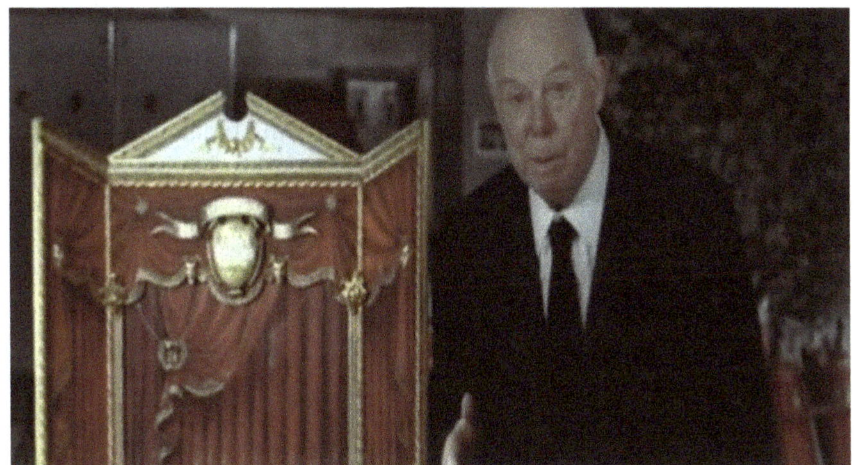

FIGURE 19.1. Jean Renoir standing beside his red-curtained toy theater stage in *The Little Theater of Jean Renoir* (Renoir, 1975)

same with cinema, the basic principle of which is a denial of any frontiers to action."[15]

The Little Theater of Jean Renoir opens with a view of what seems to be a red-curtained proscenium. However, as the camera pulls back and reveals Renoir standing beside it, we realize that it is only a miniature toy stage (figure 19.1). In direct address, Renoir welcomes us to his "little theater" and then introduces the first episode, "The Last Christmas Eve." After seeing a page on which the title of the sequence and its actors are printed, a red curtain (again filling the frame) rises onto a winter street scene. With this conceit, Magritte's vision in *La belle captive* seems to have come true—theater drapes literally opening upon the world.

Wealthy people are celebrating the holiday, and some of them are clearly drunk. Two couples emerge, and one of the men (M. Gontran played by Roland Bertin) looks into the window of a restaurant and approves of its traditional decor. As he proclaims, "I adore the conventional" adding that Christmas is by now a "cliché." In the restaurant, the men discuss how everything in today's world is being "leveled" so that all is "the same."

Noticing an elderly homeless man on the street (played by Nino Formicola), Gontran goes outside and pays the man to peer through the restaurant window in order to increase his dining pleasure. Evidently, seeing a starving person while he is eating amuses him. The two women in Gontran's party are upset and leave, and soon the men follow them.

One of the restaurant employees tells the maître d' to get rid of the "bum" outside. They offer him gourmet leftovers, but the man (who is well spoken) talks of how he is "particular" about his champagne and cutlery. Finally, he accepts the gift-wrapped food package and says he will share it with a beautiful woman.

We then follow the homeless man to a place where his elderly female companion (played by Milly) is waiting. The two profess their love for each other and peer up at the cloudy night sky. She speaks of their past Christmases in their chateau with servants but then cries out that "this game is hideous!" and asks her partner to "stop this delirium." He asserts that she has just "forgotten" those days but she proclaims them "made up memories." He replies that those reminiscences are "the best kind."

They dance in the snow, and suddenly the street scene is transformed to that of their imaginary villa with servants bringing in trays of food. The image returns to reality, and they joke about going to sleep in their canopied bed. Instead, they lie in the snow and the man holds an umbrella above them. After a fade-out and -in, we see two other homeless people happening upon the scene, declaring the couple dead and eating the meal that the latter never consumed.

There are several aspects of this episode that are evocative of Magritte—beyond the trope of curtains parted to reveal "the world." First, there is Gontran's love of "the conventional" and his fear that society is now reduced to "the same." Of course, Magritte relished the ordinary with his depiction of quotidian objects and the sameness of his bowler-hatted clones. Furthermore, there is Gontran's encouragement of the homeless man's pitiable voyeurism (his looking into the restaurant as more fortunate people dine). Clearly, scopophilia is a theme in Magritte's work. Moreover, there is the sequence's emphasis on fantasy—the fact that the elderly couple at times imagines a life that they never lived. Using cinema's arsenal of special effects, Renoir even makes this daydream "come true."

But the most interesting feature of the film is its emphatic "staginess." Rather than filming on actual snowy streets, the mise-en-scène is obviously one created and filmed in a studio. It is patently unreal—or a mere "semblance" of the world, to borrow Magritte's word from this chapter's epigraph. At one point, for instance, when the elderly couple dances in the "snow," we notice that they leave no footprints. In this regard, the film shares Magritte's love of the artificial. Just as his red curtains open onto a pictorial mock-up of the sky or ocean, Renoir's open up to a French sound studio.

The second story rendered in *The Little Theater* is "The Electric Waxer." After the red curtain closes on the first episode, Renoir appears once more to introduce it. He says that its subject is timely, as it deals with "man versus machine." Though the sequence opens on a real street (vs. a sound studio stage), it is as artificial as the prior story. It unrolls in the form of an opera, with a chorus of men and women singing at various points. In their first appearance, they intone about the hassles of everyday life—rushing from office to subway, dealing with nylons and makeup.

Soon we focus on a female pedestrian (Émilie, played by Marguerite Cassan) who runs by and enters an apartment building, then a flat. Almost immediately she is consumed with hand polishing her parquet floor. When her husband, Gustave (Pierre Olaf), comes home, he wants to celebrate his work promotion, but all she can talk about is her desire to own an electric waxer. As she tells him, waxed floors are to a good housewife what mink and pearls are to a whore. After threatening to leave him, Gustave relents and promises to buy her the appliance.

Outside the apartment building, the chorus sings about how overhearing neighbors is a "free show," and "better than the movies." The members assert that "other people's troubles are our blessed breed." Several of the male singers hold baguettes (for no apparent reason), and soon seven men pass by carrying more of the same.

Inside Gustave and Émilie's apartment, the doorbell rings and a neighbor (who happens to be a salesman of electric waxers) appears, saying that he hears everything that goes on in their flat. He comes with one of the machines and says that Émilie can try it. He proceeds to sing the instructions for using it. She starts waxing and insists that her husband come in and watch. He walks into the room, slips on the floor, and dies. When friends show up for the wake, she complains that they are marking up her floors.

While she is still in mourning, her childhood sweetheart Jules (Jacques Dynam) shows up, and in the next scene they are living together. When she waxes the floor, he complains of the racket, reminding her that she promised not to do so when he was home. She continues to wax, singing an erotic love song to the machine:

> Oh waxer dear let me hug you tight
> What exquisite intoxication . . .
> I feel it in my skin,
> I feel it in my breasts.
> I'm going to blossom.

She follows the song by hugging and caressing the device. Angered, Jules enters the room, grabs the waxer, and throws it out the window. A few moments later,

Émilie jumps off the balcony. The chorus on the street below breaks out in song, speaking of Jules' "sacrilege":

> Dead machines do not revive
> Irremediable is their demise
> Men are born and they grow
> They grow like mushrooms
> It's necessary to stop them

The episode ends with a couple who walk by, kiss, and pledge their affection, declaring that they will have children. It ends with them seen against a cloud-filled blue sky. The curtain lowers on the scene.

There are again many Magrittian elements to this sequence. Though some of it is shot "on location," it is entirely fantastical—with people breaking out in song and the characterization of the dramatis personae over the top. All this squares with Magritte's antirealism.

There is also the story's focus on routine bourgeois existence (e.g., the repetitive journey from subway to office) as well as on everyday objects. In particular, we think of the endless parade of baguettes that we have seen, reminding us of Magritte's painting *The Golden Legend* (1958), in which breads fill the sky. Once more, Renoir's universe is consonant with the synthetic world represented (in a different form) on Magritte's canvases.

There is also an allusion to auditory "voyeurism"—people snooping on their neighbors who enact a free "show." Here we recall Magritte's *The Spy* (1928) (see figure 5.1) as well as *The Month of the Grape Harvest* (1959) (see figure 3.6), in which numerous men peer into someone's window. That the film ends on the image of a cloudy blue sky is also evocative of the mise-en-scène of so many Magritte paintings.

Finally, there is the film's message about human proliferation—that men are born and grow and multiply like mushrooms. Once more we think of Magritte's endless duplicate gentlemen. But while Renoir's political theme is all too evident (that modern society is vapid and values the mechanical more than the human), Magritte's rhetoric is always enigmatic and (like all Surrealists), unconcerned with conventional ethics.

Having discussed several of Magritte's paintings that employ the conceit of the red curtain, there is one more to consider, *The Memoirs of a Saint* (1960) (figure 19.2). In it, the red curtains do not simply open onto the universe (a blue sky again) but wrap it up on the underside of the fabric. Significantly, the curved shape of the curtains is reminiscent of the wide-screen novelty

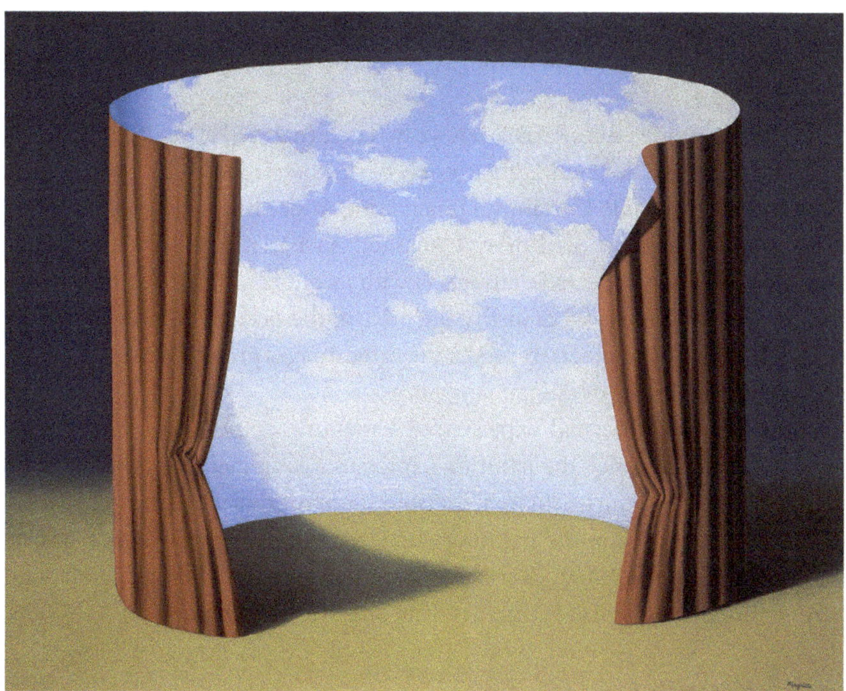

FIGURE 19.2. *Memoirs of a Saint* (*The Memoirs of a Saint*/*Les mémoires d'un saint*) (1960)

Cinerama, a production/exhibition system that premiered in New York City in 1952. With its rounded screen, it promised to envelop the viewer in the projected filmic world.

At the time of Cinerama's debut (with a screening of Merian C. Cooper's *This Is Cinerama* [1952]), *New York Times* film critic Bosley Crowther gushed:

> Somewhat the same sensations that the audience in Koster and Bial's Music Hall must have felt on that night, years ago, when motion pictures were first publicly flashed on a large screen were probably felt by the people who witnessed the first public showing of Cinerama the other night . . . the shrill screams of the ladies and the pop-eyed amazement of the men when the huge screen was opened to its full size and a thrillingly realistic ride on a roller-coaster was pictured upon it, attested to the shock of the surprise. People sat back in spellbound wonder as the scenic program flowed across the screen. It was really as though most of them were seeing motion pictures for the first time. . . . [T]he effect of

> Cinerama in this its initial display is frankly and exclusively "sensational," in the literal sense of that word.[16]

Cinerama arrived in Paris a few years later, in 1955, at the Empire Theater,[17] so it is possible that Magritte knew of or experienced it before painting *The Memoirs of a Saint*. Certainly, French critic André Bazin was familiar with it but not as impressed as Bosley Crowther. As Bazin writes, "Cinerama is scarcely more than a spectacle attraction with its quota of surprises, of novelty, and of physical splendor that justify the price of the tickets."[18] He critiqued its technical difficulty to precisely match the three images projected but did admit its possibilities for the documentary genre.[19]

Whether Magritte had experienced Cinerama or not, however, is ultimately immaterial since the painting expresses a long-standing aspiration of Magritte's to enfold the world in his art and thereby eradicate the gap between reality and fiction. That the painting's imagery mimics the Cinerama screen also attests to the fact that, over the years, Magritte's work ranged from suggesting the silent cinema to a then cutting-edge film technology.

20

FILM HISTORY, TECHNIQUES, PROCESSES, AND MODES OF RECEPTION

> The cinema showed moving pictures on a screen, and this amazing novelty inspired [painters] to rival it.
>
> René Magritte[1]

IN ADDITION TO creating canvases that took on major themes, concepts, and issues circulated in the movies (e.g., voyeurism, magic, words vs. images, the face, etc.), Magritte's works can be understood figuratively to invoke signal moments in early film history as well as to emulate numerous film techniques, processes, and modes of reception.

Primitive Cinema

The Lost Jockey series

When instructors begin to teach film history, they often start with the pre-cinema, including such movement-simulating devices as the zoetrope, thaumatrope, and phenakistoscope. But they also discuss nineteenth-century photographic experiments, such as those of Étienne-Jules Marey and his photo gun. Most important, however, were the studies conducted by Eadweard Muybridge, who in 1872, at the behest of California governor Leland Stanford, set up multiple trip-wired cameras to record the gait of a horse. When animated by a zoopraxinoscope, Muybridge's photographs reproduced the horse's trot. When stopped on a particular frame, they proved that, at one moment while galloping, a horse is, in fact, airborne.

Here a particular series of paintings by Magritte is suggestive. Beginning in 1926 with *The Lost Jockey* (figure 20.1) and lasting into the 1960s, one of Magritte's favored images was that of a rider galloping on a horse. His version of the animal was most likely copied from an illustration in the Larousse dictionary.[2] His 1960 painting on the theme (*The Anger of Gods*) is especially comical since the horse and jockey are positioned on top of a car, ostensibly negating their need to move on their own steam. For anyone steeped in film history, this series of Magritte paintings cannot help but bring to mind the photographic experiments of Muybridge. Interestingly, however, Magritte always depicts the animal with one foot on the ground—a cunning revolt against realism.

Time Transfixed (1938)

While the photographic studies of Muybridge mark a seminal moment in precinematic history, another work marks the point at which cinema emerges on its own. It is the movie *The Arrival of a Train* (1895), made by August and Louis Lumière—one of the first ever publicly exhibited.

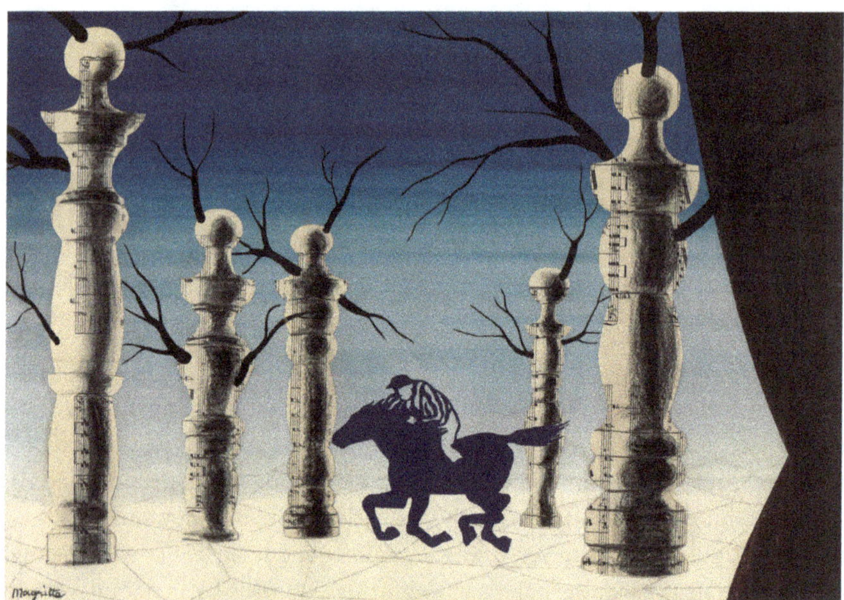

FIGURE 20.1. *The Lost Jockey* (1926)

As mentioned in the preface, as a graduate student I took the class Dada, Surrealism, and Film with the late Annette Michelson. In it, she showed a slide of Magritte's *Time Transfixed* (1938) (figure 20.2) as a means of invoking *The Arrival of a Train*. At one point, film historians believed that when spectators first saw the train rushing toward them in the theater, many of them recoiled—a tale that is now regarded as semiapocryphal.

Before discussing the image that Magritte depicts in the canvas, it is noteworthy that the title of the work has ties to the cinema, as the notion that time could be "transfixed" speaks to the medium's ability to control temporality. That Magritte chose to depict a train incongruously racing through a fireplace into a parlor is significant, since the movies brought the outside world (including its new mechanical wonders) inside—be it to a cafe, saloon, nickelodeon, or home. Nonetheless, cinema made such behemoths as locomotives "harmless" for indoor consumption, as they existed only as light and shadow.

Beyond this, throughout film history the train has served as an omnipresent part of cinematic mise-en-scène—be it in silent serials like *The Perils of Pauline* (Louis J. Gasnier and Donald MacKenzie, 1914), in which a heroine might be tied to the tracks; in melodramas like *The Mother and the Law* (D. W. Griffith, 1919), in which a train might function as part of an extended chase finale; in dramas like *La roue* (Abel Gance, 1923), in which the protagonist is a train engineer; in mysteries like *Murder on the Orient Express* (Sidney Lumet, 1974; Kenneth Branagh, 2017, in which enigmatic events take place during a rail journey); or in experimental films like *Pacific 231* (Jean Mitry, 1949), in which the beauty of rotating wheels and axles fashions a study of shape and movement. Significantly, one of the earliest (and most idiosyncratic) venues for film viewing was offered by Hale's Tours (shown, for instance, at the St. Louis Exhibition of 1904), whose "theater" resembled a railway coach from which viewers watched movies (as though looking at passing scenery) through its front window.

Film Techniques, Processes, and Modes of Reception

Shot Distance and Scale

One way that Magritte's works suggest film technique is to mimic the medium's variable shot distance—which can range (in an instant) from close-up to medium shot to long shot. Magritte's brilliant take on this was to combine different "shot distances" within a single canvas—playing with scale in one image the way that film does over a series of sequential ones.

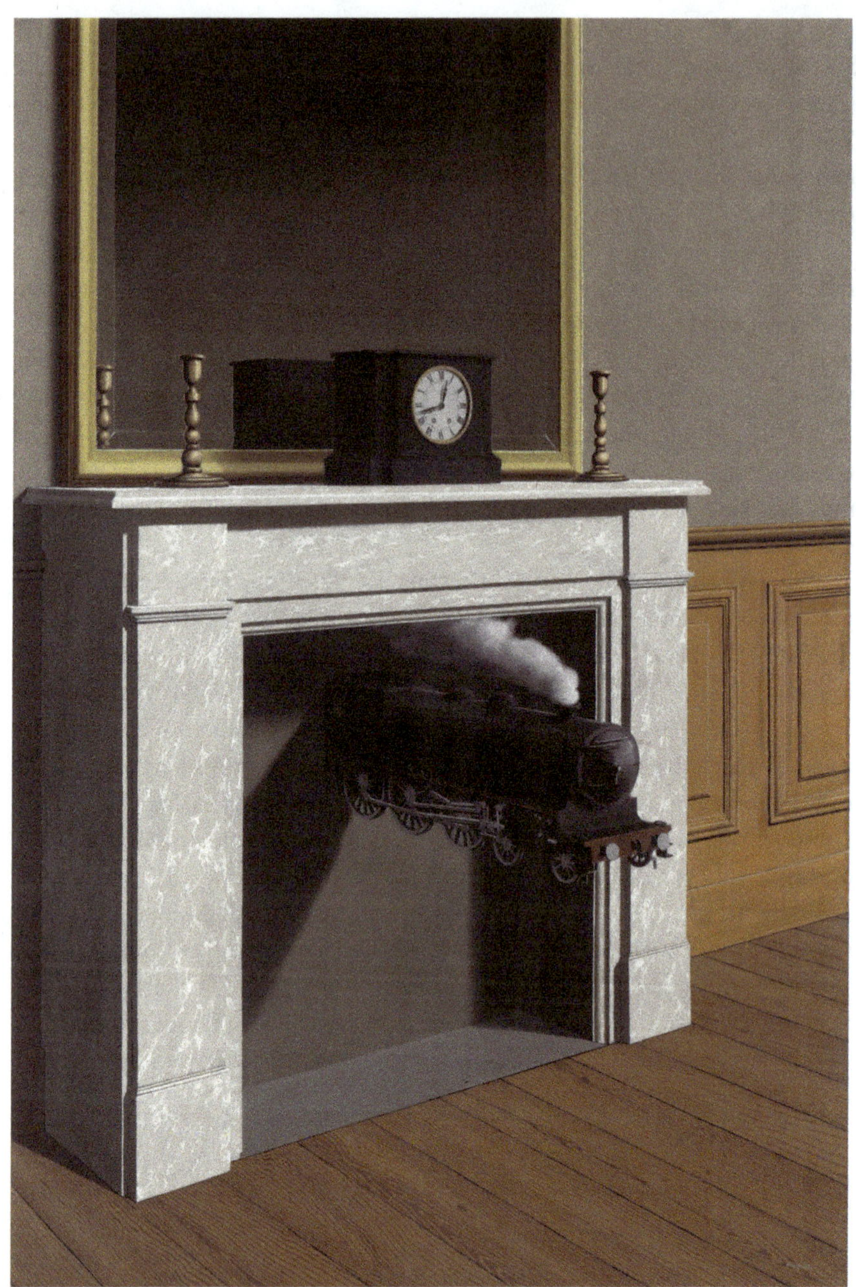

FIGURE 20.2. *Time Transfixed* (*La durée poignardée*) (1938)

Here one thinks of *Stimulation Objective* (1938–39), in which a small image of a statue is inserted into a larger identical one. The smaller one might be imagined to have been shot from a distance while the larger version from closer up. Similarly, in *Representation* (1962), we find a canvas in which a scene (of boys playing ball) is repeated twice—with one version larger than the other. Again, it is as though the smaller one was filmed in extreme long shot, while the larger one from a closer perspective. One is also reminded of *The Cascade* (1961) (figure 20.3), which depicts a framed picture on an easel up against the leaves of trees. What is interesting is that the framed picture depicts a long shot of the very foliage against which it is tightly wedged. Thus, while a movie might have presented consecutive images—first, a long shot of a group of trees and, second, a close shot of some foliage—Magritte combines the two images into one.

But there are additional iterations of this trope in Magritte's work. *Personal Values* (1952) (see figure 20.13) depicts a room containing a group of apparently oversized objects: a comb, a shaving brush, a glass, a match, and a bar of soap. Why they appear to be so large is that the furniture pieces in the room (a bed and a wardrobe) are tiny in comparison. It is as though we are simultaneously seeing a long shot of the room and an extreme close-up of the objects within it. This is not to say that we apprehend the room as real (given that its walls are decorated with the sky). Furthermore, the size of some of the objects seems puzzling in relation to others. For instance, the comb seems too big in comparison with the stemmed glass. Nonetheless, the simultaneous play with scale can be seen to mirror the sequential one in film discourse.

A room is also depicted in *The Giantess* (1931) (see figure 10.5), but this time Magritte uses human figures to show the contrast in size. A tiny man is pictured in the foreground while a huge woman appears a just a bit behind him making their relative size impossible. From a filmic perspective, we might, however, imagine that he is shot in long shot while she from a nearer vantage point. Clearly, the furniture in the room is also strangely sized. The sofa is way too large for the man while being too small for the woman.

Magritte's eccentric play on dimension occurs in two other paintings. In *The Tomb of Wrestlers* (1960) a room is populated by a gargantuan rose. He repeats this motif in *The Listening Room* (1952) in which a giant apple fills a chamber as well. In both cases, it is as though Magritte again combines a long shot of the room with an extreme close-up of an item within it. Clearly, there is also a discourse of nature versus culture going on here, in the collision of natural objects with the built environment.

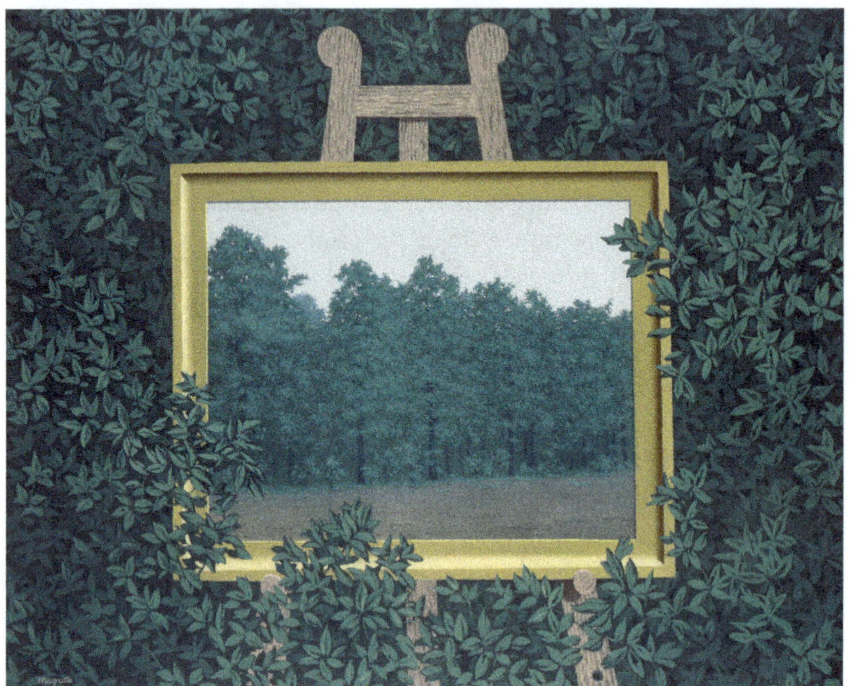

FIGURE 20.3. *The Cascade* (*La cascade*) (1961)

Finally, there is Magritte's *Megalomania* (*Delusions of Grandeur*) (1962). It depicts three different components of a female body in one image: the legs and hips, the torso, and the upper body (including breasts and arm stumps). The pieces are nested together in the manner of Russian dolls, ascending from largest (at the sculpture's base) to smallest (at its top). The sculptural segments might also be seen as moving from a close-up of the legs and hips (which assume a large size), to a medium shot of the torso (which is smaller) to a long-shot of the upper body (which is smallest, as though seen from a distance). Here, of course, one should also note the painting's implicit violence to the female subject who is sliced into parts and is missing her lower limbs and head (echoing the theme of dismemberment discussed in chapter 16).

Aside from the fact that all movies have the potential to shift scale by simply adjusting camera distance (or using a zoom lens), there are a few films that do so in an exaggerated fashion, drawing on an arsenal of cinematic special effects. Several of these are works of fantasy and depend upon the conceit of human beings shrinking in size so that everything in the world appears huge to them. (I have referenced a brief sequence of this kind in *The Eternal*

Sunshine of the Spotless Mind [Michel Gondry, 2004], discussed in chapter 10, in which to portray a character's memory of childhood, an oversized set is employed making the person seem tiny.) While there are some Magritte paintings in which humans are portrayed as miniscule (e.g., *The Giantess* or *Portrait of Stephy Langui* [1961], discussed below), most of his manipulation of scale involves objects. One of the first feature films to miniaturize a person was *The Incredible Shrinking Man* (Jack Arnold, 1957), a sci-fi/horror movie in which a man is exposed to a radioactive cloud while vacationing on a boat. Some six months later, he notices that he is getting smaller, a process that continues until he can fit into a dollhouse. Then in 1981, Joel Schumacher made *The Incredible Shrinking Woman*, a comedy in which a suburban wife and mother is diminished in size after being exposed to some experimental perfume.

Most popular of all in this genre, however, was another comedy, *Honey, I Shrunk the Kids* (Joe Johnson, 1989), in which an inventor father who is fashioning a miniaturizing machine accidentally shrinks his and his neighbor's children. Most of the narrative involves the adventures of the quasi-microscopic kids in their backyard—battling insects, a lawn sprinkler, a lawn mower, and the footsteps of their parents. Finally, the family dog rescues them and brings them into the house, only to have one of them land in his dad's cereal bowl—barely avoiding being eaten.

The film begins with a graphic animated sequence that links it a bit to painting and involves the children's struggles with everyday objects (e.g., a saltshaker and a pencil). In the live-action sequences, the children encounter nature—for instance, landing in a flower and being covered with pollen or taking cover under a mushroom.

Finally, *Downsizing* (2017), directed by Alexander Payne, is a recent satirical work that imagines people willing to have themselves shrunken to acquire more things and live more affluent lives.

The Frame/Montage

In chapter 9, I considered Magritte's use of the empty frame as a subject for paintings and have raised parallels to the film frame. But there are other works in which the frame plays a major role. For instance, many critics have noted how Magritte's *Man with a Newspaper* (1928) (figure 20.4) seems to present us with four cinematic frames or shots. Together (as though through film editing), they propose a kind of narrative and mystery. In the first frame, a man sits reading a newspaper; but as of the second, he has disappeared, never to resurface again. We wonder why.

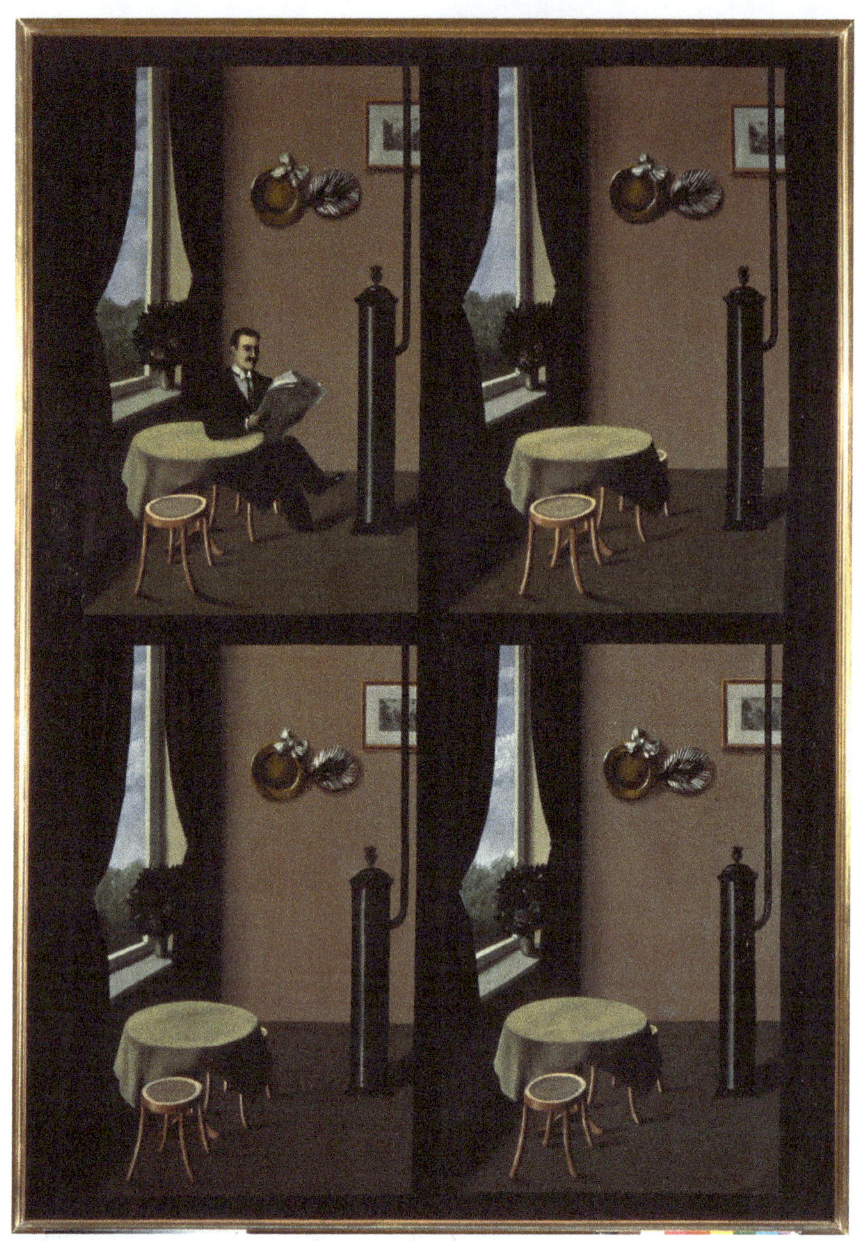

FIGURE 20.4. *Man with a Newspaper* (1928)

There is also Magritte's multiframe painting *The Eternally Obvious* (1930). Like *Megalomania*, it is problematic in its carving a woman into pieces—though it grants her all her body parts, as though she could be reassembled. The five sections of the work (each individually framed) are mounted vertically on a wall with spaces in between them. Here we might conceive of five consecutive cinematic shots of a naked woman as seen from the same camera distance: her head, her breasts and chest, her belly button and pubis, her thighs, and her legs and feet; no major manipulation of scale is involved. Rather, it is as though each view were shot in close-up and edited together through filmic montage.[3]

There is another multiframe painting that also speaks to montage: *The Depths of the Earth* (1930). The top- and bottom-left framed paintings seem to consist of separate "shots" of the same foliage, while the top- and bottom-right panels seem to consist of two shots of another tree. One can imagine them edited together in a variety of ways—so as to highlight aspects of the same landscape.

Finally, there is *The Six Elements* (1929) (figure 20.5), which depicts a framed picture, standing in a three-dimensional space containing six diverse internal frames. Reading from left to right, and top to bottom, the images included are those of flames, a female torso, trees, windows, the sky, and bells—many of them standard elements of Magritte's repetoire. Interestingly, the external frame is unconventional and irregular in shape, as are all the internal ones. On one level, we can imagine this painting as a modernist storyboard for some experimental film that juxtaposes shots of varied objects and scenes combined through montage. On another, the assorted forms of the frames inside can be seen analogous to the multiple shapes and aspect ratios that have been used in cinema over time—ranging from the standard (e.g., the Academy ratio or 11:8) to panoramic (21:9) and everything in between.

Especially, in the silent era, through the use of matting, filmmakers could alter the sense of the frame to their liking (if not its actual outside borders). French director Abel Glance makes extensive use of this strategy in *La roue*. In some shots, the image we view is encased within a round internal frame, while in others an oval one. There are even a few instances of a diagonal matte when picturing the rails of a train yard. Additionally, there is one shot that contains multiple differently shaped mattes—approximating most closely the mode of collocation that Magritte employs in *The Six Elements* (figure 20.6).

One work by Magritte seems especially relevant to the silent cinema, *The Viewpoint* (1927). In it, four landscapes (apparently the same) are encased in irregular, roundish frames that seem to mimic the blurry outlines of early film mattes. Gance, of course, further experimented with image framing and

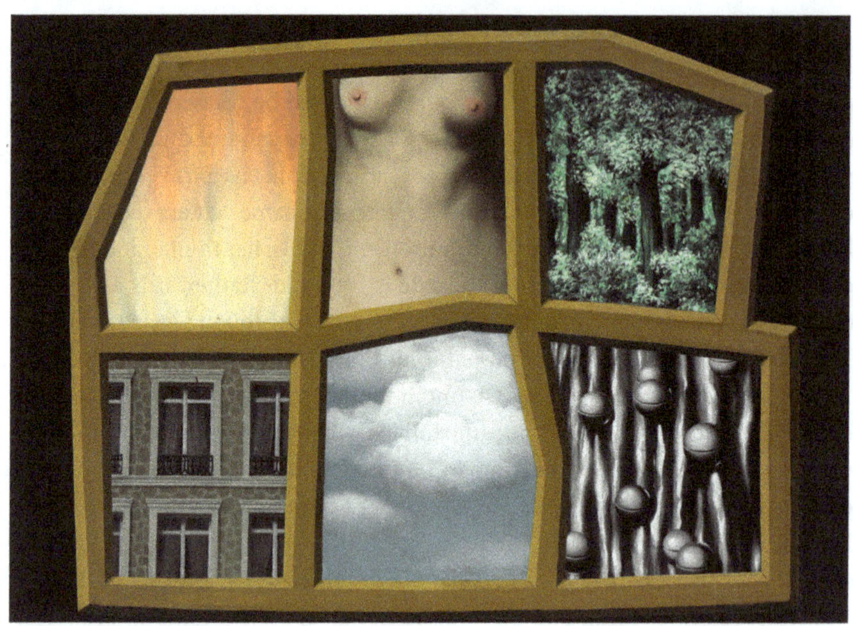

FIGURE 20.5. *The Six Elements* (1929)

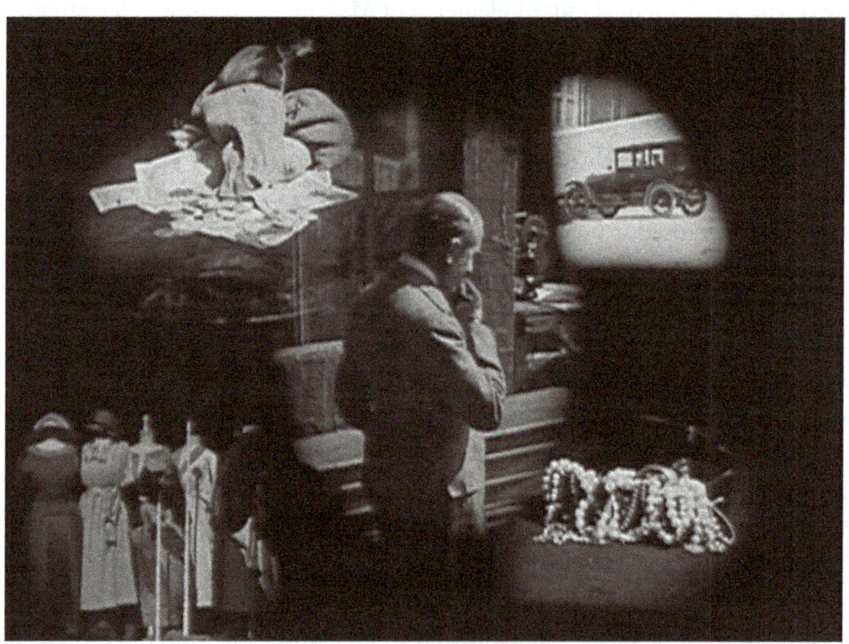

FIGURE 20.6. This shot from *La roue* (Gance, 1923) entails five multishaped matted images depicting different scenes, reminiscent of Magritte's use of irregular frames.

juxtaposition in his later groundbreaking film *Napoleon* (1927), whose finale constitutes a triptych of imagery. Gance achieved this by shooting with Polyvision (which employed three interlocked cameras), and then screening the sequence utilizing three projectors.

Of course, in later decades, it became possible to split the screen through optical printing or CGI. An interesting use of the effect occurs in the 1959 film *Pillow Talk*, directed by Michael Gordon. The credit sequence employs a triptych of rectangles, but a later episode of the film, depicting three people talking on telephones, uses triangular shapes to encase them. Finally, the multiplication of frames reaches excessive proportions in *OSS 117: Lost in Rio* (Michel Hazanavicius, 2009), in which one shot contains twelve internal frames of varying size and shape, again depicting people on the telephone.

Lighting: Day for Night

One of Magritte's most famous series of paintings is called *The Domain of Light* (figure 20.7), which he began to create in 1949 and worked on until his death in 1967. Each canvas portrays a dimly lit night scene that includes a house and an illuminated streetlamp. The sky is blue and filled with white cumulus clouds. What is clearly strange about these works is the lighting, which simultaneously signals both day and night. Thus, it uproots our conventional sense of time and is distressing for that reason.

Of his series of paintings, Magritte opines, "This evocation of night and day seems to me to have the power to surprise and delight us. I call this power: poetry."[4] He also states that the paintings reflect "the idea that night and day exist together, that they are one."[5] Here Magritte unites temporal dimensions as he does spatial realms in other works—for instance, showing that inside and outside are one and the same. In fact, there is a painting that subverts spatial oppositions while invoking the iconography of *The Domain of Light*—*The Night Owl* (1928). The canvas shows an interior scene, but an item that is usually associated with the outside (a lit lamppost) appears on the inside. This makes the lighting of the chamber peculiar—bright at the level of the lamppost but dark almost everywhere else.

Beyond its interest for Modernist art history, the *Domain of Light* series sparks several associations to the cinema. First, there is the technique called "day for night," by which a scene that takes place in the evening (according to the narrative) is actually shot during the day, with the lighting darkened unnaturally in postproduction. This strategy was historically utilized when it was too difficult to shoot at night, either logistically or because of technical limitations. In recent years, as the light sensitivity of film stocks has improved,

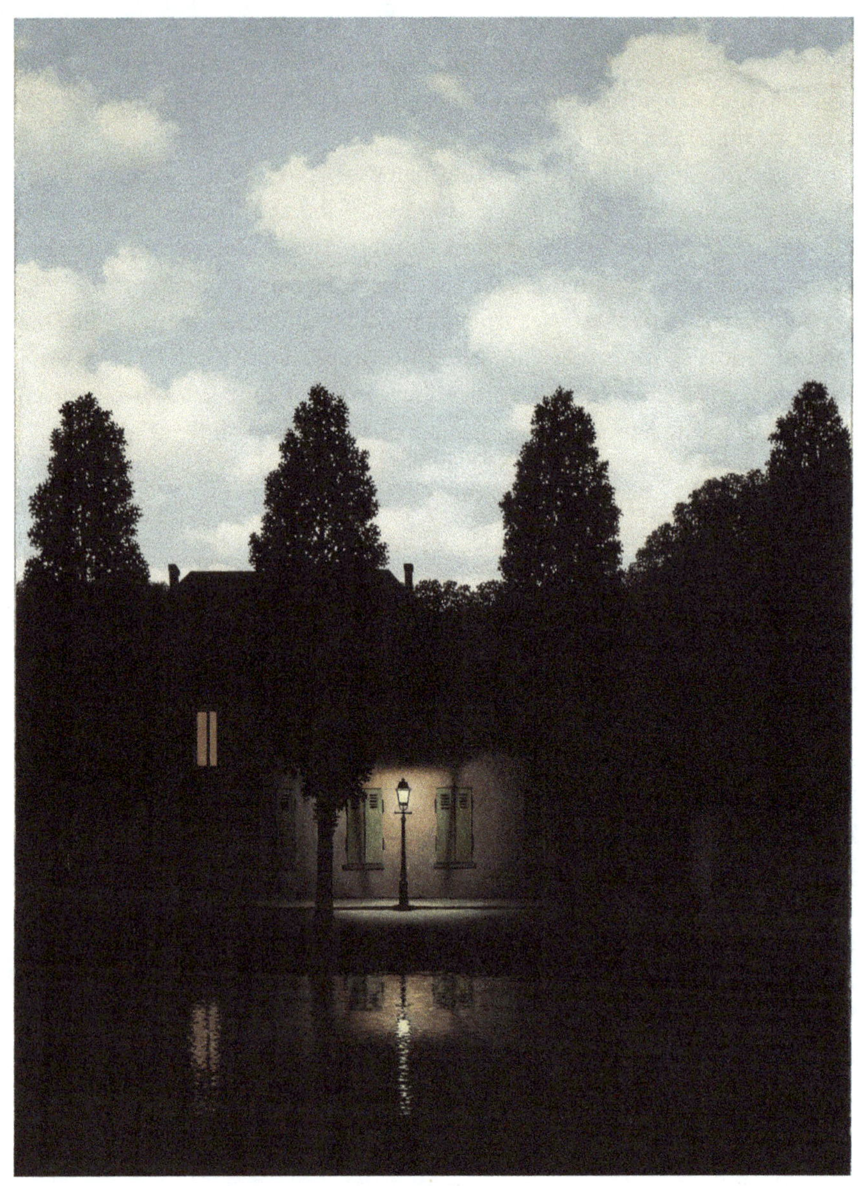

FIGURE 20.7. *The Domain of Light* (*The Dominion of Light*/*L'empire des lumières*) (1954)

"day for night" shooting has become less common. It is the *conception* of this type of filmmaking practice (where day and night are, on some level, equalized) that relates to the *Domain of Light* paintings, not the final film product, which generally completely resembles night.

But there are specific films in which the lighting is peculiar in the manner of the famous Magritte series. Strangely, the François Truffaut movie, which is named *Day for Night* (1973), does not contain any scene of this kind, though it does have a production sequence in which this technique is enacted (though we never see the result). As for other films, many commentators have noted similarities between a scene in the horror film *The Exorcist* (William Friedkin, 1973), in which the priest arrives at the stricken girl's home, and the *Domain of Light* series—one that seems a clear homage to Magritte. In fact, the film's poster highlights this very shot.

But there are movies that, in a more thorough way, attempt to mimic the eerie brand of light that Magritte captures in the *Domain of Light* series. One such work is the Italian film *The Spider's Stratagem* (Bernardo Bertolucci, 1962). It concerns a man who returns to his home town many years after his anti-Fascist father's murder during the Mussolini era to learn who killed him. Beyond the lighting, the film has other parallels with Magritte: a confusion of temporalities, a fascination with doubles or "duplicate" identities and bizarre statues., Here is what Bertolucci, says about his preparation for shooting:

> I like to show paintings to [Vittorio] Storaro, my cinematographer, before we shoot. In *A Spider's Stratagem* [*sic*] we looked at a lot of naif paintings—like the ones seen over the titles. And we discovered that the way the naif artists painted the night was similar to *the way Magritte painted it*—a night-blue in which you can see everything, discovering each and every detail. So we used to *shoot between light and dark*. And if you shoot without the filter you get a kind of liquid blue that bathes the people.[6]

And in another interview, Bertolucci is even more specific about the ties to Magritte:

> On the set I talked a lot with Vittorio Storaro, my director of photography, about the *two visual reference points for the film: Magritte and the naive painters*. For example, we shot the night scenes, as you remember, in a coloration that is quite unusual for the cinema, that is completely in azure. That is, they are nights in which you can see everything, nights

> when you can see a house three hundred meters away hidden in the landscape. . . . *[I]n Magritte's work there is the same type of night "eclairage." There's a painting by Magritte, called "The Empire of Light"* [The Domain of Light] *in which you can see a rectangular, almost horizontal house, with a tree, and two lighted street lamps just like in the scene at the train station when [the protagonist] is getting ready to leave at the end of the film.*[7]

In showing the village during the evening in the film, while streetlights are turned on (signaling nighttime) the sky is still entirely clear and illuminated (figure 20.8). In one such shot, the protagonist carries a lantern (signaling nighttime) while everything around him is amply lit. Finally, the mise-en-scène of a sequence shot at a train station at night perhaps most approximates Magritte's *Domain of Light* series.

To return to a film discussed in chapter 10, *Eternal Sunshine of the Spotless Mind* has moments that tend to mimic aspects of the *Domain of Light* series. When the protagonist, Joel (Jim Carrey), is recollecting an evening he spent frolicking on the frozen Charles River with his now ex-girlfriend, though it is nighttime, he is brightly illuminated as though in a spotlight. A similar day-for-night brand of lighting occurs as Joel recollects another evening with his ex-girlfriend, when the two break into a shuttered summerhouse on the beach. Again, he is bathed in a Surreal floodlit glow.

Point of View

The issue of point of view is one of the most complex in cinema, with entire scholarly books devoted to the subject. In one of them, Edward Branigan introduces the notion by tying it to the question of subjectivity: "When a text [like a movie] is considered as an *object* for contemplation, there must of necessity be some conception of a *subject* who presents the text (author), tells the story (narrator), [and] lives in the fictional world (character)."[8] Depending on how we understand a particular shot in a film, it will generally be attributed to one or the other of the above "points of view." For example, when we watch the trailer for *Citizen Kane* (1941), we hear the recognizable voice of Orson Welles offscreen; therefore, what we view seems to be from his (the author's) point of view. Alternatively, when in Alain Resnais's *Night and Fog* (1956) a disembodied voice (not the director's) describes the terrible things that we see onscreen, we assume that we are observing from the narrator's perspective. Much more common, however, are examples of character point of view. When in *The Diving Bell and the Butterfly* (Julian Schnabel, 2007), Jean-Dominique Bauby (Mathieu Amalric) opens his eyes after suffering a

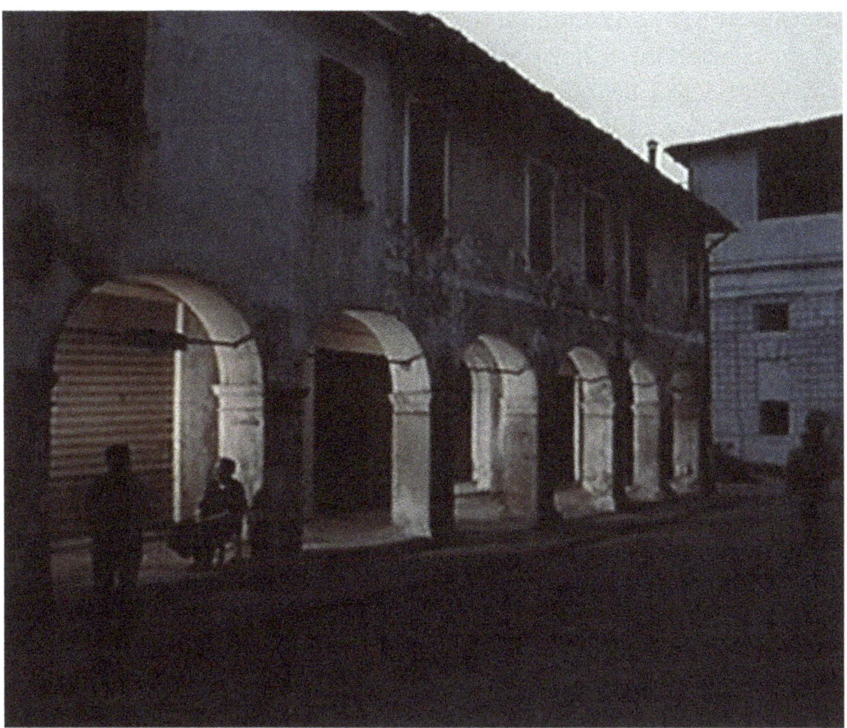

FIGURE 20.8. This shot from *The Spider's Stratagem* (Bertolucci, 1962) mimics the strange lighting in Magritte's *Domain of Light* series (1949–67).

stroke and the next shot we see is a blur of faces, we realize that we are seeing a group of doctors from his impaired viewpoint. While these are clear examples of various categories of point of view, in fact the catalog of possibilities is wide ranging in cinema (including so-called omniscient point of view not identified with any dramatis persona) and far too complicated to consider fully now.

The important thing to realize, however, is that unlike literature—which is based on language and can easily indicate, if the author so desires, a text's point of view (e.g., "Sally regarded the bleak scene outside her window"), the cinema has no access to precise linguistic terminology, for, as Susan Sontag points out, "We see on screen what the camera sees. In the cinema, narration proceeds by ellipsis (the 'cut' or change of shot). The camera eye is a unified point of view that continually displaces itself. *But the change of shot can provoke questions, the simplest of which is: 'from whose point of view is the shot seen?'*" Hence, she talks of "the ambiguity of the point of view latent in the cinema."[9]

Obviously, by utilizing such standard editing tropes as shot/countershot, movies are often able to indicate rather plainly a particular point of view. Using the linguistic example I gave above, shot 1 would portray the character of Sally looking offscreen, and shot 2 would depict what she saw (a bleak scene outside the window). In traditional cinema, the rendering of point of view tends to be realistic. The shot sequence just delineated would only make sense if we knew that Sally was in a room with a window. But some films of a more experimental nature play with improbable points of view. For example, in Luis Buñuel and Salvador Dalí's *Un chien andalou* (1929), a man standing inside an urban apartment looks at his outstretched hand, and the next shot reveals ants crawling on his palm—an impossible vision.

It is clear from Branigan's language that when he discusses point of view, he does so within the context of narrative texts—ones that tells a story (defined as involving an "account of connected events"). This implies a temporal medium that can string together actions over time.

While a multipaneled canvas can depict action over time, and a single-panel painting can have narrative elements (as in a picture of a person playing the piano or riding a horse), painting is not generally considered a temporal medium, and questions of point of view are understood quite differently than they are in film. On one level, the term in art tends to refer to the spatial position from which a subject is represented (e.g., eye level, aerial, frontal, or oblique). Furthermore, space may be rendered in terms of linear perspective (as in the Renaissance) or not (as in Byzantine art). There may also be an observer figure within a canvas who is understood to be viewing the rest of the scene. Finally, on another level, point of view may simply refer to the painter's ideological stance on a subject. For instance, caricaturist George Grosz often takes a satirical stance, making his subjects appear sinister or grotesque. When it comes to Modernist painting, the rules of realistic point of view are often scrambled. Cubism, for instance, renders numerous spatial perspectives simultaneously. Surrealism can also employ techniques of distortion.

Three Magritte canvases, in particular, are of interest here. In *Not to Be Reproduced* (1937) (see figure 12.5), a man, viewed from the rear, looks into a mirror, but rather than seeing his face, he sees the back of his head. Thus, he seems to be both inside and outside himself at once. This painting reminds us of a paradox of the human condition. Without a mirror, we can never actually see our face or the back of our head. Our eyes are trapped within our skull, unable to regard ourselves externally. To produce the view that Magritte renders in *Not to Be Reproduced*, a man would have to stand with his back to a mirror, holding up a second mirror over his shoulder. For once, a Magritte title makes sense.

Another provocative canvas is *The Glass House* (1939). Again, a man is seen from the rear, but this time part of the front of his face protrudes from the back of his head. Clearly, he seems to be occupying two positions at once. A third mystifying work is *Dangerous Connections* (1935). It portrays a woman, pictured frontally, holding up a mirror (facing the viewer) that shows part of her body as seen from the rear. Thus, it conceives of the woman as standing in two places simultaneously, since only if her duplicate had its back turned to her would the mirror reflect the image that it does.

In all three works, Magritte seems to go beyond the kind of spatial displacement created by an artist like Picasso, who in *Head of a Woman with Blue Hat and Red Ribbon* (1939) paints part of a woman's face in profile and the rest in a frontal view. While Picasso's depiction seems to disrupt purely spatial rules, Magritte's seems to violate metaphysical ones concerning subjectivity and identity.

While no film offers a one-to-one analogy to either of these Magritte paintings, there is a movie that provides tantalizing resonances to both: *Being John Malkovich*, directed by Spike Jonze in 1999. Written by Charlie Kaufman (also the scriptwriter for *Eternal Sunshine of the Spotless Mind*), the film tells the bizarre tale of Craig Schwarz (John Cusack), an unemployed puppeteer who gets a temporary clerical job working for LesterCorp. We know that the office will be strange when he is told to take the elevator to floor 7½. As we might suspect, the ceilings of rooms there are exceedingly low, and everyone must walk around bent at the waist. One day, while moving a filing cabinet, Craig discovers a small door in the wall. When he opens it and crawls into the tunnel-like space, he is sucked in, as though by a vortex, only to find himself within the mind of actor John Malkovich (played by himself). Thus, we watch (as though from Craig's perspective and signified by an oval matte) Malkovich read the newspaper, wash dishes, and prepare to leave the house. When Craig's session in the "portal" is complete, he is dumped by the side of a road in New Jersey.

Over the course of the film, various people that Craig tells about his experience venture into the portal and inhabit Malkovich's mind: for instance, Craig's wife, Lotte (Cameron Diaz), who finds Malkovich in the shower, and his coworker and love object, Maxine (Catherine Keener). Soon word gets out about the opportunity to inhabit a celebrity's consciousness, and hordes of people line up at LesterCorp after hours and pay admission to spend time in Malkovich's brain.

Eventually, Malkovich suspects that something odd is happening to him, because when Craig inhabits him, he gets jerked around, as though a puppet on a string. Finally, he learns of the scam that Craig and Maxine are running and appears at LesterCorp demanding to enter the portal himself. When he does so, the world he encounters is entirely populated with duplicate John Malkoviches who continually repeat the words "Malkovich, Malkovich"—a vision of narcissism if there ever was one. Furthermore, the cloned Malkoviches remind us of Magritte's endless duplicate men in bowler hats.

Many other interesting events take place in the film (involving lesbianism, transgender identification, animal consciousness, reincarnation, and possession), but the ones just described are most relevant to comparisons with Magritte. First, it is important to note how the film makes use of mirrors (as does *Not to Be Reproduced* and *Dangerous Connections*). When people enter Malkovich's mind they see through his eyes; therefore, the audience does not see his face. The only way we are sure that a character is inside Malkovich is when the actor looks into a mirror and we recognize him. Here again, the fact that humans need a reflective surface to see their own countenance is emphasized. In utilizing this prop, the film takes advantage of a strategy pioneered in *The Lady in the Lake* (Robert Montgomery, 1947)—a work that sought to depict first-person consciousness throughout the narrative.

Moreover, the positionality of the two figures in *Not to Be Reproduced*—a "real" man standing "behind" his artificial reflection—is reminiscent of the sense of Malkovich (back to us), entering the portal in order to enter himself. Magritte's warning "not to be reproduced" hits home when, in so doing, Malkovich is greeted by a nightmare world of Malkovich doubles, endlessly repeating his name.

Similarly, the film can be seen to have intimations of Magritte's *The Glass House* as well. As noted, that painting depicts a man (seen from the rear) whose face should be invisible to us. Instead, the man's face partially pokes through the back of his skull and regards us. This protrusion is not simply absurd "but aggressive (as suggested by the opened skull, the image comparable to a person breaking into his own house)."[10] In a sense, this canvas implies something like the troubling brand of dual consciousness that Malkovich experiences in inhabiting his own mind. It also engages Magritte's obsession with the gaze. Ordinarily, when one views the rear of an individual he or she cannot look back. But in *The Glass House*, he does.

There are two other works by Magritte with intriguing ties to the issue of point of view. In *The Alarm Clock* (1957) (figure 20.9), a painting that depicts a bowl of fruit is placed upside down on an easel for no apparent reason. And in *Portrait of Stephy Langui*, a woman, her head upside down, peers through an archway into a room that contains two tiny people and a large boulder. What is most interesting here is not the contents of the room but rather the sense of an inverted perspective on the world—one that also characterizes *The Alarm Clock*.

These paintings spark associations to two movies that also render the world topsy-turvy. One is Ernie Gehr's experimental film *Side/Walk/Shuttle* (1991), in which documentary images of skyscrapers are turned on their head (figure 20.10). This short color film was shot in San Francisco with the camera located in a three-sided glass elevator in the Fairmont Hotel—ascending or descending. It consists of twenty-five shots, most of them under ninety seconds each. Many are accompanied by ambient urban sound.

The first shot establishes a normal perspective as the camera, in a rising elevator, travels up the surface of a building across the street. We know that things are right side up by the position of the ocean and sky. After that,

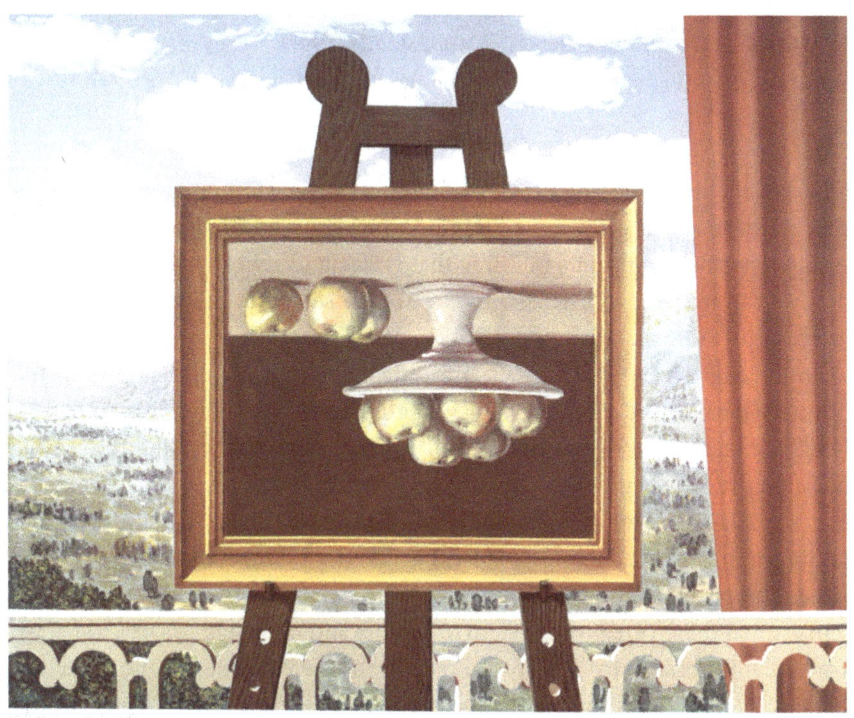

FIGURE 20.9. *The Alarm Clock* (*Le réveille-matin*) (1957)

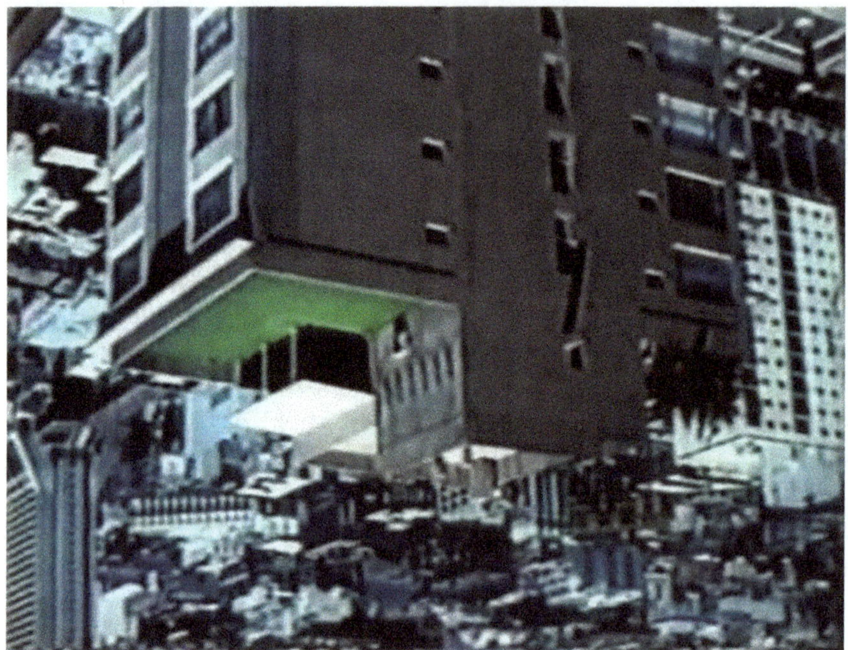

FIGURE 20.10. In Gehr's *Side/Walk/Shuttle* (1991), scenes of buildings in San Francisco, as photographed from a moving elevator, often appear upside down.

however, the directionality of images is either nonsensical or ambiguous. One shot seems to show us a building that is lowering itself into the ocean and sky. Another seems to present a building that is rising to street level. The only way that we can make spatial sense of what we are seeing is either to look at the images upside down (like the woman in Magritte's *Portrait of Stephy Langui*) or to flip the screen on which we are watching—thus restoring views to the ordinary perspective of an elevator going up or down. Otherwise, as Steven Higgins notes, "the city swoops and tilts before our eyes, making the viewer question the laws of gravity."[11]

The 2012 feature film *Upside Down*, directed by Juan Solanas, takes the notion of an inverted world to an extreme. The premise of this rather silly fantasy movie is that in a distant solar system twin planets revolve around the same sun and are ruled by a system of double and opposing gravity. Thus, we are told, it is possible to "fall up and rise down" there. What this means is that the tips of each world meet in the center and appear reversed to those in the other realm. The only thing connecting the dual dominions is a tower belonging to the capitalist Trans World Corporation.

Utilizing a conventional spatial hierarchy, the film conceives of the upper sphere as belonging to the rich and the lower as relegated to the poor. People from one zone are forbidden to travel to the other without permission; if they do, the pull of opposing gravity will set them on fire—shades of Magritte's burning tubas (as in the 1947 version of *La belle captive*). Drawing on another cliché, the film imagines a cross-class love affair between a man from one territory and a woman from the other.

Given the parameters of the fictional cosmos, shots in the film often portray objects inverted, including the heroine, Eden (Kirsten Dunst). Moreover, within the selfsame image, things are often portrayed both right side up and upside down, according to the world to which an individual or object belongs. In one shot, for instance, the hero, Adam (Jim Sturgess), has been allowed to work in an office in the upper domain. While he is seen from a normal point of view, his supervisor appears upended.

Certainly, in both films and in Magritte's canvases, there is a call to view the world from a fresh perspective—unhampered by normal visual or spatial constraints. Significantly, in discussing Gehr's *Side/Walk/Shuttle*, P. Adams Sitney draws upon a relevant quote from Ralph Waldo Emerson: "Turn the eyes upside down, by looking at the landscape through your legs. . . . [H]ow agreeable is the picture, though you have seen it any time these twenty years!"[12]

Detached Displays

According to Noël Carroll, one of cinema's important features (though not one exclusive to it) is its presentation of "detached displays," which contrast to the manner in which we perceive things in the real world. As he writes: "When I see an image of the Kremlin in cinema, I cannot, on the basis of the spatial image, orient myself to that precinct of Moscow. . . . If we are, in a manner of speaking, attached to the arrays that surround us visually in our lives off screen, the cinematic images are *detached displays* . . . phenomenologically detached from the actual space of our bodies."[13] Why this notion rings true (in a different sense and on a figurative level) with so much of Magritte's iconography is that he continually offers us images of the world in which items are entirely detached from their surroundings (as well as from us, given that they appear in discrete pictures).

In *The Waking State* (1958), we see unmoored windows floating in the sky, as we do in *The Female Guest* (1956). In *The Scars of Memory* (1926 or 1927), *Victory* (1939) (figure 20.11), and *The Foundling* (1967), we similarly find unanchored doors; in *The Misanthropes* (1942) and *Organ Tones of Evening* (1965), we have a series of half curtains standing on the ground. Here we also

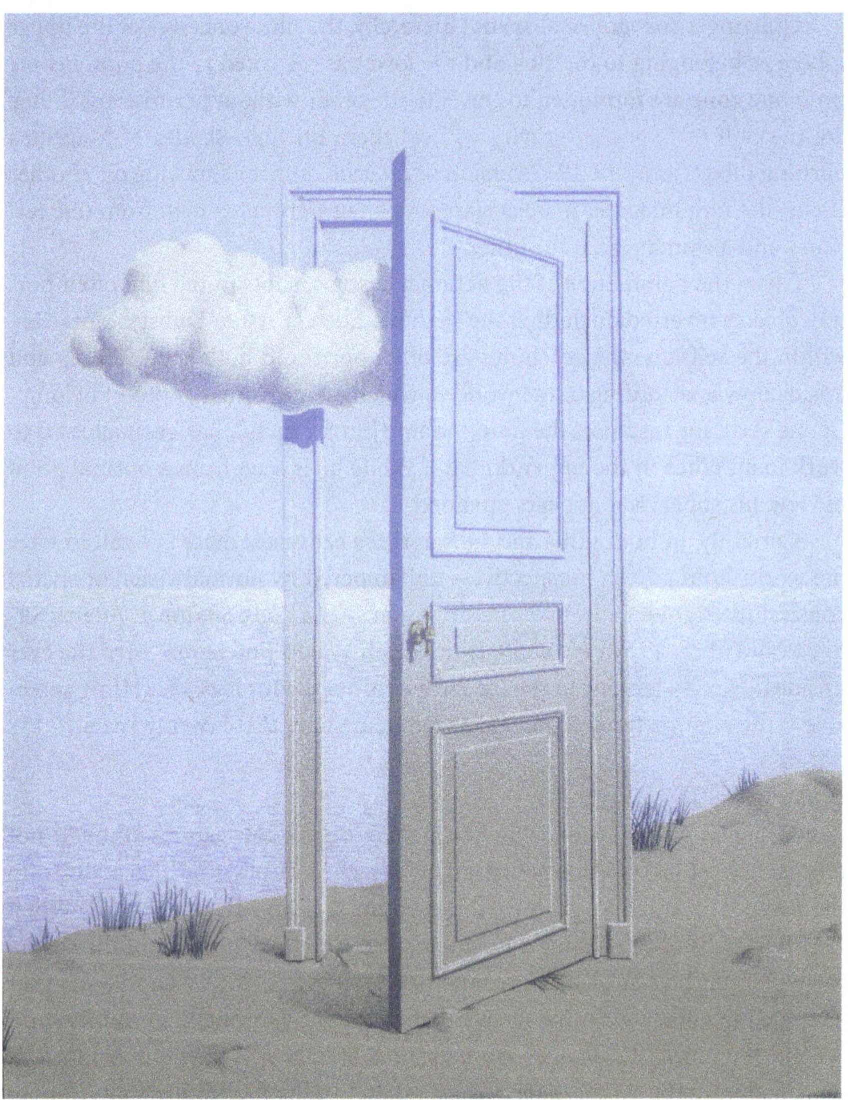

FIGURE 20.11. *Victory* (*La victoire*) (1939)

recall the unmoored objects in *Porky in Wackyland* (Robert Clampett, 1938), discussed in chapter 8, or in *Monsieur Fantômas* (Ernst Moerman, 1937), examined in chapter 4.

On one level, such spatial disconnection is related to Surrealism's interest in locating objects in new contexts, making them strange and disarming. On the other, as seen through the lens of cinema, it is as though Magritte were presenting us (metaphorically) with items the way we see them in the movies—detached from their placement in the actual physical world. As we would be at pains to spatially navigate a window hanging in midair, so a window projected on the film screen confounds our attempts to affix it (and us in relation to it) to the real world. Such an image remains a "detached display."

Realism

From the earliest days of theoretical writing about film, the medium was associated with realism—for its ability to allegedly capture life unawares. As stated in chapter 1, André Bazin likened the cinematic image to a "decal" or "transfer" of reality onto celluloid.[14] Likewise, Siegfried Kracauer saw film as offering a "redemption of physical reality."[15] Significantly, we have highlighted Magritte's surface pictorial accuracy, though, of course, the subject of his paintings belie any sense of the world as we know it. While objects on his canvas may be painted with accuracy, their context and combination are weird. Thus, on many levels, his work constitutes a critique of naive realism.

Most famous, of course, in this respect is his *The Treachery of Images* (1929) which depicts a smoking pipe and the words "Ceci n'est pas une pipe" (This is not a pipe). Obviously, the canvas warns us not to fall for the illusion of reality—that we are actually seeing a pipe. Rather, it alerts us to the fact that we are merely viewing a picture or reproduction of a pipe. Clearly, the same goes for imagery in the cinema—a medium of far greater verisimilitude than painting.

Another work comments on the trap of realism more obliquely—*The Uncertainty Principle* (1944) (figure 20.12)—already discussed in chapter 15 in relation to human-animal hybrids. It constitutes a sketch of a woman standing in the foreground who projects a shadow on the wall. But the shadow is not consonant with her body; rather, it traces the outlines of a bird. As stated earlier, the work's title plays on Heisenberg's "uncertainty principle" in physics, which asserts that one can never simultaneously know the exact position and the exact speed of an object. While this type of uncertainty has no relevance to the picture, doubt haunts the relation of the figure to the shadow depicted on the canvas.

As Victor I. Stoichita has noted, in general the shadow serves many functions in the history of art. On one level, it affirms the carnality of a body portrayed in a painting. On another (as in German Expressionism), it projects a subject's psyche onto the exterior world in the form of the terrifying and uncanny double.[16] Interestingly, Magritte uses few shadows in his work (as

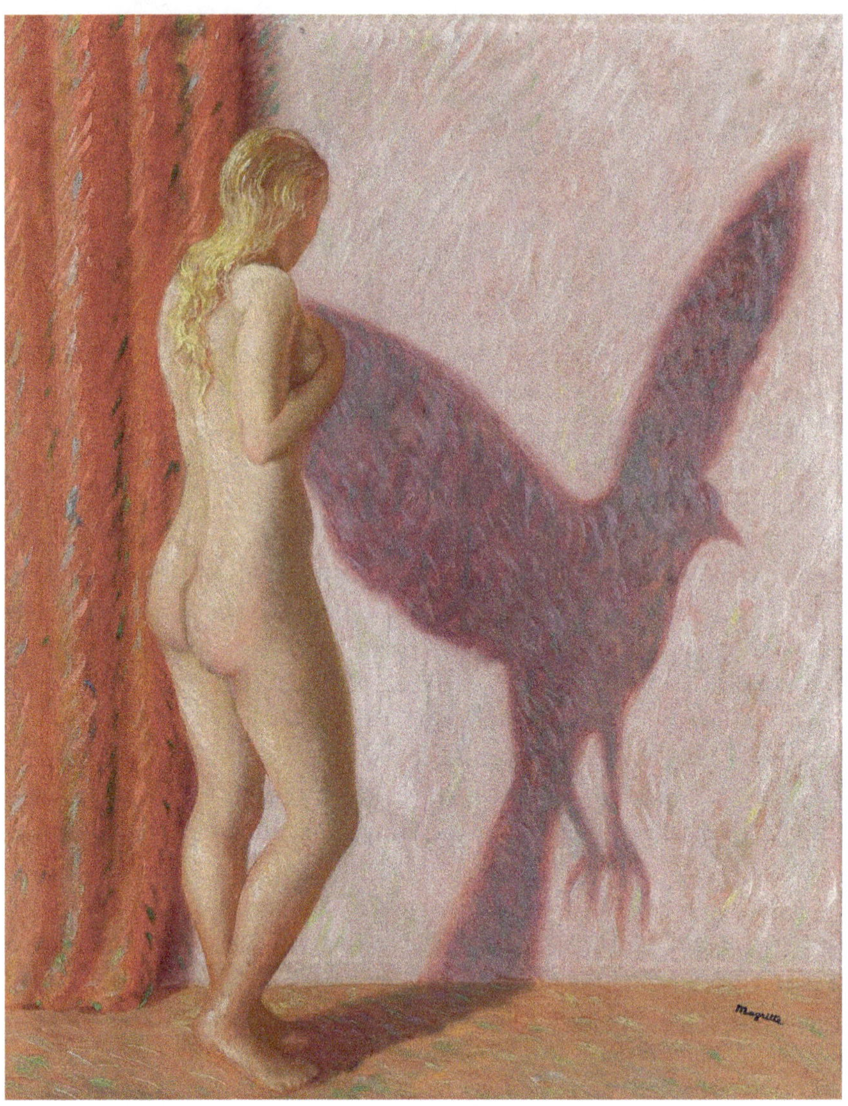

FIGURE 20.12. *The Uncertainty Principle* (1944)

opposed to another Surrealist—Giorgio de Chirico—whom Soichita cites).[17] This in itself is interesting, since when Magritte wants to get a sense of the doppelganger, he simply multiplies the figure (often his man in a bowler hat). When shadows are used at all, they are often employed realistically, as when in the painting *The Survivor* (1950), a rifle, leaning against a wall, casts a shadow on the latter's surface. But clearly in *The Uncertainty Principle* something else is going on, as Magritte takes pains to create a mismatch between the woman and her projection. As he once noted: "We cannot be sure from the shadow of an object what that object is in reality. (For example: you can make a bird's shadow with your hands and fingers.)"[18]

Here it is worthwhile to turn attention to the cinema, which has often been conceived as involving a play of light and shadow. Perhaps what *The Uncertainty Principle* is telling us is that we should beware of any naive notions of realism—that (to use a filmic metaphor) the figure before the lens and the one projected on the screen may be (or seem) quite different from each other from the perspective of the viewer. For instance, if Stan Brakhage's 1963 experimental movie were not called *Mothlight*, we would have no idea that what we were viewing on screen were insect wings. Rather, we might assume that we were watching a hand-painted animated Abstract Expressionist film. On a different note, when Dziga Vertov in *Man with a Movie Camera* (1929) shows us images of a day in the life of "a city," in truth, we are viewing pictures of *multiple* cities shot at different times but made to appear as one locale through editing and graphic matches.

We might also view the dual but opposing figures in *The Uncertainty Principle* as invoking the filmmaking technique of employing a "body double" (instead of the star) for certain sequences of a movie that entail danger or perhaps nudity. While the spectator views the bodies seen on screen as identical from shot to shot or scene to scene, in truth they may be vastly different.

Finally, with the use of green screen, CGI, and motion (or performance) capture, what the camera films in the studio and what the spectator sees in the play of light and shadow on the movie screen are entirely dissimilar. While shooting a scene for *Dawn of the Planet of the Apes* (Matt Reeves, 2014), Andy Serkis stands before multiple cameras wearing a dark bodysuit emblazoned with markers, what is projected on the screen for the viewer is the image of Caesar the Ape. Clearly, this is not so different from what we see in *The Uncertainty Principle*—a woman whose shadow resembles a bird.

Props

It would be impossible to discuss the work of Magritte without emphasizing his interest in objects, which fill his paintings as much as (or even more than) human subjects. In fact, he once talked about wanting to make "everyday objects shriek out loud."[19] Here, in particular, one thinks of his paintings that depict *only* objects—like *The Discovery of Fire* (1934–35), with its flaming tuba (which Magritte deemed an "object painting"[20]), or *Personal Values* (figure 20.13) with its comb, shaving brush, glass, and bar of soap—or canvases in which objects (a valise, a clock, a pitcher) are accompanied by words (mismatched, of course), as in *The Interpretation of Dreams* (1935). Clearly, in some of Magritte's artworks the objects do "shriek out loud," as, for instance, when a tuba burns. This is because, for Magritte, painting the world of things involved "creating new objects; transforming ordinary objects; [or] changing the substance of some objects."[21] Furthermore, he once stated (echoing a quote mentioned in chapter 1): "An object, any subject taken as a question is a matter of finding another object as answer, secretly connected to the first by links which are sufficiently complex to serve as verification of the answer. If the answer is imperative, obvious, the bringing together of the two objects is striking."[22]

Magritte's interest in objects is, of course, consonant with the broader Surrealist valorization of them. As André Breton writes in his 1936 "The Crisis of the Object," the movement's mode of thought "is distinguished above all by the fact that it is dominated by an unprecedented *desire to objectify*."[23] For Breton, Surrealist objects are derived from dreams, and he recalls how, in 1924, he proposed actually manufacturing such eccentric items for circulation.[24] Primary in the Surrealist characterization of objects was the "depreciation of . . . [their] often dubiously accepted usefulness."[25] Rather, Surrealists tapped into the "latent possibilities" of objects, which allow their "transformation." In so doing, their "conventional value . . . becomes entirely subordinate . . . to [their] dramatic value."[26] Finally, Breton discusses a May 1936 exhibit in which such bizarre items were displayed.[27] We have already mentioned a few of such Surrealist items: Salvador Dalí's lobster telephone (1936) and Man Ray's nail-embellished clothing iron (1921).

In a few of his art works, Magritte moved from painted objects to actual ones. Noteworthy is *This Is a Piece of Cheese* (1936), in which a framed painting of a cheese slice is placed inside a dome-lidded transparent glass food server, thus confusing representation with reality. Here the server functions as a literal "prop" for his canvas. At other times, he produced sculptures based on iconography from his canvases, as in the bronze *Megalomania* (1967) based on the earlier canvas *Megalomania* (*Delusions of Grandeur*).

But, in general, objectification in Magritte's work resides in the things he paints—objects that share the kind of alteration of which Breton speaks as well as distance from their ordinary use. Magritte, however, did not generally create from his unconscious; rather, as noted in chapter 1, he talks of rationally solving the "problem" of individual objects—be it a window or a shoe. As he wrote, "I felt that the objects themselves had to reveal their vigorous existence, and

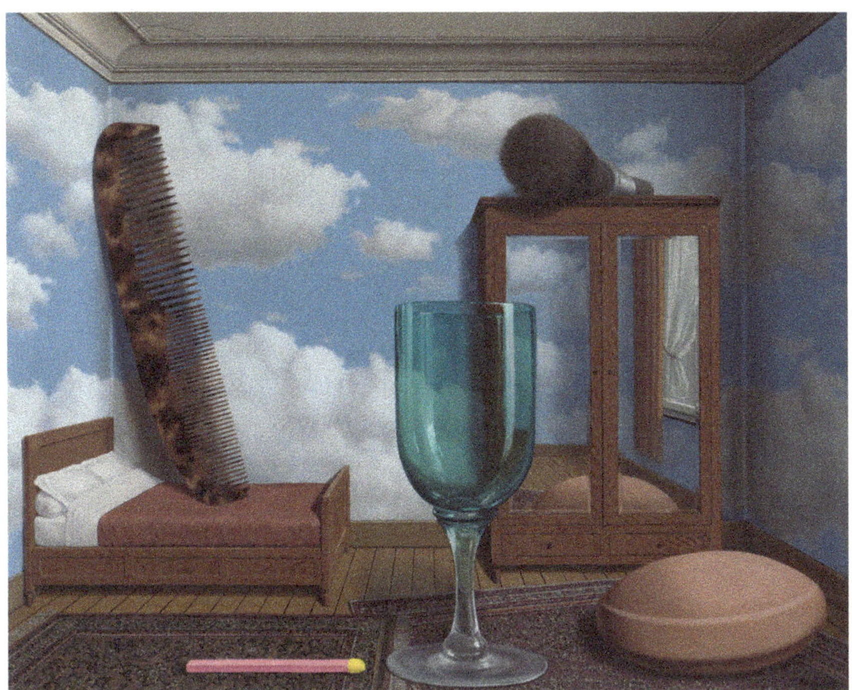

FIGURE 20.13. *Personal Values* (*Les valeurs personnelles*) (1952)

I searched for the answer."[28] For this reason, critics have spoken of Magritte's "philosophy of objects" and his "art of the problem."[29]

Unlike some Surrealists who tended toward abstraction, Magritte represented objects with great veracity. Thus, around 1924, Magritte decided "only to paint objects with the details that were visible."[30] As Breton notes, "Certainly, Magritte's initial concern is to reproduce the objects . . . which make up our everyday world in order to reconstitute its [*sic*] appearance for us with absolute fidelity. But far beyond this, Magritte is concerned to make us conscious of the latent life of all these components by drawing attention to the constant fluctuation of their interrelationships."[31]

Turning to cinema, we have already mentioned in chapter 1 that film theorists acknowledged how the world of things could achieve a more major role in cinema than on the stage, since the camera can focus on them in close-up, often at the expense of framing people. Here one thinks of the function of a key in Alfred Hitchcock's *Notorious* (1946), or the role of a telephone in Anatole Litvak's *Sorry, Wrong Number* (1948), or the use of bull rushes in F. W. Murnau's *Sunrise* (1927). In film parlance, of course, many objects in the cinematic mise-en-scène are deemed *props*, which are defined as "furnishings, fixtures, hand-held objects, decorations, or any other moveable items that are seen or used on a film . . . set but that are not a structural part of the set."[32]

As we know, movie props can be employed in many ways. On one level, they function to create a credible atmosphere—for instance, a scene in a classroom may require desks, a chalkboard, and books. Similarly, a film set in the 1920s must be populated with items consonant with that era. Here a set dresser operates with the same kind of attention to verisimilitude as does Magritte in his portrayal of most objects. On the other hand, props can also signify fantasy—as when we find a talking candelabra in Disney's *Beauty and the Beast* (Gary Trousdale and Kirk Wise, 1991). Here we might think of Magritte's bizarre shoe with human toes in *The Red Model* (1935). If one were looking for a whimsical prop that might approach such eccentric Magritte objects, we might think of the typewriter in David Cronenberg's *Naked Lunch* (1991)—a cross between an insect and a machine. Props can also mark nation or social class: a British flag may signify that the scene takes place in the United Kingdom; a tattered chair may indicate that its owner is poor. Sometimes props can have narrative resonance. For instance, if a bomb is highlighted in an early episode of a film, it is likely that it will be detonated in a later one. Props can also be placed within the frame for purely aesthetic purposes, as when a lovely vase graces a credenza. Finally, props can serve a symbolic purpose. When early in *The Blue Angel* (1930, Josef von Sternberg), Professor Rath (Emil Jannings) finds his caged songbird dead, it harbors bad luck for his relationship with the singer Lola Lola (Marlene Dietrich).

What I wish to conjecture is that, like certain objects shown within the film frame, those in Magritte's canvases can be seen as iconographic "props." They are not generally placed there to depict a realistic scene (since Magritte's universe is often fanciful). Rather, they are chosen for their role as elements in the intellectual or phantasmagoric discourse that Magritte articulates (in a sense they "prop" them up). Thus, when in *The Human Condition* (1933), a canvas on an easel is positioned in front of a window, it is not there to show a believable view of a painter's studio (though this reading is plausible). Instead, it serves as a "prop" to trouble the relationship between inside and outside, between illusion and reality. When in *Hegel's Holiday* (1958) a glass of water is placed atop an open umbrella, we recognize its location as fundamentally absurd. In truth, it is a prop to destabilize the connection between cause and effect: an umbrella is opened as a protective device against falling rain; but liquid does not fall from an upright glass of water, negating the need for protection. Similarly, in *Elective Affinities* (1933) an egg placed inside a birdcage is not shown for reasons of verisimilitude (as this is not a scene that we would find in the quotidian world). Rather the objects are used as props to illustrate the reversal of the usual sequence of events. Obviously, there is no sense caging an egg (which exists *before* a bird is born). It only makes sense to cage the bird *after* it emerges from the egg. As Magritte wrote, "Given my wish to make the most familiar objects jar . . . I obviously had to upset the order in which objects are usually placed."[33] Furthermore, like props stored in a Hollywood "property room," Magritte's objects are recycled from work to work—be they canvases, bilboquets, apples, bells, rocks, or statues.

Magritte's preference for objects over humans (or equalization of the two) becomes more comprehensible when we consider props in the manner of theater historian Melissa Mueller who writes: "As actors, stage objects vest nonhuman elements in the . . . text with physical presence. . . . When we see objects as actors, we discover that they are vital to the performance."[34] This notion of objects (or props) as "actors" is certainly applicable to the cinema where they often are as essential as their human counterparts. What, for instance, would the thriller or crime film be without a gun—a performer in its own right? Similarly, the apple that hangs in front of a person's face in Magritte's *The Son of Man* (1964) has pride of place over the individual. Its location "acts" to tell us that the human countenance cannot be trusted and is always obscured, even when seen unobstructed. Magritte might have communicated this by showing us an ambiguous visage, but he chose to foreground the apple instead. Here again, Mueller's point of view is useful in that she observes that "props [can] take on uncanny agency."[35]

Finally, as we have seen, in Magritte's home movies, *he transposes pictorial aspects of his paintings quite literally into three-dimensional props for his films*. Thus, in the opening of *Tuba* (1960), a reclining woman holding a mask takes a tuba out from under her bedsheets—thus utilizing two elements of Magritte's iconographic catalog (mask and instrument). Similarly, in *Paul Colinet* (1956–57), the poet wears a German helmet exactly like the one Magritte utilizes in *Homage to Erich von Stroheim* (1957). And in other Magritte movies, people play around with bowler hats—a signature head covering in Magritte's oeuvre and one that he often sported himself. Significantly, in these last two instances, the headgear operate more as props than as elements of costume. Thus, the objects represented on Magritte's canvases are fully materialized and revealed as props when he turns to the cinematic medium.

Interpretation

The interpretative act is one engaged in by many movie *viewers* who attempt to make sense of what they are seeing; thus, we can include it as a mode of reception.

We should first note that Magritte was no fan of the explanatory act as applied to art and especially to his own work. This is clear from his *Interpretation of Dreams* series (e.g., 1927, 1930, 1935), in which pictures and word labels are often mismatched. What he required was a spectator whose "intelligence [was] freed from the obsessive will to give things a meaning in order to use or master them."[36] Though he admitted that "riddles and *puzzles* have a charm for the mind," he felt that "the game [should] not affect the images whose meaning remains unknown."[37]

Magritte's use of "puzzle" is especially interesting because some of his paintings approximate puzzle frames, with or without their pieces being present. The former is true of *The Imp of the Perverse* (1927), which looks like a wooden puzzle missing its inserts. Alternatively, *The Daring Sleeper* (1928) (figure 20.14) resembles a puzzle whose pieces are snugly secured in its frame. Here it seems significant that the latter work's title is *The Daring Sleeper*, possibly a warning to the man who slumbers. And given Magritte's negative attitude toward interpretation (as well as psychoanalysis), it would seem that the sleeper is being chastised for dreaming in symbols that too easily fit some prefabricated slots. Thus, there is considerable irony to this work—one created by an artist who purposely scrambled words and images in other canvases. Here we sense that, once more, Magritte rebels against all signifiers (verbal or visual) that too easily connect to their signifieds. Hence, we might consider retitling the work *The Daring Spectator*—pointing to the viewer who dares to look for comforting exegeses of art, analyses that assign coherent meaning to works imbued with inherent ambiguity. We might also note that in recent years critics have discussed the so-called puzzle film, such as *Memento* (Christopher Nolan, 2000), whose narrative structure toys with the viewer's desire or ability to comprehend its narrative structure and logic.[38] Magritte would have been pleased to know that, quite frequently, these movies entirely frustrate that urge.

One other of Magritte's paintings can be read as a parable on interpretation: *Clairvoyance* (1936) (figure 20.15). It depicts an artist (who exactly resembles Magritte) looking at an egg on a table while painting a bird. On the one hand, the canvas seems explained by its title: the artist foresees what the egg will become and hence paints it—upsetting the temporality of the present. But, on the other hand, it can be read as invoking the interpretive

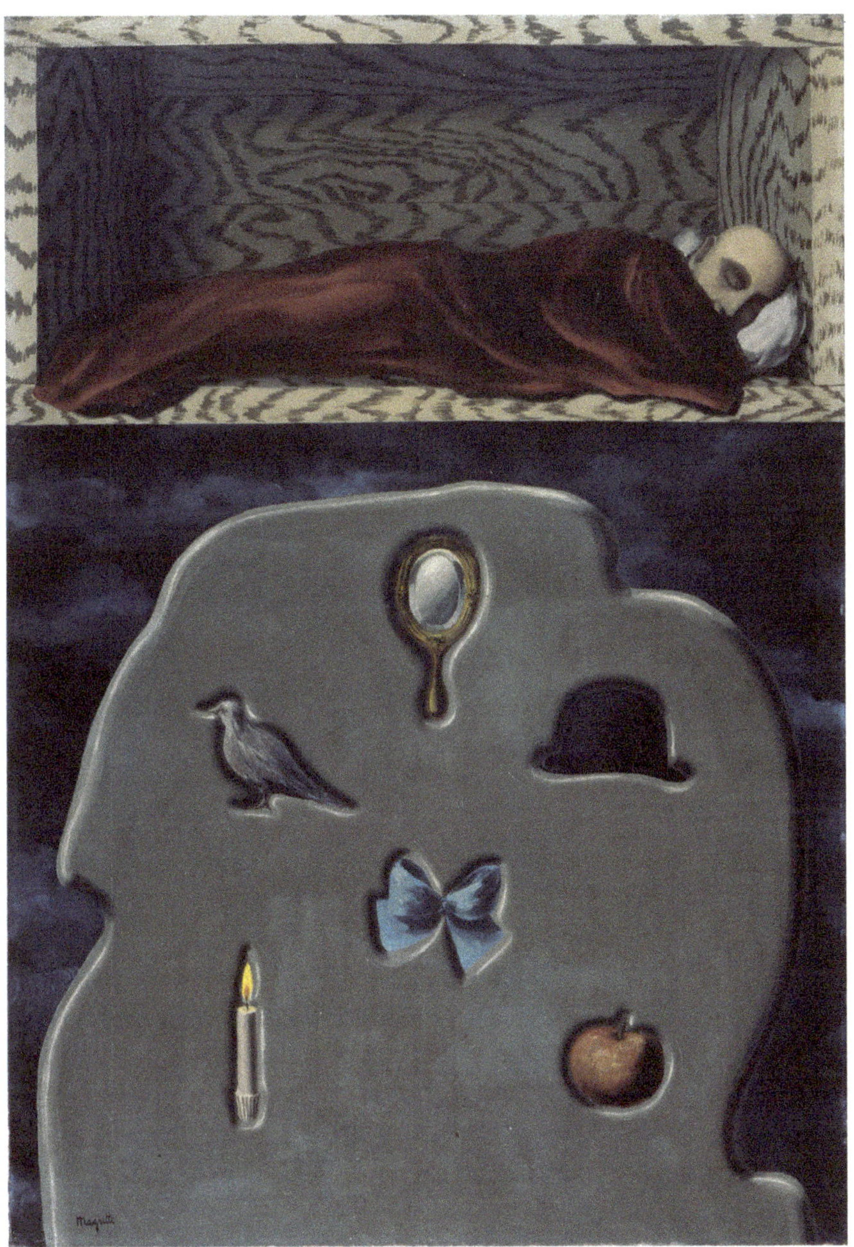

FIGURE 20.14. *The Daring Sleeper* (*The Reckless Sleeper*) (1928)

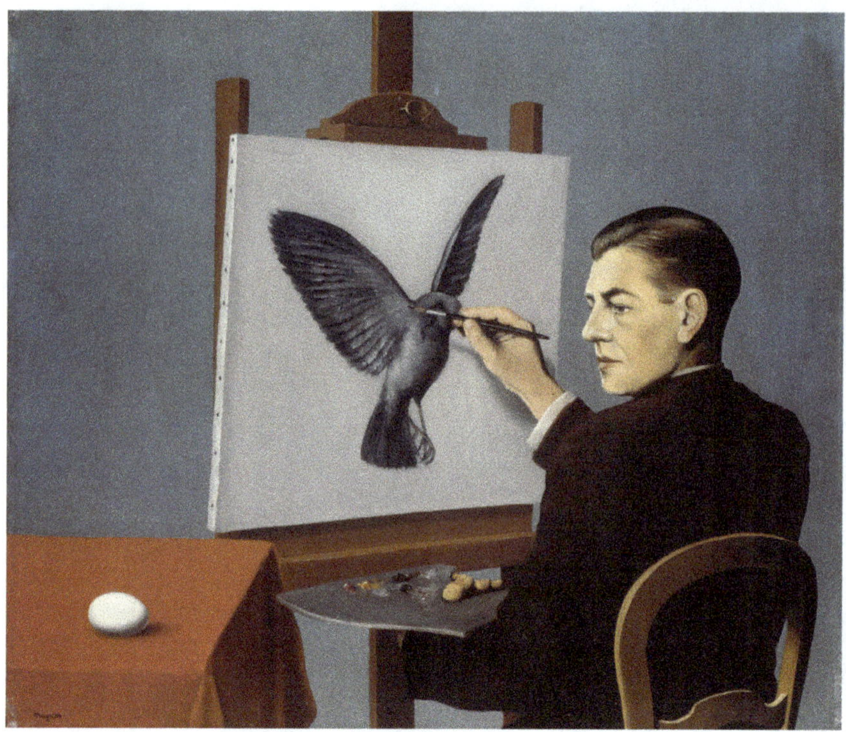

FIGURE 20.15. *Clairvoyance* (*La clairvoyance*) (1936)

act: how we do not always "read" things literally. In a work of silent cinema, one may see an image of flower on screen but read it as a symbol of innocence.

In sum, there are ways in which various paintings by Magritte can be seen figuratively as suggesting important moments of film history as well as aspects of film techniques, processes, and even modes of reception. Ultimately, this is not surprising as Magritte was a lover of movies and came of age in the cinematic era. Furthermore, as he notes in this chapter's epigraph, with the motion picture's birth, painters sought to "rival" it in a variety of inspired ways.

21

CONCLUDING THOUGHTS

> The conception of a picture is an idea about one thing or several things which can be realized visually in my painting.
>
> René Magritte[1]

I HAVE TRIED to show in *Cinemagritte* how the work of Modernist/Surrealist artist René Magritte is productive to consider in relation to cinema theory and practice—this, despite the fact that it has largely been ignored in the annals of film history and criticism. I have asserted this because (1) Magritte's oeuvre (as the epigraph demonstrates) is highly conceptual, and in ways that prove evocative for film studies, (2) his realistic pictorial style is quasi-"photographic" and therefore related to film, (3) his use of objects finds a parallel in cinema where objects are often as important as people, and (4) he was an avid moviegoer throughout his life, so cinematic tropes may have entered his work via "osmosis."

While many film critics have mentioned Magritte's art in passing (stating how a certain movie or scene within one sparks association to his work), hardly any have considered the issue in depth. Furthermore, what few insights there have been are often endlessly repeated, including Magritte's obvious links to the Surrealist cinema of Luis Buñuel or Salvador Dalí and the fact that several of his works draw on his love for the *Fantômas* serials of his youth.

While I have copiously cataloged such allusions (in order to give credit where credit is due), my own work has moved far beyond them in a variety of ways. I have tried to situate my discussion of Magritte within the field of intermedial studies, especially that of painting and film. I have also attended to the numerous art documentaries that have taken Magritte as their subject—viewing them as critical essays in film form. Furthermore, I have examined the home movies made by Magritte and his friends and analyzed them from both a film and art critical perspective.

While these have been rather traditional scholarly pursuits, *Cinemagritte* has also involved some innovative approaches. Rather than seek out documented influences of films on the work of Magritte or the work of Magritte on films (though these are sometimes mentioned), I have looked for resonances of his oeuvre in various cinematic texts—arguing that certain paintings and movies share some themes, iconography, and/or concerns. Hence, the preceding chapters have considered how Magritte's love of word/image play has been echoed in particular avant-garde films, how his fixation on the masking of faces has found parallels in movies, or how his interest in voyeurism finds its match in the history of cinematic practice. In all these chapters, I have taken what I deem "imaginative leaps," which I hope unearth insightful and fruitful associations unavailable through other methods.

Furthermore, I have gone beyond simply linking works by Magritte to particular films. In the final section, I have argued that some of Magritte's oeuvre draws upon central film techniques or elements of the medium: a play with framing, scale, editing, point of view, lighting, or codes or realism. Moreover, his work can be seen to comment on such issues as interpretation as experienced by the viewer. Finally, while not mimicking any particular film, in some of Magritte's paintings we find provocative intimations of important moments of film history, such as the role of the horse and jockey in pre-cinema or the filming of trains in early movies.

Throughout *Cinemagritte* I have tried to communicate my love for and admiration of Magritte's work—its beauty, intelligence, and wit. My desire has been to expand its purview—to "unframe" it from the hermetic world of art history so as to "repurpose" it for the broader world of film. If this has seemed to some an uncanny juxtaposition, I would remind them of Surrealism's love of apposition. If to others it has seemed an unholy intermixing of scholarly fields, I remind them that Magritte may well have enjoyed such a transgression. Here I take heart in Magritte's own words: "I hope that the critic or historian will elucidate, by the written word, the *unforeseen possibilities* that my pictures call forth."[2] This is precisely what I have attempted to do.

Notes

Preface: Magritte and Me

1 Lucy Fischer, "Homo Ludens: An Analysis of Four Films by Jacques Tati" (PhD diss., New York University, 1978).
2 Xavier Canonne, *René Magritte: The Revealing Image* (Antwerp: Ludion, 2017), 135.
3 Lucy Fischer, *Designing Women: Cinema, Art Deco and the Female Form* (New York: Columbia University Press, 2003); Lucy Fischer, ed., *Art Direction and Production Design* (New Brunswick, NJ: Rutgers University Press, 2015); and Lucy Fischer, *Cinema by Design: Art Nouveau, Modernism, and Film History* (New York: Columbia University Press, 2017).
4 Lucy Fischer, "The Savage Eye: Edward Hopper and the Cinema," in *A Modern Mosaic: Essays in American Modernism*, ed. Townsend Ludington (University of North Carolina Press, 2000), 334–56.

Chapter 1: Introduction

1 René Magritte, *Selected Writings*, ed. Kathleen Rooney and Eric Plattner, trans. Jo Levy (Minneapolis: University of Minnesota Press, 2016), 69.
2 Xavier Canonne, *René Magritte: The Revealing Image* (Antwerp: Ludion, 2017), 117.
3 Robert Short, "Magritte and the Cinema," in *Surrealism: Surrealist Visuality*, ed. Silvano Levy (Keele, UK: Keele University Press, 1996), 95–108.
4 A. M. Hammacher, *René Magritte*, trans. James Brockway (New York: Harry Abrams, 1986), 18.
5 Ellen Handler Spitz, *Museums of the Mind* (New Haven, CT: Yale University Press, 1994), 7.
6 Ibid., 18.
7 Magritte, *Selected Writings*, 200.
8 Ibid., 211.

9 Ibid., 65.

10 Ibid., 200.

11 Bruce Elder, *Dada, Surrealism and the Cinematic Effect* (Waterloo, ON: Wilfred Laurier Press, 2013), 269, 270.

12 André Breton, *Manifesto of Surrealism (1924)*, 1999, www.tcf.ua.edu/Classes/Jbutler/T340/SurManifesto/ManifestoOfSurrealism.htm.

13 André Bazin, "The Ontology of the Photographic Image," in *Film Theory and Criticism*, ed. Leo Braudy and Marshall Cohen (New York: Oxford University Press), 126–30.

14 Siegfried Kracauer, *Theory of Film: The Redemption of Physical Reality* (London: Oxford University Press, 1960).

15 Magritte, *Selected Writings*, 64.

16 André Bazin, "Theater and Cinema, Part Two," in *What Is Cinema?*, trans. Hugh Gray, vol. 1 (Berkeley: University of California Press, 1967), 106.

17 Canonne, *René Magritte*, 120.

18 Short, "Magritte and the Cinema," 96.

19 Silvano Levy, "Introduction," in *Surrealism: Surrealist Visuality*, ed. Silvano Levy (Keele, UK: Keele University Press, 1996), 8.

20 Anne Umland, "This Is How Marvels Begin," in *Magritte: The Mystery of the Ordinary: 1926–1938*, ed. Anne Umland (New York: Museum of Modern Art, 2013), 26–41, 33.

21 *The Barbarian*, which hung at the London Gallery, was destroyed in the 1940 Blitz. Only a photograph of Magritte in front of it remains to document it. wwww.tate.org.uk/context-comment/blogs/Magritte-and-surrealism-london.

22 Uwe M. Schneede, *René Magritte, Life and Work*, trans. W. Walter Jaffe (New York: Barron's Educational Series, 1982), 9.

23 Canonne, *René Magritte*, 120.

24 Short, "Magritte and the Cinema," 99.

25 Umland, "This Is How Marvels Begin," 33.

26 Canonne, *René Magritte*, 120.

27 Ibid. The film is sometimes called *L'homme du large.*

28 Ibid., 121.

29 Peter Wollen, "Magritte and the Bowler Hat," *New Left Review* (January–February 2000): 104–21, 110.

30 Ibid, 141.

31 Ibid., 135.

32 Ibid., 134.

33 Marco Borroni, "Il fuori di nessun dentro," *Cineforum* 406 (2016): 12.

34 Canonne, *René Magritte*, 121.

35 Ibid., 119.

36 William Jeffett, "Magritte and Dalí," in *Magritte and Dalí* (St. Petersburg, FL: Dalí Museum and Ludion, 2018), 13–34, 13.

37 Levy, "Introduction," 8.

38 Ibid.

39 Rob Stone, "Eye to Eye: The Persistence of Surrealism in Spanish Cinema," in *The Unsilvered Screen: Surrealism on Film*, ed. Graeme Harper and Rob Stone (London: Wallflower, 2007), 23–37, 35.

40 Barbara Creed, "Untamed Eye and the Dark Side of Surrealism: Hitchcock, Lynch, and Cronenberg," *The Unsilvered Screen: Surrealism on Film*, ed. Graeme Harper and Rob Stone (London: Wallflower, 2007), 131.

41 Raymond Durgnat, *Franju* (Berkeley: California University Press, 1968), 32.

42 Susan Felleman, "The Mystery . . . The Blood . . . The Age of Gold: Sculpture in Surrealist and Surreal Cinema," in Steven Jacobs, Susan Felleman, Vito Adriaensens, and Lisa Colparet, *Screening Statues, Sculpture and Cinema* (Edinburgh: Edinburgh University Press, 2017), 46–64, 47–48.

43 P. Adams Sitney, *Visionary Film: The American Avant-Garde, 1945–2000*, 3rd ed. (New York: Oxford University Press, 2002), 149, 431, 60.

44 Jonathan Rosenbaum, "Chantal Akerman: The Integrity of Exile and the Everyday," *Lola* 2 (June 2012), www.lolajournal.com/2/integrity_exile.html.

45 Catherine Fowler, "All Night Long: The Ambivalent Text of Belgianicty," in *Identity and Memory: The Films of Chantal Akerman*, ed. Gwendolyn Audrey Foster (Southern Illinois University Press, 2003), 77–93.

46 Lenuta Giukin, "Cinematic Transgressions: André Delvaux and the Surrealist Dilemma," *French Review* 81, no. 6 (May 2008): 1174–86.

47 Georgiana M. M. Colvile, "Between Surrealism and Magic Realism: The Early Feature Films of André Delvaux," *Yale French Studies* 109 (2006) 115–28, 120.

48 Ibid.

49 Ibid., 116.

50 Philip Mosley, "Anxiety, Memory, and Place in Belgian Cinema," *Yale French Studies* 102 (2002), 160–74.

51 Short, "Magritte and the Cinema," 95.

52 Ágnes Pethő, *Cinema and Intermediality: The Passion for the In-Between* (Cambridge: Cambridge Scholars Publishing, 2014), 204.

53 Dalí did create a painting titled *The Eye*, but it was done in 1945, the same year as *Spellbound*.

54 John Walker, *Art and Artists on Screen* (Manchester, UK: Manchester University Press, 1994), 244.

55 Jeffrey Longacre, "The Difference between Crows and Blackbirds: Alfred Hitchcock and the Treason of Images," *Post Script* 34, no. 2–3 (Summer, 2015): 53–70.

56 Trevor H. Maddock and Ivan Krisjansen, "Surrealist Poetics and the Cinema of Evil: The Significance of the Expression of Sovereignty in Catherine Breillat's *A ma soeur* (2001)," *Studies in French Cinema* 3, no. 3 (2014): 161–71.

57 Ibid.

58 Wollen, "Magritte and the Bowler Hat," 110.

59 Enoch Brater, *Beyond Minimalism: Beckett's Late Style in the Theater* (New York: Oxford University Press, 1987), 76.

60 Timothy Corrigan and Patricia White, *The Film Experience: An Introduction*, 3rd ed. (Boston: Bedford/St. Martin's, 2012), 416.

61 Garrett Stewart, *Between Film and Screen: Modernism's Photo Synthesis* (Chicago: University of Chicago Press, 1999), 202.

62 Maryann DeJulio, "Ageing and Memory in Agnès Varda's *Les plages d'Agnès*," *Senses of Cinema* 67, (July 2013), sensesofcinema.com/2013/feature-articles/ageing-and-.

63 Rosemarie Trentinella, "*The Spider's Stratagem*" (senior project, Vassar College, May 14, 2001), italian.vassar.edu/resources/magritte/spider.html.

64 Pethő, *Cinema and Intermediality*, 94.

65 "13 Great Movie Posters You Didn't Know Were Inspired by Famous Artworks," Taste of Cinema, August 19, 2016, www.tasteofcinema.com/2016/13-great-movie-posters-you-didnt-know-were-inspired-by-famous-artworks/2/.

66 Short, "Magritte and the Cinema," 95–108.

67 See José Vovelle, "Magritte et le cinéma," *Cahiers dada surréalisme* 4 (1970): 1-3-110; and Germain Viatte, ed. *Peinture, cinéma, peinture* (Marseille: Hazan, 1990).

68 Short, "Magritte and the Cinema," 97.

69 Ibid., 99.

70 Ibid., 100.

71 Ibid., 101.

72 Ibid., 102.

73 Ibid.

74 Canonne, *René Magritte*, also mentions *Four Troublesome Heads* (Méliès, 1898) and *The Tramp and the Mattress Makers* (Méliès, 1906) in relation to Magritte's paintings, 124.

75 Short, "Magritte and the Cinema," 102.

76 Ibid.

77 Ibid.

78 Ibid., 104.

79 Michel Draguet and Claude Goormans, "Once the Image Is Isolated, What Happens to the Mind?" in *Magritte: The Mystery of the Ordinary*, ed. Anne Umland (New York: Museum of Modern Art, 2013), 150–163, 152, 153.

80 Canonne, *René Magritte*, 119.

81 Ibid.

82 They were eventually transferred to 16 mm and restored, appearing as *La fidélité des images*. They do not, however, seem to be available at this time.

83 Short, "Magritte and the Cinema," 104–5.

84 Ibid., 105.

85 Daniel Urban, "Relaxed and Playful," *SchirnMag*, May 18, 2017, www.schirn.de/en/magazine/context/magritte/rene_magritte_super_8_film. Magritte's use of 8 mm technology is also mentioned in Victoria Laurie, "Eye for the Camera: Surrealist René Magritte's Rarely Exhibited Photographs and Films Begin Their World Tour in Country Victoria," *Australian*, August 19, 2017, www.theaustralian.com.au/arts/review/rene-magritte-revealing-image-photos-and-films-at-latrobe-gallery/news-story/60b16ff702fa2880f0f18495d909f98d.

86 *Imitation du cinéma* is not readily available, but you can read a description of it on Wikipedia, last modified May 31, 2017, translate.google.com/translate?sl=auto&tl=en&js=y&prev=_t&hl=en&ie=UTF-8&u=https%3A%2F%2Fnl.wikipedia.org%2Fwiki%2FL%2527imitation_du_cin%C3%A9ma&edit-text=. There is also some unedited footage of it on YouTube: *L'imitation du cinema—Marcel Marien—1960*, posted by TheSuLizhen, YouTube, September 4, 2011, www.youtube.com/watch?v=dIEEkFABfYQ.

87 "Le palais idéal," Atlas Obscura, www.atlasobscura.com/places/le-palais-ideal, accessed March 8, 2019.

88 Ibid., 106.

89 Ibid., 107.

90 Siegfried Gohr, *Magritte: Attempting the Impossible* (New York: D.A.P./Distributed Art Publishers, 2009), 46.

91 Ibid.

92 Roger Rothman, "René Magritte and 'The Shop Window Quality of Things,'" *The Space Between* 3, no. 1 (2007): 11–28, 12.

93 Stephanie D'Alessandro, "Mirrors That Become Paintings: Magritte's Commissions for Edward James," in *Magritte: The Mystery of the Ordinary: 1926–1938*, ed. Anne Umland (New York: Museum of Modern Art, 2013), 194–209, 195. The mural no longer exists.

94 Ibid. See also Umland, "This Is How Marvels Begin," 35.

95 Alastair Sooke, "René Magritte: The Artist Who Turned the World on Its Head," *Telegraph*, June 21, 2011, www.telegraph.co.uk/culture/art/art-features/8582472/Rene-Magritte-The-artist-who-turned-the-world-on-its-head.html.

96 Ibid.

97 Ibid.

98 Gohr, *Magritte*, 46.

99 Rothman, "René Magritte," 12.

100 Ibid., 22.

101 Sooke, "René Magritte."

102 Short, "Magritte and the Cinema," 96.

103 Ibid., 95.
104 Canonne, *René Magritte*, 134.
105 Ibid., 127.
106 Short, "Magritte and the Cinema," 95–96.
107 Canonne, *René Magritte*, 127.
108 Short, "Magritte and the Cinema," 98.
109 Ibid., 95.
110 Though we think of Magritte as a painter, he also produced sculptures and collages.
111 Pethő, *Cinema and Intermediality*, 31.
112 Ibid., 38.
113 Ibid., 39.
114 Ibid., 68.
115 Ibid., 65–66.
116 André Bazin, "Theater and Cinema," in *Theater and Film: A Comparative Anthology*, ed. Robert Knopf (Yale University Press, 2005), 110–33; and Susan Sontag, "Film and Theater," in *Theater and Film: A Comparative Anthology*, ed. Robert Knopf (Yale University Press, 2005), 134–51.
117 There are four works in French that deal with film and painting: Pascal Bonitzer, *Peinture et cinéma: Décadrages* (Paris: Editions d'l'Etoile), 1985; Jacques Aumont, *L'oeil interminable* (Paris: Éditions de la Différence), 2007; Alain Bonfand *Le cinéma saturé. Essai sur les relations de la peinture et des images en movement* (Paris: Vrin, 2012); and Raymond Bellour, *Cinéma et peinture: Approches* (Paris: Presses Universitaires de France, 1990). There is also a book on a single filmmaker that is worthy of note, Hava Aldouby's *Federico Fellini: Painting in Film, Painting on Film* (Toronto: University of Toronto Press, 2013), but it focuses largely on arguing that certain images in Fellini's films (e.g., *Juliet of the Spirits* [1965]) are influenced by particular painting or design styles (in this case, Symbolism and Art Nouveau). There is also Allister Mactaggart's *The Film Paintings of David Lynch: Challenging Film Theory* (Bristol, UK: Intellect, 2010).
118 Vachel Lindsay, *The Art of the Moving Picture* (New York: Liveright, 1970), 108.
119 Ibid., 125.
120 Ibid., 127.
121 Ibid.
122 Ibid., 139.
123 Ibid., 128.
124 Bazin, "Painting and Cinema," in *What Is Cinema?*, trans. Hugh Gray, vol. 1 (Berkeley: University of California Press, 1967), 164.
125 Ibid., 164–65.
126 Ibid., 167.

127 Angela Dalle Vacche, "The Art Documentary in the Postwar Period," *Aniki: Portuguese Journal of the Moving Image* 1, no. 2 (2014): 292–313.

128 Ibid., 295, 299.

129 Ibid., 294.

130 Ibid., 299.

131 Ibid., 300.

132 Ibid., 302.

133 Walker, *Art and Artists on Screen*, 1.

134 Brigitte Puecker, *Incorporating Images: Film and the Rival Arts* (Princeton, NJ: Princeton University Press, 1994), 3.

135 Ibid., 80.

136 Ibid., 81.

137 Ibid., 148.

138 Brigitte Puecker, *The Material Image: Art and the Real in Film* (Stanford, CA: Stanford University Press, 2007).

139 Ibid., 21, 24–25.

140 Ibid., 31.

141 Ibid., 58.

142 Ibid., 69.

143 Angela Dalle Vacche, *Cinema and Painting: How Art Is Used in Film* (Austin: University of Texas Press, 1996), 1.

144 Angela Dalle Vacche, *The Visual Turn: Classical Film Theory and Art History* (New Brunswick, NJ: Rutgers University Press, 2002).

145 Rudolf Arnheim, "Painting and Film," in *The Visual Turn: Classical Film Theory and Art History*, ed. Angela Dalle Vacche (New Brunswick, NJ: Rutgers University Press, 2002), 151–54.

146 Susan Felleman, *Art in the Cinematic Imagination* (Austin: University of Texas Press, 2006), 4.

147 Susan Felleman, *Real Objects in Unreal Situations: Modern Art in Fiction Film* (Bristol, UK: Intellect, 2014).

148 Steven Jacobs, *Framing Pictures Film and the Visual Arts* (Edinburgh: Edinburgh University Press, 2011), x.

149 Nancy Mowll Mathews (with Charles Musser), *Moving Pictures: American Art and Early Film, 1880–1910* (Manchester, VT: Hudson Hills Press, 2005).

150 Ibid., 2.

151 Dominique Païni and Guy Cogeval, eds., *Hitchcock and Art: Fatal Coincidences* (Montreal: Montreal Museum of Fine Arts, 2000).

152 Nathalie Bondil-Poupard, "Such Stuff as Dreams Are Made On: Hitchcock and Dali, Surrealism and Oneiricism," in ibid., 155–71. Magritte is mentioned on pp. 160 and 171.

153 Ibid., 16.

154 Gillian McIver, *Art History for Filmmakers: The Art of Visual Storytelling* (London: Bloomsbury, 2016), 8.
155 Ibid.
156 Ibid.
157 Ibid., 97–99.
158 Ibid., 99.
159 Magritte, *Selected Writings*, 213, 210.
160 David Sylvester, ed., *René Magritte: Catalogue raisonné*, vols. 1–6 (London: Menil Foundation, Philip Wilson, 1993).

Chapter 2: Art Documentaries/Home Movies

1 René Magritte, *Selected Writings*, ed. by Kathleen Rooney and Eric Plattner, trans. Jo Levy (Minneapolis: University of Minnesota Press, 2016), 69.
2 André Bazin, "Painting and Cinema," in *What Is Cinema?*, trans. Hugh Gray, vol. 1 (Berkeley: University of California Press, 2005), 164.
3 Marcella Biserni, *Magritte e il cinema . . . Chapeau!* (Perugia: Morlacchi University Press, 2011). See also Marcella Biserni, "Le polyèdre de Magritte: Reflets littéraires de l'objet peint, filmé et scénarisé" (PhD diss., Aix-Marseille Université, Marseille, and Università degli studi, Verona, 2013); and Marcella Biserni, "Le Titre Performatif Peint et Filmé Chez Magritte" in *Ceci n'est pas un titre: Les artistes et l'intitulation*, ed. Laurence Brogniez, Marianne Jakobi, and Cédric Loire (Lyon, France: Fage Editions, 2014), 123–32.
4 The *Catalogue raisonné* of Magritte's work says that it appeared on "invitation cards." David Sylvester, ed., *René Magritte: Catalogue raisonné*, vol. 5 (London: Menil Foundation, Philip Wilson, 1993), 97.
5 Jonathan Coulthart, "The Magic Toyshop," *Feuilleton*, December 20, 2012, www.johncoulthart.com/feuilleton/2012/12/20/the-magic-toyshop/2.
6 Sonya Andermahr and Lawrence Philips, eds., *Angela Carter: New Critical Readings* (London: Bloomsbury, 2012), 202, 206.

Chapter 3: Honoring the Artist

1 René Magritte, cited in BrainyQuote, www.brainyquote.com/authors/rene_magritte, accessed March 8, 2019.
2 André Bazin, "Theater and Cinema, Part Two," in *What Is Cinema?*, trans. Hugh Gray, vol. 1 (Berkeley: University of California Press, 1967), 95.
3 Alain Robbe-Grillet and René Magritte, *La belle captive: A Novel*, trans. Ben Stolzfus (Berkeley: University of California Press, 1996).
4 Ibid., 7 and 9.
5 Ibid., 15.

6 Ibid., 20.

7 Ibid., 24.

8 Ibid., 32.

9 Suitcases appear in several versions of Magritte's *The Interpretation of Dreams*, sometimes labeled correctly as "the valise" (1935) and sometimes not (e.g., "le ciel" [1927]). A suitcase also appears in *The Virgin's Chariot* (1965) in which it sits on a mirror.

10 Roch C. Smith, "Generating the Erotic Dream Machine: Robbe-Grillet's *L'Eden et après* and *La belle captive*," *French Review* 63, no. 3 (February 1990): 494.

11 Lisa K. Broad, "Prisoners of Possibility: Robbe-Grillet's *La belle captive* as 'Quantum Text,'" Senses of Cinema, August 2008, sensesofcinema.com/2008/feature-articles/robbe-grillet-belle-captive/.

12 Ibid.

13 *Thomas Crown Affair* plot summary, Wikipedia, last edited February 13, 2019, en.wikipedia.org/wiki/The_Thomas_Crown_Affair_(1999_film)#Plot.

14 *The Lovers Magritte*, posted by Ana López, YouTube, April 8, 2016, www.youtube.com/watch?v=CH64p8Hc_4Y.

15 *Step Inside: René Magritte's "le groupe silencieux,"* posted by Christie's, YouTube, February 27, 2018, www.youtube.com/watch?v=gaT3boaird0.

16 *Magritte Animation*, posted by Joel Remy, YouTube, November 6, 2016, www.youtube.com/watch?v=i0obs9cPTgo.

17 *Magritte "False Mirror" Video Interpretation*, posted by Nathaniel Holt, YouTube, 2014, www.youtube.com/watch?v=V0fNjIWMKLI.

18 *This Is Not a Film*, posted by focomoso, YouTube, November 6, 2006, www.youtube.com/watch?v=0qCVIelcIYE.

Chapter 4: Belgian Surrealist Cinematic Avant-Garde

1 René Magritte, *Selected Writings*, ed. by Kathleen Rooney and Eric Plattner, trans. Jo Levy (Minneapolis: University of Minnesota Press, 2016), 217.

2 Patricia Allmer and Hilde van Gelder, "The Forgotten Surrealists: Belgian Surrealism Since 1924," *Image [&] Narrative* 13 (November 2005), www.imageandnarrative.be/inarchive/surrealism/surrealism.htm.

3 Ibid.

4 Ibid.

5 Quote taken from the now defunct Art Haps website, www.arthaps.com/show/magritte_and_beyond_1, accessed 2018.

6 John Coulthart claims that the artist is played by Magritte, but it does not look like Magritte to me. Also, the IMDb credits for the film do not list Magritte in the cast. John Coulthart, "Monsieur Fantômas by Ernst Moerman," *Feuilleton*, May 24, 2010, www.johncoulthart.com/feuilleton/2010/05/24/monsieur-fantomas-by-ernst-moerman/.

7 “Pour vos beaux yeux,” PointCulture, www.pointculture.be/mediatheque/documentaires/pour-vos-beaux-yeux-tw07412, accessed March 8, 2019.

Chapter 5: Voyeurism and the Gaze

1 René Magritte, *Selected Writings*, ed. Kathleen Rooney and Eric Plattner, trans. Jo Levy (Minneapolis: University of Minnesota Press, 2016), 211.
2 Stanley Cavell, *The World Viewed: Reflections on the Ontology of Film* (Cambridge, MA: Harvard University Press, 1979), 40–41.
3 Laura Mulvey, “Visual Pleasure and Narrative Cinema,” in *Film Theory and Criticism: Introductory Readings*, ed. Leo Braudy and Marshall Cohen (New York: Oxford University Press, 1999), 833–46, 835–36.
4 Ibid., 837.
5 Here one thinks of *The Blue Angel* (1930), *Scarlet Empress* (1934), *The Devil Is a Woman* (1935), and so on.

Chapter 6: Fictional versus Real Persons and Spaces

1 René Magritte, *Selected Writings*, ed. Kathleen Rooney and Eric Plattner, trans. Jo Levy (Minneapolis: University of Minnesota Press, 2016), 17.
2 The photograph is in the private collection of Isadora and Isy Gabriel Brachot. See Anne Umland, “Magritte’s Grand Illusions,” *ArtNews*, September 5, 2013, www.artnews.com/2013/09/05/magrittes-grand-illusions/.
3 I am using quotation marks for the film-within-a-film and italics for Allen’s film itself.

Chapter 7: Word versus Image

Part of this chapter is a revised version of a section of my book *Body Double: The Author Incarnate in the Cinema* (New Brunswick, NJ: Rutgers University Press, 2013).

1 René Magritte, *Selected Writings*, ed. Kathleen Rooney and Eric Plattner, trans. Jo Levy (Minneapolis: University of Minnesota Press, 2016), 10.
2 René Magritte, “Words and Images,” *La révolution surréaliste* 12 (December 1929).
3 In Magritte’s *Selected Writings*, 54–55, there is a lecture on words and images that seems similar to his 1929 publication.
4 Ibid., 112.
5 Ibid., 115.
6 Ibid., 116.

7 Ibid., 65.

8 Michel Foucault, *This Is Not a Pipe*, trans. James Harkness (Berkeley: University of California Press, 1982), 38.

9 Ibid., 112.

10 Will Eisner, *Comics & Sequential Art* (New York: W. W. Norton, 2008), 8.

11 Sergei Eisenstein, "The Cinematographic Principle and the Ideogram," in *Film Form: Essays in Film Theory*, trans. Jay Leyda (New York: Harcourt, 1969).

12 Gil Maia, "When What You See Is What You Read," *Writing and Seeing: Essays on Word and Image*, ed. Rui Manuel G. de Carvalho Homem and Maria de Fátima Lambert (Amsterdam: Rodop, 2006), 381.

13 W. J. T. Mitchell, *Picture Theory* (Chicago: University of Chicago Press, 1994), 95.

14 Ibid., 150.

15 James Monaco, *How to Read a Film* (New York: Oxford University Press, 1979).

16 Alastair Sooke, "René Magritte: The Artist Who Turned the World on Its Head," *Telegraph*, June 21, 2011, www.telegraph.co.uk/culture/art/art-features/8582472/Rene-Magritte-The-artist-who-turned-the-world-on-its-head.html.

17 "*Zorn's Lemma* (film)," Wikipedia, last edited March 3, 2019, en.wikipedia.org/wiki/Zorns_Lemma_(film).

18 Federico Windhausen, "Words into Film: Toward a Genealogical Understanding of Hollis Frampton's Theory and Practice" *October* 109 (2004): 82.

19 Peter Wollen, *Signs and Meaning in the Cinema* (Bloomington: Indiana University Press, 1969).

20 Christian Metz's *Film Language: A Semiotics of the Cinema* (Chicago: University of Chicago Press, 1974).

21 Wollen, *Signs and Meaning*, 122.

22 André Bazin, "The Ontology of the Photographic Image," in *What Is Cinema?*, trans. Hugh Gray, vol. 1 (Berkeley: University of California Press, 2005), 14.

23 Hollis Frampton, *On the Camera Arts and Consecutive Matters: The Writings of Hollis Frampton*, ed. Bruce Jenkins (Cambridge, MA: MIT Press, 2009), 67.

24 Ibid.

25 Hollis Frampton, "(nostalgia)," hollisframpton.org.uk/nostalgia.htm, accessed September 19, 2017; my emphasis.

26 Foucault, 40.

27 For an excellent an in-depth analysis of *Poetic Justice,* see Bruce Jenkins, "The Films of Hollis Frampton: A Critical Study" (PhD diss., Northwestern University, 1984), 244–58.

28 The published script for the film is in Scott MacDonald, *Screen Writings: Scripts and Texts by Independent Filmmakers* (Berkeley: University of California Press, 1995), 70–90.
29 Jenkins, "Films of Hollis Frampton," 258.
30 Magritte, *Selected Writings*, 35.
31 The narrator of the art documentary *Rene Magritte* (*Artists of the 20th Century* series) points this out. *Artists of the 20th Century: Rene Magritte*, directed by DPM, Kultur Video, 2004.

Chapter 8: Pictures and Landscapes

1 René Magritte, *Selected Writings*, ed. Kathleen Rooney and Eric Plattner, trans. Jo Levy (Minneapolis: University of Minnesota Press, 2016), 200.
2 Ibid., 169.
3 David Pescoe, *Peter Greenaway: Museums and Moving Images* (London: Reaktion Books, 1997), 77–78.
4 In articles about art history, this device is sometimes called a perspective frame, a drawing tool, or a drawing grid.
5 André Bazin, "Theater and Cinema, Part Two," in *What Is Cinema?*, trans. Hugh Gray, vol. 1 (Berkeley: University of California Press, 1967), 95–124.
6 Leon Steinmetz and Peter Greenaway, *The World of Peter Greenaway* (Boston: Journey Editions, 1998), 43; and Douglas Keesey, *The Films of Peter Greenaway: Sex, Death and Provocation* (Jefferson, NC: McFarland, 2006), 10.
7 Steinmetz and Greenaway, *World*, 43.
8 I am thinking here of Jean Cocteau's film *The Blood of a Poet* (1930) and of such paintings as Magritte's *Memory* (1948).
9 Alan Woods, *Being Naked Playing Dead: The Art of Peter Greenaway* (Manchester, UK: Manchester University Press, 1996), 113–14.
10 Ibid., 114.
11 Ibid.

Chapter 9: Empty Frames and X-Ray Vision

1 *René Magritte: An Attempt at the Impossible*, directed by Bernard Crutzen and Pierre Sterckx, Kultur, 1999.
2 See Scott Curtis, "Between Photography and Film: Early Uses of Medical Cinematography," Remedia, January 19, 2016, remedianetwork.net/2016/01/19/medicine-in-transit-between-photography-and-film-early-uses-of-medical-cinematography/.
3 John Macintyre, "X-Ray Records for the Cinematograph," *Archives of Skiagraphy* 1, no. 2 (April 1897).

4 *Skiagraphy* is the use of shading and the projection of shadows to show perspective in architectural or technical drawing. *Dr. Macintyre's X-Ray Film*, National Library of Scotland, movingimage.nls.uk/film/0520, accessed October 23, 2017.
5 Ibid. More on sound in *Special Effects* can be found in Melissa Ragona, "Hidden Noise: Strategies of Sound Montage in the Films of Hollis Frampton," *October* 109 (Summer 2004): 96–118. She focuses on the issue of sound/image asynchronization, which she feels leads to a comic sense.
6 Hollis Frampton, "Hollis Frampton's *Hapax Legomena*," Harvard Film Archive program, hcl.harvard.edu/hfa/films/2011janmar/frampton.html, accessed October 23, 2017.
7 Manohla Dargis, "No Blockbusters Here, Just Mind Expanders," *New York Times*, November 11, 2011, www.nytimes.com/2011/11/13/movies/ernie-gehrs-films-traffic-in-images-and-light.html.

Chapter 10: Mindscreens

1 René Magritte, *Selected Writings*, ed. Kathleen Rooney and Eric Plattner, trans. Jo Levy (Minneapolis: University of Minnesota Press, 2016), 189.
2 Salomon Resnik, *Mental Space* (London: Karnac Books, 1994).
3 Ibid., 55.
4 Ibid., 38. He mistakenly calls the painting *The Poison*.
5 Ibid., 35.
6 Ibid., 38.
7 Ibid., 109.
8 Ibid., 52.
9 Ibid., 81.
10 Ellen Handler Spitz, *Museums of the Mind* (New Haven, CT: Yale University Press, 1994), 17.
11 Ibid., 29.
12 Ibid., 42.
13 Ibid., 17.
14 Ibid., 11.
15 Ibid., 21.
16 Ibid., 10.
17 Ibid., 19–20.
18 Ibid., 6.
19 Magritte, *Selected Writings*, 210.
20 Ibid., 204.
21 For instance, the *Interpretation of Dreams* series (e.g., 1927, 1930, 1953, etc.).
22 Ibid., 202.
23 Ibid., 173.

24 Ibid., 101.

25 Hugo Munsterberg, *The Film: A Psychological Study* (Mineola, NY: Dover, 1970), 41.

26 Ibid.

Chapter 11: Petrification, Horror, and Fantasy

1 René Magritte, *Selected Writings*, ed. Kathleen Rooney and Eric Plattner, trans. Jo Levy (Minneapolis: University of Minnesota Press, 2016), 145.

2 "Magritte's 1949–1960 Gallery," Matteson Art, www.mattesonart.com/1949-1960-mature-period.aspx, accessed March 7, 2019.

3 René Magritte, cited in BrainyQuote, www.brainyquote.com/quotes/rene_magritte_378857, accessed March 8, 2019.

4 Abraham Hammacher, *Magritte* (London: Thames and Hudson, 1974), 140.

5 André Bazin, "The Ontology of the Photographic Image," in *What Is Cinema?*, trans. Hugh Gray, vol. 1 (Berkeley: University of California Press, 2005), 9.

6 Ibid.

7 Ibid., 10.

8 "Freeze frame," Dictionary.com, www.dictionary.com/browse/freeze-frame, accessed September 14, 2017.

9 Laura Mulvey, *Death24X a Second: Stillness and the Moving Image* (London: Reaktion Books, 2006).

10 Ibid., 22.

11 Ibid., 15.

12 Ibid., 32.

13 For a study of the use of statues in film, see Steven Jacobs, Susan Felleman, Vito Adriaensens, and Lisa Colpaert, *Screening Statues: Sculpture and Cinema* (Edinburgh: Edinburgh University Press, 2017).

14 Emmanuel Levinas, "Reality and Its Shadow," in *The Levinas Reader*, ed. Seán Hand (London: Basil Blackwell), 129–43, 141.

15 Helmutt Wohl, "Memory, Oblivion, and the 'Invisibility' of Monuments," in *Memory & Oblivion: Proceedings of the XXIXth International Congress of the History of Art*, ed. Wessel Reinink and Jeroen Stumple (Amsterdam: Kluwer, 1999), 925–28, 926.

16 Michael Atkinson, "Love in Ruins," essay booklet accompanying DVD release of *Les visiteurs du soir* (New York: Criterion Collection, 2012).

17 Edward Baron Turk, "The Politics of Cinematic Reception: *Les visiteurs du soir*, Narrative Tempo, and the Debacle," *French Review* 61, no. 4 (March 1988): 598.

18 *The Wonders of Nature*, Rene Magritte: Biography, Paintings, and Quotes, ReneMagritte.org, www.renemagritte.org/the-wonders-of-nature.jsp, accessed September 14, 2017.

19 Michelle Bolduc, "Levinas and 'Medieval' Film: Memory and Time in Marcel Carné's *Les visiteurs du soir*," *French Review* 83, no. 5 (April 2010): 100.
20 Danièle Gasiglia-Lasteur, "*Les visiteurs du soir*: Une date peut en chacher un autre," *Cahiers de l'Association internationale d'études françaises* 47 (1995): 80.
21 Turk, "Politics," 600.
22 There are multiple versions of this painting: five from 1950, one from 1955, one from 1956, one from 1962, and one from 1963.
23 "Gorgons," Myth Encyclopedia, www.mythencyclopedia.com/Go-Hi/Gorgons.html, accessed September14, 2017.

Chapter 12: Animation

1 "Poetry Is a Pipe: Selected Writings of René Magritte," Literary Hub, September 29, 2016, lithub.com/poetry-is-a-pipe-selected-writings-of-rene-magritte/.
2 Van Norris: "Interior Logic: The Appropriation and Incorporation of Popular Surrealism into Classical American Animation," in *The Unsilvered Screen: Surrealism on Film*, ed. Graeme Harper and Rob Stone (London: Wallflower, 2007).
3 This film was mentioned as interesting in another context in David Sylvester, ed., *René Magritte: Catalogue raisonné*, vol. 3 (London: Menil Foundation, Philip Wilson, 1993), 413.
4 "Magritte Gallery 1947–1948 Vache Period," www.mattesonart.com/1947-1948-vache-period.aspx, accessed March 8, 2019.
5 Dani Cavallaro, *The Anime Art of Hayao Miyazaki* (Jefferson, NC: McFarland, 2006), 191.
6 Marina Warner, "Dream Works," *Guardian*, June 16, 2007, www.theguardian.com/film/2007/jun/16/film.
7 Caryn James, "Review/Film; Aggressive Objects Take It Out on Helpless People," *New York Times*, May 3, 1989, www.nytimes.com/1989/05/03/movies/review-film-aggressive-objects-take-it-out-on-helpless-people.html.
8 Mentioned in James Thrall Soby, *René Magritte* (New York: Doubleday, 1965).

Chapter 13: Faces and Masks

1 René Magritte, "Gallery 1949–1960 Mature Period," Matteson Art, www.mattesonart.com/1949-1960-mature-period.aspx, accessed March 8, 2019.
2 Richard Calvocoress, *Magritte* (London: Phaidon, 1984), 106.
3 In the *Catalogue raisonné*, it has no official title, just [Portrait of Rena Schitz] denoted as provisional and purely descriptive by the use of brackets. David

Sylvester, ed., *René Magritte: Catalogue raisonné*, vol. 2 (London: Menil Foundation, Philip Wilson, 1993), 247.

4 Magritte did render countless paintings of his wife, Georgette, though she was not identified as such. On some level, these might be considered portraits (often, nude ones). But rarely do they provide entrée into her thoughts, emotions, or attitude.

5 Shearer West, *Portraiture* (Oxford: Oxford University Press, 2004), 36.

6 Ibid., 33.

7 Béla Balázs, "The Close-Up" and "The Face of Man," in *Film Theory and Criticism*, 7th ed., ed. Leo Braudy and Marshall Cohen (Oxford: Oxford University Press, 2009), 273–281, 277 and 280.

8 Ibid., 278.

9 Jacques Aumont, "The Face in Close-Up," in *The Visual Turn, Classical Film Theory and Art History*, ed. Angela Dalle Vacche (New Brunswick, NJ: Rutgers University Press, 2003), 145.

10 Roland Barthes, "The Face of Garbo," in *Sean Redmond, Stardom and Celebrity: A Reader*, ed. Sean Redmond and Su Holmes (London: Sage, 2007), 261–62.

11 Noa Steimatsky, *The Face on Film* (New York: Oxford University Press, 2017).

12 Ibid.

13 Ibid., 13.

14 Therese Davis, *The Face on the Screen* (Bristol, UK: Intellect, 2004), 1.

15 Eric Rohmer, *The Taste for Beauty*, trans. Carol Volk (Cambridge: Cambridge University Press, 1989), 50–51.

16 Paul Coates, *Screening the Face* (Basingstoke, UK: Palgrave Macmillan), 2012.

17 Hans Belting, *Face and Mask: A Double History*, trans. Thomas S. Hansen and Abby J. Hansen (Princeton, NJ: Princeton University Press, 2017), 2.

18 Ibid., 6.

19 Ibid., 22.

20 Richard Brilliant, *Portraiture* (Cambridge, MA: Harvard University Press, 1991), 66.

21 Ibid., 8.

22 Ibid., 17.

23 Ibid., 18.

24 Ibid., 19.

25 Ibid., 214.

26 Quoted in Aumont, "Face in Close-Up," 142.

27 André Bazin, "Theater and Cinema, Part Two," in *What is Cinema?*, trans. Hugh Gray, vol. 1 (Berkeley: University of California Press, 1967), 95–124.

28 See the 1924 image from Siegfried Gohr, *René Magritte* (San Francisco: San Francisco Museum of Modern Art, 2000); and the 1925 "Arlequinade" image

from "Rene Magritte's Early Art Deco Advertising Posters, 1924–1927," Open Culture, www.openculture.com/2013/09/rene-magrittes-early-art-deco-advertising-posters-1924-1927.html.

29 Raymond Durgnat, *Franju* (Berkeley: California University Press, 1968), 80.

30 Ibid., 81.

31 "Georges Franju Le Visionnaire," episode of a *Cinema of Our Time* broadcast, posted by Justyna Szewczuk, YouTube, July 18, 2018, www.youtube.com/watch?v=XVvaDnTqr98. Note: In 1964, film critic and filmmaker André S. Labarthe, together with Janine Bazin, widow of influential film theorist André Bazin, approached the French television channel ORTF about starting a program that would resemble the long, in-depth interviews with film directors that magazines such as *Cahiers du cinéma* and *Positif* regularly published. ORTF gave the green light, and *Cinéastes/Cimema of Our Time* was born, www.filmlinc.org/series/nyff50-cineastes-de-notre-temps-cinema-de-notre-temps/.

32 Ibid.

33 Ibid.

Chapter 14: Science Fiction

1 René Magritte, *Selected Writings*, ed. Kathleen Rooney and Eric Plattner, trans. Jo Levy (Minneapolis: University of Minnesota Press, 2016), 3.

2 Despina Kakoudaki, *The Anatomy of a Robot: Literature, Cinema and the Cultural Work of Artificial People* (New Brunswick: Rutgers University Press, 2014).

3 Ibid., 103.

4 William Wordsworth, *Lines Written a Few Miles above Tintern Abbey*, Poetry Foundation, www.poetryfoundation.org/poems/45527/lines-composed-a-few-miles-above-tintern-abbey-on-revisiting-the-banks-of-the-wye-during-a-tour-july-13-1798.

5 W. J. Lillyman, "The Blue Sky: A Recurrent Symbol," *Comparative Literature* 21, no. 2 (Spring 1969): 124.

Chapter 15: Human-Animal Hybrids

1 René Magritte, *Selected Writings*, ed. by Kathleen Rooney and Eric Plattner, trans. Jo Levy (Minneapolis: University of Minnesota Press, 2016), 9.

2 Gavin Parkinson, *Surreaism Art and Modern Science: Relativity, Quantum Mechanics and Epistemology* (New Haven, CT: Yale University Press), 2008.

3 The 1977 film was directed by Don Taylor; the 1996 film was directed by John Frankenheimer (with Richard Stanley uncredited).

4 A. M. Hammacher, *René Magritte*, trans. James Brockway (New York: Harry Abrams, 1974), 76.

Chapter 16: Magic

1 René Magritte, *Selected Writings*, ed. Kathleen Rooney and Eric Plattner, trans. Jo Levy (Minneapolis: University of Minnesota Press, 2016), 59.
2 Ibid., 175.
3 René Magritte, quoted in William Jeffett, "Magritte and Dalí" in *Magritte and Dalí* (St. Petersburg, FL: Dalí Museum and Ludion, 2018), 13-34, 26.
4 Comparisons between Magritte and Méliès were mentioned in our examination of an essay by Robert Short in chapter 1 and in relation to the commentary of one art documentary discussed in chapter 2. In each case, such references by critics were very brief.
5 Magritte, *Selected Writings*, 175.
6 Ibid., 99.
7 Noam Elcott, *Artificial Darkness: An Obscure History of Modern Art and Media* (Chicago: University of Chicago Press, 2016).
8 Ibid., 137.
9 Sigmund Freud, "Medusa's Head," in *The Medusa Reader*, ed. Marjorie Garber and Nancy J. Vickers (New York: Routledge, 2003), 84–86.
10 Robin Adèle Greeley, "Image, Text and the Female Body: René Magritte and the Surrealist Publications," *Oxford Art Journal* 15, no. 2 (1992): 48.
11 Susan Gubar quoted in ibid., 50.
12 "The Dali Murder Mystery," *Guardian*, March 8, 2000, www.theguardian.com/theguardian/2000/mar/09/features11.g23.
13 Flemish-Netherlands Foundation, *The Low Countries*, vol. 8 (Rekkem, Belgium: Stichting Ons Erfdeel, 2000).
14 "Guillotine," Wikipedia, last edited March 7, 2009, en.wikipedia.org/wiki/Guillotine.
15 Sandra Zalman, "The Double Agent: A Preface," in *Selected Writings*, ed. Kathleen Rooney and Eric Plattner, trans. Jo Levy (Minneapolis: University of Minnesota Press, 2016), xi.
16 The definition of cloning is from *Macmillan Dictionary*, www.macmillandictionary.com/us/dictionary/american/clone_1.

Chapter 17: Windows

1 René Magritte, *Selected Writings*, ed. Kathleen Rooney and Eric Plattner, trans. Jo Levy (Minneapolis: University of Minnesota Press, 2016), 4.
2 Ibid., 65–66.
3 "Poetry Is a Pipe: Selected Writings of René Magritte," Literary Hub, September 29, 2016, lithub.com/poetry-is-a-pipe-selected-writings-of-rene-magritte/.
4 Magritte, *Selected Writings*, 217.

Chapter 18: Bells and Belle

1 René Magritte, *Selected Writings*, ed. Kathleen Rooney and Eric Plattner, trans. Jo Levy (Minneapolis: University of Minnesota Press 2016), 221.

2 Sigmund Freud, "Medusa's Head," in *The Medusa Reader*, ed. Marjorie Garber and Nancy J. Vickers (New York: Routledge, 2003), 84–86.

Chapter 19: Curtains

1 René Magritte, cited in Good Reads, www.goodreads.com/quotes/820011-we-are-surrounded-by-curtains-we-only-perceive-the-world, accessed March 8, 2019.

2 See, for instance, *Movie Theater Curtain Opening Video*, posted by StephBuan, YouTube, www.youtube.com/watch?v=StWifzzcy2Q, accessed January 23, 2018.

3 Magritte, *Selected Writings*, 114.

4 "Magritte's Influence on Lynch's Red Room," Sixty East, September 28, 2015, ryc.me/art/magrittes-influence-on-lynchs-red-room.

5 Ibid.

6 Freire Barnes, "David Lynch Interview: 'There is something so incredibly cosmically magical about curtains," TimeOut, January 13, 2014, www.timeout.com/london/art/david-lynch-interview-there-is-something-so-incredibly-cosmically-magical-about-curtains.

7 Prairie Miller, "Interview with David Lynch," NYRock, October 2001, www.lynchnet.com/mdrive/nyrock.html.

8 Allister Mactaggart, *The Film Paintings of David Lynch: Challenging Film Theory* (Bristol, UK: Intellect, 2010).

9 André Bazin, "Theater and Cinema, Part Two," in *What Is Cinema?*, trans. Hugh Gray, vol. 1 (Berkeley: University of California Press, 1967), 96.

10 Ibid., 97.

11 Ibid, 98.

12 Ibid., 101.

13 Ibid.

14 Ibid., 102.

15 Ibid., 104.

16 Bosley Crowther, "New Movie Projection Shown Here; Giant Wide Angle Screen Utilized; Novel Technique in Films Unveiled," *New York Times*, October 1, 1952, movies.nytimes.com/movie/review?res=9E0DE6DF1E3CE23BBC4953DFB6678389649EDE.

17 Xavier Delamar, "Empire," Cinema Treasures, cinematreasures.org/theaters/7275, accessed March 8, 2019.

18 André Bazin, *Andre Bazin's New Media*, ed. Dudley Andrew (Berkeley: University of California Press, 2014).

19 Ibid.

Chapter 20: Film History

1 René Magritte, *Selected Writings*, ed. Kathleen Rooney and Eric Plattner, trans. Jo Levy (Minneapolis: University of Minnesota Press, 2016), 123.

2 Anne Uland, "This Is How Marvels Begin," in *Magritte: The Mystery of the Ordinary*, ed. Anne Uland (New York: Museum of Modern Art, 2013), 24–41, 27.

3 One of the few times any critic mentioned parallels to cinematic shots is when Josef Helfenstein talks of close-ups in this painting. See Josef Helfenstein, "A Lightning Flash Is Smoldering beneath the Bowler Hat," in *Magritte: the Mystery of the Ordinary, 1926–1938*, ed. Anne Uland (New York: Museum of Modern Art, 2013), 83.

4 Silvano Levy, *Surrealism: Surrealist Visuality* (Keele, UK: Keele University Press, 1996).

5 Letter from Magritte to M. Marion, 27 July 1952; see Sarah Whitfield, *Magritte* (London: South Bank Centre, 1992), explanatory text for plate 111, *The Domain of Light* (1952).

6 Jonathan Cott, "A Conversation with Bernardo Bertolucci," *Rolling Stone*, June 21 1973, www.rollingstone.com/movies/features/a-conversation-with-bernardo-bertolucci-19730621; my emphasis.

7 Fabien S. Gerard, Thomas Jefferson Kline, Bruce H. Sklarew, eds., *Bernardo Bertolucci: Interviews* (Jackson: University of Mississippi Press, 2000), 53; my emphasis.

8 Edward Branigan, *Point of View in the Cinema* (Berlin: Mouton de Gruyter, 2010).

9 Susan Sontag, "Film and Theater," in *Theater and Film: A Comparative Analysis*, ed. Robert Knopf (New Haven, CT: Yale University Press, 2005), 134–51; my emphasis.

10 *The Glass House*, Rene Magritte: Biography, Paintings, and Quotes, Rene Magritte.org, www.renemagritte.org/the-glass-house.jsp, accessed March 8, 2019.

11 Steven Higgens, quoted by MoMA, "Ernie Gehr, *Side/Walk/Shuttle*, 1991," www.moma.org/collection/works/107463, accessed March 8, 2019. See also P. Adams Sitney, *Eyes Upside Down-Visionary Filmmakers and The Heritage of Emerson* (New York: Oxford University Press, 2008).

12 Ralph Waldo Emerson, "Nature (Chap. 6)," Genius, genius.com/Ralph-waldo-emerson-nature-chap-6-annotated, accessed March 8, 2019.

13 Noël Carroll, *The Philosophy of Motion Pictures* (Malden, MA: Blackwell, 2008), 57.

14 André Bazin, "The Ontology of the Photographic Image," in *Film Theory and Criticism*, ed. Leo Braudy and Marshall Cohen (New York: Oxford University Press), 126–30.

15 Siegfried Kracauer, *Theory of Film: The Redemption of Physical Reality* (New York: Oxford University Press, 1960).

16 Victor I. Stoichita, *A Short History of the Shadow* (London: Reakton Books, 2013), 127, 133, 139.

17 Ibid., 148.

18 "Poetry Is a Pipe: Selected Writings of René Magritte," Literary Hub, September 29, 2016, lithub.com/poetry-is-a-pipe-selected-writings-of-rene-magritte.

19 "How Magritte Made 'Everyday Objects Shriek Aloud,'" Phaidon, www.phaidon.com/agenda/art/articles/2013/september/24/how-magritte-made-everyday-objects-shriek-aloud/, accessed March 8, 2019; also mentioned in Uland, D'Alessandro, and Helfenstein, "Magritte's Essential Surrealist Years," 16–23.

20 Magritte, quoted in William Jeffett, "Magritte and Dalí," in *Magritte and Dalí* (St. Petersburg, FL: Dalí Museum and Ludion, 2018), 13–34, 28.

21 Magritte, *Selected Writings*, ed. Kathleen Rooney and Eric Plattner, trans. Jo Levy (Minneapolis: University of Minnesota Press, 2016), 65.

22 "Poetry Is a Pipe."

23 André Breton, "The Crisis of the Object," in *Surrealism and Painting*, trans. Simon Watson Taylor (New York: Harper and Row, 1972), 277–80.

24 Ibid.

25 Ibid.

26 Ibid., 279.

27 Ibid.

28 Magritte, *Selected Writings*, 61.

29 Michel Draguet and Claude Goormans, "Once the Image Is Isolated, What Happens to the Mind?" in *Magritte: The Mystery of the Ordinary*, ed. Anne Unland (New York: Museum of Modern Art, 2013), 150–63, 153.

30 Ibid., 61.

31 André Breton, "Magritte," in *Surrealism and Painting*, trans. Simon Watson Taylor (New York: Harper and Row, 1972), 269–70.

32 Film Terms Glossary, Film Site, www.filmsite.org/filmterms15.html, accessed March 8, 2019.

33 Magritte, *Selected Writings*, 64.

34 Melissa Mueller, *Objects as Actors: Props and the Poetics of Performance in Greek Tragedy* (Chicago: University of Chicago Press, 2016), 1.

35 Ibid.

36 Magritte, *Selected Writings*, 161.

37 Ibid., 189; my emphasis.

38 See Warren Buckland, ed., *Puzzle Films: Complex Storytelling in Contemporary Cinema* (West Sussex, UK: Blackwell, 2009).

Chapter 21: Concluding Thoughts

1 René Magritte, *Selected Writings*, ed. by Kathleen Rooney and Eric Plattner, trans. Jo Levy (Minneapolis: University of Minnesota Press, 2016), 167.
2 Ibid., 182; my emphasis.

Magritte Works and Credits

Figures are identified by the title of the work as it is referred to in the text and used as the primary caption. Titles are based on the *Catalogue raisonée* of Magritte's work (David Sylvester, ed., *René Magritte: Catalogue raisonné*, vols. 1–6 [London: Menil Foundation, Philip Wilson, 1993]). The titles in parentheses represent variant titles used by the image source. Sometimes titles and dates of the latter will vary from the *Catalogue raisonée*. That is also noted.

Cover. *The False Mirror* (1929) (1928 per image source)
Oil on canvas, 21¼ × 31⅞ in.
Purchase © C. Herscovici, Brussels/Artist Rights Society, New York
The Museum of Modern Art
Digital Image © The Museum of Modern Art/Licensed by SCALA/Art Resource, New York

Figure 1.1. *The Flame Rekindled* (*Le retour de flamme/The Return of the Flame*) (1943)
Oil on canvas, 65 × 50 cm
Private collection
Photo credit: Banque d'Images ADAGP/Art Resource, New York

Figure 2.2. *The Lovers* (*Les amants*) (1928)
Oil on canvas, 54 × 73 cm
Photo credit: Banque d'Images ADAGP/Art Resource, New York

Figure 3.2. *La belle captive* (1967)
Gouache and pencil on paper, 29.8 × 45.2 cm
Photo credit: Banque d'Images ADAGP/Art Resource, New York

Figure 3.6. *The Month of the Grape Harvest* (*Le moi des vendanges*) (1959)
Private collection
Photo credit: Banque d'Images ADAGP/Art Resource, New York

Figure 5.1. *The Spy* (*L'espion*) (1928)
Oil on canvas, 54 × 73 cm
Londres, The Mayor Gallery
Photo credit: Banque d'Images ADAGP/Art Resource, New York

Figure 6.1. *Attempting the Impossible* (*La tentative d'impossible/The Impossible Attempt*) (1928)
Oil on canvas, 116 × 81 cm
Private collection
Photo credit: Banque d'Images ADAGP/Art Resource, New York

Figure 6.3. *The Key to the Fields* (*The Key of the Fields*) (1936)
Private collection
Photo credit: Banque d'Images ADAGP/Art Resource, New York

Figure 7.1. *The Treachery of Images* (*La trahison des images*) (1929)
Gouache on card, 5¾ × 7 in.
Access #: 5217
The Menil Collection, Houston
Photographer: Paul Hester

Figure 8.1. *The Human Condition* (*La condition humaine*) (1933)
Oil on canvas, 39⅜ × 31⅞ × ⅝ in.; framed: 45¾ × 38 × 1¾ in.
Gift of the Collectors Committee
National Gallery of Art, 1987.55.1

Figure 8.2. *La belle captive* (1931)
Oil on canvas, 38 × 55 cm
Private collection
Photo credit: Banque d'Images ADAGP/Art Resource, New York

Figure 9.1. *The Blood-letting* (*La saignée*) (1938 or 1939) (1939 per image source)
Gouache, 37 × 43 cm
Signed on the top right. Rotterdam Museum Boymans-van Beuningen.
Photo credit: Banque d'Images ADAGP/Art Resource, New York

Figure 10.1. Poster for the Brussels Film and Fine Arts World Festival (Brussels International Festival of Film and Fine Arts, Exhibition Poster) (1949) (1947 per image source)
Photo credit: Herscovici/Art Resource, New York

Figure 10.2. *Memory* (1948)
©ARS, New York
Photo credit: Banque d'Images ADAGP/Art Resource, New York

Figure 10.5. *The Giantess* (*La géante*) (1931)
Gouache and India ink on hardboard, 53 × 73 cm
Photo credit: Banque d'Images ADAGP/Art Resource, New York

Figure 11.3. *The Wonders of Nature* (*Les merveilles de la nature*) (1953)
Collection of the Museum of Contemporary Art Chicago. Gift of Jory and Joseph Shapiro, 1982.48
Photo credit: Nathan Keay

Figure 12.3. *The Ellipsis* (*L'ellipse/The Ellipse*) (1948)
Oil on canvas, 50 × 73 cm
Private collection
Photo credit: Banque d'Images ADAGP/Art Resource, New York

Figure 12.5. *Not to Be Reproduced* (*La reproduction interdite*/Portrait of Edward James) (1937)
Oil on canvas, 81 × 65 cm
Museum Boijmans van Beuningen
Photo credit: Banque d'Images ADAGP/Art Resource, New York

Figure 13.1. *Bauci's Landscape* (*Le paysage de Bauci*) (1966)
Oil on canvas, 27⅞ × 18 in.
Access #: Y207
Photo credit: Paul Hester
The Menil Collection, Houston

Figure 13.2. *The Sage's Carnival* (*Le carnaval du sage*) (1947)
Photo credit: Herscovici/Art Resource, New York

Figure 14.1. *The Double Secret* (*Le double secret/The Secret Double*) (1927)
Oil on canvas, 114 × 62 cm. Inv. AM1980-2
Musée National d'Art Moderne
© CNAC/MNAM/Dist. RMN-Grand Palais/Art Resource, New York

Figure 14.3. *Castle in the Pyrenees* (*Le château des Pyrénées*) (1959)
Israel Museum
Photo credit: Banque d'Images ADAGP/Art Resource, New York

Figure 15.1. *Collective Invention* (*L'invention collective*) (1934) (1935 per image source)
Oil painting, 73 × 116 cm
Private collection
Photo credit: Banque d'Images ADAGP/Art Resource, New York

Figure 16.1. *The Magician* (*Le sorcier/The Sorcerer, Self-Portrait with Four Arms*) (1951)
Oil on canvas, 35 × 46 cm
Private collection
Photo credit: Banque d'Images ADAGP/Art Resource, New York

Figure 16.2. *The Double Reality* (1936)
Oil on canvas, 50 × 65 cm
Private collection
Photo credit: Banque d'Images ADAGP/Art Resource, New York

Figure 16.3. *Rape* (*Le viol/The Rape*) (1935) (Listed as 1934 by The Menil Collection)
Oil on canvas, 28⅞ × 21½ in.
Access #: 1976-06 DJ
Photo credit: Paul Hester
The Menil Collection, Houston

Figure 17.1. *In Praise of the Dialectic* (*L'éloge de la dialectique*) (1937)
From the portfolio *La philosophie de la peinture de René Magritte* (vol. 1)
Lithograph on paper, 30 × 22 in. (76.2 × 55.88 cm)
Collection of the Albright-Knox Art Gallery, Buffalo, NY. Gift of Wade Stevenson, 1983 (P1983:42.7a).
© Estate of René Magritte/Artists Rights Society (ARS), New York

Figure 18.1. *The Voice of the Air* (*La voix des airs/The Voice of Space*) (1928)
Oil on canvas, 25½ × 19½ in. (64.77 × 49.53 cm)
Collection of the Albright-Knox Art Gallery, Buffalo, NY. Albert H. Tracy Fund, by exchange, and George B. and Jenny R. Mathews Fund, 1976 (1976:13).
© Estate of René Magritte/Artists Rights Society (ARS), New York

Figure 18.3. *Titanic Days* (*Gigantic Days/Les jours gigantesques*) (1928)
Oil on canvas, 116 × 81 cm
Kunstsammlung Nordhein-Westfalen
Photo credit: Banque d'Images ADAGP/Art Resource, New York

Figure 19.2. *Memoirs of a Saint* (*The Memoirs of a Saint/Les mémoires d'un saint*) (1960)
Oil on canvas, 31½ × 39¼ in.
Access #: X2105
Photo credit: Paul Hester
The Menil Collection, Houston

Figure 20.1. *The Lost Jockey* (1926)
Collage, gouache, watercolor, pencil on paper, 38.7 × 55.4 cm
Private collection
Photo credit: Banque d'Images ADAGP/Art Resource, New York

Figure 20.2. *Time Transfixed* (*La durée poignardée*) (1938)
Oil on canvas, 57⅞ × 38⅞ in.
Joseph Winterbotham Collection, 1970.426
The Art Institute of Chicago
Photo credit: The Art Institute of Chicago
Art Resource, New York

Figure 20.3. *The Cascade* (*La cascade*) (1961)
Oil on canvas, 81 × 100 cm
Private collection
Photo credit: Banque d'Images ADAGP/Art Resource, New York

Figure 20.4. *Man with a Newspaper* (1928)
Oil on canvas, 115.6 × 81.3 cm
Tate Gallery
© Tate, London/Art Resource, New York

Figure 20.5. *The Six Elements* (1929)
Oil on canvas, 28¾ × $39\frac{5}{16}$ inches; framed: $35\frac{7}{16} \times 45\frac{13}{16} \times 3\frac{11}{16}$ inches
Philadelphia Museum of Art, The Louise and Walter Arensberg Collection, 1950-134-127
© Artists Rights Society (ARS), New York/ADAGP, Paris

Figure 20.7. *The Domain of Light* (*The Dominion of Light/L'empire des lumières*) (1954)
Oil on canvas, 51⅛ × 37¼ in.
Access #: V 616
Photo credit: Paul Hester
The Menil Collection, Houston

Figure 20.9. *The Alarm Clock* (*Le réveille-matin*) (1957)
From the portfolio *La philosophie de la peinture de René Magritte* (vol. 1)
Lithograph on paper, 30 × 22 inches (76.2 × 55.88 cm)
Collection of the Albright-Knox Art Gallery, Buffalo, NY. Gift of Wade Stevenson, 1983 (P1983:42.7g).
© Estate of René Magritte/Artists Rights Society (ARS), New York

Figure 20.11. *Victory* (*La victoire*) (1939) (1938 or 1939 per image source)
Gouache, 45 × 35 cm
Private collection
Photo credit: Banque d'Images ADAGP/Art Resource, New York

Figure 20.12. *The Uncertainty Principle* (1944)
Oil on canvas, 65 × 50 cm
Private collection
Photo credit: Banque d'Images ADAGP/Art Resource, New York

Figure 20.13. *Personal Values* (*Les valeurs personnelles*) (1952)
Oil on canvas, 31½ × 39⅜ in.
San Francisco Museum of Modern Art. Gift of Phyllis C. Wattis.
Charly Herscovici, Brussels Artist Rights Society, New York
Photo credit: Katherine Du Tiel

Figure 20.14. *The Daring Sleeper* (*The Reckless Sleeper*) (1928)
Tate Gallery
©Tate, London/Art Resource, New York

Figure 20.15. *Clairvoyance* (*La clairvoyance*) (1936)
Private collection
Photo credit: Herscovici/Art Resource, New York

Index

CPSIA information can be obtained
at www.ICGtesting.com
Printed in the USA
BVHW062235071119
563215BV00001B/4/P

9 780814 346365